Lecture Notes in Computer Science   11378

Commenced Publication in 1973
Founding and Former Series Editors:
Gerhard Goos, Juris Hartmanis, and Jan van Leeuwen

More information about this series at http://www.springer.com/series/7410

Chang D. Yoo · Yun-Qing Shi
Hyoung Joong Kim · Alessandro Piva
Gwangsu Kim (Eds.)

Digital Forensics and Watermarking

17th International Workshop, IWDW 2018
Jeju Island, Korea, October 22–24, 2018
Proceedings

 Springer

Editors
Chang D. Yoo
Korea Advanced Institute of Science
and Technology
Daejeon, South Korea

Alessandro Piva (iD)
University of Florence
Florence, Italy

Yun-Qing Shi
New Jersey Institute of Technology
Newark, NJ, USA

Gwangsu Kim
Korea Advanced Institute of Science
and Technology
Daejeon, South Korea

Hyoung Joong Kim
Korea University
Seoul, South Korea

ISSN 0302-9743 ISSN 1611-3349 (electronic)
Lecture Notes in Computer Science
ISBN 978-3-030-11388-9 ISBN 978-3-030-11389-6 (eBook)
https://doi.org/10.1007/978-3-030-11389-6

Library of Congress Control Number: 2018968011

LNCS Sublibrary: SL4 – Security and Cryptology

This Springer imprint is published by the registered company Springer Nature Switzerland AG
The registered company address is: Gewerbestrasse 11, 6330 Cham, Switzerland

Preface

The 17th International Workshop on Digital Forensics and Watermarking (IWDW 2018) was held in Jeju, South Korea, during October 22–24, 2018. IWDW 2018, following the principles of the IWDW series, aimed at providing a technical program covering the latest and most sophisticated technological developments in the fields of digital watermarking, steganography and steganalysis, forensics and anti-forensics, visual cryptography, and other multimedia-related security issues. Among 46 submissions from Europe, Asia, and North America, 28 papers for regular sessions and a special session were selected for publication, including three papers for the best paper awards. The selection was based on the reviews provided by 36 Program Committee members, the general chair, and two Special Session Committee members.

Besides the regular presentations, one special session was held. "Deep Generative Models (DGM) for Forgery and Its Detection" was organized by the general chair, Chang D. Yoo. The aim of the session was to introduce up-and-coming issues related to forgery with regard to the generative models considered in artificial intelligence. The session provided a wonderful platform to exchange ideas regarding DGM and to identify key challenges in detecting forged generated data including text as well as image.

In addition to the paper presentations, the workshop featured congratulatory remarks from the dean of Jeju University, Kyung Youn Kim, and three talks: (1) plenary talk "Opportunities and Challenges for Blockchain," presented by Professor Yongdae Kim (Korea Advanced Institute of Science and Technology); (2) tutorial "Introduction to Deep Neural Networks, Convolutional Neural Networks, and Generative Adversarial Networks," presented by Professor Junmo Kim (Korea Advanced Institute of Science and Technology); and (3) a special guest talk "Forensic Watermarking Application in Media Business by MarkAny," presented by Go Choi (VP of MarkAny Strategy and Business Development).

The best paper awards were given to the papers titled "VPCID – A VoIP Phone Call Identification Database" by Yuankun Huang et al. (Shenzhen University, China); "Comparison of DCT and Gabor Filters in Residual Extraction of CNN-Based JPEG Steganalysis" by Huilin Zheng et al. (Sun Yat-sen University, China; New Jersey Institute of Technology, USA); and "Reconstruction of Fingerprints from Minutiae Using Conditional Adversarial Networks" by Hakil et al. (Inha University, South Korea).

We would like to thank all of the authors, reviewers, lecturers, and participants for their valuable contributions to IWDW 2018. Our sincere gratitude also goes to all the members of the Technical Program Committee, special session reviewers, and our local volunteers for their careful work and great efforts made in the wonderful organization of this workshop.

Finally, we are certain that the readers will enjoy this volume and hope that it will provide inspiration and opportunities for future research.

November 2018

Chang D. Yoo
Yun-Qing Shi
Alessandro Piva
Hyoung Joong Kim
Gwangsu Kim

Organization

General Chair

Chang D. Yoo · · · · · · · · · · · · · · · Korea Advanced Institute of Science and Technology, South Korea

Technical Program Chairs

Yun-Qing Shi · · · · · · · · · · · · New Jersey Institute of Technology, USA
Hyoung Joon Kim · · · · · · · · · Korea University, South Korea
Alessandro Piva · · · · · · · · · · · University of Florence, Italy
Gwangsu Kim · · · · · · · · · · · · · Korea Advanced Institute of Science and Technology, South Korea

Technical Program Committee

Akira Nishimura · · · · · · · · · · · Tokyo University of Information Sciences, Japan
Andreas Westfeld · · · · · · · · · · Dresden University of Applied Sciences, Germany
Anja Keskinarkaus · · · · · · · · · University of Oulu, Finland
Athanassios Skodras · · · · · · · · University of Patras, Greece
Chang-Tsun Li · · · · · · · · · · · · University of Warwick, UK
Claude Delpha · · · · · · · · · · · · University of Paris-Sud XI, France
Christian Kraetzer · · · · · · · · · Otto von Guericke – University of Magdeburg, Germany
Dawen Xu · · · · · · · · · · · · · · · · Ningbo University of Technology, China
Feng Liu · · · · · · · · · · · · · · · · · Chinese Academy of Sciences, China
Guopu Zhu · · · · · · · · · · · · · · · Shenzhen Institutes of Advanced Technology, Chinese Academy of Sciences, China
Isao Echizen · · · · · · · · · · · · · · National Institute of Informatics, Japan
James C. N. Yang · · · · · · · · · · National Dong Hwa University, Taiwan
JongWeon Kim · · · · · · · · · · · · Sangmyung University, South Korea
Krzysztof Szczypiorski · · · · · · Warsaw University of Technology/Institute of Telecommunications, Poland
Minoru Kuribayashi · · · · · · · · Okayama University, Japan
Mohan Kankanhalli · · · · · · · · · National University of Singapore, Singapore
Pascal Schöttle · · · · · · · · · · · · University of Innsbruck, Austria
Pedro Comesaña Alfaro · · · · · · University of Vigo, Spain
Rainer Böhme · · · · · · · · · · · · · University of Innsbruck, Austria
Sabah A. Jassim · · · · · · · · · · · University of Buckingham, UK
Stefan Katzenbeisser · · · · · · · · Technical University of Darmstadt, Germany
Steffen Wendzel · · · · · · · · · · · Worms University of Applied Sciences, Germany
Tomás Pevný · · · · · · · · · · · · · · Czech Technical University in Prague, Czech Republic

Ton Kalker	DTS, Inc., USA
Wojciech Mazurczyk	Warsaw University of Technology, Poland
Xiangui Kang	Sun Yat-sen University, China
Xiaotian Wu	Jinan University, China
Xinghao Jiang	Shanghai Jiao Tong University, China
Xinpeng Zhang	Shanghai University, China
Yao Zhao	Beijing Jiaotong University, China
Yong-Man Ro	Korea Advanced Institute of Science and Technology, South Korea

Local Arrangements Chair

Gwangsu Kim	Korea Advanced Institute of Science and Technology, South Korea

Special Session Committee

Chang D. Yoo	Korea Advanced Institute of Science and Technology, South Korea
Gwangsu Kim	Korea Advanced Institute of Science and Technology, South Korea
Dong Eui Chang	Korea Advanced Institute of Science and Technology, South Korea
Junmo Kim	Korea Advanced Institute of Science and Technology, South Korea

Contents

Reversible Data Hiding

Steganographic Algorithms

Identification and Security

Special Session: Deep Generative Models for Forgery and Its Det

Deep Neural Networks for Digital Forensics

A Convolutional Neural Network Based Seam Carving Detection Scheme for Uncompressed Digital Images

Jingyu Ye[(⊠)], Yuxi Shi, Guanshuo Xu, and Yun-Qing Shi

Department of Electrical and Computer Engineering,
New Jersey Institute of Technology, Newark, NJ 07102, USA
jy58@njit.edu

Abstract. Revealing the processing history that a given digital image has gone through is an important topic in digital image forensics. Detection of seam carving, a content-aware image scaling algorithm commonly implemented in commercial image-editing software, has been studied by forensic experts in recent years. In this paper, a convolutional neural network (CNN) architecture is proposed for seam carving detection. Unlike the existing forensic works in detecting seam carving, where the feature selection and the pattern classification are two separated procedures, the proposed CNN-based deep learning architecture learns and then uses more effective features via joint optimization of feature extraction and pattern classification. Experimental results conducted on a large dataset have demonstrated that, compared with the current state-of-the-art, the proposed CNN based deep learning scheme can largely boost the classification rates as the seam carving rate is rather low.

Keywords: Seam carving detection · Digital image forensics ·
Content-aware image scaling · Convolutional neural network · Deep learning

1 Introduction

Due to the rapid development of image-editing techniques in the past years, digital images can be easily edited or tampered with popular software such as Photoshop. To reveal malicious image editing, digital image forensics [1] have been extensively studied for the past decade. In this paper, we present a novel forensic approach to detect the operation of seam carving [2] in digital images, specifically in uncompressed images. Seam carving, also known as content-aware scaling, is one popularly utilized image scaling algorithm and has been included in many predominant image editing software, such as Photoshop and GIMP. By recursively deleting a seam (a horizontal or vertical path of 8-connected pixels) with the lowest energy, the image size is altered and the visually more important image contents can be well-preserved.

A few forensic works have been reported in the past several years to reveal traces of seam carving in digital images. In the first piece of forensic work for seam carving detection [3], Sarkar et al. proposed to utilize Markov transition probability to reveal the trace of seam carving in digital images, specifically in JPEG compressed images.

© Springer Nature Switzerland AG 2019
C. D. Yoo et al. (Eds.): IWDW 2018, LNCS 11378, pp. 3–13, 2019.
https://doi.org/10.1007/978-3-030-11389-6_1

Later in [4], a hybrid statistical feature model was proposed by Fillion et al. to track the operation of seam carving in uncompressed images based on energy distribution, seam behavior and wavelet absolute moments. In [5], Lu et al. proposed an active forensic approach to determine whether a received uncompressed image has been attacked by seam carving or not by comparing the SIFT features pre-extracted by the sender with the SIFT features extracted at the receiver end. Chang et al. [6] later presented a series of statistical features based on the blocking artefact characteristics matrix to differentiate non-seam carved JPEG images from seam carved JPEG images. This work was further extended in [7]. In [8], Liu et al. proposed to employ the calibrated neighboring joint density of DCT coefficients for the detection of seam carving in JPEG images, and the extended works were reported in [9, 10]. In Ryu et al.'s work [11], the authors designed a set of features based on energy bias and noise level to unveil the operation of seam carving in uncompressed images. In [12], Wei et al. presented an interesting approach to detect seam carving in uncompressed images. By dividing images into 2×2 mini-squares and categorizing each of the squares into nine types of predefined patches, each square was possibly recovered to its original form. Then, Markov transition probability was applied to discriminate seam carved images from non-seam carved images. Yin et al. [13] proposed a blind forensic technique to detect seam carving in uncompressed images based on the similar idea proposed in [11]. In [13], twenty-four features consisting of six newly designed features and eighteen features proposed in [11] were extracted from the local binary pattern pre-processed images for seam carving detection in uncompressed images. In [14], Ye and Shi proposed to employ a set of energy features which extracted from local derivative pattern encoded images to identify seam carved images. In [15], an advanced statistical model, consisting of local derivative pattern, Markov transition probabilities, and subtractive pixel adjacency model, are designed to determine if an image has been gone through seam carving or not. The extended work of [14, 15] was presented in [16]. In [17], Zhang et al. designed forty-two features to unveil the statistical properties of spatial and spectral entropies (SSE). They were combined with local binary pattern (LBP)-based energy features to detect seam carving image with low scaling ratio.

Most of the existing methods for seam carving detection as introduced, except [5], are focusing on feature engineering, a Support Vector Machines (SVM) based classification scheme is applied to ensure better performance. In this paper, inspired by the substantial successes achieved by convolutional neural networks (CNN) in computer vision [18–20], and the success obtained by the CNN-based steganalysis work [21], we propose and report a CNN architecture that includes both the feature extraction and classification in a joint optimization framework to unveil the process of seam carving in uncompressed digital images. As far as we know, this is the first work that successfully applies deep learning for seam carving detection. Furthermore, as indicated by experimental results, the proposed approach achieves almost perfect results at higher scaling rates, and largely outperforms the state-of-the-art at lower scaling rates. The rest of the paper is organized as follows: In Sect. 2, seam carving is briefly introduced. Then, the proposed CNN structures are described in Sect. 3. The experimental results are reported in Sect. 4. The conclusion is made in Sect. 5.

2   Background of Seam Carving

The image scaling is a process to resize a digital image so as to satisfy certain geometric requirement. However, the conventional image scaling schemes could not always provide a promising visual quality after resizing because the image content is not considered carefully by these algorithms. One example is shown in Fig. 1. As a result, seam carving is designed to protect image content from being destroyed while scaling is conducted.

For a given energy function $e(.)$, e.g., gradient, the importance of a pixel in image I can be evaluated with its energy as shown below,

$$e(I(x,y)) = \left| \frac{\partial}{\partial x} I(x,y) \right| + \left| \frac{\partial}{\partial y} I(x,y) \right| \tag{1}$$

where x and y are the corresponding row and column coordinates, respectively. By assuming the less important image content consists of lower energy pixels, seam carving is to delete a seam with the lowest cumulative energy recursively so as to alter

(a)   (b)

(c)   (d)

Fig. 1. (a) an original image from UCID with a size of 384 × 512. (b), (c) and (d) are the resized copies of (a) with the same size of 384 × 411 but processed by different scaling techniques respectively: (b) bilinear interpolation, (c) cropping, (d) seam carving.

the size of a given image. Note that a seam is a path of 8-connected pixels crossing the image either from top to bottom (vertical seam), or from left to right (horizontal seam). For instance, a horizontal seam s^H in an n × m (height × width) image I can be defined as:

$$s^H = \{s_i^H\}_{i=1}^m = \{(x(i), i)\}_{i=1}^m, s.t. \forall i, |x(i) - x(i-1)| \le 1 \tag{2}$$

where s_i^H represents the coordinates of each included pixel. Therefore, the optimal horizontal seam s^* can be shown below,

$$s^* = \min_s E(s) = \min_s \sum_{i=1}^m e\left(I\left(s_i^H\right)\right) \tag{3}$$

where $E(s)$ is the cumulative energy of seam s. As the optimal seam always has the lowest cumulative energy, it is considered to be the least visually important and unnoticeable in the image. Therefore, by removing multiple such optimal seams, either horizontal seams or vertical seams, not only can the image size be altered, but also the important image content could be well-preserved consequently.

3 Proposed CNN Architecture

CNNs has aroused tremendous interests since a remarkable success was achieved in the ILSVRC-2012 competition by utilizing this advanced artificial intelligence technology [18]. A typical CNN hierarchical architecture starts with multiple stages of convolutional modules and ends with a classification module. A common convolutional module includes a convolutional layer, an activation layer, and a pooling layer. The convolutional layer is a trainable filter bank which can be considered as a feature extractor. The activation layer brings non-linearity to the network and bounds the extracted features. The pooling layer reduces the quantity of features extracted from immediately prior convolutional layer to avoid overfitting. By stacking a series of convolutional modules, hierarchical feature maps are extracted and then fed into the classification module composed of one or more fully-connected layers, and the Softmax layer with cross-entropy loss. The classification module can transform feature vectors to output probabilities for each class. Through back-propagation, weights and biases in convolutional layers will be optimized so as to reduce the training loss, and the power of the network will then be enforced to predict the labels of unseen data.

The overall architecture of the proposed CNN is illustrated in Fig. 2. Instead of directly feeding the original images into the network, a high-pass filtering (HPF) layer with kernel size of 5 × 5 × 1 (height × width × number of input feature maps) [21] is employed to pre-process input images. In this way, we use the first convolutional layer of CNN model as a pre-processing module. The trace of seam carving, i.e. imperceptible discontinuity of image content, is a kind of weak high frequency signal, which is greatly impacted by image content. Therefore, high-pass filter is employed at the beginning so as to boost the signal-to-noise ratio. This can provide a good initialization to drive the whole network, hence achieve good performance as compared to without doing it.

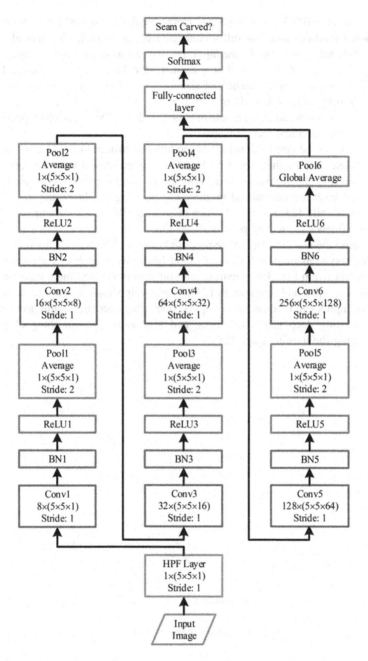

Fig. 2. The proposed CNN architecture. Parametric setting of each layer is included in the corresponding box.

Following the HPF layer is the CNN hierarchical structure which consists of six convolutional modules and one fully- connected linear classification module. In the first convolutional layer (Conv1), the input, i.e., the pre-processed input image, is to be filtered by 8 kernels of size $5 \times 5 \times 1$ each. In the following convolutional layers (Conv2–Conv6), there are 16 kernels of size $5 \times 5 \times 8$ in Conv2, 32 kernels of size $5 \times 5 \times 16$ in Conv3, 64 kernels of size $5 \times 5 \times 32$ in Conv4, 128 kernels of size $5 \times 5 \times 64$ in Conv5 and 256 kernels of size $5 \times 5 \times 128$ in Conv6 respectively so as to generate hierarchical feature maps.

Different from the conventional CNN module as introduced in [18], an additional layer, called batch normalization (BN) layer [23], is employed between each convolutional layer and the following activation layer. As the outputs generated by the convolutional layer are normalized by the corresponding BN layer, the so called 'internal covariate shift' [23] is reduced which helps to accelerate the training speed and to reduce the influence caused by poor initialization.

To increase the non-linearity of the proposed deep architecture, rectified linear units (ReLU) are served as the non-linear activation functions in each of the convolutional modules, as shown in Fig. 3. Comparing with other popular non-linear functions, such as hyperbolic tangent and Sigmoid, ReLU has relatively simple form, i.e., gradient is 1 for positive inputs and 0 for negative inputs. Such characteristics could accelerate the speed on training deep neural networks, and also avoid the vanishing of gradient happens during the training stage [24].

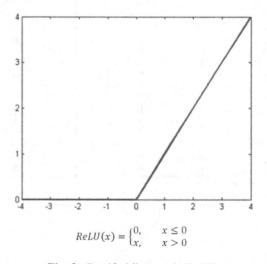

$$ReLU(x) = \begin{cases} 0, & x \leq 0 \\ x, & x > 0 \end{cases}$$

Fig. 3. Rectified linear unit (ReLU).

Since the process of seam carving will remove lower energy pixels, those higher energy pixels which normally have large intensity value are more likely remained in the image. Due to this characteristic, focusing on the maximum pixel value of a local region which is normally considered in computer vision intuitively insufficient to discover the trace of seam carving. Therefore, average pooling is employed in the proposed CNN framework for spatial sub-sampling instead of max pooling popularly utilized in computer vision. In the last pooling layer, namely, Pool6, the kernel size for pooling is fixed to the spatial size of the input feature maps. Therefore, each input feature map will be aggregated to one single number, which serves as a feature for the classification. As there are 256 input feature maps to Pool6, 256 features are generated and fed into the fully-connected linear classification module for each image.

$$ReLU(x) = \begin{cases} 0, x \leq 0 \\ x, x > 0 \end{cases}$$

4 Experimental Results

Since there is no any image database which is publicly available and designed for the forensic research on detecting seam carving, we implemented the seam carving algorithm [2] in MATLAB and established 12 seam carved image sets based on the BOSSbase 1.01 [25], which is a benchmark image database for the research of steganalysis. It contains 10,000 never-compressed grayscale images with the size of 512×512. For each image from the BOSSbase, the pre-implemented seam carving algorithm was utilized to reduce the height by 5%, 10%, 20%, 30%, 40% and 50%, respectively. Therefore, 6 groups of seam carved copies were acquired. Similarly, by scaling the width of each original image with aforementioned various scaling rates, another 6 groups of seam carved copies were generated. Consequently, 12 seam carved copies were obtained for each image in the BOSSbase and thus 12 seam carved image sets were formed, i.e., '5%H', '10%H', '20% H', '30%H', '40%H', '50%H', '5%V', '10%V', '20%V', '30%V', '40%V' and '50%V'. Specifically, '5%H' stands for the height of each original image was scaled by 5%, '5%V' mean the width was decreased by 5%. As a result, each seam carved set contains 10,000 seam carved images.

To evaluate the performance of the proposed CNN architecture, the experiments were conducted to detect the 12 designed seam carving cases. In the experiments, the proposed CNN architecture was constructed with Caffe toolbox [26], and stochastic gradient descent was applied to train all the CNNs with the batch size of 64 images. We fixed the momentum as 0.9 and the weight decay as 0.0005. The learning rate was initialized to 0.001 and forced to decrease 10% after each 5000 iterations. To fairly compare the performance with the state-of- the-art, we not only implemented and tested methods proposed for seam carving detection [11, 13], but also examined the performance of rich model [22] which represents the state-of- the-art of steganalysis. Each method was tested on the 12 seam carving cases with linear SVM as the classifier [27]. Additionally, 2-fold cross validation was applied throughout the experiments.

As shown in Table 1, the proposed CNN architecture performs significantly better than the two state-of-the-art of seam carving detection [11, 13] when the scaling rate is below 30%. In particularly, our method achieves, respectively, 90% and 93% detection accuracies in the experiments of testing '5%H' and '5%V', the two toughest cases, which are 20% higher than performance achieved by both state-of-the-art.

The receiver operating characteristic curves (ROC) together with the corresponding area under ROC curves (AUC) shown in Fig. 4 indicate that the proposed method

Table 1. The performance of proposed CNN architecture and the state-of-the-art [11, 13, 22], on detecting 12 seam carving cases.

	5%H	10%H	20%H	30%H	40%H	50%H
Ref. [11]	65.92%	72.88%	82.78%	90.31%	95.01%	97.77%
Ref. [13]	70.26%	83.60%	94.35%	97.90%	99.16%	**99.71%**
Ref. [22]	86.89%	93.22%	96.95%	97.98%	98.60%	99.07%
Proposed	**90.37%**	**95.18%**	**97.84%**	**98.76%**	**99.21%**	99.56%
	5%V	10%V	20%V	30%V	40%V	50%V
Ref. [11]	71.13%	79.83%	88.36%	93.18%	96.08%	97.79%
Ref. [13]	58.74%	71.50%	85.68%	93.31%	97.25%	98.97%
Ref. [22]	87.06%	94.74%	97.98%	98.82%	99.34%	**99.60%**
Proposed	**93.99%**	**96.71%**	**98.55%**	**99.08%**	**99.45%**	**99.60%**

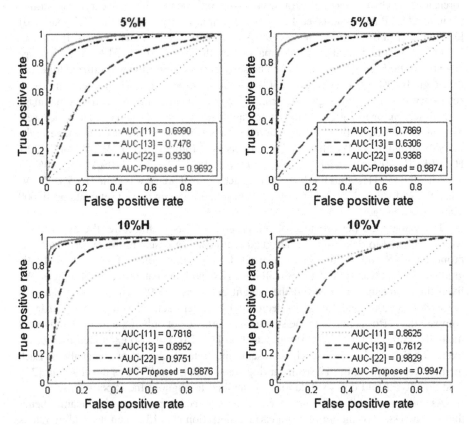

Fig. 4. The ROC curves and their corresponding AUC illustrating all four tested methods on detecting '5%H', '5%V', '10%H' and '10%V', respectively.

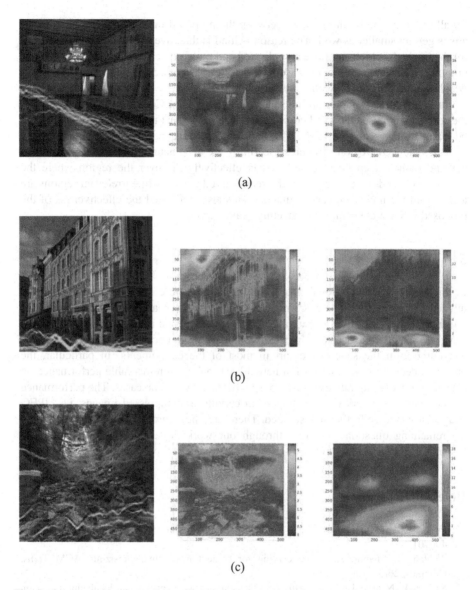

Fig. 5. Images in the first column illustrate the ground truth of carved seams in the original images with the carving rate equal to 5%. Heat maps in the second column are learnt from the original non-seam carved images by the proposed CNN, while heat maps learnt from the seam carved copies are shown in the third column.

outperforms the two seam carving forensic methods dramatically on detecting both '5%' and '10%' cases. It is also observed that rich model outperforms the [11, 13] on those low carving rate cases although it still underperforms the proposed CNNs. Notably, the detection accuracy increases monotonically with the increased carving rate for all tested methods, and the gap between the proposed method and the tested prior arts is getting smaller as well. The reason behind is that, overfitting is more significant for the methods which are more complicated and more powerful on modelling, such as proposed CNN and rich model as well, on detecting easy cases, i.e., detecting images in which a large number of seams are carved out.

In Fig. 5, three samples are presented. The outputs of Conv5 for each sample and the corresponding seam carved copies are visualized as heat maps to illustrate what can be learnt by the proposed CNN. The region in the heat maps which has large value indicates the ROI (region of interest) learnt by the deep neural network. It is observed that the trained deep neural network can effectively discover the region where the seams are deleted by learning from the seam carved copies, while irrelevant regions are learnt from the non-seam carved images. This also illustrated the effectiveness of the proposed CNN architecture on detecting seam carving.

5   Conclusion

In this paper, a convolutional neural network architecture has been established and utilized for seam carving detection. It is the first deep learning framework on this research topic as far as we know. Indicated by experimental results, the proposed deep learning method can successfully detect seam carving in uncompressed digital images and outperform the state-of-the- art in most of the experiments. In particular, the proposed deep convolutional neural network has achieved remarkable performance on detecting low carving rate cases, i.e., 5% and 10% carving rate cases. The performance of deep neural network on detecting seam carving in compressed images, i.e., JPEG images, needs to be further investigated. Therefore, the future work will be focusing on the remaining questions. Overall, through our work, it has been shown that deep learning could be a new direction for the forensic research on seam carving detection.

References

1. Piva, A.: An overview on image forensics. ISRN Sig. Process. **2013** (2013). Article ID 496701
2. Avidan, S., Shamir, A.: Seam carving for content-aware image resizing. ACM Trans. Graphics, **26**(3) (2007)
3. Sarkar, A., Nataraj, L., Manjunath, B.S.: Detection of seam carving and localization of seam insertions in digital images. In: Proceedings of 11th ACM Workshop on Multimedia and Security, MM&Sec 2009, New York, NY, USA, pp. 107–116 (2009)
4. Fillion, C., Sharma, G.: Detecting content adaptive scaling of images for forensic applications. In: Media Forensics and Security, SPIE Proceedings, p. 75410. SPIE (2010)
5. Lu, W., Wu, M.: Seam carving estimation using forensic hash. In: Proceedings of 13th ACM multimedia workshop on Multimedia and Security, MM&Sec 2011, New York, NY, USA, pp. 9–14 (2011)
6. Chang, W., Shih, T.K., Hsu, H.: Detection of seam carving in JPEG images. In: Proceedings of iCAST-UMEDIA (2013)

7. Wattanachote, K., Shih, T.K., Chang, W., Chang, H.: Tamper detection of JPEG image due to seam modification. IEEE Trans. Inf. Forensics Secur. **10**(12), 2477–2491 (2015)
8. Liu, Q., Chen, Z.: Improved approaches with calibrated neighboring joint density to steganalysis and seam-carved forgery detection in JPEG images. ACM Trans. Intell. Syst. Technol. **5**(4) (2014)
9. Liu, Q.: Exposing seam carving forgery under recompression attacks by hybrid large feature mining. In: 23rd International Conference on Pattern Recognition (ICPR), pp. 1036–1041 (2016)
10. Liu, Q.: An approach to detecting JPEG down-recompression and seam carving forgery under recompression anti-forensics. Patt. Recogn. **65**, 35–46 (2016)
11. Ryu, S., Lee, H., Lee, H.: Detecting trace of seam carving for forensic analysis. IEICE Trans. Inf. Syst. **E97-D**(5), 1304–1311 (2014)
12. Wei, J., Lin, Y., Wu, Y.: A patch analysis method to detect seam carved images. Patt. Recogn. Lett. **36**, 100–106 (2014)
13. Yin, T., Yang, G., Li, L., Zhang, D., Sun, X.: Detecting seam carving based image resizing using local binary patterns. Comput. Secur. **55**, 130–141 (2015)
14. Ye, J., Shi, Y.Q.: A local derivative pattern based image forensic framework for seam carving detection. In: Proceedings of 15th International Workshop on Digital Watermarking, pp. 172–184 (2016)
15. Ye, J., Shi, Y.Q.: An effective method to detect seam carving. J. Inf. Secur. Appl. **35**, 13–22 (2017)
16. Ye, J., Shi, Y.Q.: A hybrid feature model for seam carving detection. In: Proceedings of 16th International Workshop on Digital Watermarking, pp. 77–89 (2017)
17. Zhang, D., Yin, T., Yang, G., Xia, M., Li, L., Sun, X.: Detecting image seam carving with low scaling ratio using multi-scale spatial and spectral entropies. J. Vis. Commun. Image Represent. **48**, 281–291 (2017)
18. Krizhevsky, A., Sutskever, I., Hinton, G.: ImageNet classification with deep convolutional neural networks. In: Proceedings of Advances in Neural Information Processing Systems, pp. 1106–1114 (2012)
19. Szegedy, C., et al.: Going deeper with convolutions. In: Proceedings of IEEE International Conference on Computer Vision and Pattern Recognition, pp. 1–9 (2015)
20. Russakovsky, O.: ImageNet large scale visual recognition challenge. Int. J. Comput. Vis. **115**, 211–252 (2015)
21. Xu, G., Wu, H., Shi, Y.Q.: Structural design of convolutional neural networks for steganalysis. IEEE Sig. Process. Lett. **23**(5), 708–712 (2016)
22. Fridrich, J., Kodovsky, J.: Rich models for steganalysis of digital images. IEEE Trans. Inf. Forensics Secur. (2012)
23. Ioffe, S., Szegedy, C.: Batch normalization: accelerating deep network training by reducing internal covariate shift (2015)
24. Glorot, X., Bordes, A., Bengio, Y.: Deep sparse rectifier neural networks (2011)
25. Bas, P., Filler, T., Pevný, T.: "Break our steganographic system": the ins and outs of organizing BOSS. In: Filler, T., Pevný, T., Craver, S., Ker, A. (eds.) IH 2011. LNCS, vol. 6958, pp. 59–70. Springer, Heidelberg (2011). https://doi.org/10.1007/978-3-642-24178-9_5
26. Jia, Y.: Caffe: convolutional architecture for fast feature embedding. In: Proceedings of ACM International Conference on Multimedia, pp. 675–678 (2014)
27. Chang, C.C., Lin, C.J.: LIBSVM: a library for support vector machines. ACM Trans. Intell. Syst. Technol. **2**, 1–27 (2011)

Convolutional Neural Network for Larger JPEG Images Steganalysis

Qian Zhang[1,2], Xianfeng Zhao[1,2(⊠)], and Changjun Liu[1,2]

[1] State Key Laboratory of Information Security,
Institute of Information Engineering, Chinese Academy of Sciences,
Beijing 100093, China
zhaoxianfeng@iie.ac.cn
[2] School of Cyber Security, University of Chinese Academy of Sciences,
Beijing 100093, China

Abstract. This paper proposes an effective steganalytic scheme based on CNN in order to detect steganography on larger JPEG images. Most of the CNN schemes were designed very deep to achieve high accuracy, resulting in inability to train large size images due to the limitation of GPUs' memory. Most existing network architectures use small images of 256×256 or 512×512 pixels as their detection objects which are far from meeting the needs of practical applications. Meanwhile, the resizing operation on stegos will make the slight noise signal caused by steganography become difficult to detect. In our proposed network architecture, we try to solve the problem by compressing the depth of network structure. And in order to reduce the data dimension, we apply a histogram layer to transform the feature maps to feature vectors before the fully connected layer. We test our network on images of size 512×512, 1024×1024 and 2048×2048. For different application scenes, we take two methods to generate large samples. The result demonstrates that the proposed scheme can make directly training the steganalysis detectors on large images feasible.

Keywords: JPEG steganalysis · Larger images · Histogram layer · Convolutional Neural Networks (CNN)

1 Introduction

Steganography is a covert communication method which uses multimedia files to hide message imperceptibly. On the contrary, steganalysis is designed for detecting the existence of secret information. JPEG format image is one of the most popular digital media in our daily life, and there are many steganographic algorithms designed for JPEG format, such as F5 [14], JRM [8], UED [3] and J-UNIWARD [6]. To counter these algorithms, some feature-based steganalysis methods have been widely used. The feature of steganalysis is a statistic that distinguishes between a normal image and a secret image, we can get the

C. D. Yoo et al. (Eds.): IWDW 2018, LNCS 11378, pp. 14–28, 2019.
https://doi.org/10.1007/978-3-030-11389-6_2

statistics feature based on the Discrete Cosine Transform (DCT) coefficients or transform the DCT coefficients to spatial domain, then form the JPEG-phase-aware features from the spatial domain residuals. The latter method has better effect. DCTR [5] and GFR [12] are the representative methods which exhibit competitive performance.

Great success achieved by deep learning in other areas of image processing has lead researchers to apply deep learning frameworks, such as Convolutional Neural Networks (CNN) on detecting steganography. But the CNN was only used in spatial-domain steganalysis at the beginning. Qian et al. [9] proposed a pioneering architecture, the method integrates feature extraction and classification into a CNN framework, and uses backpropagation methods to optimize parameters. Qian et al. [10] improve the detection performance of low payload tasks through transfer learning, at first they pre-trained the CNN model using stego with high payload, then fine-tuning for stego with low payload, they proved that the auxiliary information from the high payload model can be used to help analyze the stego with a low payload. Xu et al. [16] improved the network model's capability by using more effective network structure units, for example, batch-normalization layer, which is used to avoid falling into a local minimum. TanH layer, which is used for preventing overfitting. Sedighi et al. [11] proposed a histogram layer to simulate PSRM [4] models within the CNN framework. The proposed method indicated that it may reduce the dimensionality of the PSRM by using the kernels trained in CNN structure.

Research on steganalysis of JPEG Images is still insufficient, Xu et al. [15] constructed a 20-layer network to detect J-UNIWARD, borrowed idea from Resnet which is an excellent method in the field of computer vision. Mo et al. [2] proposed a JPEG-Phase-Aware Convolutional Neural Network, which inserted a PhaseSplit module to split the feature map by JPEG phase for boosting the detection accuracy.

In order to obtain better detection effect, existing schemes generally use deep network structures, but with the limitation of GPUs' memory, it is not possible to train the deep CNN net using large images. We can only train the model with small images, typically 256×256 or 512×512 pixels. This is far from meeting the needs of practical applications. To steganalyze large images, [13] proposed an approach in which modified an existing CNN detector. They output statistical moments (the average, minimum, maximum, and variance) of the feature maps before entering the fully-connected layers of the network, trained the network with moments on small tiles, then regarded the front part of the network as a "universal feature extractor" and retrained the fully-connected layers of the network to adapt to a different input image size. This is an indirect method to detect large images.

In this paper, we propose an architecture to directly detect steganography on large images. We reduce the depth of network structure, and apply histogram layer to reduce data dimension. People often get images from the Internet as steganography covers, but these images are usually small. To embed more messages, people resize the images to the larger sizes. On the other hand, people take photos themselves as steganography covers, these images are usually very large. For the convenience of processing and transmission, people resize the images to appropriate size. So we take two methods to generate large samples. The experiment, examining J-UNIWARD on standard datasets of size 512×512, 1024×1024, 2048×2048, has shown that directly detecting large images can achieve a good performance.

The rest of this paper is organized as follows. In Sect. 2 we will overview the rich model and introduce the function of histogram layer. The architecture of our network is presented in Sect. 3. Experiments and discussion are presented in Sect. 4. Conclusion and future work are contained in Sect. 5.

2 Overview of Rich Models and the Function of Histogram Layer

Rich models are the most widely used method in steganalysis, and it can be used for reference in design of CNNs network. We will give an overview of rich model, and gather insight from it. DCTR and GFR are the most popular handcrafted features to detect steganography on JPEG images, the extraction process is shown in Fig. 1.

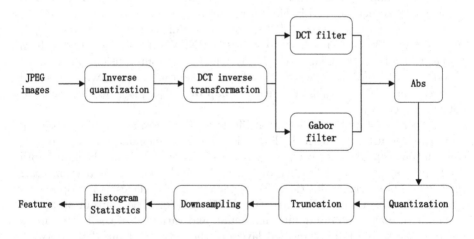

Fig. 1. The extraction process of rich model features.

First, transform the input data of JPEG format to the spatial domain. Then let the images pass through a set of filter banks, DCT filters or Gabor filters. Next, take the absolute values of the residual. And for convenience of calculation, quantify its value and further truncate with a threshold value. After that, generate a series of small feature maps through down sampling. Finally, project the residual maps to the histogram to get the histogram features.

Histogram feature has been proved to be effectual in rich models, so researchers try to use histogram structure in CNN framework. [11] implements a new layer that simulates the formation of histogram to obtain the histogram feature in CNN. They select Gaussian kernel as histogram bin to allow the back flow of gradients through the layer, then use the back-propagation algorithm to optimize the parameters. The values of the histogram bin B(k) of each histogram bin center at $\mu_k \in \{-3.5, -2.5, ..., 2.5, 3.5\}$, the values are computed by (1).

$$B(k) = \frac{1}{MN} \sum_{i=1}^{M} \sum_{i=1}^{N} e^{-\frac{(x_{ij} - \mu_k)^2}{\sigma^2}} \qquad (1)$$

x_{ij} is the element of feature maps, this operation projects each feature map onto a vector which only has 8 values (Fig. 2).

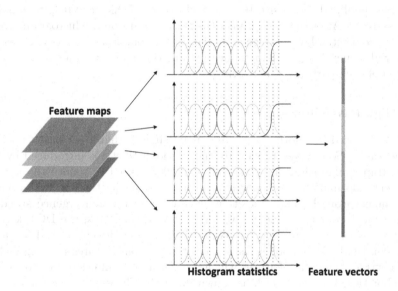

Fig. 2. Reducing dimension using histogram layer.

In the previous network structure, pooling layer is used to reduce the feature dimensions and retain main properties of input data, which will undoubtedly loss a lot of useful information. In our network structure, we modify the histogram layer and put it before fully connected layer to replace the pooling layer, which can make full use of all information and greatly decrease parameters to make it possible to detect steganography directly on large images. In next section we will illustrate the using method of histogram layer in detail.

3   Network Architecture

In this section, we experiment two kinds of structures with histogram layer to get the best capability. The two structures are shown in Figs. 3 and 4.

In both structures, we first transform the images from the frequency domain to the spatial domain, then let the images go through a set of filter banks to project single input to different frequency bands. Afterward we use an absolute value activation (ABS) layer in structure II to facilitate statistical modeling and match different histogram layer. A truncation layer is used in both structures to limit the range of input data. The most important block convolutional layers are used to extract feature maps. In structure I, each block is formed by a convolutional layer of 3 × 3 kernel, a TanH activation function layer, and a batch normalization layer. Different from structure I, we use ReLU activation function in structure II. After we get the feature maps, we introduce an average pooling layer of size 16 × 16 with stride 1, which can help to enhance model stability. After that, we project the feature maps on the histogram layers. The fully connected layer is placed at the end to complete the tasks of classification. Subsequently, we will introduce the function and the detailed parameter selection of each part of the network.

3.1   High Pass Filter

The signal caused by information hiding is far slighter than the content itself in steganography. So in order to capture the subtle distinctions introduced by the steganography algorithm, high pass filter (HPF) is used to reduce the impact of content information. It is worth mentioning that the type of HPFs has a great influence on the final detection accuracy and the convergence speed of the network. In our experiments, we test two kinds of HPFs, the DCT kernels of size 4 × 4 used in [15] and the Gabor kernels of 8 directions and 5 scales. In general, small size Gabor kernels extract the global features and big Gabor kernels extract the detail features which are sensitive to interference. So we use the Gabor kernel of size 8 × 8, as shown in Fig. 5. The experiments show that simple application of Gabor kernel does not improve the detection performance, on the contrary, it reduces the detection accuracy and slows the convergence speed. It should be researched for further study.

3.2   Truncation

After passing through the high-pass filters, we take a truncate operation, it can limit the range of input data to avoid the effects of extreme values. We test the global threshold value of 6, 8, 12 the threshold of 8 achieves the best experimental result.

3.3   ABS Layer

In the structure II, we add an ABS layer after the HPF. An absolute value operation is performed on each input data, this operation can eliminate the influence of symbol, just as the traditional methods do. We don't do quantification, it will slow the convergence.

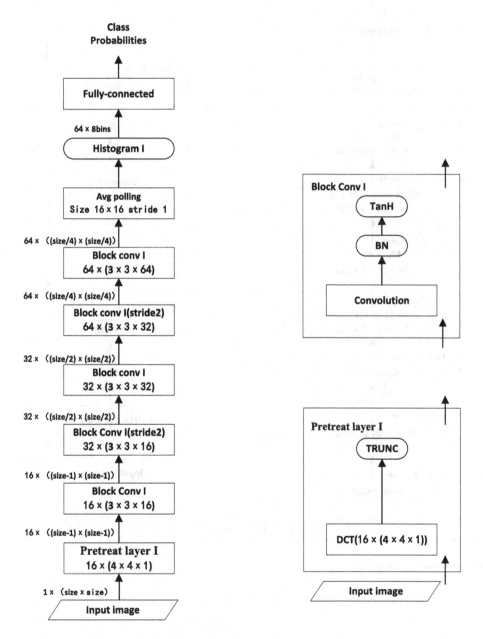

Fig. 3. Proposed CNN architecture I.

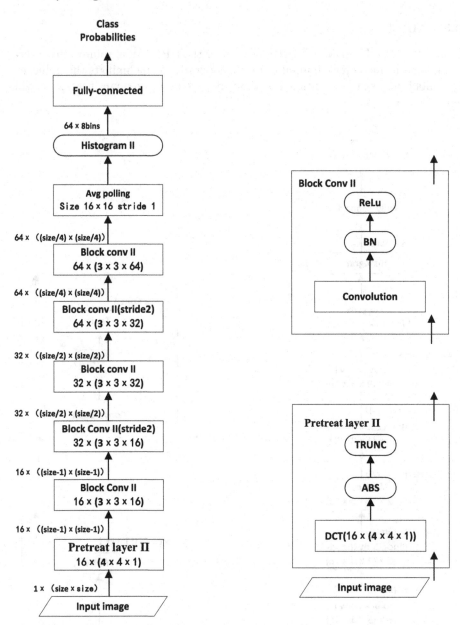

Fig. 4. Proposed CNN architecture II.

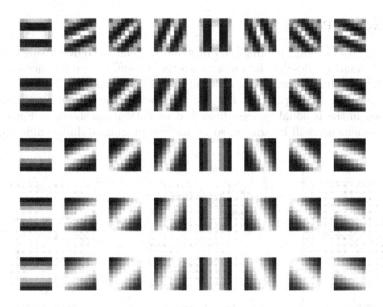

Fig. 5. 8 directions and 5 scales Gabor kernels.

3.4 Convolutional Layer

The convolutional layer is the main component in CNN. In our proposed network, we use convolutional layers of size 3×3 and stride 1 to capture the features of input data. In the rich model methods, they obtain small feature maps through down sampling. To get better results, we use convolutional layer of stride 2 to get small feature maps through learning.

3.5 Batch Normalization Layer

The Batch Normalization layer (BN layer) is widely used in CNN to solve the problem of gradient disappearing and gradient explosion. Besides, it can decrease the danger of overfitting, accelerate the speed of convergence and increase the detection accuracy. It is usually placed before the activation layer.

3.6 Activation Function

In order to increase the expressiveness of the model, we introduce nonlinear factors through the activation function in eaYch convolutional block. TanH and ReLU is the most commonly used activation function. TanH can effectively limit the range of input data, and remove sparse or unfavorable values to the statistical model. ReLu can avoid the problem of gradient disappearing as the network go deep and accelerate training. According to different symbolic characteristics, we use TanH in structure I, and ReLU in structure II.

3.7   Average Pooling

We introduce an average pooling layer of stride 1, it can avoid overfitting without losing information. Besides, it can enhance the capability of difference - awareness. When we change one DCT coefficient in JPEG images, it will cause changes of corresponding 8×8 pixels in the decompressed images, then more changes are caused in the residual images through convolutions, as shown in Fig. 6, but many positions are still invariable, so we use the pooling to diffuse difference.

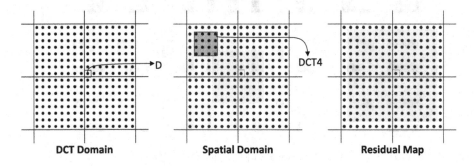

DCT Domain   **Spatial Domain**   **Residual Map**

Fig. 6. Effect of modifying DCT coefficient on residual filter image.

3.8   Histogram Layer

In structure I, we use the same histogram layer as [11], as shown in Fig. 7(a), it obtain the positive and negative values at the same time. In structure II, we modified the histogram layer like Fig. 7(b), it only obtain the positive values, and we test the threshold value of 4, 6, 8. Although increasing the threshold value can slightly improve the accuracy, the speed of training is going to drop a lot, so we set the threshold value to 4.

3.9   Fully Connected Layer

In the network, the function of the fully connected layer is to implement the classification. It maps the features to the label space of samples. The parameters of FC layer account for 80% of the entire network. So reducing the parameters of the fully connected layer is important to detect large images.

3.10   The Depth of the Network

Generally, the deeper the network is, the more expressive it is, and the more training data it can handle. Researchers try to get a high detection rate by using a very deep network, which makes the parameters of a model increase a lot. In the field of computer vision, one view has been point that when the depth reaches a certain level, simply superposing the same architecture can't

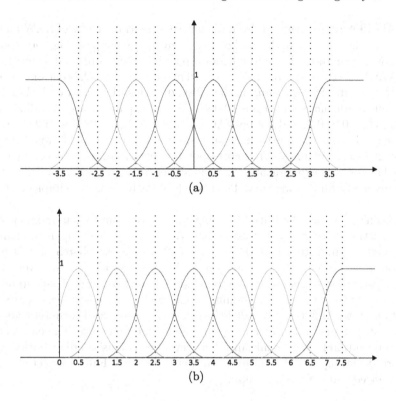

Fig. 7. Histogram layer: (a) Original histogram layer. (b) New histogram layer.

significantly improve the performance, new architecture and new component is essential. And through compressing model, we can get a small network with good performance, the deep of network should match the difficulty of the task.

Obviously, it is not possible to train very deep network on large images. In order to reduce the number of parameters to an acceptable range, we must reduce the depth of the network. Convolution blocks' number of 3, 4, 5 and 6 has been tested. Finally, to balance the detection accuracy with memory constraints, we use three convolutions of stride 1, and two convolutions of stride 2. We managed to fit this CNN in a single GPU with 16GB memory. It is essential for the CNNs to reduce the spatial resolutions by pooling layer. In our CNN, reduction of dimension is achieved by convolutional layers of stride 2, after which the spatial sizes of data are cut by half and the number of channels doubles.

4   Experiments

4.1   Dataset and Setting

In this paper we use the dataset BOSSbase v1.01 [1] which includes 10,000 uncompressed cover images. To generate covers for JPEG steganography, the images are compressed with QF75, and then resized to 1024 × 1024 and 2048 × 2048 from

512 × 512 BOSSbase images or from the native resolution images of RAW format to illustrate the influence of the method to generate large samples. The corresponding stegos are generated through embedding data into the compressed images using J-UNIWARD as the steganographic method in our study, which is one of the most secure steganography algorithms in the JPEG domains. Hence, for each classification problem, the dataset contains 10,000 cover-stego pairs. The embedding rates are set to 0.1, 0.2, 0.3, and 0.4 bpnzAC on 512 × 512 and 1024 × 1024 images. Because it takes a lot of time to make large sample images, we use 0.2 and 0.4 bpnzAC on 2048 × 2048 images. The corresponding performances achieved by GFR are used as contrast experiments. We train all networks on a NVIDIA Tesla P100 GPU with 16G graphics memory. The Caffe toolbox [7] is used to implement the CNNs.

In training, we set the initial learning rate to 10^{-3} and we use exponential decay function with a decay rate of 0.9. Additionally, learning rate changes every 5000 training iterations. For 512 × 512 images, the batch size of each iteration is 32 (16 cover/stego pairs) in training stage, and 10 (5 cover/stego pairs) in validation stage. For 1024 × 1024 images, the batch size of each iteration is 16 (8 cover/stego pairs) in training stage, and 10 (5 cover/stego pairs) in validation stage. And for 2048 × 2048 images, the batch size of each iteration is 4 (2 cover/stego pairs) in both training stage and validation stage. The parameters of the convolution layers are initialized via zero-mean Gaussian distribution with standard deviation of 0.01, and bias learning is disabled. Fully-connected layers are initialized using Xavier method.

4.2   Results

Tables 1, 2, 3 and 4 show the final ensemble results on the BOSSBase using the CNN in Fig. 4. As we can see, the performance of the proposed CNN outperforms the feature-based method GFR in almost all experiments, except for the experiments on the 2048 × 2048 images resized from the native resolution images of RAW format. Obviously, we can see the accuracy rates detecting the large images directly are excellent, which illustrates that our scheme is feasible. Different from the [13], which detects steganography on larger spatial domain images, our method achieves the detection of steganography on larger JPEG images. Furthermore, the time cost does not increase significantly when we train the models on large images. The method of resize has a great influence on the results of the experiments. The large stego images resized from 512 × 512 BOSSbase images are easier to detect. The performance is not satisfactory when we directly detect the 2048 × 2048 images of low embedding rate and the images resized from the native resolution images of RAW format. Instead of training from scratch, we use parameters obtained from the tasks of higher embedding rates or the task of small images to fine-tine the model, and get a better result (Fig. 8).

Table 1. Classification errors on 512×512 images

	Embedding rates (bpnzAC)			
	0.1	0.2	0.3	0.4
GFR	0.4082	0.2866	0.1785	0.1026
Proposed	0.3718	0.2432	0.1502	0.0632

Table 2. Classification errors on 1024×1024 images resized from small images

	Embedding rates (bpnzAC)			
	0.1	0.2	0.3	0.4
GFR	0.358	0.1945	0.0817	0.0507
Proposed	0.3184	0.1656	0.054	0.0255

Table 3. Classification errors on 1024×1024 images resized from large images

	Embedding rates (bpnzAC)			
	0.1	0.2	0.3	0.4
GFR	0.378	0.255	0.156	0.0737
Proposed	0.361	0.236	0.142	0.0526

Table 4. Classification errors on 2048×2048 images resized from small(S) or large(L) images

	Embedding rates (bpnzAC)			
	(S)0.2	(S)0.4	(L)0.2	(L)0.4
GFR	0.0902	0.0272	0.1936	0.0652
Proposed	0.0682	0.0121	0.2265	0.0956

Table 5. Comparison of memory requirement with XU's net

	Memory requirement (MB)		
	512×512	1024×1024	2048×2048
XU's net	10361	-	-
Proposed	5917	12319	13933

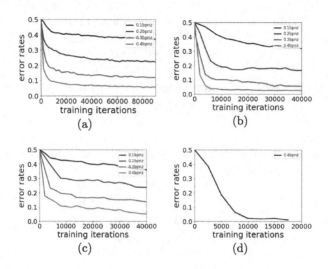

Fig. 8. Validation errors versus training iterations of proposed CNN at different embedding rate. (a) 512 (b) 1024 (Resize from small images) (c) 1024 (Resize from large images) (d) 2048 (Resize from small images)

4.3   Memory Size Comparison

Table 5 shows the needed memory compared with Xu's net, and we can see that the proposed structure greatly reduces memory requirements, which can bring a lot of benefits, such as enhancing the network training speed, quickly testing the effects of some structures, facilitating the adjustment of parameters. We can train the model with even less memory by reducing the size of batchsize.

5   Conclusions

CNN-based Steganalysis has exceeded the performance of detectors using the rich model. However, the inability to directly detect large images limits its application. The leading CNN detectors for steganalysis use a rather small tile as their input or fine-tune the model trained on small tiles to indirectly handle larger images. Aiming at this issue, we propose a shallow steganalytic network which contains histogram layer to detect steganography on large JPEG images. We test two different structures based on the histogram layer characteristics, then we select the better scheme and do further optimization. The experiment show detecting large images has better detection accuracy and faster convergence speed, which demonstrates directly train on large images is feasible and effective.

In our future work, we will further optimize our CNN scheme to detect larger images directly. We will use different steganography algorithm, and further improve the accuracy by using more effective HPF kernels.

Acknowledgments. This work was supported by National Key Technology R&D Program under 2016YFB0801003, NSFC under U1636102 and U1736214, Fundamental Theory and Cutting Edge Technology Research Program of IIE, CAS, under Y7Z0371102, and National Key Technology R&D Program under 2016QY15Z2500.

References

1. Bas, P., Filler, T., Pevný, T.: "Break our steganographic system": the Ins and outs of organizing BOSS. In: Filler, T., Pevný, T., Craver, S., Ker, A. (eds.) IH 2011. LNCS, vol. 6958, pp. 59–70. Springer, Heidelberg (2011). https://doi.org/10.1007/978-3-642-24178-9_5

2. Chen, M., Sedighi, V., Boroumand, M., Fridrich, J.: JPEG-phase-aware convolutional neural network for steganalysis of JPEG images. In: Proceedings of the 5th ACM Workshop on Information Hiding and Multimedia Security, IH&MMSec 2017, Philadelphia, PA, USA, 20–22 June 2017, pp. 75–84. ACM (2017)

3. Guo, L., Ni, J., Shi, Y.Q.: Uniform embedding for efficient JPEG steganography. IEEE Trans. Inf. Forensics Secur. **9**(5), 814–825 (2014)

4. Holub, V., Fridrich, J.: Random projections of residuals for digital image steganalysis. IEEE Trans. Inf. Forensics Secur. **8**(12), 1996–2006 (2013)

5. Holub, V., Fridrich, J.: Low-complexity features for JPEG steganalysis using undecimated DCT. IEEE Trans. Inf. Forensics Secur. **10**(2), 219–228 (2015)

6. Holub, V., Fridrich, J., Denemark, T.: Universal distortion function for steganography in an arbitrary domain. EURASIP J. Inf. Secur. **2014**(1), 1 (2014)

7. Jia, Y., et al.: Caffe: convolutional architecture for fast feature embedding. In: Proceedings of the ACM International Conference on Multimedia, MM 2014, Orlando, FL, USA, 03–07 November 2014, pp. 675–678. ACM (2014)

8. Kodovský, J., Fridrich, J.: Steganalysis of JPEG images using rich models. In: Media Watermarking, Security, and Forensics 2012, Burlingame, CA, USA, 22 January 2012, Proceedings, vol. 8303, p. 83030A. SPIE (2012)

9. Qian, Y., Dong, J., Wang, W., Tan, T.: Deep learning for steganalysis via convolutional neural networks. In: Media Watermarking, Security, and Forensics 2015, San Francisco, CA, USA, 9–11 February 2015, Proceedings, vol. 9409, p. 94090J. International Society for Optics and Photonics (2015)

10. Qian, Y., Dong, J., Wang, W., Tan, T.: Learning and transferring representations for image steganalysis using convolutional neural network. In: 2016 IEEE International Conference on Image Processing, ICIP 2016, Phoenix, AZ, USA, 25–28 September 2016, pp. 2752–2756. IEEE (2016)

11. Sedighi, V., Fridrich, J.: Histogram layer, moving convolutional neural networks towards feature-based steganalysis. In: Proceedings of IS&T, Electronic Imaging, Media Watermarking, Security, and Forensics 2017, San Francisco, CA, USA, pp. 50–55 (2017)

12. Song, X., Liu, F., Yang, C., Luo, X., Zhang, Y.: Steganalysis of adaptive JPEG steganography using 2D gabor filters. In: Proceedings of the 3rd ACM Workshop on Information Hiding and Multimedia Security, IH&MMSec 2015, Portland, OR, USA, 17–19 June 2015, pp. 15–23. ACM (2015)

13. Tsang, C.F., Fridrich, J.: Steganalyzing images of arbitrary size with CNNs. In: Proceedings of IS&T, Electronic Imaging, Media Watermarking, Security, and Forensics 2018, San Francisco, CA, USA, pp. 1–8 (2018)

14. Westfeld, A.: F5—a steganographic algorithm. In: Moskowitz, I.S. (ed.) IH 2001. LNCS, vol. 2137, pp. 289–302. Springer, Heidelberg (2001). https://doi.org/10.1007/3-540-45496-9_21
15. Xu, G.: Deep convolutional neural network to detect J-UNIWARD. In: Proceedings of the 5th ACM Workshop on Information Hiding and Multimedia Security, IH&MMSec 2017, Philadelphia, PA, USA, 20–22 June 2017, pp. 67–73. ACM (2017)
16. Xu, G., Wu, H.Z., Shi, Y.Q.: Structural design of convolutional neural networks for steganalysis. IEEE Sig. Process. Lett. **23**(5), 708–712 (2016)

Comparison of DCT and Gabor Filters in Residual Extraction of CNN Based JPEG Steganalysis

Huilin Zheng[1], Xuan Li[1], Danyang Ruan[1], Xiangui Kang[1(✉)],
and Yun-Qing Shi[2]

[1] Guangdong Key Lab of Information Security Technology,
School of Data and Computer Science, Sun Yat-sen University, Guangzhou, China
353166851@qq.com, isskxg@mail.sysu.edu.cn
[2] Department of ECE, New Jersey Institute of Technology, Newark, NJ, USA

Abstract. An effective feature selection method to capture the weak stego noise is essential to image steganalysis. In the conventional JPEG steganalysis, Gabor filter and DCT filter are both used for residual extraction. However, there are few comparisons in existing convolutional neural networks (CNNs) based JPEG steganalysis using Gabor filter or DCT filter in the pre-processing stage to extract residuals. In this paper, we compare the performance of DCT filter with Gabor filter in the pre-processing phase of the steganalysis CNN. Firstly, we choose the parameters empirically and theoretically for Gabor filters which are used in CNN. Secondly, we improve the performance by removing the ABS layer in the original XuNet. Finally, the experimental results show that using Gabor filters or DCT filter can achieve comparable performance whenever the parameters of pre-processing filters are fixed or learnable. It's different from the conventional steganalysis method where Gabor filters have advantages over DCT filters. When the parameters of the pre-processing filters are learnable, both Gabor filter and DCT filter can achieve better performance compared with the condition where the parameters are fixed.

Keywords: JPEG steganalysis · Gabor filter · Convolutional neural networks (CNNs)

1 Introduction

Steganography is a kind of covert communication method which embeds a secret message into a cover object to hide the presence of the message itself. Steganalysis, contrary to the steganography, is the technique to detect messages hidden in digital media. Owing to the convenient access to digital images on the Internet

This work was supported by NSFC (Grant Nos. U1536204, NSFC 61772571) and the special funding for basic scientific research of Sun Yat-sen University (Grant No. 6177060230).

© Springer Nature Switzerland AG 2019
C. D. Yoo et al. (Eds.): IWDW 2018, LNCS 11378, pp. 29–39, 2019.
https://doi.org/10.1007/978-3-030-11389-6_3

and the extensive use of JPEG format images, the research on JPEG steganography and steganalysis has academic significance and application value.

Modern JPEG steganographic schemes are usually content adaptive, e.g. UED [8], UERD [9] and J-UNIWARD [10]. They minimize a carefully designed distortion function such that embedding changes are restricted to complex regions which are difficult to be modeled. The JPEG-phase-aware features, which are assembled as the histogram of noise residuals split by the 8×8 pixel grids, are widely used by content adaptive steganalysis methods like Phase Aware Rich Model (PHARM) [12], DCT Residuals (DCTR) [11], and Gabor Filter Residuals (GFR) [18]. Remarkably, GFR extracts the statistical features from multiple scales and orientations, and significantly improves the detection performance against the content adaptive JPEG steganography. By incorporating the channel selection knowledge into GFR, the selection-channel-aware(SCA)-GFR [5] has achieved the most accurate detection among the conventional methods.

Due to the overwhelming superiority of CNN in computer vision, the novel detection architectures with CNN have been proposed for spatial steganalysis [16,20,21] and JPEG steganalysis [2,19,24]. Zeng et al. [24] designed a hybrid deep-learning framework containing three sub-CNNs with 5×5 DCT filters to extract image residual. Xu [19] proposed a 20-layer CNN (XuNet in short) which extract the residuals by 4×4 DCT filter bank and achieves the state-of-the-art JPEG steganalysis performance in detecting J-UNIWARD. Chen et al. [2] proposed JPEG-phase-aware steganalysis and used a combination of Gabor filter, F_{kv} filter 'SQUARE5 $\times$ 5' from the spatial rich model [6] and its complementary point high-pass filter to suppress the image content and increase the high-frequency stego signals.

In this paper, the performance of CNN using Gabor filters and that using DCT filters in the residual extraction of JPEG steganalysis has been compared in two different cases: filter parameters are learnable or fixed during the training phase. In the next section, we give a brief introduction of the Gabor filter and its property, then present the overall CNN architecture. In Sect. 3, we evaluate the performance of Gabor filters and DCT filters in image residual extraction of CNN architecture and the paper is summarized in Sect. 4.

2   The CNN Architecture with Gabor Filters

In this section, we firstly introduce 2D Gabor filter and its important properties and then the CNN architecture of JPEG steganalysis is presented.

2.1   Gabor Filters

Based on Gabor transform, Daugman proposed 2D Gabor filters [4] and pointed out that the family of 2D Gabor filters can achieve the theoretical lower bound of joint uncertainty in the two conjoint domains of visual space and spatial frequency. 2D Gabor filter is a sinusoidal plane wave modulated by a Gaussian kernel function:

$$G_{\lambda,\theta,\phi,\sigma,\gamma}(x,y) = e^{\left(-\frac{u^2+\gamma^2 v^2}{2\sigma^2}\right)} \cos(2\pi\frac{u}{\lambda} + \phi) \tag{1}$$

where

$$u = x\cos\theta + y\sin\theta, v = -x\sin\theta + y\cos\theta \tag{2}$$

λ represents the wavelength of the sinusoidal factor, $\sigma = 0.56\lambda$ is the standard deviation of the Gaussian modulation and represents the scale parameter, the θ represents the orientation of the 2D Gabor filter, γ represents the spatial aspect ratio and specifies the ellipticity of the support of the Gabor function, and ϕ is the sinusoidal wave phase offset.

For $\phi = \{0, \pi/2\}$, Gabor filter satisfies the property:

$$G_{\lambda,\theta,0,\sigma,\gamma}(x,y) = G_{\lambda,\theta+\pi,0,\sigma,\gamma}(x,y) \tag{3}$$

$$G_{\lambda,\theta,\pi/2,\sigma,\gamma}(x,y) = -G_{\lambda,\theta+\pi,\pi/2,\sigma,\gamma}(x,y) \tag{4}$$

the absolute value of residuals extracted with $G_{\lambda,\theta,\phi,\sigma,\gamma}(x,y)$ is the same as that with $G_{\lambda,\theta+\pi,\phi,\sigma,\gamma}(x,y)$. Besides, the parameters of $G_{\lambda,\theta,\phi,\sigma,\gamma}(x,y)$ equal to the filter parameters of horizontally flipped $G_{\lambda,\pi-\theta,\phi,\sigma,\gamma}(x,y)$.

GFR [18] uses 256 Gabor filters to extract multiple residual, in which the Gabor filter has 32 directions $\theta = \{0, \frac{\pi}{32}, \frac{2\pi}{32}, ..., \frac{31\pi}{32}\}$, two phase offset parameters $\phi = \{0, \pi/2\}$. Parameter $\sigma = \{0.5, 0.75, 1, 1.25\}$ for JPEG quality factor(QF) 75 and $\sigma = \{0.5, 1, 1.5, 2\}$ for QF 95. Besides, all the Gabor filters in GFR are made zero-meaned by subtracting the kernel mean from all its elements to form high-pass filters.

It's of significance to extract steganography signal from multiple orientations and scales for steganalysis. Orientation θ and scale σ are the most important parameters in Gabor filter. Considering the property of Gabor filter and the priori knowledge of GFR, we select the orientation parameter θ in CNN pre-processing stage from $0 \leq \theta \leq \pi/2$ to reduce feature redundancy and computer resource. And σ is selected from the set $\sigma = \{0.5, 0.75, 1, 1.25\}$. The experimental results with different parameter selection are shown in the third part of the next section.

2.2   The CNN Model

For the case where the pre-processing filters' parameters are fixed, we adopt the CNN architecture of XuNet [19], which uses sixteen 4×4 DCT kernels $B^{(k,l)}$ to extract image residual:

$$B^{(k,l)}_{mn} = \frac{w_k w_l}{4} \cos(\frac{k\pi(2m+1)}{8}) \cos(\frac{l\pi(2n+1)}{8}) \tag{5}$$

where

$$w_0 = 1, w_x = \frac{1}{\sqrt{2}} \, for \, x > 0, \, 1 \leq k,l \leq 4, \, 1 \leq m,n \leq 4$$

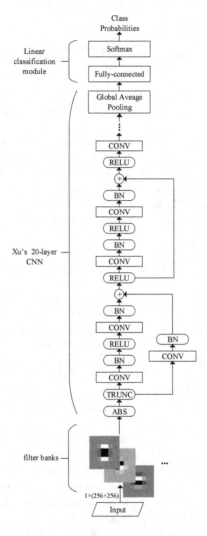

Fig. 1. The steganalysis method with Gabor filters and XuNet.

We replace the DCT kernels in XuNet with the Gabor filters to make comparison between the filters. The CNN architecture is shown in Fig. 1, which consists of the residual extraction and a 20-layer CNN. In the pre-processing stage, an input JPEG image is firstly decompressed into the spatial domain without rounding, then is convolved by twenty 8 × 8 Gabor filters. An ABS layer follows the residual extraction to obtain the absolute value of coefficients in frequency subbands. Then the residual is further truncated by a global threshold to limit the range of input data and speed up the convergence. After the residual extraction, all the convolutional layers adopting 3 × 3 kernels and each convolutional layer is followed by Batch Normalization (BN) [13] layer and Rectified

Linear Unit (ReLU) activation function [15]. All pooling operations except the last global average pooling are carried out by 3 × 3 convolution kernels with stride of 2. The structure of shortcut connections is used in the architecture to overcome the gradient vanishing problem. In this work, we remove the ABS layer in XuNet(Fig. 1) to further enhance the detecting performance. Similar to [22] and [23], we also consider using learnable pre-processing filters' parameters to extract more effective residual while filters parameters in XuNet are fixed during network training.

3   Experiment and Analysis

3.1   Datasets

In this paper, we focus on the detection of UED, UERD, and J-UNIWARD. All images of each dataset are shuffled first and then embedded with payload sizes 0.1, 0.2, 0.3 and 0.4 bpnzAC respectively to create the corresponding stego images. Two image datasets are used for experiments.

BOSSbase. The standard database BOSSbase v1.01 [1] contains 10,000 raw images with size of 512 × 512. The images are first cropped from the central 256 × 256 block and then JPEG compressed with quality factor 75. For each payload, 6,000 cover-stego pairs are randomly selected as training set, 1,500 cover-stego pairs are selected for validation and the remaining 2,500 pairs are selected for testing.

ImageNet. 100,000 images are randomly selected from large-scale ImageNet ILSVRC 2013 classification dataset [17]. All the images are cropped from the central part to resize to 256 × 256, then convert to grayscale and JPEG compressed with quality factor 75. For each payload, 85% of images are randomly selected for training, 5% for validation and 10% for testing.

3.2   Platform and Hyperparameter Settings

Caffe toolbox [14] is used to implement the proposed method. We use mini-batch stochastic gradient descent optimizer (SGD) to train the CNNs in this paper. A batch, containing 32 cover-stego pairs in ImageNet or 16 cover-stego image pairs in BOSSbase, is fed to network for each training iteration. The momentum is set to 0.9, the learning rate is initialized to 0.001 and then decreased by 10% every 5000 training iterations. A zero-mean Gaussian distribution with standard deviation of 0.01 is used to initialize the parameters of the convolutional kernels. Bias learning is disabled in convolutional layers but fulfilled in BN layers. Parameters in the final fully-connected (FC) layer are initialized using "Xavier" [7] initialization. Weight decay (L2 regularization) for the FC layer and the updated filter layer is set to 0.01.

Each input image pair is randomly rotated by a multiple of 90 degrees or horizontally flipped in a synchronized manner to ensure that the difference caused by data embedding can be learned by the proposed CNN. The maximum number of iterations is 90000 and the parameters of the CNN are saved after every 500 training iterations. Five models performing best on validation set are selected for testing and the ensemble result of them is regarded as the final result.

3.3   Gabor Filter Settings

XuNet adopts sixteen DCT filters in the pre-processing stage, the number of Gabor filters in the variant CNN should be set as a similar number to adapt to the network architecture. We set $\phi = \{0, \pi/2\}$, and then choose σ from $\{0.5, 0.75, 1, 1.25\}$, and select θ from $0 \le \theta \le \pi/2$. Firstly, we set orientation $\theta = \{0, \pi/8, 2\pi/8, 3\pi/8, 4\pi/8\}$ and test the influence of σ. Table 1 shows the performance of detecting J-UNIWARD with different sigma parameters, $\sigma = 0.75$ and $\sigma = 1$ obtain the best performance for both high and low payload, and $\sigma = 1.25$ is obviously worse than the others. The results on combination of two different sigma parameters are shown in Table 2. It can be found that using more scale values can enhance the detection performance. The best performance is achieved when $\sigma = \{0.75, 1\}$, i.e. σ is chosen to be both 0.75 and 1.

Table 1. Detection Accuracy (%) of Gabor filter bank with different σ parameters for J-UNIWARD on BOSSbase

Payload (bpnzAC)	$\sigma = 0.5$	$\sigma = 0.75$	$\sigma = 1$	$\sigma = 1.25$
0.1	55.45	55.5	**55.98**	54.46
0.4	82.3	**83.94**	82.8	78.78

Table 2. Detection Accuracy (%) of Gabor filter bank with different combination of σ parameters for J-UNIWARD on BOSSbase

Payload (bpnzAC)	$\sigma = \{0.5, 0.75\}$	$\sigma = \{0.5, 1\}$	$\sigma = \{0.75, 1\}$
0.1	57.92	57.4	**58.16**
0.4	84.6	84.9	**85.54**

For $\sigma = \{0.75, 1\}$, the J-UNIWARD detection accuracies with different orientations are shown in Table 3. For example, the orientation $\{0, 1, 2\} \times \pi/4$ in Table 3 means that the orientations are 0, $\pi/4$ and $\pi/2$ and each orientation corresponds to two different scales and two phase offsets, totally 12 filters are contained in the filter bank. It can be observed from the first three rows in Table 3 that the detection accuracy increases and then gets down along with the increasing number of orientation. The turning point is $\theta = \{0, 1, 2, 3, 4\} \times \pi/8$. By comparing the performance of $\theta = \{0, 1, 2, 3, 4\} \times \pi/8$ with $\theta = \{0, 1, 2, ..., 7\} \times \pi/8$, we can observe that the Gabor filter with orientation range $[0, \pi)$ has no advantage

Table 3. Detection Accuracy (%) of Gabor filter bank with different orientations for J-UNIWARD on BOSSbase

Embedding rates (bpnzAC)	0.1	0.2	0.3	0.4
$\{0, 1, 2\} \times \pi/4$	58.40	69.32	78.2	84.18
$\{0, 1, 2, 3, 4\} \times \pi/8$	58.16	**69.42**	**79.40**	**85.54**
$\{0, 1, 2, ..., 7, 8\} \times \pi/16$	57.78	68.70	78.44	85.40
$\{0, 1, 2, ..., 7\} \times \pi/8$	**58.44**	69.16	78.20	84.16

Table 4. Detection Accuracy (%) of Gabor filter bank with different γ parameters for J-UNIWARD on BOSSbase

Payload (bpnzAC)	$\gamma = 0.5$	$\gamma = 1$
0.1	57.06	**57.4**
0.4	83.9	**84.9**

over $[0, \pi/2]$, which verifies our analysis in Sect. 2 that θ should be within $[0, \pi/2]$. For the following experiments, we set orientation $\theta = \{0, \pi/8, 2\pi/8, 3\pi/8, 4\pi/8\}$.

Noticeably, the aspect ratio γ is set as 1 in this paper, where the support of the Gabor function is circular. The performance of Gabor filter with $\gamma = 1$ and $\gamma = 0.5$ is compared in Table 4. With $\phi = \{0, \pi/2\}$, $\sigma = \{0.75, 1\}$ and $\theta = \{0, \pi/8, 2\pi/8, 3\pi/8, 4\pi/8\}$, we can find that Gabor filter with $\gamma = 1$ achieves better performance on detecting both 0.1 and 0.4 bpnzAC payload.

Based on theoretical analysis and experimental results, the Gabor filters parameters used in the following experiments are set as: $\gamma = 1$, $\phi = \{0, \pi/2\}$, $\sigma = \{0.75, 1\}$, $\theta = \{0, \pi/8, 2\pi/8, 3\pi/8, 4\pi/8\}$.

3.4   Results on the BOSSbase

The DCT filters used in this paper are the same as the setting of XuNet [19] which adopts sixteen 4×4 DCT basis patterns. As indicated above, the amount of the 8×8 Gabor filters is 20. The steganalysis method with Gabor filters and XuNet is shown in Fig. 1. In the architecture of XuNet one ABS layer is used. When the DCT and Gabor filter parameters are fixed, the detection results on UED, UERD, and J-UNIWARD are shown in Table 5, where "DCT" and "Gabor" mean the filter used in residual extraction.

We remove the ABS layer in the original XuNet, which is shown in Fig. 1. The other settings are the same as that in Table 5. From Tables 5 and 6, it can be observed that both the CNN architecture with DCT filters and the CNN with Gabor filters achieve a significant improvement when the ABS layer is removed from the framework. So in the sequel, the ABS layer is removed in CNN. It may be because absolute value operation may reject some efficient information, the residual extraction without ABS layer can help the CNN learn more resultful feature. The performance of Gabor filter and DCT filter are comparable in all

Table 5. Detection Accuracy (%) for UED, UERD and J-UNIWARD with fixed filters and ABS layer on BOSSBase

Payload (bpnzAC)		0.1	0.2	0.3	0.4
Steganography	Filter				
UED	DCT	73.48	84.98	90.64	94.64
	Gabor	**74.40**	**85.48**	**91.10**	**95.02**
UERD	DCT	**67.56**	**82.1**	87.16	**91.28**
	Gabor	66.46	81.36	**88.28**	90.98
J-UNIWARD	DCT	56.68	67.99	77.73	84.00
	Gabor	**58.07**	**69.22**	**78.66**	**85.21**

Table 6. Detection Accuracy (%) for UED, UERD and J-UNIWARD with fixed filters and without ABS layer on BOSSBase

Payload (bpnzAC)		0.1	0.2	0.3	0.4
Steganography	Filter				
UED	DCT	80.48	88.06	92.60	94.16
	Gabor	**80.96**	**88.42**	**92.40**	**95.06**
UERD	DCT	68.4	81.44	87.66	91.78
	Gabor	**70.1**	**81.64**	**87.94**	**91.86**
J-UNIWARD	DCT	58.77	71.40	79.47	85.26
	Gabor	**60.18**	**71.53**	**79.74**	**85.32**

Table 7. Detection Accuracy (%) for UERD and J-UNIWARD with learnable filters on BOSSBase

Payload (bpnzAC)		0.1	0.2	0.3	0.4
Steganography	Steganalysis				
J-UNIWARD	CNN+DCT	59.58	**72.32**	80.20	**86.69**
	CNN+Gabor	**62.42**	72.02	**80.30**	85.87
	SCA-GFR+EC	56.93	68.07	72.05	78.85
UERD	CNN+DCT	**70.42**	81.94	88.46	**92.4**
	CNN+Gabor	69.24	**81.96**	**89.04**	92.22

cases. It is because CNN method has the characteristic of rotation invariant [3], thus the directional selection of Gabor filter has no advantage in CNN.

We also evaluate the performance when the parameters of DCT or Gabor filter are learnable during training, with the performance of the most secure conventional steganalysis SCA-GFR as reference. The results on detecting J-UNIWARD and UERD are shown in Table 7. Comparing with the fixed filter parameters, updating the parameters in the training phase can enhance the performance of both Gabor filter and DCT filter. The most significant improvement is achieved when detecting J-UNIWARD with 0.1 bpnzAC payload, where the CNN with learnable Gabor filters achieves 2.24% improvement than the CNN with fixed Gabor filters. When the filter parameters are learnable, the detection accuracy of DCT filters and Gabor filters are comparable. It is because that in this case, the performance of CNN with learnable filter parameters mostly depends on the stochastic gradient descent rather than the parameters of the initialized filters.

3.5   Results on the ImageNet

We train the CNN model with 250,000 iterations on dataset ImageNet which containing 100,000 JPEG images. Table 8 lists the comparative results for the CNN with learnable DCT and Gabor filters. Also, ABS layer is removed in CNN in this experiment. Similar to the results on BOSSBase, using both filters achieves comparable performance. It further states that initializing the residual filter using Gabor filter may bring no advantage over DCT filter in CNN method.

Table 8. Detection Accuracy (%) for J-UNIWARD with learnable filters and without ABS layer on ImageNet

Embedding rates (bpnzAC)	0.1	0.2	0.3	0.4
DCT	52.60	**81.14**	**90.90**	**95.54**
Gabor	**53.50**	79.84	88.18	94.76

4   Conclusion

In this work, we evaluate the performance of DCT filters and Gabor filters when they are used in residual extraction of CNN steganalysis method. In addition, the performance with learnable DCT filter and Gabor filter is also compared. Firstly, the experimental results that detecting J-UNIWARD, UED, UERD under different conditions show that using Gabor filters or DCT filters brings no obvious difference in steganalysis with CNN. It is because CNN has the characteristic of rotational invariant, the directional selection of Gabor filters has no advantage in CNN. Secondly, removing the ABS layer of original XuNet significantly improves the detection accuracy of the architecture. Finally, a better detection performance of the architecture can be achieved when the parameters of preprocessing filters are learnable than that are fixed.

References

1. Bas, P., Filler, T., Pevný, T.: "break our steganographic system": the ins and outs of organizing BOSS. In: Proceedings of Information Hiding - 13th International Conference, IH 2011, Prague, Czech Republic, 18–20 May 2011, Revised Selected Papers, pp. 59–70 (2011)

2. Chen, M., Sedighi, V., Boroumand, M., Fridrich, J.J.: JPEG-phase-aware convolutional neural network for steganalysis of JPEG images. In: Proceedings of the 5th ACM Workshop on Information Hiding and Multimedia Security, IH&MMSec 2017, Philadelphia, PA, USA, 20–22 June 2017, pp. 75–84 (2017)

3. Chen, Y., Lyu, Z., Kang, X., Wang, Z.J.: A rotation-invariant convolutional neural network for image enhancement forensics. In: Proceedings of 2018 IEEE International Conference on Acoustics, Speech and Signal Processing, ICASSP, pp. 2111–2115 (2018)

4. Daugman, J.G.: Uncertainty relation for resolution in space, spatial frequency, and orientation optimized by two-dimensional visual cortical filters. J. Opt. Soc. Am. Opt. Image Sci. **2**(7), 1160 (1985)

5. Denemark, T., Boroumand, M., Fridrich, J.J.: Steganalysis features for content-adaptive JPEG steganography. IEEE Trans. Inf. Forensics Secur. **11**(8), 1736–1746 (2016)

6. Fridrich, J.J., Kodovský, J.: Rich models for steganalysis of digital images. IEEE Trans. Inf. Forensics Secur. **7**(3), 868–882 (2012)

7. Glorot, X., Bengio, Y.: Understanding the difficulty of training deep feedforward neural networks. In: Proceedings of the 13th International Conference on Artificial Intelligence and Statistics, AISTATS 2010, Chia Laguna Resort, Sardinia, Italy, 13–15 May 2010, pp. 249–256 (2010)

8. Guo, L., Ni, J., Shi, Y.: An efficient JPEG steganographic scheme using uniform embedding. In: Proceedings of the 2012 IEEE International Workshop on Information Forensics and Security, WIFS 2012, Costa Adeje, Tenerife, Spain, 2–5 December 2012, pp. 169–174 (2012)

9. Guo, L., Ni, J., Su, W., Tang, C., Shi, Y.: Using statistical image model for JPEG steganography: uniform embedding revisited. IEEE Trans. Inf. Forensics Secur. **10**(12), 2669–2680 (2015)

10. Holub, V., Fridrich, J.J.: Digital image steganography using universal distortion. In: Proceedings of ACM Information Hiding and Multimedia Security Workshop, IH&MMSec 2013, Montpellier, France, 17–19 June 2013, pp. 59–68 (2013)

11. Holub, V., Fridrich, J.J.: Low-complexity features for JPEG steganalysis using undecimated DCT. IEEE Trans. Inf. Forensics Secur. **10**(2), 219–228 (2015)

12. Holub, V., Fridrich, J.J.: Phase-aware projection model for steganalysis of JPEG images. In: Proceedings of Media Watermarking, Security, and Forensics 2015, San Francisco, CA, USA, 9–11 February 2015, Proceedings, p. 94090T (2015)

13. Ioffe, S., Szegedy, C.: Batch normalization: accelerating deep network training by reducing internal covariate shift. In: Proceedings of the 32nd International Conference on Machine Learning, ICML 2015, Lille, France, 6–11 July 2015, pp. 448–456 (2015)

14. Jia, Y., et al.: Caffe: convolutional architecture for fast feature embedding. In: Proceedings of the ACM International Conference on Multimedia, MM 2014, Orlando, FL, USA, 03–07 November 2014, pp. 675–678 (2014)

15. Nair, V., Hinton, G.E.: Rectified linear units improve restricted Boltzmann machines. In: Proceedings of the 27th International Conference on Machine Learning (ICML-10), 21–24 June 2010, Haifa, Israel, pp. 807–814 (2010)

16. Qian, Y., Dong, J., Wang, W., Tan, T.: Deep learning for steganalysis via convolutional neural networks. In: Proceedings of Media Watermarking, Security, and Forensics 2015, San Francisco, CA, USA, 9–11 February 2015, Proceedings, p. 94090J (2015)

17. Russakovsky, O., et al.: Imagenet large scale visual recognition challenge. Int. J. Comput. Vis. **115**(3), 211–252 (2015)

18. Song, X., Liu, F., Yang, C., Luo, X., Zhang, Y.: Steganalysis of adaptive JPEG steganography using 2D gabor filters. In: Proceedings of the 3rd ACM Workshop on Information Hiding and Multimedia Security, IH&MMSec 2015, Portland, OR, USA, 17–19 June 2015, pp. 15–23 (2015)
19. Xu, G.: Deep convolutional neural network to detect J-UNIWARD. In: Proceedings of the 5th ACM Workshop on Information Hiding and Multimedia Security, IH&MMSec 2017, Philadelphia, PA, USA, 20–22 June 2017, pp. 67–73 (2017)
20. Xu, G., Wu, H., Shi, Y.Q.: Ensemble of CNNs for steganalysis: an empirical study. In: Proceedings of the 4th ACM Workshop on Information Hiding and Multimedia Security, IH&MMSec 2016, Vigo, Galicia, Spain, 20–22 June 2016, pp. 103–107 (2016)
21. Xu, G., Wu, H., Shi, Y.: Structural design of convolutional neural networks for steganalysis. IEEE Sig. Process. Lett. **23**(5), 708–712 (2016)
22. Yang, J., Shi, Y., Wong, E.K., Kang, X.: JPEG steganalysis based on DenseNet. Computing Research Repository abs/1711.09335 (2017)
23. Ye, J., Ni, J., Yi, Y.: Deep learning hierarchical representations for image steganalysis. IEEE Trans. Inf. Forensics Secur. **12**(11), 2545–2557 (2017)
24. Zeng, J., Tan, S., Li, B., Huang, J.: Large-scale JPEG steganalysis using hybrid deep-learning framework. Computing Research Repository abs/1611.03233 (2016)

A Deep Residual Multi-scale Convolutional Network for Spatial Steganalysis

Shiyang Zhang[1,2], Hong Zhang[1,2(✉)], Xianfeng Zhao[1,2], and Haibo Yu[1,2]

[1] State Key Laboratory of Information Security, Institute of Information Engineering, Chinese Academy of Sciences, Beijing 100093, China
zhanghong@iie.ac.cn
[2] School of Cyber Security, University of Chinese Academy of Sciences, Beijing 100093, China

Abstract. Recent studies have indicated that Convolutional Neural Network (CNN), incorporated with certain domain knowledge, is capable of achieving competitive performances on discriminating trivial perturbation introduced by spatial steganographic schemes. In this paper, we propose a deep residual multi-scale convolutional network model, which outperforms several CNN-based steganalysis schemes and hand-crafted rich models. Compared to CNN-based steganalyzers proposed in recent studies, our model has a deeper network structure and it is integrated with a series of proven elements and complicated convolutional modules. With the intention of abstracting features from various dimensions, multi-scale convolutional modules are designed in three different ways. Besides, inspired by the idea of residual learning, shortcut components are adopted in the proposed model. Extensive experiments with BOSSbase v1.01 and LIRMMBase are carried out, which demonstrates that our network is able to detect multiple state-of-the-art spatial embedding schemes with different payloads.

Keywords: Spatial steganalysis · Convolutional Neural Network · Deep residual network · Multi-scale convolutional module

1 Introduction

Image steganography is the technique of hiding confidential messages through the procedure of embedding data into cover digital images [4]. The algorithms in the spatial domain nowadays usually conceal secret information in the region with high content complexity, which makes the stego signal less noticeable [7,9,12]. To cope with the development of steganography algorithms, Spatial Rich Model (SRM) [5] and its variants [3,8] are proposed. Although these schemes achieve better performance by utilizing the heuristic knowledge, it is very challenging to design hand crafted feature sets with more complexity.

© Springer Nature Switzerland AG 2019
C. D. Yoo et al. (Eds.): IWDW 2018, LNCS 11378, pp. 40–52, 2019.
https://doi.org/10.1007/978-3-030-11389-6_4

Inspired by the successful application of deep neural networks in the computer vision field [6,10,16,19,34], a number of CNN-based steganalyzers were proposed. Tan and Li [21] presented a structure with stacked auto-encoders to detect secret messages. However, the result turned out to be worse than rich model methods. In [14,15], Qian et al. proposed a 5-layer CNN with Gaussian activation function and average pooling, which achieved a slightly worse detection error than SRM. The structure was then shrunk to 2 broader layers [13] and obtained a better performance. Xu et al. [27] presented a CNN model incorporated with the absolute operation and tanh activation function. It received a comparable performance with traditional methods and the result was further improved by ensembling techniques [26]. In [28,29], the knowledge of selection channel was fused into CNN-based steganalyzers. Moreover, the network model proposed by [29] was trained on an augmented dataset and achieves a more competitive detection result of spatial-domain steganography. Wu et al. [22–24] proposed two CNN models with identity mapping, which led to a noticeable improvement in terms of detection accuracy. Lately, Yedroudj et al. [31] empirically designed a CNN-based steganalysis scheme which outperformed several CNN-based spatial steganalysis schemes, and the influence of data augmentation on this network structure was thoroughly investigated in [30].

Recent studies indicate that deep learning steganalysis methods have obtained a superior performance over traditional schemes. Yet, we have not discovered any deep residual network models equipped with complicated convolutional modules and newly presented network components in the field of spatial steganalysis. In this paper, we propose a modified deep residual network model for spatial steganalysis. The network is empirically designed with multi-scale convolutional modules and a series of proven propositions, such as high-pass filters and truncated linear activation functions. The main contribution of this work is summarized as follows: First, according to [11,19,20], employing more types of receptive fields usually results in better performance for image classification. Inspired by this, three kinds of multi-scale convolutional modules are implemented in the proposed scheme. In addition, aggregation operations are set to fuse features of various scales and the dimension of each convolutional module's input is reduced by a 1×1 convolution. Second, from previous researches [2,16,17], it is observed that the network model with larger depth can abstract complex optimal functions more efficiently. However, deep networks are usually plagued with the performance degradation problem. He et al. [6] proposed the idea of residual learning and overcome this issue. Follow the last two notions, we repeat the convolutional module twice in the same block and design the network model with shortcut components. Our experimental results demonstrate that the proposed network model obtains considerable improvement in terms of detection performance. For multiple steganographic algorithms with a wide range of payloads, our network outperforms various previous steganalyzers.

The rest of this paper is organized as follows. Section 2 elaborates the overall structure and the module design of the proposed deep residual network model. Section 3 introduces the experimental results and analysis. Finally, the conclusion and future works are drawn in Sect. 4.

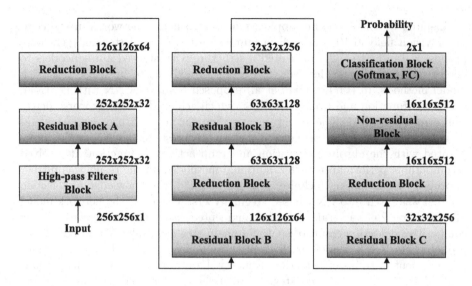

Fig. 1. The overall architecture of the proposed DRMCN model. Detailed implementations of each block are displayed in Figs. 2, 3 and 4.

2 The Proposed Deep Residual Multi-scale Convolutional Network Model

The overall architecture of the proposed network model is illustrated in Fig. 1, it is referred as DRMCN. The network consists of a high-pass filter block, four residual blocks, four reduction blocks, a non-residual block and a classification block. Implement details will be described in the rest of this section. To better distinguish models used in subsequent experiments, DMCN represents networks that share the same structure with DRMCN but without identity mapping shortcut components. The network model with the half depth of DMCN is named MCN, which also doesn't contain any shortcut components.

2.1 High-Pass Filter Block

Input cover/stego images are first convolved with a set of predefined kernels in the high-pass filter block (Fig. 2). These HPF kernels are initialized with the filter set adopted in SRM [5]. This residual computation process helps compressing image content and restraining the dynamic range of parameters. Therefore, the signal-to-noise ratio between the trivial stego disturbance and the image content increased significantly and the network is able to concentrate on a more robust stego signal. Previous studies [29,31,32] have shown that using more types of high-pass filter in the preprocessing step tends to yield better results than using fewer or only one filter. Similar to [29,31], the high-pass filter block employs all 30 basic linear filters in SRM. Furthermore, it is important to note that the weight matrix of all filters are optimized during network training. In addition, the truncated linear unit (TLU) is implemented as activation functions to take account of the sign symmetry existed in noise residuals [29]. The TLU function is defined by

$$\mathrm{TLU}\,(x) = \begin{cases} -T\,, & x < -T \\ x\,\,, & -T \le x \le T \\ T\,, & x > T \end{cases} \tag{1}$$

where T is the threshold, and it is set to 3 in the proposed network model. Truncated operation restrict the feasible parameter space of feature maps, which prevent the network from concentrating on excessive values.

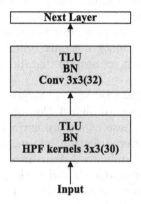

Fig. 2. The high-pass filter block of the proposed DRMCN.

Table 1. The detection errors P_E comparison between deep DRMCN and shallow MCN on BOSSLIRM_crop. The embedding payload is 0.4 bpp.

	DRMCN	MCN
HUGO	**0.1722**	0.2502
WOW	**0.2028**	0.2826
S-UNIWARD	**0.2539**	0.3352

2.2   Residual Block and Reduction Block

The next four residual blocks, as well as four reduction blocks, are of the essence in abstracting features and acquiring the optimum function. Figures 3 and 4 illustrate their structures respectively. Residual blocks are responsible for extracting productive features, while reduction blocks are used to reduce the dimension of features and diversifying the characterization of output feature maps. For each block, convolution operations are reused in order to introduce more parameters into the network model and increase the depth of DRMCN. The essentiality of network depth is confirmed in Table 1. Compared to shallower MCN, deeper DRMCN usually obtains superior results. Taking consideration of the balance between the limitation of computing facilities and the effectiveness of feature extraction, we repeat every convolution operation twice. Each residual block correspond to one kind of convolutional module, e.g., residual block A only use convolutional module A. The detailed architecture of convolutional modules is shown in Fig. 5. Then, each convolution operation is followed by a batch normalization layer (BN) and a non-linear activation function. Through BN layers, the output feature map is first normalized to zero mean and unit variance. Then, it is recovered with scaling and shifting parameters. Both parameters are optimized during network training, therefore, the phenomenon of internal covariant shift is alleviated [11]. We choose ReLU as activation function since it has a faster gradient computation procedure compared with TLU. Additionally, inspired by [6,11,18–20], each block not only contains two convolutional modules but also includes a shortcut connection that directly links the input and the output of this block.

With the purpose of adapting to different stages in feature extraction, three types of convolutional modules are designed. Convolutional module A (Fig. 5(a)), corresponding to the initial phase of feature extraction, is required to handle large feature maps with scattered feature information. Taking computational complexity into consideration, only 3×3 size convolution kernel is put into use. The purpose of convolutional module B and C (Fig. 5(b) and (c)), however, is to capture features at a higher abstraction level. In these two models, feature information is processed with various scales of convolution kernels and then aggregated by a 1×1 size kernel. Meanwhile, although the number of feature maps is strictly restrained, multi-scale convolution operation will inevitably make convolution computation prohibitively expensive. This issue leads to the application of 1×1 convolutions as dimension reduction and projection procedures. The number of each 1×1 size reduction filters is set to 32 in the first convolutional module B whereas 64 in the second module B and 128 in the module C. According to [18,29], the size of convolution kernels is empirically selected in each convolutional module. The multi-scale convolutional structure comprising three kinds of kernel (1×1, 3×3, 5×5) in convolutional module B and two kinds of kernel (1×1, 7×7) in convolutional module C, which enables the next layer to absorb features from different scales. For the sake of saving computational cost, based on the suggestions in [20], 5×5 convolution is replaced with two 3×3 convolution layers and 7×7 convolution is replaced by a 1×7 and a 7×1 convolution. At the end of each module, The aggregation operation allows each convolutional module for compressing the number of feature maps to the same level as the input.

Results in Table 2 indicate an evident superiority for multi-scale convolution over single-scale convolution, the detection error rate decrease about 2%. And in Table 3, the utility of the combination of multi-scale convolutional modules is further verified. The network equipped with only one kind of multi-scale convolutional modules (denoted as Multi-scale B and Multi-scale C) always achieve

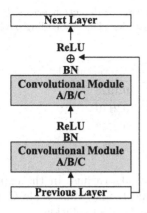
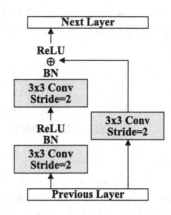

Fig. 3. The schema of residual block A/B/C of the proposed DRMCN. Detailed implementations of convolutional modules are displayed in Fig. 5.

Fig. 4. The structure of reduction blocks in DRMCN.

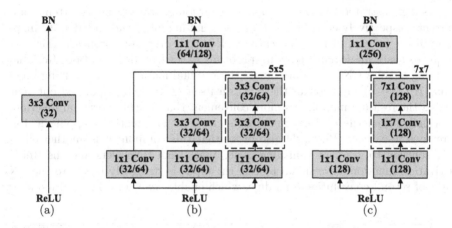

Fig. 5. The implementation of the convolutional modules adopted in residual blocks of the proposed DRMCN. (a) Convolutional module A. (b) Convolutional module B. (c) Convolutional module C.

Table 2. The performance on BOSSLIRM_crop in terms of detection errors P_E of the proposed DRMCN when multi-scale convolutional modules are replaced with 3×3 and 5×5 convolution. The embedding payload is 0.4 bpp.

	Multi-scale	3×3	5×5
HUGO	**0.1812**	0.2026	0.1984
WOW	**0.2128**	0.2367	0.2253
S-UNIWARD	**0.2559**	0.2824	0.2841

Table 3. The performance on BOSSLIRM_crop in terms of detection errors P_E of different strategies in using multi-scale convolutional modules. The embedding payload is 0.4 bpp.

	Multi-scale	Multi-scale B	Multi-scale C
HUGO	**0.1812**	0.1874	0.1925
WOW	**0.2128**	0.2169	0.2110
S-UNIWARD	**0.2559**	0.2592	0.2743

higher detection error among three steganography algorithms. In the experiment of Table 3, under the condition of Multi-scale B and Multi-scale C, the unemployed convolutional module is replaced with 5×5 convolution.

Following the residual block, the reduction block subsequently decreases the grid size of feature maps while doubles the channel of the network filters. It corresponds to the pooling operation in traditional CNN [20,25]. Inspired by [6,25], 3×3 convolution with stride 2, instead of max or average pooling, is employed in reduction blocks.

As demonstrated in Figs. 3 and 4, convolution operations and shortcut components respectively correspond to the residual mapping and the identity mapping in the process of residual learning. He et al. originally proposed this idea in [6] to avert inadequate training problems caused by degeneration. Residual learning enables CNN to approximate the residual mapping of underlying function $(H(x) - x)$ rather than the function itself $(H(x))$. It is pointed out that fitting the residual mapping is more convenient than learning original function, especially when the optimal function is closer to an identity mapping [6,18]. Previous researches [18,23,25] also prove that this component is another effective solution to gradient vanishing issue, apart from BN layers and the ReLU activation function. In residual blocks, the input is straightly linked to the BN layer of second convolutional module, which enables two convolutional modules

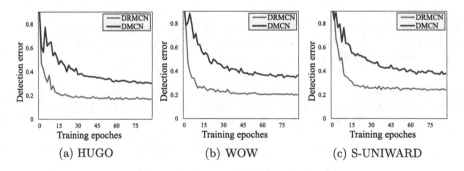

(a) HUGO   (b) WOW   (c) S-UNIWARD

Fig. 6. The validation errors comparison between network model with and without shortcut component. The network model is trained and validated on BOSSLIRM_crop at 0.4 bpp embedding rate.

to concentrate more on the stego signal [25]. Nevertheless, in reduction blocks (Fig. 4), the pooling procedure mentioned before is added to the shortcut components with the intention of accommodating feature map's scale variation. At the end of the shortcut component, element-wise addition is conducted. Figure 6 shows the performance comparison the between network model with shortcut component (DRMCN) and without shortcut component (DMCN). It is prominent that the identity mapping structure guarantees a lower detection error rate and helps facilitate network convergence.

2.3 Non-residual Block and Classification Block

With respect to the non-residual block, it shares the same structure with the residual block but not equipped with a shortcut component. The 5×5 convolution is employed in this block. At last, with the consideration of involving fewer parameters into the classification stage and avoiding over-fitting problems, only one fully connected layer with two necessary neurons are implemented in the classification block. Softmax layer then eventually generates posterior probability distribution between two labels, i.e. cover and stego.

3 Experimental Results

3.1 The Datasets

The dataset used in this paper consists of the BOSSbase v1.01 [1] and the LIR-MMBase [13]. The original BOSSbase includes 10000 natural grey-level images of size 512×512, which are captured by 17 different cameras and never compressed. As regards the LIRMMBase, it comprises 9388 grey-level images of size 512×512, which are captured by 7 cameras that differ from those in BOSSbase and remain uncompressed. In the early stage of the experiment, it is observed that feeding images with a resolution of 512×512 pixels usually lead to a sharp increase in training time and constantly make network models exceed the limitation of the computing platform. Consequently, three datasets with 256×256 pixels images are generated from the combination of two datasets above. We conduct datasets transformation as below:

(1) Using the *imcrop()* function with default settings in Matlab to crop random part of the original images with a size of 256×256. The dataset is named as BOSSLIRM_crop.
(2) Using the *imresize()* function with default settings in Matlab to resize original images into the size of 256×256. The dataset is named as BOSSLIRM_resize.
(3) Each image is first randomly cropped or resized into the size of 256×256. Then, half of the images in the dataset are flipped or rotated with equal probability. Flipping operation includes horizontal flop and vertical flip. Rotating operation includes three angles: $90°$, $180°$ and $270°$. This dataset is denoted as BOSSLIRM_aug.

During experiments, we divide each dataset into three parts, 50% of the cover/stego pairs is assigned to the training set, 30% of the cover/stego pairs is treated as the validation set, remaining 20% of the dataset is allocated to the testing set. Three well known content-adaptive steganographic algorithms – HUGO [12], S-UNIWARD [9], WOW [7] are selected to assess the discrimination validity of steganalysis methods.

3.2 Platform and Hyperparameters Setting

We implement the proposed DRMCN architecture on Tensorflow platform. The network model use AdaDelta [33] optimizer to update parameters. The decay rate and the "epsilon" value for the optimizer are set to 0.95 and 1×10^{-8}, respectively. A mini-batch of 32 images with 16 cover images and 16 stego images are used as the input for each iteration. We set the initial value of the learning rate to 1×10^{-1}, and make it decay exponentially by a factor of 0.95 for every 2000 iterations. All weights in convolution kernels are initialized using "Xavier" initialization and the initial biases are set to 0.2. Unlike convolutional layers, weight matrices in the classification block are initialized by zero-mean Gaussian distribution with standard deviation of 0.01, their bias is set to be zero.

3.3 General Performance Comparisons with State-of-the-Art Steganalyzer

In this experiment, we compare our proposed network model with several state-of-the-art steganalysis schemes including maxSRMd2 [3], XuNet [27] and YeNet [29]. Similar to [15,29], for steganalysis tasks with low payload, transfer learning strategy is adopted. It is noticed that, from Tables 4, 5 and 6, our DRMCN outperforms other CNN-based steganalyzers and hand-craft rich models on all three datasets.

Table 4. The detection errors P_E comparison of involved steganalysis schemes. All methods are trained and validated on BOSSLIRM_crop at different embedding rates.

	Payload	maxSRMd2	XuNet	YeNet	DRMCN
HUGO	0.4	0.2235	0.2473	0.2119	**0.1812**
	0.2	0.2892	0.3038	0.2849	**0.2787**
WOW	0.4	0.2709	0.2685	0.2464	**0.2128**
	0.2	0.3513	0.3389	0.3222	**0.3033**
S-UNIWARD	0.4	0.2978	0.3180	0.2917	**0.2539**
	0.2	0.3893	0.4025	0.3771	**0.3452**

Experimental results demonstrate the superior performance of DRMCN over maxSRMd2, the detection error rate is decreased by an average of 4%. In contrast with XuNet and YeNet, there is also a clear drop in P_E, especially on

Table 5. The detection errors P_E comparison of involved steganalysis schemes. All methods are trained and validated on BOSSLIRM_resize at different embedding rates.

	Payload	maxSRMd2	XuNet	YeNet	DRMCN
HUGO	0.4	0.1638	0.1362	0.1430	**0.1011**
	0.2	0.2342	0.2095	0.2253	**0.1914**
WOW	0.4	0.2021	0.1833	0.1675	**0.1425**
	0.2	0.2638	0.2697	0.2564	**0.2469**
S-UNIWARD	0.4	0.2369	0.2374	0.2186	**0.1859**
	0.2	0.3105	0.3339	0.3089	**0.2764**

Table 6. The detection errors P_E comparison of involved steganalysis schemes. All methods are trained and validated on BOSSLIRM_aug at different embedding rates.

	Payload	maxSRMd2	XuNet	YeNet	DRMCN
HUGO	0.4	0.1895	0.1924	0.1806	**0.1681**
	0.2	0.2614	0.2527	0.2319	**0.2256**
WOW	0.4	0.2363	0.2103	0.2084	**0.1957**
	0.2	0.2946	0.2716	0.2682	**0.2623**
S-UNIWARD	0.4	0.2415	0.2494	0.2624	**0.2083**
	0.2	0.3295	0.3268	0.3371	**0.2832**

BOSSLIRM_crop dataset. Under the condition of 0.4 payload, the proposed network model achieves 1.2–3.5% improvement in detection error among three datasets. While payload is 0.2, The average performance gap various from different datasets and different embedding schemes, but never below 0.5%. The most prominent decline of 3.5% is observed under the circumstance of HUGO algorithm with 0.4 payloads on BOSSLIRM_resize dataset. Note that it is of necessity for XuNet to acquire optimal results by adopting ensemble method [26], and extra operations, such as training set enlarging and cautious hyperparameters choosing, need to be taken during the training process of YeNet [29]. The proposed DRMCN does not require any additional operation and obtains a better result.

4   Conclusion

In this paper, a deep residual multi-scale convolutional network (DRMCN) is proposed to detect the minor disturbance introduced by multiple spatial steganographic schemes for various payloads. Multi-scale convolutional modules are equipped in the proposed network model. For the purpose of abstracting features from various dimensions, the multi-scale convolutional module is designed in three different ways. And, the effectiveness of this structure in elevating the detection accuracy is experimentally verified.

In addition, a series of proven elements, such as high-pass filters and truncated linear activation functions, are employed for the sake of facilitating network convergence. Inspired by the idea of residual learning, the proposed DRMCN also adopts shortcut components.

Extensive experiments conducted on images from BOSSbase and the LIRMMBase has demonstrated that the proposed deep residual network model achieves superior performance over other CNN-based steganalyzers and maxS-RMd2.

Based on the design paradigm mentioned above, in the future, we will integrate more essential domain knowledge, such as projection spatial rich model, into the network and develop convolutional modules that provide a higher level of robustness in feature extraction.

Acknowledgments. This work was supported by NSFC under 61802393, U1636102, U1736214 and 61872356, National Key Technology R&D Program under 2016YFB0801-003 and 2016QY15Z2500, and Project of Beijing Municipal Science & Technology Commission under Z181100002718001.

References

1. Bas, Patrick, Filler, Tomáš, Pevný, Tomáš: "Break our steganographic system": the ins and outs of organizing BOSS. In: Filler, Tomáš, Pevný, Tomáš, Craver, Scott, Ker, Andrew (eds.) IH 2011. LNCS, vol. 6958, pp. 59–70. Springer, Heidelberg (2011). https://doi.org/10.1007/978-3-642-24178-9_5
2. Bianchini, M., Scarselli, F.: On the complexity of neural network classifiers: a comparison between shallow and deep architectures. IEEE Trans. Neural Netw. Learn. Syst. **25**(8), 1553–1565 (2014)
3. Denemark, T., Sedighi, V., Holub, V., Cogranne, R., Fridrich, J.: Selection-channel-aware rich model for steganalysis of digital images. In: Proceedings of the 2014 IEEE International Workshop on Information Forensics and Security, Atlanta, GA, USA, pp. 48–53 (2014)
4. Filler, T., Judas, J., Fridrich, J.: Minimizing additive distortion in steganography using syndrome-trellis codes. IEEE Trans. Inf. Forensics Secur. **6**(3–2), 920–935 (2011)
5. Fridrich, J., Kodovský, J.: Rich models for steganalysis of digital images. IEEE Trans. Inf. Forensics Secur. **7**(3), 868–882 (2012)
6. He, K., Zhang, X., Ren, S., Sun, J.: Deep residual learning for image recognition. In: Proceedings of the 2016 IEEE Conference on Computer Vision and Pattern Recognition, Las Vegas, NV, USA, pp. 770–778 (2016)
7. Holub, V., Fridrich, J.: Designing steganographic distortion using directional filters. In: Proceedings of the 2012 IEEE International Workshop on Information Forensics and Security, Costa Adeje, Tenerife, Spain, pp. 234–239 (2012)
8. Holub, V., Fridrich, J.: Random projections of residuals for digital image steganalysis. IEEE Trans. Inf. Forensics Secur. **8**(12), 1996–2006 (2013)

9. Holub, V., Fridrich, J., Denemark, T.: Universal distortion function for steganography in an arbitrary domain. EURASIP J. Inf. Secur. **2014**, 1 (2014)
10. Huang, G., Liu, Z., van der Maaten, L., Weinberger, K.Q.: Densely connected convolutional networks. In: Proceedings of the 2017 IEEE Conference on Computer Vision and Pattern Recognition, Honolulu, HI, USA, pp. 2261–2269 (2017)
11. Ioffe, S., Szegedy, C.: Batch normalization: accelerating deep network training by reducing internal covariate shift. In: Proceedings of the 32nd International Conference on Machine Learning, Lille, France, pp. 448–456 (2015)
12. Pevný, T., Filler, T., Bas, P.: Using high-dimensional image models to perform highly undetectable steganography. In: Proceedings of the 12th International Workshop on Information Hiding, Calgary, AB, Canada, pp. 161–177 (2010)
13. Pibre, L., Pasquet, J., Ienco, D., Chaumont, M.: Deep learning is a good steganalysis tool when embedding key is reused for different images, even if there is a cover sourcemismatch. In: Proceedings of the 2016 IS&T, Electronic Imaging, Media Watermarking, Security, and Forensics, San Francisco, CA, USA, pp. 1–11 (2016)
14. Qian, Y., Dong, J., Wang, W., Tan, T.: Deep learning for steganalysis via convolutional neural networks. In: Proceedings of the 2015 IS&T, Electronic Imaging, Media Watermarking, Security, and Forensics, San Francisco, CA, USA, p. 94090J (2015)
15. Qian, Y., Dong, J., Wang, W., Tan, T.: Learning and transferring representations for image steganalysis using convolutional neural network. In: Proceedings of the 2016 IEEE International Conference on Image Processing, Phoenix, AZ, USA, pp. 2752–2756 (2016)
16. Simonyan, K., Zisserman, A.: Very deep convolutional networks for large-scale image recognition. CoRR abs/1409.1556 (2014). http://arxiv.org/abs/1409.1556
17. Sun, S., Chen, W., Wang, L., Liu, X., Liu, T.: On the depth of deep neural networks: a theoretical view. In: Proceedings of the 30th AAAI Conference on Artificial Intelligence, Phoenix, AZ, USA, pp. 2066–2072 (2016)
18. Szegedy, C., Ioffe, S., Vanhoucke, V., Alemi, A.A.: Inception-v4, inception-resnet and the impact of residual connections on learning. In: Proceedings of the 31st AAAI Conference on Artificial Intelligence, San Francisco, CA, USA, pp. 4278–4284 (2017)
19. Szegedy, C., et al.: Going deeper with convolutions. In: Proceedings of the 2015 IEEE Conference on Computer Vision and Pattern Recognition, Boston, MA, USA, pp. 1–9 (2015)
20. Szegedy, C., Vanhoucke, V., Ioffe, S., Shlens, J., Wojna, Z.: Rethinking the inception architecture for computer vision. In: Proceedings of the 2016 IEEE Conference on Computer Vision and Pattern Recognition, Las Vegas, NV, USA, pp. 2818–2826 (2016)
21. Tan, S., Li, B.: Stacked convolutional auto-encoders for steganalysis of digital images. In: Proceedings of the 2014 Asia-Pacific Signal and Information Processing Association Annual Summit and Conference, Chiang Mai, Thailand, pp. 1–4 (2014)
22. Wu, S., Zhong, S., Liu, Y.: Steganalysis via deep residual network. In: Proceedings of the 22nd IEEE International Conference on Parallel and Distributed Systems, Wuhan, China, pp. 1233–1236 (2016)
23. Wu, S., Zhong, S., Liu, Y.: Residual convolution network based steganalysis with adaptive content suppression. In: Proceedings of the 2017 IEEE International Conference on Multimedia and Expo, Hong Kong, China, pp. 241–246 (2017)
24. Wu, S., Zhong, S., Liu, Y.: Deep residual learning for image steganalysis. Multimedia Tools Appl. **77**(9), 10437–10453 (2018)

25. Xu, G.: Deep convolutional neural network to detect J-UNIWARD. In: Proceedings of the 5th ACM Workshop on Information Hiding and Multimedia Security, Philadelphia, PA, USA, pp. 67–73 (2017)
26. Xu, G., Wu, H., Shi, Y.Q.: Ensemble of CNNs for steganalysis: an empirical study. In: Proceedings of the 4th ACM Workshop on Information Hiding and Multimedia Security, Vigo, Galicia, Spain, pp. 103–107 (2016)
27. Xu, G., Wu, H., Shi, Y.: Structural design of convolutional neural networks for steganalysis. IEEE Signal Process. Lett. **23**(5), 708–712 (2016)
28. Yang, J., Liu, K., Kang, X., Wong, E.K., Shi, Y.: Steganalysis based on awareness of selection-channel and deep learning. In: Proceedings of the 16th International Workshop on Digital Forensics and Watermarking, Magdeburg, Germany, pp. 263–272 (2017)
29. Ye, J., Ni, J., Yi, Y.: Deep learning hierarchical representations for image steganalysis. IEEE Trans. Inf. Forensics Secur. **12**(11), 2545–2557 (2017)
30. Yedroudj, M., Chaumont, M., Comby, F.: How to augment a small learning set for improving the performances of a CNN-based steganalyzer? CoRR abs/1801.04076 (2018). http://arxiv.org/abs/1801.04076
31. Yedroudj, M., Comby, F., Chaumont, M.: Yedrouj-net: an efficient CNN for spatial steganalysis. CoRR abs/1803.00407 (2018). http://arxiv.org/abs/1803.00407
32. Yuan, Y., Lu, W., Feng, B., Weng, J.: Steganalysis with CNN using multi-channels filtered residuals. In: Proceedings of the 3rd International Conference on Cloud Computing and Security, Nanjing, China, pp. 110–120 (2017)
33. Zeiler, M.D.: ADADELTA: an adaptive learning rate method. CoRR abs/1212.5701 (2012). http://arxiv.org/abs/1212.5701
34. Zhu, X., Liu, J., Wang, J., Li, C., Lu, H.: Sparse representation for robust abnormality detection in crowded scenes. Pattern Recogn. **47**(5), 1791–1799 (2014)

Steganalysis and Identification

Provably Secure Generative Steganography Based on Autoregressive Model

Kuan Yang, Kejiang Chen, Weiming Zhang$^{(\boxtimes)}$, and Nenghai Yu

CAS Key Laboratory of Electromagnetic Space Information,
University of Science and Technology of China, Hefei, China
zhangwm@ustc.edu.cn

Abstract. Synthetic data and generative models have been more and more popular with the rapid development of machine learning and artificial intelligence (AI). Consequently, generative steganography, a novel steganographic method finishing the operation of steganography directly in the process of image generation, tends to get more attention. However, most of the existing generative steganographic methods have more or less shortcomings, such as low security, small capacity or limited to certain images. In this paper, we propose a novel framework for generative steganography based on autoregressive model, or rather, PixelCNN. Theoretical derivation has been taken to prove the security of the framework. A simplified version is also proposed for binary embedding with lower complexity, for which the experiments show that the proposed method can resist the existing steganalytic methods.

Keywords: Steganography · Provable security · Steganalysis · Generative model · PixelCNN

1 Introduction

Steganography is a collection of techniques for covert communication, which aims to hide secret message into the host media without arousing suspicion by an eavesdropper. In the last decade, the vast majority of work on steganography has focused on digital images, with a large number of image steganographic algorithms investigated. A famous non-adaptive steganographic method is LSB replacement. For the sake of minimizing statistical detectability, adaptive steganographic methods have been adopted, such as HUGO [1], WOW [2], SUNIWARD [3], HILL [4] and MiPOD [5]. In the meanwhile, the opposite of steganography, called steganalysis, has made advances recently. Various steganalytic methods are designed to detect the presence of secret messages, like SPAM [6], SRM [7], maxSRM [8], Xu-Net [9] and so on.

This work was supported in part by the National Natural Science Foundation of China under Grant U1636201 and 61572452.

© Springer Nature Switzerland AG 2019
C. D. Yoo et al. (Eds.): IWDW 2018, LNCS 11378, pp. 55–68, 2019.
https://doi.org/10.1007/978-3-030-11389-6_5

With the rapid development of machine learning and artificial intelligence (AI), it is increasingly popular to produce synthetic images with generative models. There are even some mature products. For example, Microsoft has unveiled an artificial artist, drawing bot, and Prisma is world famous App using style generative art. In order to eventually generate images with highly realistic quality, many generative models are proposed. The most prominent ones are variational auto-encoder (VAE) [10], generative adversarial network (GAN) [11], and autoregressive model (NAME [12], RIDE [13], and recently, PixelCNN [14]), each with its own strengths and weaknesses.

Image synthesis and generative models bring about new opportunities for steganography. With image synthesis more and more popular, it's a good idea to cover up information hiding with image generation. Generative steganography is a novel steganographic method, which finishes the operation of steganography directly in the process of image generation. It modifies the generative models and directly generates images containing secret messages, called stego images. The security of generative steganography lies in the indistinguishability between the normally-generated images and stego images.

There are some generative steganographic methods proposed. Hayes et al. [15] proposed a generative steganographic algorithm based on adversarial training and the stego images were generated by a neural network. Wu et al. [16] focused on texture synthesis and embedded message by selecting the non-optimal patches for texture image synthesis. Coverless image steganography [17] generated stego images by searching for appropriate images of which hash sequences are equivalent to the secret message (I take image searching as a special case of image generation). However, most of the existing generative steganographic methods have more or less shortcomings, such as low security, small capacity or limited to certain images.

We propose a novel framework of generative steganography with the help of autoregressive model, or rather, PixelCNN. The original PixelCNN models the conditional distributions of pixels and samples stochastically to generate an image pixel by pixel. We weave the image generation process into steganography using rejection sampling to encode secret messages. To improve the security, we adopt the decoding algorithm of adaptive arithmetic coding to encode the secret message based on the probability distribution calculated in the process of Pixel-CNN. Theoretical analysis is given to prove the security of our framework. With the purpose of reducing the complexity, we also propose a simplified version of the proposed framework, with slightly weaker security. To show the effectiveness of this framework, we test on two image sets. Experimental results have verified that our proposed algorithm can resist the existing steganalysis methods, including SPAM [6], SRM [7] and Xu-Net [9].

The remainder of this paper is organized as follows. After introducing notations, we review the autoregressive generative model, PixelCNN. In Sect. 3, the proposed framework and its simplified version are detailed. We experiment with two image sets and the results are elaborated in Sect. 4. Conclusions are given in Sect. 5.

2   Preliminaries and Related Work

2.1   Notations

Throughout the paper, matrices, vectors and sets are written in bold face. The image (of size $n_1 \times n_2$) is denoted by $\mathbf{X} = (x_{i,j})^{n_1 \times n_2}$, where the signal $x_{i,j}$ is an integer, such as the 8-bit gray value of a pixel. As we use the autoregressive model, the image is often scanned as a one-dimensional sequence $(x_j)^N$ with $N = n_1 \times n_2$, and the corresponding steganographic image (stego image) is denoted by $(y_j)^N$. The n bits secret message is denoted by $\mathbf{m} = (m_j)^n$. Before being embedded, the message usually should first be encrypted, so we can assume that $\mathbf{m}$ is binary pseudo-random sequence.

2.2   PixelCNN

The PixelCNN family [14] is a powerful class of autoregressive generative models that factorize the distribution of a natural image using the elementary chains rule over pixels. The network scans the image one row at a time and one pixel at a time within each row. The scan is according to a raster order: from left to right and from top to bottom. For each pixel it predicts the conditional distribution based on the scanned pixel values. The joint distribution over the image pixels is factorized into a product of conditional distributions:

$$p(\mathbf{X}) = \prod_{j=1}^{n^2} p(x_j | x_1, x_2, ..., x_{j-1}). \tag{1}$$

The value $p(x_j | x_1, x_2, ..., x_{j-1})$ is the probability distribution of the j-th pixel x_j, given all the previous pixels $x_1, x_2, ..., x_{j-1}$. For the sake of simplification, this conditional distribution is written as p_{x_j}.

A similar setup has been used by other autoregressive models such as NADE [12] and RIDE [13]. The difference lies in the way the condition distribution p_{x_j} is constructed. In PixelCNN, every conditional distribution is modeled by a convolutional neural network. Due to the operation of convolution, the distributions over the pixel values are computed in parallel during training and evaluation, while the generation has to be proceeded pixel by pixel [18]. As shown in the left part of Fig. 1, the process of generation for each pixel can be divided into two steps: Firstly, the autoregressive model predicts the distribution of the current pixel p_{x_j} given all the previously generated ones. Secondly, the model samples in the distribution and outputs a certain pixel value, denoted by

$$x_j = O\left(p_{x_j}\right), \tag{2}$$

in which $O\left(p_{x_j}\right)$ stands for the basic random sampling algorithm according to the distribution p_{x_j}.

To improve the speed and the quality of the generative model, some followup researches are conducted after original PixelCNN. Condition PixelCNN [18] replaces the original activation function, removes the blind spot, and adds a latent vector **h** for better performance and conditional image generation. PixelCNN++ [19] uses a discrete logistic mixture likelihood on the pixels, rather than a 256-way softmax, which speeds up training significantly.

3   Proposed Method

3.1   Motivation

As shown in the last section, PixelCNN is a sequential generative model, with random sampling for each pixel. What's more, PixelCNN can output explicit probability distribution. Based on the characteristics above, we modify the structure of PixelCNN and adopt rejection sampling and the decoding algorithm of a entropy encoder to embed the secret message. In this paper, we propose to use adaptive arithmetic decoding (AAD) [20].

3.2   A Novel Framework for Generative Steganography

We propose a provably secure generative steganographic framework based on PixelCNN, shown in Figs. 1 and 2. Assuming that the training process of Pixel-CNN has finished, we focus on the generation of images. As introduced in Sect. 2, the generation proceeds pixel by pixel, and the generation for each pixel can be divided into two steps, predicting the distribution and sampling. We embed the secret message by modifying the sampling process.

Rejection Sampling Algorithm. Before elaborating the details of our framework, we introduce a sampling algorithm, which helps embed the secret message. In numerical analysis, rejection sampling algorithm works by repeating the basic sampling until a value satisfies the acceptable condition [21]. The construction suggested in [22] is adopted in this paper. In this construction, the acceptable condition is defined by a mapping function $F(x)$ where x is the sampling value. Then rejection sampling algorithm is denoted by $G(b, p_x)$ while the original sampling on p_x is denoted by $O(p_x)$. To finish $G(b, p_x)$, we obtain a sample x using $O(p_x)$ and check whether the acceptable condition $F(x) = b$ is satisfied. If it holds true, we accept x as a sample of $G(b, p_x)$. Otherwise we reject the value of x and return to the sampling step. In this paper, we take $F(x)$ as a modular function with modular $L = 2, 3, \cdots$, or 255. For a given L, the corresponding $F(x)$ is denoted by $F_L(x)$ such that

$$F_L(x) \equiv x \mod L . \tag{3}$$

Obviously, $F_L(x)$ is L-ary number, and its distribution $p_{F_L(x)}$ can be easily derived from p_x and the definition of F_L as follows.

$$P(F_L(x) = b) = \sum_{\substack{a=0 \\ b \equiv a \mod L}}^{255} P(x = a), \quad b = 0, 1 \cdots, L - 1 . \tag{4}$$

With F_L, we will embed a L-ary digit into each pixel. To do that, we will transform the binary message sequence $\mathbf{m}$ into a L-ary sequence $\mathbf{M} = (M_j)^N$ according to the distribution $p_{F_L(x_j)}$ with Adaptive Arithmetic Decoding (AAD).

Adaptive Arithmetic Decoding. Now we describe how to transform the binary message $\mathbf{m}$ into the L-ary message $\mathbf{M}$. Because the message should be encrypted, the message $\mathbf{m}$ is a binary pseudo-random sequence. Therefore we can suppose that $\mathbf{m}$ is the compression result of a L-ary sequence $\mathbf{M} = (M_j)^N$ with Adaptive Arithmetic Encoding (AAE) [20] according to the distribution $(p_{F_L(x_j)})^N$. Therefore, we can decompress $\mathbf{m}$ into $\mathbf{M} = (M_j)^N$ with Adaptive Arithmetic Decoding (AAD) [20] according to the distribution $(p_{F_L(x_j)})^N$.

The PixelCNN first yields the distribution p_{x_1} from which we derive the distribution $p_{F_L(x_1)}$ with Eq. (4). For simplicity, we denote $\mathbf{m}_1 = \mathbf{m}$. According to $p_{F_L(x_1)}$, we decompress $\mathbf{m}_1$ with AAD to yield M_1 such that

$$M_1 = AAD\left(\mathbf{m}_1, p_{F_L(x_1)}\right). \tag{5}$$

And then embedding M_1 into the first pixel by the rejection sampling $G(M_1, p_{x_1})$ such that

$$y_1 = G\left(M_1, p_{x_1}\right), \tag{6}$$

where y_1 is the first pixel of the stego image, and $F_L(y_1) = M_1$. With y_1 as the condition, the PixelCNN can yield the distributions p_{x_2} from which we derive $p_{F_L(x_2)}$.

Assume that the first k_1 bits, $(m_1, \cdots, m_{k_1})$, of $\mathbf{m}_1$ have been decompressed into M_1 in Eq. (5). Denote the rest bits of $\mathbf{m}_1$ as $\mathbf{m}_2$. Decompressing $\mathbf{m}_2$ according to $p_{F_L(x_2)}$, we will get M_2 such that

$$M_2 = AAD\left(\mathbf{m}_2, p_{F_L(x_2)}\right), \tag{7}$$

which is embedded into the second pixel by the rejection sampling such that

$$y_2 = G\left(M_2, p_{x_2}\right). \tag{8}$$

Repeating the above process, we will get $(M_1, \cdots, M_N)$ and then the pixels $(y_1, \cdots, y_N)$ which composes of the stego image.

Embedding Process. The embedding process has been detailed when we introduce the adaptive arithmetic decoding above. We also show the whole process in Fig. 1. To further clarify the framework of steganography at the microscale, in Algorithm 1 we provide a pseudo-code that describes the implementation of embedding.

Extraction Process. At the receiver side, we inverse the operation to restore the original secret message, shown in Fig. 2, in which the PixelCNN model should be shared by the sender and the receiver. In fact, the PixelCNN model

Algorithm 1. Embedding process

Input: A cover image $(x_j)^N$; n bits of message $\mathbf{m}$; start with $j = 1$, $\mathbf{m}_1 = \mathbf{m}$
Output: The stego image $(y_j)^N$.

1: The PixelCNN yields the distribution of the current pixel x_j, denoted by p_{x_j}.
2: Derive the distribution $p_{F_L(x_j)}$ with Eq. (4).
3: Decompress $\mathbf{m}_j$ with AAD to yield M_j based on $M_j = AAD\left(\mathbf{m}_j, p_{F_L(x_j)}\right)$. Assume that the first k_j bits of $\mathbf{m}_j$ have been decompressed into M_j. Denote the rest bits of $\mathbf{m}_j$ as $\mathbf{m}_{j+1}$.
4: Embed M_j into the current pixel by the rejection sampling to yield $y_j = G(M_j, p_{x_j})$.
5: Update j with $j + 1$ and repeat the above process until the last pixel.

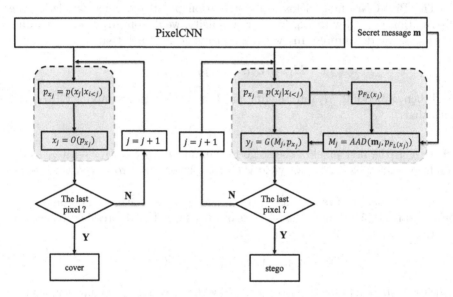

Fig. 1. This is the diagram of embedding process in the proposed framework. The left part is the original generation using PixelCNN. We modify the structure to embed secret message as the right part. Rejection sampling and adaptive arithmetic decoding (AAD) are adopted.

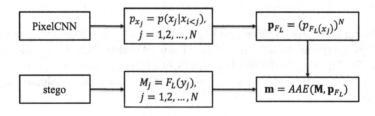

Fig. 2. This is the diagram of extraction process in the proposed framework. Different from the embedding has to proceed pixel by pixel, the extraction can be calculated by one-step.

can be open, because we will prove that the generating processes of the cover image and the stego image are statistically indistinguishable in the next subsection. With the PixelCNN model, the receiver can predict the distributions $\mathbf{p}_x = (p_{x_1}, \cdots, p_{x_N})$ and derive $\mathbf{p}_{F_L} = (p_{F_L(x_1)}, \cdots, p_{F_L(x_N)})$.

After receiving the stego image $\mathbf{y} = (y_1, \cdots, y_N)$, the receiver restores the sequence $\mathbf{M} = (M_j)^N$ by

$$M_j = F_L(y_j), \quad j = 1, 2, \cdots, N. \tag{9}$$

Then the adaptive arithmetic encoding (AAE) is used to encode $\mathbf{M}$ to the original secret message $\mathbf{m}$ such that

$$\mathbf{m} = AAE\left(\mathbf{M}, \mathbf{p}_{F_L}\right), \tag{10}$$

Different from the generation in which stego has to be proceeded pixel by pixel, the extraction can be calculated by one-step. To further detail the extraction process, we provide a pseudo-code as shown in Algorithm 2.

Algorithm 2. Extraction process

Input: A cover image $(y_j)^N$.
Output: n bits of message $\mathbf{m}$.
  1: The PixelCNN yields the distribution of all pixels, $\mathbf{p}_x = (p_{x_1}, \cdots, p_{x_N})$.
  2: Derive $\mathbf{p}_{F_L} = (p_{F_L(x_1)}, \cdots, p_{F_L(x_N)})$ with Eq. (4).
  3: Restore the sequence $\mathbf{M} = (M_j)^N$ with Eq. (9).
  4: Resrore the original secret message $\mathbf{m}$ with Eq. (10).

3.3   Proof of Security

In this subsection, we try to prove the security of the proposed framework. Because the proposed method is based on a generative model, we only need to prove that the generating processes of the cover image and the stego image are statistically indistinguishable, that is, $p_{y_j} = p_{x_j}$ for $j = 1, 2, \cdots, N$.

Note that y_j is generated by the rejection sampling algorithm according to the distribution p_{x_j} with F_L as the acceptable condition, so for any $0 \le a \le 255$ and $0 \le b \le L - 1$ we have

$$P\left(y_j = a \mid F_L(y_j) = b\right) = P\left(x_j = a \mid F_L(x_j) = b\right), \quad j = 1, 2 \cdots, N. \tag{11}$$

On the other hand, M_j is obtained by AAD according to the distribution $p_{F_L(x_j)}$, therefore M_j has the same distribution as $F_L(x_j)$, that is,

$$p_{M_j} = p_{F_L(x_j)}, \quad j = 1, 2 \cdots, N. \tag{12}$$

Thus, for any $0 \leq a \leq 255$, we have

$$P\left(y_j = a\right)$$

$$= \sum_{b=0}^{L-1} P\left(y_j = a | F_L(y_j) = b\right) P\left(F_L(y_j) = b\right) \tag{13}$$

$$= \sum_{b=0}^{L-1} P\left(x_j = a | F_L(x_j) = b\right) P\left(M_j = b\right) \tag{14}$$

$$= \sum_{b=0}^{L-1} P\left(x_j = a | F_L(x_j) = b\right) P\left(F_L(x_j) = b\right) \tag{15}$$

$$= P\left(x_j = a\right) \tag{16}$$

Herein, Eq. (14) holds due to Eq. (11) and $M_j = F_L(y_j)$. And Eq. (15) holds due to Eq. (12).

Therefore, we prove out that $p_{y_j} = p_{x_j}$ for $j = 1, 2, \cdots, N$, which means that a steganalyzer cannot distinguish the generating process of a stego image from that of a cover image.

3.4　A Simplified Version for $L = 2$

As shown in Figs. 1 and 2, both the embedding and extracting processes of the proposed framework have high complexity. At the sender side, we should transform $\mathbf{m}$ to $\mathbf{M}$ with AAD and then embed pixel by pixel. And at the receiver side, the complexity is due to predict p_{x_j} with PixelCNN. In fact, for $L = 2$, we can also achieve nearly perfect security with a simple method.

When $L = 2$, we essentially embed the message into the LSBs (Least Significant Bits) of the pixels. We found that the LSBs of pixels generated by PixelCNN is very close to a random sequence. Because the message $\mathbf{m}$ is a pseudo-random sequence, we don't need to transform $\mathbf{m}$ to match the distributions of $((F_2(x_j))^N$. Instead, we can directly embed $\mathbf{m}$ by using rejection sampling algorithm with F_2 as the acceptable condition. At the receiver side, the message can be extracted by directly reading the LSBs of the pixels $(y_j)^N$. In this simplified method, we proposed to keep the confidentiality of the PixelCNN model used by the sender. The diagram of the simplified method is shown in Fig. 3, with the pseudo-code given in Algorithms 3 and 4.

Algorithm 3. Embedding process of the simplified version

Input: A cover image $(x_j)^N$; n bits of message $\mathbf{m} = (m_j)^n$; start with $j = 1$.
Output: The stego image $(y_j)^N$.

　1: The PixelCNN yields the distribution of the current pixel x_j, denoted by p_{x_j}.
　2: Embed m_j into the current pixel by the rejection sampling to yield $y_j = G(m_j, p_{x_j})$.
　3: Update j with $j + 1$ and repeat the above process until the last pixel.

Algorithm 4. Extraction process of the simplified version

Input: A cover image $(y_j)^N$.
Output: n bits of message **m**.

1: Repeat $m_j = F_2(y_j)$ for $j = 1, 2, ..., n$.
2: Restore the original secret message **m**$= (m_j)^n$.

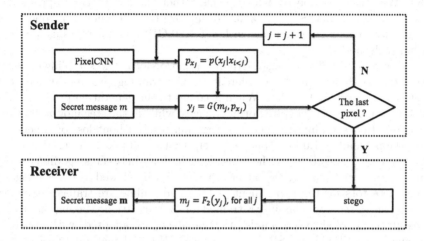

Fig. 3. A simplified method for $L = 2$, without adaptive arithmetic coding.

4 Experiment

We experiment on two image sets, gray images and color images respectively. Since the framework using AAD as the embedding method is proved to be security theoretically, here, we only verify the effectiveness of the simplified version for $L = 2$.

4.1 Setup and Datasets

The gray image set in this paper is Frey [23], which is a series of 1,965 images of Brendan Frey's face taken from sequential frames of a video. The color image set is chosen as Anime [24], containing 51,223 anime character faces crawled from a famous anime website. The datasets are listed in Table 1.

Table 1. The two image sets used in our experiment.

Dataset	Type	Dimension	Quantity
Frey	8-bit grayscale	20×28	1,965
Anime	8-bit RGB	96×96	51,223

A separate PixelCNN model is trained for each dataset. For the sake of faster training speed, we improve original Condition PixelCNN to model Frey by replacing the 256-softmax with a continuous Gaussian distribution, as a weakened version of PixelCNN++. However, different from the easy-to-model dataset, Anime has many patterns and a single gauss is hard to fit the distribution of pixels. So we use a mixture of 12 logistic distributions to model the likelihood better. We also condition on whole pixels rather than R/G/B sub-pixels and resize the original images to 32 × 32 to improve the efficiency. We collect our experimental results on a machine with 4 T K80 GPUs and it takes us 5–8 days to train each model.

As shown in Sect. 3, the steganography operation locates in sampling of image generation, so there is nothing different for the training process between our PixelCNNs and original models. When it comes to the generation process, basic sampling is adopted to generate normal images, while in the steganography case, we use rejection sampling to generate stego images. Without loss of generality, we set the payload as 1.0 bpp (bit per pixel), that is, all pixels are used to carry messages. Our goal is to verify the indistinguishability between stego images and normally-generated images, the latter of which can be viewed as cover images.

The detectors for the experiment of Frey and Anime are trained as binary classifiers and a separate classifier is trained for each situation. Making the results representative enough, three kinds of steganalysis are adopted, with two conventional ones (SPAM [6], SRM [7]) and a CNN-based method (Xu-Net [9]). Note that original Xu-Net is designed on high-resolution images with dimension 512 × 512, while the size of our generated images is much smaller. So we modify the original network and propose two shallow versions, with 5 layers for Frey and 6 layers for Anime. We report the detection error which computes the average of the false-alarm probability and missed-detection probability by 10 times of randomly splitting the training and the testing images.

4.2 Frey Results

Given the gray image set Frey with 1,965 images, we train a PixelCNN model and generate 2,000 natural-generated images (denoted by COVER) and 2000 message-embedded-generated ones (denoted by STEGO), with a payload of 1.0 bpp. We show some samples of the three image sets in Fig. 4.

Then SPAM, SRM and Xu-Net are adopted respectively to detect between the two generated image sets, with the results shown in the last column of Table 2. All of the three steganalysis methods get a detection error probability near 0.5, verifying the indistinguishability between cover images and stego images.

However, there is a logical loophole that all of the steganalysis above may not be suitable to detect steganography on this kind of image sets, especially our proposed Xu-Net. That is to say, the generated images are secure covers, the same as what happens in SGAN [25] and SSGAN [26]. Making the inference more rigorous, we conduct some follow-up experiments. We use the basic LSB-Replacement steganography with a payload of 0.4 bpp to experiment on the original Frey images (denoted by TRAIN) and the two generated image sets

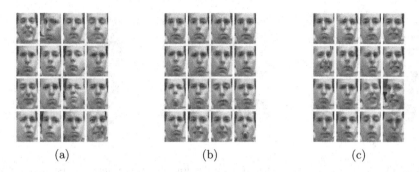

(a)   (b)   (c)

Fig. 4. The results in Frey, with 16 samples of each set. Image (a) is the training images. Image (b) is the generative cover images. And image (c) is the generative stego images.

Table 2. Detection error of different steganalysis in terms of frey dataset.

	TRAIN/ LSB_TRAIN	COVER/ LSB_COVER	STEGO/ LSB_STEGO	COVER/ STEGO
SPAM	0.3782	0.3868	0.3899	0.5001
SRM	0.3392	0.3350	0.3436	0.4996
Xu-Net	0.3594	0.3627	0.3622	0.5300

respectively, obtaining three stego image sets LSB_TRAIN, LSB_COVER and LSB_STEGO. Then the steganalysis are adopted and the results are shown in Table 2. Each column is the detection error probability for the three steganalysis methods to detect the original image set and its LSB_version. It can be concluded that the three steganalysis methods work well to detect the LSB steganography. So we can draw a conclusion that the assumption of the logical loophole is not true and our generated images are not secure covers. Above all, our proposed system succeed in finishing secure generative steganography on Frey.

4.3   Anime Results

When it comes to the color image set Anime, we train a new PixelCNN model and generate 5,000 cover images and 5,000 stego images. Some samples of the three image sets in Fig. 5.

Most of the experiments are the same as that of Frey. Note that the payload of the basic LSB-Replacement steganography is chosen as 1.0 bpp, considering the fact that the original training images have been resized and have weaker neighboring correlation. We view an RGB image as three gray images and operate only in the R channel. The results are shown in Table 3. We can draw a similar conclusion that our proposed system succeeds in finishing the secure generative steganography on the color image set Anime, rather than generating secure covers.

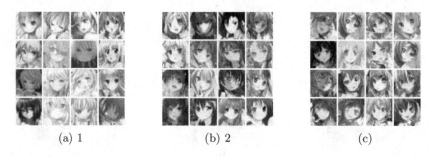

(a) 1   (b) 2   (c)

Fig. 5. The results in Anime, with 16 samples for each set. Image (a) is the training images. Image (b) is the generative cover images. And image (c) is the generative stego images.

Table 3. Detection error of different steganalysis in terms of frey dataset.

	TRAIN/ LSB_TRAIN	COVER/ LSB_COVER	STEGO/ LSB_STEGO	COVER/ STEGO
SPAM	0.3387	0.3779	0.3861	0.4943
SRM	0.2329	0.2708	0.2869	0.4987
Xu-Net	0.2656	0.3175	0.3125	0.5021

Attention to the details that the detection error probability of training image set and its LSB-Replacement version are much lower than that of the other two pairs, it can be explained that the PixelCNN cannot ideally model the distributions of Anime and cannot generate the same samples as the original training sets, even if we adopt a complicated version. However, we focus on the distinguishability between the two generated image sets, rather than the distinguishability between generated images and original source images.

5   Conclusions

In this paper, we proposed a framework for provably secure generative steganography by modifying the sampling process in PixelCNN. Theoretical derivation has been taken to prove the indistinguishability between cover and stego. We also propose a simplified version with much lower complexity, for which the experiments on the datasets Frey and Anime show that our proposed algorithm can perfectly resist the state-of-the-art steganalysis.

References

1. Filler, T., Fridrich, J.: Gibbs construction in steganography. IEEE Trans. Inf. Forensics Secur. **5**(4), 705–720 (2010)
2. Holub, V., Fridrich, J.: Designing steganographic distortion using directional filters. In: 2012 IEEE International Workshop on Information Forensics and Security (WIFS), pp. 234–239. IEEE (2012)
3. Holub, V., Fridrich, J.: Digital image steganography using universal distortion. In: Proceedings of the First ACM Workshop on Information Hiding and Multimedia Security, pp. 59–68. ACM (2013)
4. Li, B., Wang, M., Huang, J., Li, X.: A new cost function for spatial image steganography. In: 2014 IEEE International Conference on Image Processing (ICIP), pp. 4206–4210. IEEE (2014)
5. Sedighi, V., Cogranne, R., Fridrich, J.: Content-adaptive steganography by minimizing statistical detectability. IEEE Trans. Inf. Forensics Secur. **11**(2), 221–234 (2016)
6. Pevny, T., Bas, P., Fridrich, J.: Steganalysis by subtractive pixel adjacency matrix. IEEE Trans. Inf. Forensics Secur. **5**(2), 215–224 (2010)
7. Fridrich, J., Kodovsky, J.: Rich models for steganalysis of digital images. IEEE Trans. Inf. Forensics Secur. **7**(3), 868–882 (2012)
8. Denemark, T., Sedighi, V., Holub, V., Cogranne, R., Fridrich, J.: Selection-channel-aware rich model for steganalysis of digital images. In: 2014 IEEE International Workshop on Information Forensics and Security (WIFS), pp. 48–53. IEEE (2014)
9. Guanshuo, X., Han-Zhou, W., Shi, Y.-Q.: Structural design of convolutional neural networks for steganalysis. IEEE Signal Process. Lett. **23**(5), 708–712 (2016)
10. Kingma, D.P., Welling, M.: Auto-encoding variational bayes. arXiv preprint arXiv:1312.6114 (2013)
11. Goodfellow, I.: Generative adversarial nets. In: Advances in Neural Information Processing Systems, pp. 2672–2680 (2014)
12. Larochelle, H., Murray, I.: The neural autoregressive distribution estimator. In: Proceedings of the Fourteenth International Conference on Artificial Intelligence and Statistics, pp. 29–37 (2011)
13. Theis, L., Bethge, M.: Generative image modeling using spatial LSTMs. In: Advances in Neural Information Processing Systems, pp. 1927–1935 (2015)
14. van den Oord, A., Kalchbrenner, N., Kavukcuoglu, K.: Pixel recurrent neural networks. arXiv preprint arXiv:1601.06759 (2016)
15. Hayes, J., Danezis, G.: Generating steganographic images via adversarial training. In: Advances in Neural Information Processing Systems, pp. 1951–1960 (2017)
16. Wu, K.-C., Wang, C.-M.: Steganography using reversible texture synthesis. IEEE Trans. Image Process. **24**(1), 130–139 (2015)
17. Zhou, Z., Sun, H., Harit, R., Chen, X., Sun, X.: Coverless image steganography without embedding. In: Huang, Z., Sun, X., Luo, J., Wang, J. (eds.) ICCCS 2015. LNCS, vol. 9483, pp. 123–132. Springer, Cham (2015). https://doi.org/10.1007/978-3-319-27051-7_11
18. van den Oord, A., Kalchbrenner, N., Espeholt, L., Vinyals, O., Graves, A., et al.: Conditional image generation with pixelCNN decoders. In: Advances in Neural Information Processing Systems, pp. 4790–4798 (2016)
19. Salimans, T., Karpathy, A., Chen, X., Kingma, D.P.: PixelCNN++: improving the pixelCNN with discretized logistic mixture likelihood and other modifications. arXiv preprint arXiv:1701.05517 (2017)

20. Triantafyllidis, G.A., Strintzis, M.G.: A context based adaptive arithmetic coding technique for lossless image compression. IEEE Signal Process. Lett. **6**(7), 168–170 (1999)
21. https://en.wikipedia.org/wiki/Rejection_sampling#Advantages_over_sampling_using_naive_methods
22. Hopper, N.J., Langford, J., von Ahn, L.: Provably secure steganography. In: Yung, M. (ed.) CRYPTO 2002. LNCS, vol. 2442, pp. 77–92. Springer, Heidelberg (2002). https://doi.org/10.1007/3-540-45708-9_6
23. Frey dataset. http://www.cs.nyu.edu/~roweis/data/frey_rawface.mat
24. Anime dataset. https://drive.google.com/file/d/1yOrpEjEYU8LXl8h-k7gVaaQ0Z dGYfnU_/view?usp=sharing
25. Volkhonskiy, D., Borisenko, B., Burnaev, E.: Generative adversarial networks for image steganography (2016)
26. Shi, H., Dong, J., Wang, W., Qian, Y., Zhang, X.: SSGAN: Secure steganography based on generative adversarial networks. arXiv preprint arXiv:1707.01613 (2017)

A Novel Steganalysis of Steghide Focused on High-Frequency Region of Audio Waveform

Akira Nishimura[✉]

Department of Informatics, Faculty of Informatics,
Tokyo University of Information Sciences,
4–1 Onaridai, Wakaba, Chiba 265-8501, Japan
akira@rsch.tuis.ac.jp

Abstract. In this study, steganalysis of steghide embedded in Microsoft RIFF waveform audio format (WAV) data is investigated. Spectral analyses show that the conventional steganalysis utilize the statistics of high-frequency regions and silent temporal segments of the target signals intentionally or unintentionally. Moreover, the frequency components just below the Nyquist frequency are important for statistic-based steganalysis in terms of the signal-to-noise ratio where the signal corresponds to the distortion components induced by data hiding, and the noise corresponds to the cover signal. A novel steganalysis making full use of the high- frequency features is proposed, and its detection performance is compared with the conventional method, which showed the best performance so far. The results show that the proposed steganalysis outperforms the conventional method for cover data of 100 music signals and 320 speech signals mixed with background noises.

Keywords: Signal-to-noise ratio · Anti-aliasing filter · Spectral analysis · Information hiding · Covert communication

1 Introduction

Covert communication is one of the applications of steganography, and conceals secret information to be transmitted hidden in unrelated cover data in a communication channel. Cryptographic communication can keep the contents of communication as secret; however, the amount of communicated information, frequency of communication, and sending and/or receiving destination may become obvious in some cases. On the other hand, because cover data, where the secret information is to be hidden, is unrelated to the secret communication, it is difficult for a third party to detect not only the contents of the communication but also the facts of communication from the stego data where the secret information is hidden.

© Springer Nature Switzerland AG 2019
C. D. Yoo et al. (Eds.): IWDW 2018, LNCS 11378, pp. 69–82, 2019.
https://doi.org/10.1007/978-3-030-11389-6_6

Covert communication itself is a kind of communication, but it can be a threat of a personal nature, social nature, and even of national security through a computer system. For example, in an article dated 5 February 2001 [13], USA Today reported that U.S. and foreign officials said that Osama bin Laden and his colleagues were hiding maps and photographs of terrorist targets and posting instructions for terrorist activities in sports chat rooms, on pornographic bulletin boards, and at other Web sites.

The replacement and/or modification of data files can be easily detected by comparing the hash data of the original and modified files. However, when a specific user possesses the original data and uploads their stego data to the Web or social network service (SNS), the detection of such covert communication is difficult. Therefore, in order to detect undesirable covert communication using audio, video, and image files, the necessity of identifying the presence or absence of hidden information from an arbitrary content file (called steganalysis) is increasing.

Steganalysis becomes more difficult when the modification of the content accompanying hidden information is small. A representative hiding method is the least significant bit (LSB) replacement method, which replaces the LSB of the data with a secret data bit. Although this method is old-fashioned, it can hide a relatively large amount of payload with a small amount of subjective and objective quality degradation to the stego data.

In this paper, steghide [9], which is a type of LSB replacement method for the waveform data of sounds (WAV), is taken up, and conventional steganalyses for WAV data are reviewed. Conventional steganalysis have utilized high-frequency regions and silent temporal segments of the target signals intentionally or unintentionally. Moreover, the frequency components of the target signal just below the Nyquist frequency are important for statistic-based steganalysis in terms of the signal-to-noise ratio (SNR), where the signal corresponds to the distortion components induced by data hiding, and the noise corresponds to the cover signal. A novel steganalysis making full use of high-frequency features is proposed, and its detection performance is compared with the conventional method.

2   Steghide and Its Steganalysis

2.1   Steghide

Steghide [9] is a steganography program that hides data in image (JPEG, BMP) and audio (WAV, AU) files. It replaces the LSB of sampled and quantized digital waveform data with payload bits. A sequence of positions of samples in the cover file is created based on a pseudorandom number generator initialized with a passphrase. Of these positions, those that do not need to be changed (because they already contain the correct value by chance) are sorted out. Then, a graph-theoretic matching algorithm finds pairs of positions such that exchanging their values has the effect of embedding the corresponding part of the secret data. All exchanges are actually performed until the algorithm cannot find any more pairs of this type. The samples at the remaining positions (the positions that are not part of such a pair) are also modified to contain the embedded data by overwriting them. The fact that most of the embedding is done by exchanging sample values implies that the first-order statistics are not changed.

In the case of a WAV file, the maximum amount of payload bits is half the number of data samples. The number of payload bits is expressed as a ratio to the maximum amount in percentages. This is called the capacity.

2.2 Previous Studies

Several steganalyses for steghide have been proposed. These methods are classi-fied into two categories. One is extracting feature values from target signals that correspond to the cover signals and stego signals to be fed into a machine learn-ing process, typically a Support Vector Machine (SVM). The second category is a calibrated method in which the machine learning uses the difference between the feature values extracted from the target signal and its re-embedded signal. The re-embedding algorithm is usually a random LSB replacement.

The performance is expressed by precision P that represents the correct detection rate of stego signals and recall R that represents the correct detection rate of cover (clean) signals. An F-measure $F = \frac{2PR}{(P+R)}$ is used as the overall testing accuracy.

Djebbar and Ayad [2] divided each speech signal into four energetic parts using an active speech level (ASL) algorithm, as defined in ITU-T (International Telecommunication Union Telecommunication Standardization Sector) Recom-mendation P.56. Maximum entropy is computed from each energy part to gen-erate a set of features that is fed to a nonlinear SVM classifier with a radial basis function (RBF) kernel to distinguish between cover and stego speech signals. The researchers tested three LSB replacement-based steganographic methods: S-tools4, Steghide, and Hide4PGP. The experimental results showed that the detec-tion performance obtained from steghide was lowest in the F-measure at 0.797.

Ru et al. [11] investigated the wavelet coefficients obtained from a four-level 1D wavelet decomposition of the target signals for a short duration (about 20 ms) in each subband. A linear predictor for the magnitude of the wavelet subband coefficients extracted significant statistical features (mean, variance, kurtosis, and skewness), and an SVM was employed to detect the existence of hidden messages. The experimental results showed that the trained model using the stego audio embedded at 20% capacity revealed the best detection performance (F-measure of 0.957) for the stego audio embedded at 30% capacity.

Geetha et al. [4] applied wavelet noise reduction [3] to the target signals to obtain calibrated signals. After that, higher-order statistics were extracted from the Hausdorff distance between the target signal and the calibrated signal for each subband signal of a four-level wavelet decomposition. A rule-based approach with a family of six decision-tree classifiers (Alternating Decision Tree, Decision Stump, J48, Logical Model Tree, Naïve Bayes Tree, and Fast Decision Tree learner) to detect hidden audio information was introduced. An evaluation of the enhanced feature space and the decision tree paradigm on a database containing

4,800 clean and stego audio files was performed for classical steganography as well as for watermarking algorithms. The best detection score of steghide was 0.9178 in the F-measure for stego audio embedded at 5% capacity.

Ghasemzadeh et al. [5–7] proposed an audio steganalysis system based on reversed Mel-frequency cepstral coefficients (R-MFCC). This system aimed to provide high resolution in high-frequency regions and low resolution where the frequency was low. A 29-band reversed Mel-frequency filter bank was applied to second-order-differentiated and segmented target signals using a 1024-sample fast Fourier transform (FFT) with a half-overlapped hamming window. The output of filter bank was converted to a 29-band time series of R-MFCC by applying a logarithmic transform and a Fourier transform. A genetic algorithm was deployed to optimize the dimensions of the R-MFCC-based features. This sped up feature extraction and reduced the complexity of classification. The final decision was made by a trained SVM to detect suspicious audio files. The proposed method achieved F-measures of 0.954 and 0.929 for capacities of 100% and 50%, respectively. Moreover, random bits were re-embedded into the LSB of the target signals to obtain calibrated signals [5]. After that, the significant statistical features (mean, standard deviation, kurtosis, and skewness) were extracted from the difference of the R-MFCCs between the target signal and the calibrated signal for each subband signal. Simulations under a universal scenario tested a large number of steganographic and watermarking schemes at the same learning parameters. The model revealed that the detection performance of steghide at a capacity of 50% was 0.998 for the F-measure for 4,169 music and TV program signals sampled at 44.1 kHz. The performance was 0.982 for the F-measure for 1,029 speech signals sampled at 16 kHz that were recorded by themselves.

Table 1 summarizes the major previous studies on the steganalysis of steghide, including their experimental conditions and typical results of detection performance.

2.3   Effective Strategy for Steganalysis

Generally speaking, acoustic signals such as voice, music, and environmental noise have a spectral characteristic in which the power decreases by increasing the frequency. The change caused by the LSB replacement of the cover data can be approximated to an additive Gaussian random signal of relatively constant power, regardless of the amplitude and frequency of the cover signal.

In order to investigate the effect of the additive Gaussian signal induced by LSB replacement, Fig. 1 shows spectrograms of (a) the speech signal ('Ja_f4.wav' in ITU-T P.50 Appendix I), (b) the additive signal induced by 50%-capacity embedding in the speech signal by steghide, and (c) the signal-to-noise ratio where the signal and noise correspond to the additive signal and the cover speech signal, respectively. Figure 1(b) shows that the power of the additive signal spreads over the time and frequency plane uniformly. Figure 1(c) shows three types of high-SNR regions that are depicted in dark gray and black: the initial 0.4 s of zero amplitude, the highest frequency region that is just below

Table 1. Conventional steganalysis and typical results for detecting steghide. Capacity represents percentages relative to maximum amount of payload.

Researchers	Database			Capacity	F-measure
	Cover files	Duration	Sampl. Freq., Channels, Resol.		
Djebbar and Ayad [2]	620 speech	10 s	44.1 kHz, mono, 16-bit	50%	0.797
Ru et al. [11]	1,000 wavsurfer		44.1 kHz*, stereo, 16-bit	30%	0.957
Geetha et al. [4]	200 wavsurfer	10–60 s	44.1 kHz, stereo, 16-bit	5%	0.918
Ghasemzadeh and Arjmandi [6]	4,169 wavsurfer	10 s	44.1 kHz, mono, 16-bit	100% 50%	0.954 0.929
Ghasemzadeh et al. [7]	4,169 wavsurfer	10 s	44.1 kH z, mono, 16-bit	100% 50%	0.983 0.976
Ghasemzadeh et al. [5]	4.169 wavsurfer	10 s	44.1 kHz, mono, 16-bit	50% 6%	0.998 0.991
	1,029 speech	10 s	16 kHz, mono, 16-bit	50% 6%	0.982 0.741

*: Sampling frequency is not clear. It supposed to be 44.1 kHz.

the Nyquist frequency, and the silent regions of no utterance. Therefore, a steganalysis that realizes high detection performance is better for extracting and utilizing statistical features that are obtained mainly from quiet segments of low amplitude and high-frequency regions of the target signals.

In a previous steganalysis that applied wavelet filter decomposition to the target signal [4,11], the first-order detail coefficients represented a high-pass signal. The reversed Mel-frequency filter bank [5–7] also extracted high-frequency components of the target signal by narrow-band filters. Furthermore, taking the second-order derivative of the target signal [5–7] corresponded to applying a high-pass filter of $+12 \, \mathrm{dB/oct}$.

2.4 Selection of Cover Data for Steganalysis

The most critical problem of conventional research on steganalysis is that the characteristics of the audio signals used as cover data have not been clarified. Previous studies often used data sets that were supposed to be downloaded or purchased from "wavsurfer", a website that provided audio tracks of TV programs and movies as WAV or MP3 files. Both types of audio files were converted to WAV files sampled at 44.1 kHz and supplied for the cover data. However, when perceptually encoded data such as MP3s were decoded into waveform data, the high-frequency components near the Nyquist frequency will certainly be lost in the encoding and decoding processes. In addition, wavsurfer may include sound

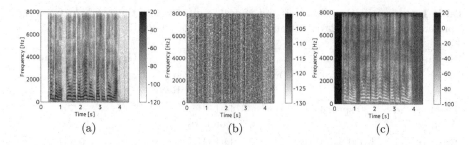

Fig. 1. Spectrogram: (a) speech signal, (b) additive signal induced by steghide, (c) signal-to-noise ratio (signal is additive signal induced by steghide, and noise is speech signal.)

files upsampled to 44.1 kHz from sampling frequencies lower than 44.1 kHz. This results in broad high-frequency regions of extremely low power. The results of a simulation shown in Sect. 3.3 show that the high-frequency components of low power, especially near the Nyquist frequency, are very effective for successful steganalysis. Even when the cover data are originally WAV files, similar problems may occur as the recording targets are audio tracks of TV programs or movies that were perceptually coded. When downloading audio files from the Internet [2], the spectral characteristics discussed above are not clear.

The following databases are suitable for research on steganalysis including music, speech, and background noise in terms of reproducibility of the experimental data. These databases are used as cover data for simulations in the next section.

The Real World Computing (RWC) music database is a copyright-cleared database that is available to researchers as a common foundation for research. It contains six original collections in audio CD format (44.1 kHz sampling, 16-bit quantization, stereo): Popular Music Database (100 songs), Royalty-Free Music Database (15 songs), Classical Music Database (50 pieces), Jazz Music Database (50 pieces), Music Genre Database (100 pieces), and Musical Instrument Sound Database (50 instruments). Music Genre Database RWC-MDB-G2001 [8] is used for spectral analysis and steganalysis by extracting the initial 60 s and the left channel of each piece of the music files.

ITU-T P.50 is a standard defined by the International Telecommunication Union Telecommunications Division for artificial voice signals in order to test the telephone system and its characteristics. Its Appendix I [10] is composed of 320 real speech files uttered in 20 languages, each of which corresponds to 8 male speech files and 8 female speech files sampled at 16 kHz in monaural format with 16-bit quantization. Their lengths are 8.8 s on average, 2.7 s for the shortest, and 17.4 s for the longest, with a standard deviation of 2.5 s. Short silent sections that are included before and after the speech sounds were removed before analysis and simulation. This database is referred to ITU-T P.50 hereafter.

Diverse Environments Multichannel Acoustic Noise Database (DEMAND) contains background noise sounds recorded for 300 s in 15 real environments by a dense microphone array of 16 channels [12]. This database is used for applications such as speech enhancement and speech recognition to be performed after controlling additive background noise. A data set of 48-kHz-sampled items and a 16-bit quantization and data set obtained by downsampling to 16 kHz by the resample command of MATLAB R2012a have been distributed. The latter database was used for the simulation.

3   Evaluation of Steganalysis

The steganalysis developed by Ghasemzadeh et al. [5], which exhibited the best detection performance among the conventional methods, was implemented. They applied a Fourier transform to the output of the reversed Mel-frequency filter bank to calculate R-MFCC. The current simulation applied a discrete cosine transform (DCT) to the output of the filter bank to calculate R-MFCC, because it showed better performance than the Fourier transform.

In addition, a novel steganalysis that utilized the frequency components just below the Nyquist frequency was developed. These steganalyses were tested to detect information hiding by steghide in music signals and speech signals with background noises.

3.1   Proposed Steganalysis

In order to extract feature values from the amplitude of frequency components just below the Nyquist frequency, N-sample Hanning windowing and an FFT were applied to a target signal by shifting half-overlapped windows. $\mathbf{x}_t$ is a N-sample vector of the target signal that begins with the t-th sample. $\mathbf{w}$ is a N-sample vector of the Hanning window. Logarithmic amplitude spectrum $X_{i,j}$ of the j-th time frame ($j = 0, 1, 2, ..., T-1$ where T is the total number of frames) and the i-th discrete frequency ($i = 0, 1, 2, ..., N/2$) are expressed as follows:

$$X_{i,j} = 20\log_{10}(\text{Abs}(\text{FFT}(\mathbf{w}\mathbf{x}_{jN/2}))) \tag{1}$$

where FFT is the fast Fourier transform that extracts frequency components below the Nyquist frequency, and $\text{Abs}(\cdot)$ is an operation taking the absolute value. The feature values are the four statistics: average (Eq. 2), standard deviation (Eq. 3), skewness (Eq. 4), and kurtosis (Eq. 5). These feature values are of the highest m discrete frequencies $i = N/2 - m + 1, N/2 - m + 2, ..., N/2$.

$$f_{\text{avg},i} = \frac{1}{T}\sum_{j=1}^{T} X_{i,j}. \tag{2}$$

$$f_{\text{std},i} = \sqrt{\frac{1}{T}\sum_{j=1}^{T}(X_{i,j} - f_{\text{avg},i})^2}. \tag{3}$$

$$f_{\text{skew},i} = \frac{\sum_{j=1}^{T}(X_{i,j} - f_{\text{avg},i})^3}{T f_{\text{std},i}^3}. \tag{4}$$

$$f_{\mathrm{kur},i} = \frac{\sum_{j=1}^{T}(X_{i,j} - f_{\mathrm{avg},i})^4}{T f_{\mathrm{std},i}^4}. \tag{5}$$

The parameter values $N = 256$ and $m = 9$ were determined by preliminary tests. The highest nine discrete frequencies were from 20,627 Hz to 22,050 Hz for the music signals sampled at 44,100 Hz, and from 7,500 Hz to 8,000 Hz for the speech signals sampled at 16,000 Hz. As a result, $9 \times 4 = 36$ feature values were used to train the model of the SVM.

3.2   Conditions of Simulation and Procedure

A simulation was conducted by a tenfold cross-validation procedure. For 100 music files, 90 embedded and 90 clean files trained the model of the SVM, and 10 embedded and 10 clean files were used for detection with the trained model.

For 320 speech files, 576 files spoken in 18 languages (which were embedded and clean files) trained the model of the SVM, and 64 embedded and clean files spoken in the remaining 2 languages were used for detection with the trained model. In order to simulate a background noise contained in an actual speech recording, a noise file was randomly chosen from 15 "ch01.wav" files of the DEMAND database. In addition, a temporal segment of the noise file whose length was equal to the speech file was randomly chosen and added to the speech file. The SNRs of the host speech signal (Signal) and the background noise (Noise) were set to ∞, 80, 60, 40, and 10 dB as the parameters. In order to simulate an anti-aliasing filter generally applied to the sound to be recorded in an actual recording, an additional experimental condition that applies an anti-aliasing filter to the background noise was applied. The cutoff frequency of the anti-aliasing filter was 7400 Hz, and its gain at the Nyquist frequency was -40 dB. This experimental condition is called "anti-alias" hereafter.

In both the conventional method and the proposed method, the RBF kernel was used for the SVM. Following the method of Ghasemzadeh et al. [5, 7], a genetic algorithm (GA) was used to select an optimal set of feature values so that the average F-measure obtained from the tenfold cross validation was maximized. The value of γ, which is the learning parameter of the SVM, was adjusted simultaneously by the GA. Because the intersection and mutation of the GA were performed based on a pseudorandom sequence for each simulation, and the noise to be added also randomly changed, the selected set of feature values, the adjusted γ value, and the resultant F-measures were slightly different among the simulations. Therefore, the simulation was repeated 10 times, and the average F-measures were obtained for each condition. The SVM library of libsvm-3.22 [1] and GA package ga-0.10.0 of Octave-Forge were used.

The embedding of random data and its capacity was set to 50% and 6%, respectively, which were often used in previous papers. In the actual use of steganalysis, the capacity of hidden messages and the power of background noises in speech sounds are not known a priori. In order to show the effects of background noise and the anti-aliasing filter on steganalysis, the best condition (when the capacity of hidden messages and the relative level of background noises were known a priori) was tested first. This means that the stego signals of the same capacity and the same levels of background noise were used to train the model and for detection by the model. After that, different capacities of embedding and different levels of background noise were used to train the model and for detection using the model. This simulated an actual scene of steganalysis.

3.3 Results of Simulation

Figure 2 shows the detection performances of information hiding by steghide for the music signals. The F-measures are compared between the conventional and proposed steganalysis by combining the capacity of steghide in the training and detection stages.

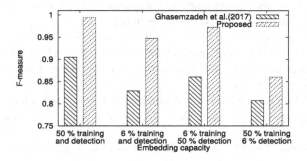

Fig. 2. Detection performances for music signals obtained from conventional and proposed steganalysis.

The proposed steganalysis outperforms the conventional one in all capacity conditions. A higher capacity in the detection stage realizes better detection performance. Different capacities of steghide in the training stage and detection stage lead to a lower detection performance. Training using the stego data of small capacity achieves better detection performance for the stego data for a wide range of capacity.

Figure 3 shows the detection performance of the previous and proposed steganalysis on the speech signals as a function of the signal-to-noise ratio (SNR), which expresses the overall power level of the speech signal to the background noise.

Without an anti-aliasing filter, the conventional steganalysis exhibits a slightly better performance than the proposed method for SNRs of 40 and 60 dB. Because the previous steganalysis utilizes the statistical features of the amplitude in all frequency bands, silent intervals among utterances of speech may be effective cues for detection. Higher levels of background noise lead to a lower detection performance for both steganalyses. This is caused by temporal and frequency segments of small amplitudes in the target signal that are filled with the background noise.

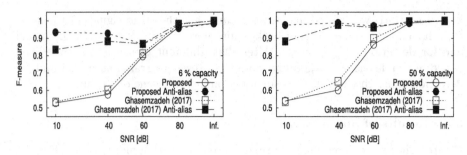

Fig. 3. Detection performances of conventional and proposed steganalysis of steghide embedded in speech signals.

When an anti-aliasing filter is applied to the background noise, a lower SNR does not lead to lower performance as the power of the cover signal at the frequency bands just below the Nyquist frequency is small enough by applying a low-pass anti-aliasing filter. The proposed steganalysis exhibited better performance than the conventional method for SNRs of 10 and 40 dB, because the proposed steganalysis made full use of the high-frequency features just below the Nyquist frequency.

The succeeding simulations are conducted only under anti-alias filtering conditions because speech recording devices generally apply an anti-aliasing filter to the sound to be recorded.

Figure 4 shows the detection performance of the conventional steganalysis. Training of the model and detection using the model were conducted in the same capacity of embedding and at different SNRs. Figure 5 shows the results of the proposed steganalysis for the same conditions as shown in Fig. 4.

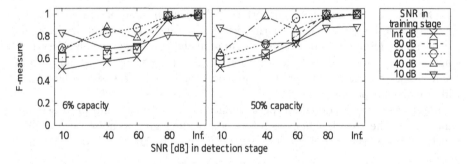

Fig. 4. Detection performance of conventional steganalysis. Training of model and detection using model were conducted in same capacity of embedding.

Figure 6 shows the detection performance of the conventional method, training of the model for 6%-capacity embedding for each SNR condition, detection using the model for a 50% capacity of stego signals for each SNR condition, and vice versa. Figure 7 shows the results of the same conditions in Fig. 6 for the proposed model.

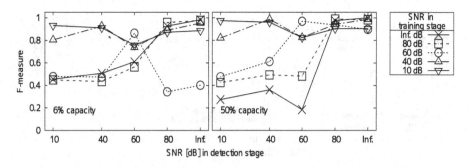

Fig. 5. Detection performance of proposed steganalysis. Training of model and detection using model were conducted in same capacity of embedding.

Figures 4 and 6 indicate that the conventional steganalysis showed good performance when the training and detection were conducted in high-SNR conditions, but the performance dropped when the SNRs of the training and detection were mismatched. By contrast, Figs. 5 and 7 show that the proposed steganalysis exhibited better performance when the training was conducted at the lowest SNR (10 dB) and with a small capacity of embedding (6%) when detecting the stego and cover signals for all combinations of capacities and SNRs.

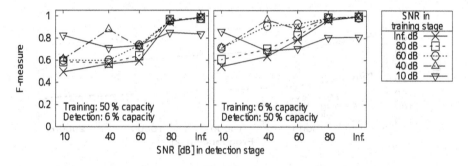

Fig. 6. Detection performance of conventional steganalysis. Training of model and detection using model were conducted for different capacities of embedding.

4   Discussion

The proposed steganalysis shows superior performance to the conventional method for both the music signals and the speech signals. This is caused by the statistics of the frequency components just below the Nyquist frequency. Figures 8 and 9 show the maximum, minimum, and average spectra of all files in RWC-MDB-G2001 and ITU-T P.50, respectively. These are the arithmetic average values of all files for each frequency. The cutoff characteristic of the anti-aliasing filter at the Nyquist frequency of the speech signal is about -40 dB

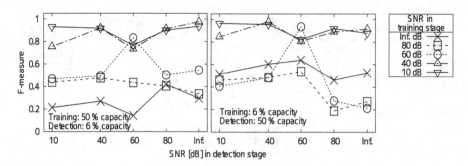

Fig. 7. Detection performance of proposed steganalysis. Training of model and detection using model were conducted for different capacities of embedding.

in Fig. 9. The power of the music signals significantly decreases as the frequency increases in Fig. 8. These characteristics are generally observed for most of the recorded sounds, thus reflecting the nature of natural sounds and recording devices. The proposed method focuses only on the highest frequency region, that is, just below the Nyquist frequency, where the artifacts of data hiding are relatively emphasized, as shown in the SNR spectrogram in Fig. 1(c). This results in superior performance.

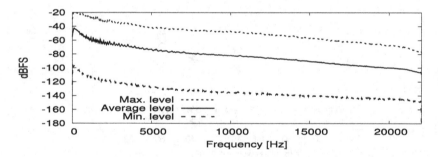

Fig. 8. Averaged spectra of minimum, arithmetic mean, and maximum of 100 music files from RWC-MDB-G2001.

The conventional method only showed a better performance for the speech signals with an SNR of ∞ dB, as shown in Figs. 4 and 6. In that condition, silent intervals with no utterance of speech that were not masked by background noises in the target signals could be a strong cue of detection because the conventional method utilized amplitude statistics in all frequency bands. However, this is not a realistic condition in actual speech recordings.

The conventional steganalysis showed better detection performance for the music and TV program sounds from wavsurfer [5] than that obtained from the music database used in the current study, as shown in Fig. 2. The reason for the better performance in the previous study may be the acoustic characteristics of

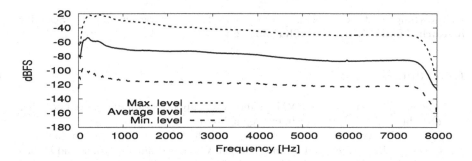

Fig. 9. Averaged spectra of minimum, arithmetic mean, and maximum of 320 speech files from Appendix I of ITU-T P.50.

the sounds included in wavsurfer. They may include upsampled WAV files and WAV files decoded from perceptually coded files. Using these sounds as cover data results in better detection performance, as discussed in Sect. 2.4.

For both the conventional and proposed steganalyses of a speech WAV file, it is difficult to detect information hiding in cover signals containing background noises without applying a steep anti-aliasing filter. From a cover signal to which an anti-aliasing filter is applied, the proposed method extracts the statistical features of the amplitude distribution just below the Nyquist frequency as significant features. Combining the statistical features of the amplitude distribution obtained from small-amplitude segments in the target signal improves the detection performance of the current steganalysis.

In this study, we examined the steganalysis of steghide for a waveform signal that is linearly quantized and not perceptually coded. However, recorded and distributed audio files on the Internet are often encoded as perceptually coded data such as MP3s or AACs. The steganalysis of such coded audio files is one of our future research targets.

5   Summary

In this paper, steganalysis for information hiding by steghide to the lower bits of the audio waveform signal were investigated. Spectral analyses of the cover data implied that the conventional steganalysis utilize the statistics of high-frequency regions and silent temporal segments of the target signals. Moreover, the frequency components just below the Nyquist frequency are important for statistic-based steganalysis in terms of the SNR when the signal corresponds to the distortion components induced by data hiding, and the noise corresponds to cover components. A novel steganalysis making full use of the high-frequency features was proposed, and its detection performance was compared with the conventional method that showed the best performance so far. The results showed that the proposed steganalysis outperformed the conventional method for cover data of 100 music signals and 320 speech signals mixed with background noises.

Acknowledgment. This work was supported by a Grant-in-Aid for Scientific Research C (JSPS KAKENHI 18K11301), 2018.

References

1. Chang, C.C., Lin, C.J.: LIBSVM - a library for support vector machines, December 2016. http://www.csie.ntu.edu.tw/~cjlin/libsvm
2. Djebbar, F., Ayad, B.: A new steganalysis method to detect information hiding in speech. In: Proceedings of 13th International Wireless Communications and Mobile Computing Conference (IWCMC), pp. 1879–1884 (2017)
3. Donoho, D.L., Johnstone, I.M.: Adapting to unknown smoothness via wavelet shrinkage. J. Am. Stat. Assoc. **90**, 1200–1224 (1995)
4. Geetha, S., Ishwarya, N., Kamaraj, N.: Audio steganalysis with Hausdorff distance higher order statistics using a rule based decision tree paradigm. Expert Syst. Appl. **37**, 7469–7482 (2010)
5. Ghasemzadeh, H., Arjmandi, M.K.: Universal audio steganalysis based on calibration and reversed frequency resolution of human auditory system. IET Signal Process. **11**(8), 916–922 (2017)
6. Ghasemzadeh, H., Arjmandi, M.K.: Reversed-Mel cepstrum based audio steganalysis. In: Proceedings of 4th International Conference on Computer and Knowledge Engineering (ICCKE), pp. 679–684 (2014)
7. Ghasemzadeh, H., Khas, M.T., Arjmandi, M.K.: Audio steganalysis based on reversed psychoacoustic model of human hearing. Digit. Signal Process. **51**(C), 133–141 (2016)
8. Goto, M., Hashiguchi, H., Nishimura, T., Oka, R.: RWC music database: music genre database and musical instrument sound database. In: Proceedings of the 4th International Conference on Music Information Retrieval (ISMIR 2003), pp. 229–230 (2003)
9. Hetzl, S., Mutzel, P.: A graph–theoretic approach to steganography. In: Dittmann, J., Katzenbeisser, S., Uhl, A. (eds.) CMS 2005. LNCS, vol. 3677, pp. 119–128. Springer, Heidelberg (2005). https://doi.org/10.1007/11552055_12
10. ITU-T: ITU-T recommendation P.50 Appendix I: Artificial voices; test signals (1998)
11. Ru, X.M., Zhang, H.J., Huang, X.: Steganalysis of audio: attacking the steghide. In: Proceedings of the Fourth International Conference on Machine Learning and Cybernetics, pp. 3937–3942 (2005)
12. Thiemann, J., Ito, N., Vincent, E.: DEMAND: Diverse environments multichannel acoustic noise database (2013). http://parole.loria.fr/DEMAND/
13. USA Today: Terror groups hide behind web encryption, 5 February 2001. https://usatoday30.usatoday.com/tech/news/2001-02-05-binladen.htm

Cycle GAN-Based Attack on Recaptured Images to Fool both Human and Machine

Wei Zhao[1,2], Pengpeng Yang[1,2], Rongrong Ni[1,2(✉)], Yao Zhao[1,2], and Wenjie Li[1,2]

[1] Institute of Information Science, Beijing Jiaotong University, Beijing 100044, China
rrni@bjtu.edu.cn
[2] Beijing Key Laboratory of Advanced Information Science and Network Technology, Beijing 100044, China

Abstract. Recapture can be used to hide the traces left by some operations such as JPEG compression, copy-move, etc. However, various detectors have been proposed to detect recaptured images. To counter these techniques, in this paper, we propose a method that can translate recaptured images to fake "original images" to fool both human and machines. Our method is proposed based on Cycle-GAN which is a classic framework for image translation. To obtain better results, two improvements are proposed: (1) Considering that the difference between original and recaptured images focuses on the part of high frequency, high pass filter are used in the generator and discriminator to improve the performance. (2) In order to guarantee that the images content is not changed too much, a penalty term is added on the loss function which is the L1 norm of the difference between images before and after translation. Experimental results show that the proposed method can not only eliminate traces left by recapturing in visual effect but also change the statistical characteristics effectively.

Keywords: Recaptured images · Cycle-GAN · Fool human and machine

1 Introduction

Nowadays, with the popularity of digital cameras and the rapid development of Internet technology, it is an indisputable fact that digital images have become important carriers. And image editing software is widely used with the advantage of operability and practicability, which makes it easy to tamper an image.

This work was supported in part by the National Key Research and Development of China (2016YFB0800404), National NSF of China (61672090, 61332012, 61532005), Fundamental Research Funds for the Central Universities (2017YJS054, 2018JBZ001). We greatly acknowledge the support of NVIDIA Corporation with the donation of the GPU used for this research.

C. D. Yoo et al. (Eds.): IWDW 2018, LNCS 11378, pp. 83–92, 2019.
https://doi.org/10.1007/978-3-030-11389-6_7

Some tampered images in the fields of politics, military and judicature will bring great harm to the society. Therefore, the identification of digital image authenticity is of particular importance.

One common type of image tampering is recapturing images. The process of recapture is as follows: firstly, the original image is projected onto a new media, such as computer screen, mobile phone screen or printed paper. Then a new image can be obtained by recapturing the projection. Recaptured images may bring about bad effect on the society if they are used maliciously. For example, due to that all the tampering will leave traces on the image, attackers can eliminate these traces by recapturing the forged image. To against it, the most simple and convenient way is to make a recaptured image decision in advance.

To discriminate between the recaptured and original images, numbers of algorithms have been proposed and mainly include two branches: statistical characteristics [1–3] and deep learning based [4]. In terms of statistical features, Farid et al. first proposed a scheme which can to distinguish between natural and unnatural images based on high-order wavelet statistical features. Unnatural images include recaptured images and computer generated images. Cao et al. [2] proposed three kinds of statistical features to detect good-quality recaptured images, namely local binary pattern (LBP), multi-scale wavelet statistics (MSWS), and color features (CF). Li et al. [3] proposed new features based on the block effect and blurriness effect due to JPEG compression and the screen effect described by wavelet decomposition. And the deep learning based method has been proved that it has better detection performance than that statistical characteristics based. Yang et al. [4] proposed a laplacian convolutional neural networks (L-CNN) and improved the detection performance especially for small-size recaptured image.

On the other hand, from the point of view of an attacker, if he want to translate a recaptured image to a fake original image, two goals need to be achieved: the visual effect of LCD should be avoided and it can attack various detection schemes. Generative adversarial networks have achieved many state-of-the-art results in image translation. Generative adversarial networks include generator network and discriminator network. The generator learns the potential distribution of the real data and generates new data and the discriminator is a binary classifier that determines whether the input is real or generated. In training phase, the generator need to be continuously optimized to improve its generating ability and the discriminator need to improve its discriminating ability. The learning process is to find a Nash equilibrium between the two networks. CGAN [5] adds extra information in the generator and discriminator to guide the process of training. Pix2pix-GAN [6] can achieve image-to-image translation tasks with paired images which include an input image and a corresponding target output image. Cycle-GAN [7] used two generators and two discriminators to learn mapping functions between two domains without paired images.

Considering that it is difficult to get the paired images for original images and recaptured images, in this work, a method based on Cycle-GAN is proposed. Due to the fact that the difference between original and recaptured images focuses on high frequency, generator and discriminator with high-pass filter are designed to make a better image translation. Additionally, to guarantee the content of images not change a lot after being translated, a penalty term is added to the loss function which is the L1 norm of the difference between images before and after translation. Experimental results show that the proposed method can not only fool human in visual effect but also the machine with a high probability.

The rest of the paper is organized as follows. In Sect. 2, proposed architecture and object function is introduced. Experiments are conducted in Sect. 3, and conclusions are drawn in Sect. 4.

2   Proposed Method

Our task is to translate recaptured images to target images which is similar to original images not only in visual effect but also in statistical characteristics. It can be formulated as learning a mapping G from recaptured images X to the original images Y given training samples $\{x_i\} \in X$ and $\{y_i\} \in Y$, where $i = 1, 2, ..., m$. Note that X and Y are not corresponding one by one because it is difficult to collect recaptured images which are completely same with original images.

The overall framework of the model is shown in Fig. 1, two generators and discriminators are used. x is present as recaptured image and y is present as original image. Generator G learns the distribution of Y and F learns the distribution of X. Discriminator D_X aims to distinguish between recaptured images $\{x\}$ and fake-recaptured images $\{F(y)\}$, and D_Y aims to distinguish between original images $\{y\}$ and fake-original images $\{G(x)\}$. To promise the mapping is meaningful, cycle network structure is used. As shown in dotted arrow, the translated images $\{G(x)\}$ and $\{F(y)\}$ are fed into the generator F and G. By limiting the difference between x and $F(G(x))$ and the difference between y and $G(F(y))$, the model can be further standardized. The training process is based on game theory and it aims at achieving the Nash equilibrium between generators and discriminators.

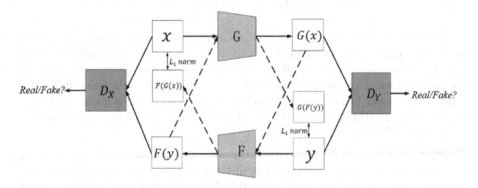

Fig. 1. The overall framework of the model.

2.1   Architecture

Generator. Two generators G and F are included. The Generator G can translate X to Y and Generator F can translate Y to X. The two generators have the same architecture which is shown in Fig. 2. Considering that the difference between original and recaptured images focus on the high frequency part, so only the part of high frequency is extracted and fed into generators. Generators are only responsible for learning the difference of high frequency, which is more easier to train than reconstructing the whole image. In this work, the laplace filter are used:

$$LF = \begin{bmatrix} 0, & -1, & 0 \\ -1, & 4, & -1 \\ 0, & -1, & 0 \end{bmatrix} \tag{1}$$

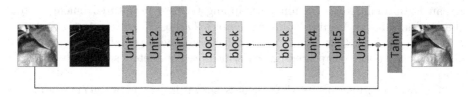

Fig. 2. The architecture of generator.

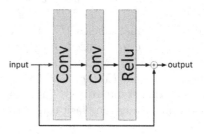

Fig. 3. The architecture of block.

In addition, six units and five residual blocks are combined together. Each of the unit 1, 2, 3 and 6 include a convolution layer, a batch normalization and a Relu function. Each of the unit 4 and 5 include a deconvolution layer, a batch normalization and a Relu function. Each residual block includes two convolution layers and a Relu function. The structure of residual block is shown in Fig. 3. In the end, a TanH activation function is used. The parameters of generator are presented in Table 1.

Discriminator. Two discriminators D_X and D_Y are included. As shown in Fig. 4, the discriminator is designed to distinguish real images and fake images. Similarly, a laplace filter is used, followed by four units and one convolution layer are used. Each unit includes a convolution layer, a batch normalization and a Leaky-ReLU function. The parameters of discriminator are presented in Table 1.

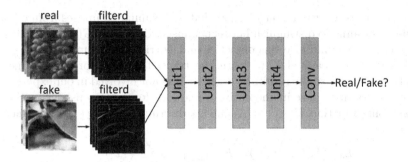

Fig. 4. The architecture of discriminator.

Table 1. The detailed parameters of the architecture

Generator	Unit 1	Conv(7*7*32), padding = 3, stride = 1; batchnorm; Relu
	Unit 2	Conv(3*3*64), stride = 2; batchnorm; Relu
	Unit 3	Conv(3*3*128), stride = 2; batchnorm; Relu
	Block	Conv(3*3*128), stride = 1; Conv(3*3*128), stride = 1; Relu
	Unit 4	Deconv(3*3*128), stride = 2; batchnorm; Relu
	Unit 5	Deconv(3*3*256), stride = 2; batchnorm; Relu
	Unit 6	Conv(7*7*3), stride = 1; batchnorm; Relu
Discriminator	Unit 1	Conv(4*4*32), stride = 2; batchnorm; Leaky-ReLU
	Unit 2	Conv(4*4*64), stride = 2; batchnorm; Leaky-ReLU
	Unit 3	Conv(4*4*128), stride = 2; batchnorm; Leaky-ReLU
	Unit 4	Conv(4*4*256), stride = 1; batchnorm; Leaky-ReLU
	Conv	Conv(4*4*1), stride = 1;

2.2 Object Function

The loss function of proposed method contains three parts: adversarial loss, cycle consistency loss and low frequency consistency loss.

Adversarial Loss. The optimization process of GAN is actually a game between two competing networks: the generator is responsible for generating data which is similar to the real data, and the discriminator is responsible for distinguishing the generated data from the real data. Formally, the game between the generator G and the discriminator D has the minimax objective. Note that the distribution of recaptured images is $P_{data}(x)$ and the distribution of original images is $P_{data}(y)$. We need to translate a recaptured image x to a target image $G(x)$ which follows the distribution of $P_{data}(y)$. Therefore, for the mapping function $G : X \rightarrow Y$ and its discriminator D_Y:

$$L_{adv}(G, D_Y, X, Y) = E_{y \sim p_{data}(y)}(\log D_Y(y)) + E_{x \sim p_{data}(x)}(1 - \log D_Y(G(x))), \tag{2}$$

where G tries to generate images $G(x)$ that look similar to images from domain Y, while D_Y aims to distinguish between translated samples $G(x)$ and real samples y. G tries to minimize this objective and D tries to maximum it.

Due to it is meaningless to learn the translation from original images to recaptured images, so the results of $F : Y \rightarrow X$ is not involved in our experiment. But it's a essential part in the entire framework for cycle consistency. So, for the mapping function $F : Y \rightarrow X$ and its discriminator D_X, there is another constraint:

$$L_{adv}(F, D_X, X, Y) = E_{x \sim p_{data}(x)}(\log D_X(x)) \\ + E_{y \sim p_{data}(y)}(1 - \log D_X(F(y))), \tag{3}$$

Cycle Consistency Loss. Compared with other generation models, the greatest advantage of GAN is that it doesn't need to formulate a target distribution, but to learn the distribution directly using two group of images. However, this mechanism also brings a shortcoming that the model is too free and uncontrollable. A generator can map the input images to any random permutation of images in the target domain, which may cause there is not any semantic links between input images and output images. Thus, it's difficult to guarantee that the learned function can map input X to desired output Y. To ensure the mapping is practical, cycle consistency loss is introduced.

For each image x from domain X, the image translation cycle should be able to bring x back to itself: $x \rightarrow G(x) \rightarrow F(G(x)) \approx x$. And for each image y from domain Y, the image translation cycle also need to bring y back to itself: $y \rightarrow F(y) \rightarrow G(F(y)) \approx y$:

$$L_{cyc}(G, F) = E_{x \sim p_{data}(x)}(\|F(G(x)) - x\|_1) \\ + E_{y \sim p_{data}(y)}(\|G(F(y)) - y\|_1), \tag{4}$$

Low Frequency Consistency Loss. It has been noted that the dataset is unpaired which is convenient to be collected. But it also bring a disadvantage that no groundtruth for recaptured images to constrain the model when training. Due to the deep learning model is driven by data, the generator may learn the difference between original image and recaptured image in training dataset. So if the dataset is not rich enough, the model is likely to be overfitting. The generator can not only learn the difference left by recapturing, but also other difference between two group of data, such as: color distribution, the content of images and so on. In that cases, the translated images may have large chromatic differences from target images. Considering the characteristic of recaptured images, the content of images is similar with original images and the main difference is focus on the high frequency. So an extra term need to be added to ensure that the low frequency part is not changed. In proposed method, median filtering is used to extract the part of low frequency:

$$L_{Low}(G, F) = E_{x \sim p_{data}(x)}(\|f(G(x)) - f(x)\|_1) \\ + E_{y \sim p_{data}(y)}(\|f(F(y)) - f(y)\|_1), \tag{5}$$

where, $f(.)$ is a median filter function which can reserve the low frequency part. In total, the full objective is:

$$\begin{aligned} L(G, F, D_X, D_Y) = & L_{adv}(G, D_Y, X, Y) \\ & + L_{adv}(F, D_X, X, Y) \\ & + \alpha L_{cyc}(G, F) \\ & + \beta L_{low}(G, F), \end{aligned} \tag{6}$$

where α, β are weight coefficients. In the experiments, α is set as 10 and β is set as 5.

Finally, by optimizing the loss function according to Eq. (7), we can get the well-trained generators and discriminators. According to the purpose of this work, only generator G is needed.

$$G^* = \min_{G, F} \max_{D_X, D_Y} L(G, F, D_X, D_Y), \tag{7}$$

where, G^* presents the well-trained generator G.

3   Experimental Results and Analysis

Image database in the experiments includes 20000 images: 10000 original images and 10000 recapture images. The size of the images is 256×256. The images derive from the image databases provided in [2]. We crop the block with size of 1024×1024 from the center of the images. Then the images are cut into non-overlapping blocks of 512×512. Finally, 256×256 images are got by center clipping. And training dataset, validation and test dataset are randomly divided by percent 40/10/50. Hyper-parameter setting in the experiment is as follows: the learning rate is 0.0001 and iteration epoch is 15. And the Adam optimizer with $\beta = 0.5$ are used. All the results shown in this section are averaged over 6 random experiments.

In the experiment, three recaptured image detection methods are involved. They include the method based on statistical characteristics: LBP feature [3] and wavelet statistical feature [3] and based on deep learning: L-CNN [4]. Firstly, these three methods are well-trained to get the different accuracies for different images. Furthermore, to analyze the validity of model modification, a contrast experiment is performed in which the model is original Cycle-GAN without any modification. Finally, in order to verify the effectiveness of proposed method, it was trained using the training dataset and the recaptured images in test set are fed into the model to be transferred to a fake images.

In Table 2, the detection accuracies using three methods for different images are presented. Noted that $IMAGE_{nor}$ means the recaptured images in test dataset without any translation. $IMAGE_{cyc}$ means the images translated by original Cycle-GAN and $IMAGE_{prop}$ means the images translated by proposed method. It can be seen that there detection methods mentioned above can all detect the recaptured images effectively. And the ability of original Cycle-GAN

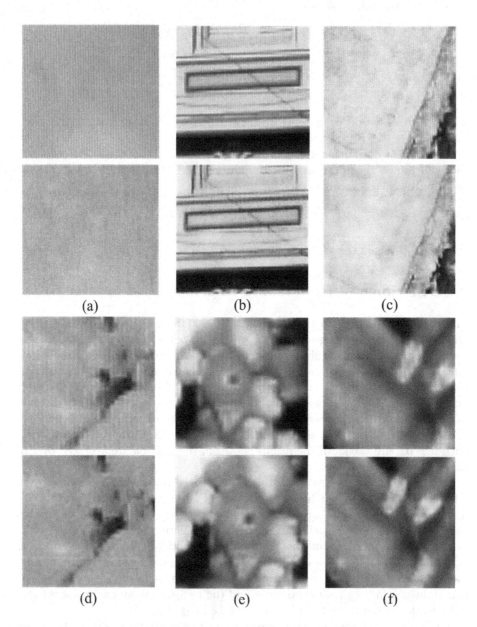

(a)   (b)   (c)

(d)   (e)   (f)

Fig. 5. The visual effect of recaptured images and corresponding translated images. In each group, recaptured image is on the top and the translated image is on the bottom.

to attack the detection methods is worse than the proposed method. It can be seen that after being transferred by proposed method, the classic schemes will be fooled with great probability. At the same time, it is noticed that the attack effect is different for three detection methods, and the proposed method can attack the L-CNN effectively but don't perform very well in attacking the methods of LBP and wavelet. We guess it is because the method of L-CNN is more similar to the discriminator of proposed method.

In the aspect of visual effects, six group of images are shown in Fig. 5. In each group, recaptured image is on the top and the translated image is on the bottom. From these images, we can find that proposed method can remove the traces of texture left by recapturing LCD screen effectively.

In conclusion, the proposed method can not only eliminate of traces left by recapturing in visual effect but also change the statistical characteristics to attack the detection methods effectively.

Table 2. The classification accuracy using three methods for different images

Image	Method		
	L-CNN	LBP	Wavlet
$IMAGE_{nor}$	99.0%	95.6%	82.0%
$IMAGE_{cyc}$	34.83%	70.96%	53.3%
$IMAGE_{prop}$	9.4%	32.85%	39.44%

4   Conclusion

In this paper, we proposed a method to translate recaptured images to fake "original images" based on Cycle-GAN. According to the characteristics of recaptured images, generator and discriminator with high-pass filter are designed to make a better image translation. Additionally, to guarantee the content of images don't change a lot after being translated, a penalty term is added to the loss function which is the L1 norm of the difference between images before and after translation. Experimental results show that the proposed method can not only fool human in visual effect but also the machine with a high probability.

References

1. Lyu, S., Farid, H.: How realistic is photorealistic? IEEE Trans. Signal Process. **53**, 845–850 (2005)
2. Cao, H., Alex, K.C.: Identification of recaptured photographs on LCD screens. In: IEEE International Conference on Acoustics, Speech and Signal Processing, pp. 1790–1793 (2010)
3. Li, R., Ni, R., Zhao, Y.: An effective detection method based on physical traits of recaptured images on LCD screens. In: Shi, Y.-Q., Kim, H.J., Pérez-González, F., Echizen, I. (eds.) IWDW 2015. LNCS, vol. 9569, pp. 107–116. Springer, Cham (2016). https://doi.org/10.1007/978-3-319-31960-5_10

4. Yang, P., Ni, R., Zhao, Y.: Recapture Image forensics based on laplacian convolutional neural networks. In: Shi, Y.Q., Kim, H.J., Perez-Gonzalez, F., Liu, F. (eds.)
   IWDW 2016. LNCS, vol. 10082, pp. 119–128. Springer, Cham (2017). https://doi.
   org/10.1007/978-3-319-53465-7_9
5. Mirza, M., Osindero, S.: Conditional generative adversarial nets. arXiv preprint
   arXiv:1411.1784 (2014)
6. Isola, P., Zhu, J.Y., Zhou, T., Efros, A.A.: Image-to-image translation with conditional adversarial networks. arXiv preprint arXiv:1611.07004 (2017)
7. Zhu, J.Y., Park, T., Isola, P., Efros, A.A.: Unpaired image-to-image translation
   using cycle-consistent adversarial networks. arXiv preprint arXiv:1703.10593 (2017)

Watermarking

Spherical Panorama Image Watermarking Using Viewpoint Detection

Jihyeon Kang[1(✉)], Sang-Keun Ji[2], and Heung-Kyu Lee[2]

[1] Graduate School of Information Security, School of Computing,
Korea Advanced Institute of Science and Technology, Daejeon, South Korea
kangji@kaist.ac.kr
[2] School of Computing, Korea Advanced Institute of Science and Technology,
Daejeon, South Korea

Abstract. Even though interest in spherical panorama content has increased rapidly, few studies have examined watermarking techniques for this content. We present a new watermarking technique to protect spherical panorama images as well as view-images that are rendered with a specific viewpoint. Solving the watermark synchronization problem in the detection process requires finding the viewpoint of a view-image. Scale Invariant Feature Transform (SIFT) and Euclidea transformation matrix are used to find viewpoint information of a detection target view-image. Using the viewpoint information, a view-image can be recovered to a source image and then we can detect watermark from it. The experimental results show robustness against several attacks such as JPEG compression, Gaussian filter, and noise addition attack.

Keywords: Image watermarking · Spherical panorama ·
Omni-directional image · 360 VR watermarking

1 Introduction

Recently, interest in spherical panorama content (a.k.a. omni-directional contents, $360 \times 180°$ contents, VR contents) has increased rapidly. Unlike other existing media content, it allows viewers to choose their viewpoint. Thanks to recent improvements in hardware and software for spherical panorama content, one can easily create, distribute, and appreciate their content. Thus, the market for spherical panoramas has grown both qualitatively and quantitatively and the copyright protection problem has become an important issue. Watermarking techniques have been proposed as a solution to the image copyright problem. However, watermarking techniques that can properly protect spherical panorama content are absent.

A view-image comes from spherical panoramas source image with a specific viewpoint. A normal user can only see view-images rather than the spherical panoramas source image, so view-images are easier to leak than the entire source image. Furthermore, a view-image can have sufficiently high content value and

© Springer Nature Switzerland AG 2019
C. D. Yoo et al. (Eds.): IWDW 2018, LNCS 11378, pp. 95–109, 2019.
https://doi.org/10.1007/978-3-030-11389-6_8

a replicated spherical panorama source image can be made using several view-images. Therefore, spherical panorama watermarking techniques should detect watermarks from view-images. However, existing watermarking techniques for 2D images or 3D stereoscopic images cannot be applied directly to spherical panoramas because its distortion varies depending on viewer's viewpoint in the rendering process.

This paper proposes a spherical panorama image watermarking technique. For the synchronization between location of embedding and location of detecting, watermark is embedded and detected on spherical panorama's source image that has a equirectangular form. Therefore, to detect watermark from a view-image, we should render the view-image into the source-image. The rendering needs the view-image's viewpoint information; we propose using the Scale Invariant Feature Transform (SIFT) feature points matching algorithm [1] and Euclidean matrix transformation to get viewpoint information of a view-image.

This paper is outlined as follows. First, we will explain related work involving image watermarking for various content in Sect. 2, we will show a spherical panorama image watermarking algorithm in Sect. 3, and Sect. 4 shows the experimental results. Finally, future research directions are proposed and the paper is concluded.

2   Related Works: Image Watermarking for Various Contents

2D image, Stereoscopic 3D, Depth Image Based Rendering (DIBR), and spherical panoramas are the examples of various types of image content. Watermarking methods have been proposed for various image content and since the various types of content each have their own characteristics, a watermarking technique should be designed that takes account of their characteristics.

To date, numerous watermarking techniques have been proposed for 2D image. Frequency domains such as DCT [2], DFT [3], DWT [4], and contourlet [5] are often used for invisibility and robustness. In various domains, various methods such as spread spectrum [6] and quantization index modulation [7] are used. Furthermore, there are many 2D image watermarking techniques that use template [12] or feature points [8] for the robustness against geometric distortion. Recently, 2D image watermarking techniques have been introduced that uses a deep learning [17,18].

3D image have two kinds of format for 3D content distribution: stereoscopic 3D (S3D) and Depth-image-based rendering (DIBR). S3D uses two images (left image, right image) to get one view and S3D image watermarking schemes emphasize the Human Visual System (HVS) to reduce visual fatigue in the 3D rendering process [11]. S3D and DIBR both use two images, but DIBR uses a center image and a depth image; DIBR makes left and right images using the center and depth images. Therefore, DIBR can control the degree of depth in an image. DIBR watermarking schemes [13–15] should consider variable depth depending on user preference. Both DIBR and spherical panorama image water-marking schemes should detect watermark from changing image according to setting, but the degree of change differs. DIBR rendering can only makes local horizontal translations; therefore, it is not adjustable to spherical panoramas.

In the case of spherical panoramas, which have recently entered the spotlight, watermarking techniques are uncommon. Miura et al. proposed a data hiding technique for omnidirectional images [20], but they did not consider robust-ness because they focused on hiding information. Furthermore, they only used equirectangular images and did not deal with view-images.

Kang et al. proposed spherical panorama image watermarking using feature points [19]; they embedded watermarks into several original images before com-bining them into an equirectangular image. The several combined watermarked images become one watermarked equirectangular image; then they could detect a watermark in the equirectangular image. Protecting only the equirectangular image can be performed using existing 2D image watermarking techniques. Usu-ally, several original images that are taken from a specific position to make one equirectangular image are taken by one person. Therefore, a different watermark is not needed for each original image. Furthermore, the view-image can easily be stolen, while the source image (mostly equirectangular image) is relatively hard to be stolen due to the characteristics of the spherical panorama. This is why we embed watermarks into equirectangular images and detect from view-images.

3   Proposed Spherical Panorama Watermarking Algorithm

This paper presents a watermarking algorithm for spherical panorama images. As mentioned in the introduction, a spherical panorama watermarking algorithm should not only be able to detect watermark from the entire source image but also from view-images. Considering rendering distortion, detecting watermarks in view-images is similar to detecting watermarks in extremely cropped and almost randomly warped 2D images. Therefore, we propose recovering detection-targeted view-image to equirectangular source image for watermark synchronization.

This section briefly explains spherical panorama images and then the water-mark embedding and detection processes are described separately.

3.1   Spherical Panorama Image

Spherical panorama images are also well known as VR images, omni-directional images, or 360° panorama images. They are very effective for expressing vir-tual space as real space. Making one spherical panorama image requires several images that include all direction views taken from one point. After that, it is necessary to combine several images into one through a process called stitching. Stitching multiple images containing all directions into one image is like express-ing a three-dimensional sphere in a 2D plane. There are many ways to project a 3D sphere into one 2D image and no method can avoid distortion, but the equirectangular form is most commonly used in spherical panorama images.

In equirectangular formed image, width refers to the 360° horizontal view and height refers to the 180° vertical view. Therefore, the length of the width is always twice that of the height in an equirectangular formed image. Common world maps are the most well-known equirectangular formed image that express the spherical Earth's surface into a single 2D image.

When someone wants to view a spherical panorama image, the equirectangular image is projected onto a sphere and then the viewer observes the partial surface of the sphere from its center. Therefore, spherical panoramas have 360° horizontal and 180° vertical fields of view. The partial image depends on the user viewpoint, which we will call the 'view-image'. Figures 1 and 2 will clarify this.

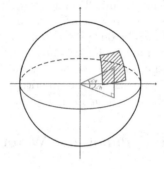

Fig. 1. Viewing a spherical panorama is like viewing a partial of surface from the center. The red area refers to 'view-image'. (Color figure online)

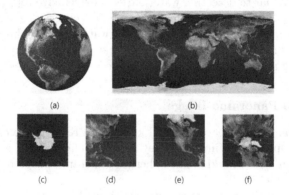

Fig. 2. (a): sphere, (b): equirectangular (source image), (c)–(f): view-images

3.2   Watermark Embedding

Watermark Patches. We embed watermark into the original source image (the equirectangular image) and we detect watermarks from view-image. This is similar to defending against a random extreme cropping attack. We want at least one complete watermark pattern in the view-image regardless of the viewpoint; we do this by dividing the source image into $n * 2n$ number of blocks, each of blocks has one watermark patch and all the blocks have same watermark patch. Since adjacent pixels are affected by each other in the spherical panorama rendering process, the edge areas of the blocks are not used and the center area of the blocks is only used as watermark patch. Figure 3 shows an example of watermark patches' area without considering watermarks' invisibility.

Fig. 3. Example of 9 × 18 watermark patches (80% of blocks)

Embedding Watermark Pattern. This proposed method can adapt to various existing 2D watermarking methods. For convenience of explanation, we will explain this using a basic DCT domain-based spread spectrum watermarking method.

The secret key (K_s) is used to make a watermark pattern (W_p) that is a random sequence that follows a Gaussian distribution with an average of 0 and a variance of 1. The length of the watermark pattern is proportional to the size of the watermark patch. W_p and the original DCT coefficients (C_o) are used to create watermarked coefficients (C_w). Making the watermarked coefficients (C_o) equation is as follows.

$$C_{w(i,k)} = C_{o(i,k)} + \alpha_w \left| C_{o(i,k)} \right| W_{p(k)} \tag{1}$$

In Eq. 1, i denotes the index of the watermark patches and k denotes index of the watermarking-targeted coefficients. Watermarking-targeted coefficients are coefficients of middle frequency in DCT domain. α_w denotes watermark strength value and this value controls the trade-off between the watermark's robustness and visibility. Original coefficients (C_o) are replaced by watermarked coefficients (C_w) and then a watermarked RGB-channel source-image is obtained through inverse-DCT (Fig. 4).

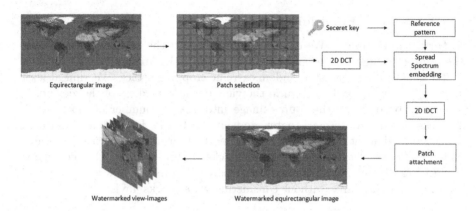

Fig. 4. Watermark embedding process

3.3 Watermark Detection

Spherical panorama watermarking schemes should be able to detect watermarks from source images and view-images. Detecting a watermark from the source image is the same as detecting a watermark from 2D image in this scheme. We propose a way to detect watermarks in a view-image by recovering a view-image to the source image. However, the recovery process needs viewpoint information from the view-image, which is why we need a viewpoint detection process. We divide the viewpoint detection process into two steps: a near-viewpoint detection step and a precise-viewpoint detection step; these are explained in detail in following subsections.

Near-Viewpoint Detection. Spherical panorama view-image is the part of a sphere's surface. Therefore, each view-image's center can be expressed as two spherical angle variables; one is horizontal ($-180°$–$180°$) and the other is vertical ($-90°$–$90°$). Obtaining a viewpoint of a view-image by comparing all the each of view-images is almost impossible. We propose a method to determine near-viewpoint using the SIFT matching technique.

We need reference view-images to obtain the near-viewpoint of a detection-targeted view-image. Reference view-images are generated from the original (or watermarked but undamaged) source image. The reference view-images represent near view-images that have a similar viewpoint. The sum of reference view-images should cover the whole spherical panorama image and there should be an overlapping region between the very next neighbor reference view-images. Too large an overlapping region increases the number of required reference view-images and means lower efficiency. Based on empirical results, we used 26 reference view-images in a source image. Figure 5 shows the example of reference view-images.

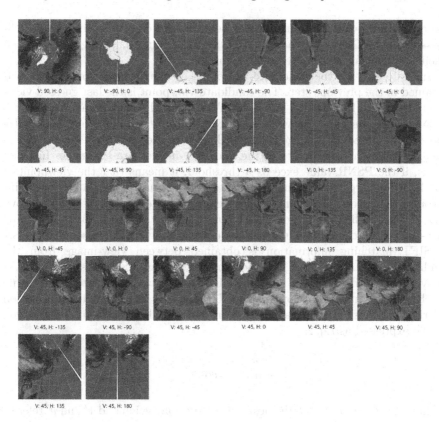

Fig. 5. Example of 26 reference view-images. V: vertical, H: horizontal

If any two view-images have a similar viewpoint, then the two view-images will likely contain several of the same objects. If there is no severe distortion, SIFT, which is robust to Rotation, Scaling, and Translation (RST) can match same objects between them. In other words, if there are many matched SIFT feature points between two view-images, then the two view-images have a similar viewpoint. A near-viewpoint can be obtained using this characteristic.

Initially, SIFT matching is performed between a detection-targeted view-image and each reference view-images. Then, the number of matching points becomes a measure of viewpoint similarity. If the maximum SIFT feature points matching number is not over a specific threshold, it is determined that the targeted view-image is not derived from the corresponding spherical panorama image. Conversely, if the maximum SIFT matching number exceeds a threshold value, the viewpoint of the reference view-image is determined as the near-viewpoint.

Precise-Viewpoint Detection. Precise-viewpoint can be obtained by searching surround of near-viewpoint. SIFT feature point matching method and Euclidean transformation are used to search.

Initially, we set the candidate-viewpoint as the near-viewpoint that was obtained in the previous step. The candidate-viewpoint is the last guessed viewpoint that could be a precise-viewpoint. After that, the Peak Signal Noise Ratio (PSNR) value between the view-image comes from candidate-viewpoint and a detection-targeted view-image is obtained. We can use the PSNR value to determine whether the viewpoints of the two view-images are the same. In other words, if the PSNR value exceeds a threshold, it means that the viewpoint of the detection-targeted view-image has been found and the candidate-viewpoint becomes the precise-viewpoint. Then, we can move on to the next step. However, if the candidate-viewpoint does not equal the viewpoint of the targeted view-image, the candidate-viewpoint should be changed to a reasonable guess.

SIFT matching information is obtained between view-image from the candidate-viewpoint and targeted view-image. This information is used to guess the vertical, horizontal, and rotation differences between the two images using the Euclidean transformation matrix. The general Euclidean transformation matrix that considers vertical translation, horizontal translation, and rotation can be expressed as Eq. 2.

$$\begin{bmatrix} x' \\ y' \end{bmatrix} = \begin{bmatrix} s \cdot \cos \theta & s \cdot -\sin \theta \\ s \cdot \sin \theta & s \cdot \cos \theta \end{bmatrix} \begin{bmatrix} x \\ y \end{bmatrix} + \begin{bmatrix} c \\ d \end{bmatrix} \tag{2}$$

In Eq. 2, x and y refer to the positions before conversion and x' and y' refer to the positions after conversion; c represents the degree of translation in the x-axis and d represents the degree of translation in the y-axis. s refers to the scale and θ represents the degree of rotation based on the origin considering the scale (s) change. After replacing $s \cdot \cos \theta$ with a and $s \cdot \sin \theta$ with b, we can expand it and then rewrite it with determinants $a, b, c,$ and d. After that, n SIFT feature point matching pairs between the two view-images can be substituted into it and then it can be expressed as Eq. 3.

$$\begin{bmatrix} x_1 & -y_1 & 1 & 0 \\ y_1 & x_1 & 0 & 1 \\ x_2 & -y_2 & 1 & 0 \\ y_2 & x_2 & 0 & 1 \\ \vdots & \vdots & \vdots & \vdots \\ x_n & -y_n & 1 & 0 \\ y_n & x_n & 0 & 1 \end{bmatrix} \begin{bmatrix} a \\ b \\ c \\ d \end{bmatrix} = \begin{bmatrix} x'_1 \\ y'_1 \\ x'_2 \\ y'_2 \\ \vdots \\ x'_n \\ y'_n \end{bmatrix} \tag{3}$$

In Eq. 3, the pseudo inverse can be used to get the best approximate values for $a, b, c,$ and d. Using c and d, we can estimate the degree of parallel translation of both x-axis and y-axis. In other words, we can estimate the degree of vertical and horizontal translation. Furthermore, we can estimate the degree of rotation (θ) using Eq. 4.

$$s = \sqrt{a^2 + b^2}, \qquad \cos \theta = \frac{a}{s} \tag{4}$$

After obtaining the guessed vertical, horizontal, and rotational transformation information, the information is used to estimate the viewpoint of the detection-targeted view-image. In other words, new candidate-viewpoint can be obtained by adjusting the transformation information.

Newly obtained candidate-viewpoints are checked for whether one is the precise-viewpoint. The method compares the PSNR value between the detection-targeted view-image and the view-image comes from the candidate-viewpoint to the threshold, and its method is the same as before. If the PSNR value exceeds a threshold, the candidate-viewpoint becomes the precise-viewpoint and we move on to the next step. Otherwise, we should repeat this step until we find the precise-viewpoint.

Recover to Source Image. The obtained precise-viewpoint is used to recover the detection-targeted view-image to the source-image. It is impossible to reconstruct the entire source image because only information used in the rendering process is recoverable. After reconstruction, an interpolation process is needed to reduce the hole-effect that interferes with watermark detection. Figure 6 presents examples of view-images and corresponding reconstructed source-images and interpolated source-images.

Watermark Detection. Watermark patches in fully recovered areas are used for detection. This paper only uses patches that have over 95% of recovered pixels. The DCT coefficients are obtained from each patch, then the correlation values between the watermark pattern and the coefficients of each patch can be obtained. As a result, one correlation value comes from one recovered patch. Optionally, some of the highest and lowest correlation values can be excluded to remove outliers.

After that, the average value of the remaining correlation is obtained, and the average value is compared to a threshold value. If the average value exceeds that threshold value, it is determined that the watermark has been detected; otherwise, it is determined that a watermark does not exist or the embedded watermark pattern and the watermark pattern that the process tried to detect are different (Fig. 7).

4   Experimental Results

The experiments used various types of a hundred equirectangular formed source images [16]. The resolutions of equirectangular images ranged from 1024 × 2048 to 3000 × 6000, the resolution of view-image was 400 × 400, and view-image's horizontal and vertical field of view values were 90°. The number of blocks of

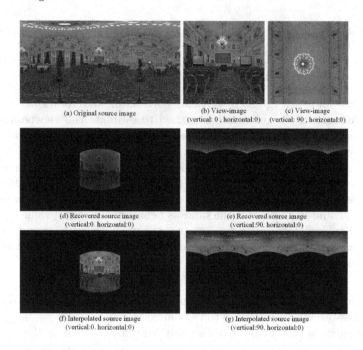

(a) Original source image

(b) View-image
(vertical: 0 , horizontal:0)

(c) View-image
(vertical: 90 , horizontal:0)

(d) Recovered source image
(vertical:0. horizontal:0)

(e) Recovered source image
(vertical:90. horizontal:0)

(f) Interpolated source image
(vertical:0. horizontal:0)

(g) Interpolated source image
(vertical:90. horizontal:0)

Fig. 6. Examples of recovering from view-image to source-image and its interpolation

a source-image was 9 × 18 and each block had one watermark patch in the center area; the patch size was equal to 75% of the block size. The length of the reference pattern equaled 40% of the number of pixels in a patch and the watermark insertion strength was 0.2.

Initially, we compared four domains to find one that was robust against spherical panorama rendering. We embedded watermark patterns into each spatial, DCT, DWT, and DFT domain patch of the source-images. Except for the spatial domain, we embedded watermark patterns into the middle frequency area. We adjusted the other variables to make the PSNR values similar (The PSNR values that were obtained were between the original view-images and the watermarked view-images).

We used 20 original source-images for this experiment. We made 80 watermarked source-images through four domains. We used four representative viewpoints to make 320 watermarked view-images in total; then, we obtained average correlation values using the proposed spherical panorama watermarking scheme. Table 1 shows the results.

As a result, DCT domains show the best performance. Therefore, watermark pattern values are inserted into DCT coefficients in the following experiments.

Table 2 shows the results of invisibility experiments using the average PSNR value between the original image and watermarked images. The source-image experiments use a hundred equirectangular formed images and the view-image experiments use 10 random-viewpoint view-images for each source-image.

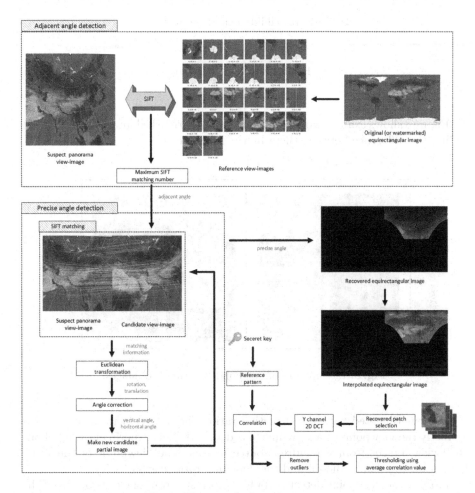

Fig. 7. Watermark detection process

Table 1. Average correlation and PSNR values depending on the domain and viewpoint

	Viewpoint (vertical, horizontal)			
	$(0°, 0°)$	$(30°, 0°)$	$(60°, 0°)$	$(90°, 0°)$
Spatial [8]	0.039	0.062	0.057	0.037
	PSNR: 42.47 dB			
DCT [2]	0.109	0.104	0.092	0.076
	PSNR: 42.35 dB			
DWT [4]	0.055	0.055	0.047	0.043
	PSNR: 40.56 dB			
DFT [3]	0.048	0.063	0.052	0.052
	PSNR: 42.61 dB			

Table 2. Invisibility experimental result

	Source-image	View-image
PSNR	45.12 dB	46.84 dB

Figure 8 shows examples of the original and watermarked images. It is difficult to find the difference between them by the human eye.

Fig. 8. Examples of original and watermarked images

We experimented with the detection ratio. The detection ratio means how correctly the viewpoint of a view-image is detected. This experiment used about 1600 view-images from a hundred source images. The viewpoint of the view-images was randomly chosen and the detection ratio was 83.15%.

Most of the viewpoint detection failures correspond to one of two types. The first type was when view-images had almost no features, such as images of the sky or ocean. The other type was when almost similar objects were repeatedly present in the image. Because the algorithm uses SIFT feature points matching technique for viewpoint detection, so the two types above can be a limitation. However, the first limitation is not a problem because the view-images that have almost no feature points are unlikely to be worth protecting. Figure 9 shows examples of the two viewpoint detection failure types; the upper lined view-images are included in the first type and the lower lined view-images are included in the second type.

We experimented on the watermarking performance; we used about 500 view-images for each test in this experiment. Initially, we obtained average correlation coefficients from correct and incorrect watermarks. A correct watermark means that the same watermark pattern is used in embedding and detecting and incorrect watermark means that different watermark patterns are used. The detection ratio result was obtained by comparing the threshold with the average correlation coefficient. Table 3 and Fig. 10 show the results; the results show the meaningful difference between the correct watermark and the incorrect watermark; we set the threshold value to 0.02 to get the detection ratio.

Fig. 9. Examples of viewpoint detection failed view-images

Table 3. Correlation results without attack

	Correct WM	Wrong WM
Average correlation	0.0796	−0.0002
Detection rate	88.8%	0%

Further experiments were conducted to determine the robustness of the watermarking against JPEG compression, noise addition attack, and blurring attack; the results are as shown in Table 4.

Table 4. Correlation result with attacks

	JPEG 90	JPEG 80	JPEG 70	JPEG 60	Noise	Gaussian
Average correlation	0.0536	0.0516	0.0466	0.0387	0.0725	0.0665
Detection rate	83.8%	85.1%	87.2%	79.7%	88.8%	90.2%
PSNR	36.34 dB	33.57 dB	32.23 dB	31.69 dB	33.15 dB	34.22 dB

Each attack experiment used about 300 random viewpoint view-images. The experiment used four types (90, 80, 70, and 60) of JPEG compression attack with different compression qualities. The noise addition attack experiments used Gaussian noise with an average of 0 and a variable of 0.0005, while the blurring attack experiments used a Gaussian filter with 0.6 sigma. The PSNR values between the watermarked view-images and watermarked and attacked view-images show the degree of attacks.

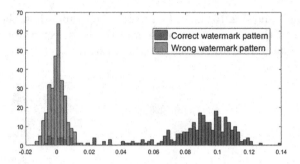

Fig. 10. Correlation histogram using correct and wrong watermark pattern

5 Conclusion

In this paper, we proposed spherical panorama image watermarking technique. We used equirectangular formed source image to synchronize embedding and detecting location. Viewpoint detection process was used to recover from view-image to source image. The experiments shows robustness against JPEG compression, Gaussian filter, and noise addition attacks. Unfortunately, this proposed scheme have limitations for some kinds of images and this is non-blind watermarking technique. As we known, this is first watermarking technique for spherical panorama contents in the right scenario and we showed the possibility of watermarking for spherical panorama contents.

Acknowledgements. This work was supported by the National Research Foundation of Korea (NRF) grant funded by the Korea government (MSIT) (NRF-2016R1A2B2009595).

References

1. Lowe, D.G.: Distinctive image features from scale-invariant keypoints. Int. J. Comput. Vis. **60**(2), 91–110 (2004)
2. Barni, M., et al.: A DCT-domain system for robust image watermarking. Signal process. **66**(3), 357–372 (1998)
3. Pereira, S., Pun, T.: Robust template matching for affine resistant image watermarks. IEEE Trans. Image Process. **9**(6), 1123–1129 (2000)
4. Xia, X.-G., Boncelet, C.G., Arce, G.R.: A multiresolution watermark for digital images. In: Proceedings of International Conference on Image Processing, vol. 1. IEEE (1997)
5. Akhaee, M.A., Sahraeian, S.M.E., Marvasti, F.: Contourlet-based image watermarking using optimum detector in a noisy environment. IEEE Trans. Image Process. **19**(4), 967–980 (2010)
6. Cox, I.J., et al.: Secure spread spectrum watermarking for multimedia. IEEE Trans. Image Process. **6**(12), 1673–1687 (1997)
7. Chen, B., Wornell, G.W.: Quantization index modulation: a class of provably good methods for digital watermarking and information embedding. IEEE Trans. Inf. Theory **47**(4), 1423–1443 (2001)

8. Lee, H.-Y., Kim, H., Lee, H.-K.: Robust image watermarking using local invariant features. Opt. Eng. **45**(3), 037002 (2006)
9. Chang, C.-C., Tsai, P., Lin, C.-C.: SVD-based digital image watermarking scheme. Pattern Recogn. Lett. **26**(10), 1577–1586 (2005)
10. Chandra, D.V.S.: Digital image watermarking using singular value decomposition. In: The 2002 45th Midwest Symposium on Circuits and Systems, 2002. MWSCAS-2002, vol. 3. IEEE (2002)
11. Ji, S.-K., Kang, J.-H., Lee, H.-K.: Perceptual watermarking for stereoscopic 3D image based on visual discomfort. In: Kim, K., Joukov, N. (eds.) ICISA 2017. LNEE, vol. 424, pp. 323–330. Springer, Singapore (2017). https://doi.org/10.1007/978-981-10-4154-9_38
12. Lu, W., Hongtao, L., Chung, F.-L.: Feature based watermarking using watermark template match. Appl. Math. Comput. **177**(1), 377–386 (2006)
13. Lin, Y.-H., Ja-Ling, W.: A digital blind watermarking for depth-image-based rendering 3D images. IEEE Trans. Broadcast. **57**(2), 602–611 (2011)
14. Wang, S., Cui, C., Niu, X.: Watermarking for DIBR 3D images based on SIFT feature points. Measurement **48**, 54–62 (2014)
15. Kim, H.-D., et al.: Robust DT-CWT watermarking for DIBR 3D images. IEEE Trans. Broadcast. **58**(4), 533–543 (2012)
16. Equirectangular flickr group. https://www.flickr.com/groups/equirectangular. Accessed 6 July 2018
17. Mun, S.-M., et al.: A robust blind watermarking using convolutional neural network. arXiv preprint arXiv:1704.03248 (2017)
18. Kim, W.-H., et al.: Convolutional neural network architecture for recovering watermark synchronization. arXiv preprint arXiv:1805.06199 (2018)
19. Kang, I.-S., Seo, Y.-H., Kim, D.-W.: Blind digital watermarking methods for omnidirectional panorama images using feature points. Korean Inst. Broadcast Media Eng. **22**(6), 785–799 (2017)
20. Miura, Y., et al.: Data hiding technique for omnidirectional JPEG images displayed on VR spaces. In: 2018 International Workshop on Advanced Image Technology (IWAIT). IEEE (2018)

Traitor Tracing After Visible Watermark Removal

Hannes Mareen$^{(\boxtimes)}$, Johan De Praeter, Glenn Van Wallendael,
and Peter Lambert

Ghent University – imec, IDLab, Department of Electronics
and Information Systems, Ghent, Belgium
hannes.mareen@ugent.be

Abstract. Watermarks are often used to protect copyright-protected videos from illegal re-distribution. More specifically, a unique watermark that represents the receiver's identifier is embedded into the video. In this way, malicious users can be identified when they leak their received version of the video. However, when the watermark is embedded as visible text in the video, it is easy for digital pirates to delete it such that they can no longer be identified. Therefore, copyright owners will benefit from a technique that allows the detection of a visible watermark when it is removed. This paper demonstrates how a visible watermark indirectly generates imperceptible variations over the entire video. As such, these variations in the non-watermarked area can be used as an alternative watermark representation, and thus enable watermark detection even after watermark removal. The experimental results prove that the watermark can be detected as long as the quality of the watermarked video is not significantly reduced, especially if the originally-distributed watermarked video has a high quality. Moreover, the watermark should be embedded into a video with sufficient motion. In conclusion, the proposed technique enables copyright-owners to identify pirates when they illegally distribute visibly-watermarked videos, even when the watermarked area is removed.

Keywords: Video security · Visible watermarking · Traitor tracing

1 Introduction

Digital watermarking is a widely-used technique that enables the identification of digital pirates when they illegally distribute copyright-protected videos.

This work was funded by the Research Foundation – Flanders (FWO) under Grant 1S55218N, IDLab (Ghent University – imec), Flanders Innovation & Entrepreneurship (VLAIO), and the European Union. Furthermore, the computational resources (STEVIN Supercomputer Infrastructure) and services used in this work were kindly provided by Ghent University, the Flemish Supercomputer Center (VSC), the Hercules Foundation and the Flemish Government department EWI.

C. D. Yoo et al. (Eds.): IWDW 2018, LNCS 11378, pp. 110–123, 2019.
https://doi.org/10.1007/978-3-030-11389-6_9

For example, watermarks are often embedded into screeners of films or TV series that are distributed to award voters and critics, before the official release date. That is, a uniquely-watermarked version of the video is sent to every authorized recipient. If a malicious award voter or critic leaks their version of the video, he or she can be identified by the watermark. Thus, watermarking enables so-called traitor tracing.

A watermark can be embedded either visibly or invisibly. The most simple and straightforward way to embed a watermark is by overlaying the identifier (ID) of the receiver as visible text in the video [3]. For example, Fig. 1a shows such a watermark with ID 260993. In this way, a human can read the watermark and thus identify the receiver. However, such visible watermarks are not robust: a malicious user can easily remove the watermark by covering the text, as visualized in Fig. 1b. After such an attack, the pirate can leak the video on the internet without being identifiable. More advanced visible watermarking techniques than overlaying text in the video exist, although even these can be destroyed relatively easily [8]. Thus, it is not recommended to use visible watermarks for traitor tracing purposes.

Although visible watermarking techniques are not useful for traitor tracing, they may be useful for other purposes [3, 9, 14]. For example, they can be used to prove ownership of intellectual property rights. More specifically, if an adversary wants to steal the video and claim ownership, he has to delete the visible logo, which inevitably leaves traces. As such, the original owner can prove that the adversary's video is derived from his video, thus proving ownership. Additionally, reversible visible watermarking techniques have been developed that enable authorized users to losslessly recover the original video [16]. As a second example, visible watermarks may be useful to discourage pirates to perform illegal re-distribution. However, it should not be the sole security measure since a pirate can easily remove the visible watermark.

For effective traitor tracing, invisible watermarking techniques should be used. In the literature, many invisible watermarking techniques have been proposed that enable the identification of digital pirates even when they attack the watermarked videos [1, 3, 4, 14]. Such methods make many small, imperceptible changes over the entire video that cannot easily be removed by pirates. Although the first invisible watermarking techniques have been proposed approximately 20 years ago [5], some pre-release screeners distributed in recent years still contained visible watermarks [12]. As a result, these videos were leaked before the official release date, with a removed watermark. In this way, they could not be identified, assuming no invisible watermarking technique was used in addition to the visible one [6, 11, 15]. Unfortunately, no state-of-the-art techniques enable traitor tracing for visible watermarking techniques when the visible watermark is removed.

As its contribution to the state-of-the-art, this paper investigates the detection possibilities of visible watermarks when they are deleted. More specifically, this paper demonstrates that embedding a visible watermark into a video has an effect on the non-watermarked area. That is, the visible watermark indirectly

(a) Watermark visible.

(b) Watermark removed.

Fig. 1. Example of simple watermark, visible as text in the video (a), which can easily be removed by covering the text with a black box (b).

results in imperceptible variations spread over the entire video. As such, these variations can be used as an alternative representation of the watermark. By detecting the alternative representation of the watermark, traitor tracing can still be performed when the visibly-watermarked area is removed.

The rest of this paper is organized as follows. First, Sect. 2 demonstrates how a visible watermark results in imperceptible variations over the entire video, and proposes to exploit it for watermark detection. Then, Sect. 3 investigates in which conditions the watermark can be detected. Lastly, the paper is concluded in Sect. 4.

2   Proposed Method

As its contribution to the state-of-the-art, this section demonstrates that a visible watermark can still be detected, even if the watermarked area was removed as in Fig. 1b. First, it proves how encoding a video with a visible watermark results in implicitly-created variations, spread over the entire video. Then, it proposes to extract the watermark using correlation-based detection techniques.

The most simple and straightforward way to embed a visible watermark in a video is by overlaying the text in an uncompressed video, and encoding the resulting video into a compressed format. As such, a watermarked video such as the one shown in Fig. 1a is created. In order to compress the video, a video encoder is used. A typical video encoder transforms the video into coding information and a residual signal. The coding information describes the structure of the video. That is, the video is divided into blocks and every block is predicted using spatially or temporally neighboring blocks. As such, intra- and inter-frame redundancies are effectively exploited. Since this prediction is usually not perfect, a residual signal is added that corrects the prediction errors. In order to provide stronger compression, this residual signal is quantized with a certain Quantization Parameter (QP). Because the compression process is lossy, many small compression artifacts are introduced. A low QP signifies a high quality level or high bitrate, and thus few compression artifacts. On the other hand, a high QP results in many compression artifacts.

This paper proposes to take advantage of the different compression artifacts that occur during the encoding process of a watermarked video, compared to those made when compressing the video without a watermark. Firstly and most notably, the region in which the text was added will be encoded differently and therefore contain different compression artifacts. However, these differences also propagate to other regions [10]. That is because the surrounding regions use information from the watermarked region for their prediction. Because the watermarked region is different, the predictions of the surrounding regions are also different. Then, similarly, those regions are used for the prediction of other regions. As such, the differences continue to propagate. Since the quantized residual of the impacted regions cannot fully correct the prediction errors, the watermarked video will contain different compression artifacts than when no watermark was added. Thus, these compression artifacts can be used as an alternative representation of the watermark.

As an example, Fig. 2 shows a visualization of the differences between the watermarked, compressed video of Fig. 1 and the corresponding unwatermarked, compressed video, for the first frame, the 100th frame, and the 200th frame. The QP used for compression is 22, i.e., the video has a high quality and thus relatively few compression artifacts. In the difference visualizations, blue means that there are no differences between the two frames, green signifies a small change in luma pixel value, and red means a pixel difference of 20 or higher. First, it can be observed that the textual watermark in the lower-right corner is visualized in red, thus meaning it is the most notable difference between the watermarked and unwatermarked video. However, one can also observe that the surrounding regions contain differences. For the first frame, in Fig. 2a, the surrounding region with differences is small and localized around the text. This is because the different compression artifacts did not have the time to propagate yet. When more frames are given for inter-frame prediction, the different distortions continue to propagate further. For example, for the 100th frame, in Fig. 2b, the differences propagated to approximately half the frame. Lastly, for the 200th frame, in Fig. 2c, the differences propagated over the entire frame.

The watermarked video does not only contain different compression artifacts compared to the unwatermarked video, but also compared to other watermarked videos. For example, Fig. 3 visualizes the differences between the 200th frame of a watermarked video with ID 260993 and ID 160993. Although the IDs only differ in their first digit, the compressed, watermarked videos contain many differences. Thus, in general, a unique visual watermark indirectly causes unique compression artifacts to be generated over the entire video.

In order to extract the watermark, existing correlation-based detection techniques can be used [3,10,17]. More specifically, the unique compression artifacts of a watermarked video are compared to the ones observed in the pirated video. A high correlation means that the watermark is present, whereas a low similarity means it is absent. Since the compression artifacts are spread over the entire video, the whole video is correlated pixel-by-pixel. Although several correlation measures exist and can be used, this paper utilizes the correlation coefficient (z_{cc}), which is an extension of the normalized correlation (z_{nc}). These measures are defined in Eq. (1), in which o and w are vectors of pixels, representing the observed and watermarked video, respectively. Additionally, $|o|$ and $|w|$ represent the Euclidean length of the vectors o and w, respectively, and $\bar{o}$ and $\bar{w}$ represent the mean pixel values of o and w, respectively.

$$z_{nc}(o, w) = \sum_i \frac{o[i]}{|o|} \cdot \frac{w[i]}{|w|},$$
$$z_{cc}(o, w) = z_{nc}(o - \bar{o}, w - \bar{w})$$

(1)

When comparing a pirated video to all watermarks, the correlation with one of the watermarked videos will be significantly higher than all others, i.e., it will be an outlier. For example, Fig. 4 shows the correlation values between a pirated (attacked) video and 100 visibly-watermarked videos of the sequence *BlowingBubbles* (with 1- and 2-digit IDs ranging from 0 to 99). The watermark in the pirated video is covered with a black box, as in Fig. 1b, and subsequently re-compressed. Although the visible watermark is covered, the correlation with watermark ID 50 is clearly higher than with all other watermarks. Thus, this means that watermark nr. 50 is detected as the present watermark, based on the unique compression artifacts that are present in the non-watermarked area.

(a) First frame.

(b) 100th frame.

(c) 200th frame.

Fig. 2. Visualizations of differences between the watermarked, compressed video of Fig. 1 and its corresponding unwatermarked, compressed video, for frame 1 (a), 100 (b), and 200 (c). Blue signifies no difference, green indicates a small change in luma pixel value, and red means a pixel difference of 20 or higher. (Color figure online)

Fig. 3. Visualization of differences between the 200th frame of the watermarked video with ID 260993 and the video with ID 160993. Although the IDs only differ in their first digit, the compressed, watermarked videos contain many differences.

It should be stressed that the black box in a pirated, attacked video completely covers the visible watermark. Thus, after re-compression, the black box will also cause different compression artifacts over the entire video. However, they are created on top of the unique compression artifacts caused by the visible watermark. As a result, they do not completely mask the unique artifacts generated by the watermark, hence enabling successful watermark detection.

In summary, this section demonstrated that the embedding of a visible watermark indirectly causes the creation of many small variations in the entire video, due to the lossy encoding process. As such, these unique compression artifacts are used to identify the visual watermark, even after watermark removal.

3   Evaluation

This section analyzes the robustness of the alternative representation of a visible watermark, described in Sect. 2. More specifically, it investigates which conditions should be met in order for the representation to be robust. Note that no comparison with related methods has been performed because, to the best of the authors' knowledge, no state-of-the-art methods exist that enable watermark detection after visible watermark removal.

In order to embed the visible watermarks, version 4.0.1 of the multimedia framework FFmpeg was used. First, a textual watermark was added to every frame of the video using the *drawtext*-filter. The font size equals to $\frac{1}{15}$ of the video height, and the color was set to white with a transparency of 50%. Two watermarked versions were created: one where the watermark is embedded in the lower-right corner of the frame, as in Fig. 5a, and one in the middle of the frame, as in Fig. 5c. Then, the videos were encoded using the *libx265*-encoder, which uses the High Efficiency Video Coding (HEVC) standard [13]. More specifically,

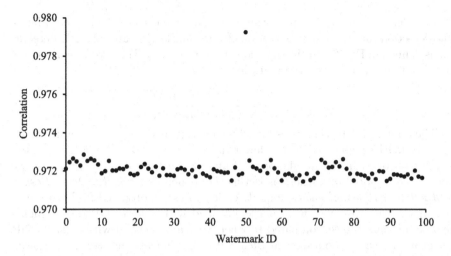

Fig. 4. The correlation values between a pirated video and 100 watermarked videos. The pirate received watermark video nr. 50, but attacked it by drawing a black box over the visible watermark, followed by a re-compression. Although the visible watermark is removed from the pirated video, the correlation with watermark ID 50 is clearly higher than with the others and is thus correctly detected.

every watermarked video was encoded with four different QPs: 22, 27, 32, and 37, further represented as QP_w. As mentioned in Sect. 2, a low QP signifies a high quality level, whereas a high QP signifies a low quality. Lastly, the length of a Group Of Pictures is set to the number of frames of the tested sequence. In other words, only the first frame is an intra-frame, whereas all other frames are inter-frames.

In order to attack the watermark, the region around the textual watermark was covered using FFmpeg's *drawbox*-filter, such as visualized in Fig. 1b. However, the proposed technique should also work if the visible watermark is removed in other ways than by covering it with a black box, such as by blurring or inpainting [7]. In this paper, a black box is used since it is considered one of the strongest attacks, as it removes a lot information and therefore leaves less traces of the watermark. In addition, the videos were re-encoded using the *libx265*-encoder with 6 QPs: 22, 27, 32, 37, 42, and 47, further represented as QP_a. Note that a QP value of 42 or 47 results in a very low quality, which pirates generally do not distribute.

In total, for every tested sequence and for both watermark locations, 100 watermarked videos were created using the 1- and 2-digit IDs ranging from 0 to 99, each encoded with the four different QP_w values. Then, each watermarked video was attacked with the six different QP_a values. As mentioned in Sect. 2, in order to extract the watermark, every attacked video is correlated to all 100 watermarked sequences, and the watermark corresponding to the highest correlation is the extracted watermark.

In order to evaluate the robustness, the Detection Rate (DR) is calculated. The detection rate signifies the fraction of watermarks that are correctly detected and is defined in Eq. (2). In the equation, TP represents a True Positive detection, meaning that the correct watermark is extracted.

$$DR = \frac{\#TP \text{ Detections}}{\text{Total Number of Detections}} \tag{2}$$

The observed detection rates for all tested sequences [2] are shown in Table 1 for watermarks embedded in the lower-right corner, and in Table 2 for watermarks embedded in the middle of the frame. From the tables, several observations can be made. First, when inspecting the sequences *BasketballDrive*, *BasketballDrill*, and *BlowingBubbles*, high detection rates are observed for both watermark locations. However, watermarks encoded with a lower QP (i.e., a higher quality) are less robust compared to when they are encoded with a higher QP. For example, when the sequence *BlowingBubbles* is watermarked in the lower-right corner and encoded with $QP_w = 22$, only 21% of the watermarks are correctly detected for an attack with $QP_a = 32$. On the other hand, when the same sequence is encoded with $QP_w = 37$, the detection rate is 100% for all $QP_a \leq 42$. Note again that (re-)encoding a video with a QP value of 42 results in a very low quality video that users generally do not enjoy to watch. Watermarked videos encoded with a lower QP are less robust because they are of higher quality and therefore contain less compression artifacts. Hence, the few unique compression artifacts are more easily deleted when the video is attacked.

A second observation that can be made is that the sequences *Traffic* and *Johnny* result in very low detection rates when the watermark is embedded in the lower-right corner. For example, when the sequence *Traffic* is watermarked in the lower-right corner and encoded with $QP_w = 32$, the detection rate is only 2% for an attack with $QP_a = 22$. This is because these sequences contain few motion, especially in the lower-right corner, which is the region in which the textual watermark is added. As a result, only few other regions are predicted based on the region in which the watermark was embedded. Thus, the different compression artifacts do not propagate over the entire video, but only within the small region in which the watermark was added.

For example, Fig. 5a visualizes the 100th frame of the sequence *Traffic*, watermarked with ID 26 and encoded with $QP_w = 32$. Moreover, Fig. 5b visualizes the corresponding implicitly-created differences with the unwatermarked video. The figures demonstrate that the variations only propagate in the lower-right corner, which contains relatively-static trees.

If the watermark is instead embedded into the middle of the frame, where there is more motion, higher detection rates are obtained. For example, when watermarking *Traffic* in the middle of the frame and encoding it with $QP_w = 32$, the detection rate is 100% for $QP_a = 22$. This is because the motion allows the implicitly-created variations to spread better. For example, Fig. 5c shows the same frame as in Fig. 5a, but watermarked in the middle of the frame instead of in the lower-right corner. Because the middle of the frame contains more motion

Table 1. Detection rates for all tested sequences, when watermarking in the *lower-right corner* of the frame. In general, the detection rates are higher when the watermarked video is encoded with a lower QP_w. Additionally, for *Traffic* and *Johnny*, low overall detection rates are obtained.

Sequence	Resolution	Frames	QP_w	Detection rate for QP_a (%)					
				$QP_a =$ 22	27	32	37	42	47
(A) Traffic	2560×1600	150	22	2	2	1	1	1	1
			27	4	2	2	1	1	1
			32	2	2	2	1	1	1
			37	3	3	3	2	1	1
(B) BasketballDrive	1920×1080	500	22	19	9	5	2	2	1
			27	100	94	20	7	4	2
			32	100	100	100	80	10	6
			37	100	100	100	100	100	48
(C) BasketballDrill	832×480	500	22	82	14	7	4	2	2
			27	100	100	72	10	5	3
			32	100	100	100	100	23	10
			37	100	100	100	100	100	100
(D) BlowingBubbles	416×240	500	22	100	99	21	5	2	1
			27	100	100	100	39	6	3
			32	100	100	100	100	56	6
			37	100	100	100	100	100	5
(E) Johnny	1280×720	600	22	3	2	2	1	1	1
			27	8	5	2	2	2	1
			32	13	10	9	4	2	2
			37	57	49	27	14	5	2

from the moving cars, the implicitly-created variations are propagated over a larger area.

Although embedding the watermark in the middle of the frame shows improvements in robustness for the sequences *Traffic* and *Johnny*, they are still not as robust as the other tested sequences. For example, when watermarking *Traffic* in the middle of the frame and encoding it with $QP_w = 27$, the detection rate is only 16% for $QP_a = 22$. These low detection rates can be explained by the general lack of motion in these sequences. The other tested sequences contain more motion either by camera movement or by larger objects moving over the entire frame. Therefore, the implicitly-created variations in those sequences propagate better and are hence more robust.

Table 2. Detection rates for all tested sequences, when watermarking in the *middle* of the frame. The detection rates for *Traffic* and *Johnny* are much higher than those of the same sequences in Table 1, although they are still low compared to the other tested sequences.

Sequence	Resolution	Frames	QP_w	Detection rate for QP_a (%)					
				$QP_a =$ 22	27	32	37	42	47
(A) Traffic	2560 × 1600	150	22	5	3	2	2	1	1
			27	16	11	5	2	2	1
			32	100	88	48	10	2	3
			37	100	100	100	100	15	5
(B) BasketballDrive	1920 × 1080	500	22	28	9	5	2	2	2
			27	100	100	31	9	4	2
			32	100	100	100	100	12	8
			37	100	100	100	100	100	76
(C) BasketballDrill	832 × 480	500	22	62	12	5	2	2	2
			27	100	100	44	10	4	2
			32	100	100	100	100	14	9
			37	100	100	100	100	100	84
(D) BlowingBubbles	416 × 240	500	22	100	78	10	5	1	1
			27	100	100	100	20	4	1
			32	100	100	100	100	23	5
			37	100	100	100	100	100	46
(E) Johnny	1280 × 720	600	22	5	2	2	2	2	1
			27	10	9	5	2	2	2
			32	54	33	16	8	3	2
			37	100	100	100	82	15	5

As a final observation, the watermark location has a negligible effect for the sequences *BasketballDrive*, *BasketballDrill*, and *BlowingBubbles*. For example, the sequence *BasketballDrill* has a detection rate of 100% when encoding it with $QP_w = 27$ for an attack with $QP_a \leq 27$, both when watermarking it in the lower-right corner and middle of the frame. The watermark location has a negligible effect in these sequences because they contain more motion in general, both in the lower-right corner and middle of the frame.

In conclusion, a visible watermark can be detected in a pirated, re-compressed video under two circumstances. First, the pirated video should not be of significantly lower quality than the distributed watermarked video, especially when the watermarked video is of high quality. Secondly, the watermark should be embedded in a video and region with sufficient motion, such that the implicitly-created variations are spread over the entire video.

(a) Watermark in lower-right corner.   (b) Differences with unwatermarked.

(c) Watermark in middle.   (d) Differences with unwatermarked.

Fig. 5. The 100th frame of the sequence *Traffic*, watermarked with ID 26 in the lower-right corner (a) and middle of the frame (c), in addition to the corresponding implicitly-created variations (b) (d). When the watermark is embedded in the lower-right corner, the variations do not propagate out of the static region with trees in which the watermark was added. In contrast, when the watermark is embedded in the middle of the frame, the implicitly-created variations propagate over a larger portion of the frame because the watermark is added in a region with more motion.

4   Conclusion

Although visible watermarking is rarely used for traitor tracing purposes, some cases exist in which it was. When these videos are illegally distributed with an apparently-deleted watermark, state-of-the-art techniques provide no solution to identify the culprits. Therefore, this paper assists the search for these traitors. More specifically, this paper demonstrated how a visible watermark indirectly causes imperceptible variations in the entire watermarked video. Hence, they are proposed to be used to detect the visible watermark, even if the visibly-watermarked area is removed.

The experimental results prove that the implicitly-created variations are robust as long as two conditions are met. First, the pirated video should not significantly reduce the quality of the video, especially when the watermarked video was originally distributed in a high quality. Secondly, the watermark should be embedded in an area that contains sufficient motion, such that the variations can propagate over the entire video. Thus, in practice, the detection should be performed on segments that contain a lot of motion.

References

1. Asikuzzaman, M., Pickering, M.R.: An overview of digital video watermarking. IEEE Trans. Circuits Syst. Video Technol. (2017). https://doi.org/10.1109/TCSVT.2017.2712162

2. Bossen, F.: Common test conditions and software reference configurations. Technical report, JCTVC-L1100, ITU-T Joint Collaborative Team on Video Coding (JCT-VC), January 2013

3. Cox, I., Miller, M., Bloom, J., Fridrich, J., Kalker, T.: Digital Watermarking and Steganography, 2nd edn. Morgan Kaufmann Publishers, San Francisco (2008)

4. Feng, B., Weng, J., Lu, W.: Improved algorithms for robust histogram shape-based image watermarking. In: Kraetzer, C., Shi, Y.Q., Dittmann, J., Kim, H.J. (eds.) IWDW 2017. LNCS, vol. 10431, pp. 275–289. Springer, Berlin (2017). https://doi.org/10.1007/978-3-319-64185-0_21

5. Hartung, F., Girod, B.: Watermarking of uncompressed and compressed video. Signal Process. 66(3), 283–301 (1998)

6. Hu, Y., Kwong, S., Huang, J.: Using invisible watermarks to protect visibly watermarked images. In: Proceedings of IEEE International Symposium Circuits Systems (ISCAS). vol. 5, pp. V-584–V-587, May 2004

7. Huang, C.H., Wu, J.L.: Inpainting attacks against visible watermarking schemes. In: Proceedings of SPIE, vol. 4314 (2001). https://doi.org/10.1117/12.435421

8. Huang, C.H., Wu, J.L.: Attacking visible watermarking schemes. In: Proceedings of IEEE International Conference on Multimedia Computing Systems (ICMCS), vol. 6, no. 1, pp. 16–30, Feburary 2004. https://doi.org/10.1109/TMM.2003.819579

9. Kankanhalli, M.S., Ramakrishnan, K.R.: Adaptive visible watermarking of images. In: Proceedings of IEEE International Conference on Multimedia Computing Systems (ICMCS), vol. 1, pp. 568–573, July 1999. https://doi.org/10.1109/MMCS.1999.779263

10. Mareen, H., De Praeter, J., Van Wallendael, G., Lambert, P.: A novel video watermarking approach based on implicit distortions. IEEE Trans. Consum. Electron. 64(3), 250–258 (2018). https://doi.org/10.1109/TCE.2018.2852258

11. Mohanty, S.P., Ramakrishnan, K.R., Kankanhalli, M.: A dual watermarking technique for images. In: Proceedings of ACM International Conference on Multimedia, pp. 49–51. ACM, New York (1999). https://doi.org/10.1145/319878.319891

12. Siddique, H.: Game of thrones fifth season episodes leaked online. The Guardian, 12 April 2015. https://www.theguardian.com/tv-and-radio/2015/apr/12/game-of-thrones-fifth-season-episodes-leaked-online

13. Sullivan, G.J., Ohm, J.R., Han, W.J., Wiegand, T.: Overview of the high efficiency video coding (HEVC) standard. IEEE Trans. Circuits Syst. Video Technol. 22(12), 1649–1668 (2012). https://doi.org/10.1109/TCSVT.2012.2221191

14. Tew, Y., Wong, K.: An overview of information hiding in H.264/AVC compressed video. IEEE Trans. Circuits Syst. Video Technol. 24(2), 305–319 (2014). https://doi.org/10.1109/TCSVT.2013.2276710

15. Wong, P.W.: A watermark for image integrity and ownership verification. In: Proceedings of IS&TS PICS, pp. 374–379. Society for Imaging Science & Tehnology (1998)

16. Yang, G., Qi, W., Li, X., Guo, Z.: Improved reversible visible watermarking based on adaptive block partition. In: Kraetzer, C., Shi, Y.Q., Dittmann, J., Kim, H.J. (eds.) IWDW 2017. LNCS, vol. 10431, pp. 303–317. Springer, Berlin (2017). https://doi.org/10.1007/978-3-319-64185-0_23

17. Zhang, X., Wang, Z.J.: Correlation-and-bit-aware multiplicative spread spectrum embedding for data hiding. In: Proceedings of IEEE International Workshop Information Forensics Security (WIFS), pp. 186–190, November 2013. https://doi.org/10.1109/WIFS.2013.6707816

Improved High Capacity Spread Spectrum-Based Audio Watermarking by Hadamard Matrices

Yiming Xue[1]([✉]), Kai Mu[1], Yan Li[2], Juan Wen[1], Ping Zhong[2], and Shaozhang Niu[3]

[1] College of Information and Electrical Engineering, China Agricultural University, Beijing 100083, China
xueym@cau.edu.cn
[2] College of Science, China Agricultural University, Beijing 100083, China
[3] School of Computer Science, Beijing University of Posts and Telecommunication, Beijing 100876, China

Abstract. Traditional spread spectrum-based audio watermarking methods usually use randomly generated pseudonoise sequences for watermark embedding and extraction. In this paper, we use Hadamard sequences, which are rows of Hadamard matrices, to embed and extract watermarks instead of pseudonoise sequences. By exploiting the orthogonality of Hadamard sequences and a technique of sign change, we propose a new spread spectrum-based audio watermarking method. Experimental results show that, compared to the newly high embedding capacity spread spectrum-based audio watermarking method, our method achieves a better perceptual quality and a higher embedding capacity while maintaining almost equal strong robustness. We also provide a theoretical analysis of the security of our method.

Keywords: Spread spectrum · Audio watermarking · Hadamard sequences · Imperceptibility

1 Introduction

Digital audio watermarking is an important research branch of information hiding, which can be used for copyright protection, authentication, and etc. The four most important factors for the evaluation of digital audio watermarking methods are imperceptibility, robustness, security, and capacity. Imperceptibility means that the watermarked signal should be indistinguishable with the host signal perceptually. Robustness represents the ability to recover the watermark information from the watermarked signal in situations with and without attacks. Security requires that the watermarks can only be extracted by the authorized parties. Capacity refers to the amount of information that can be embedded into the given host data.

© Springer Nature Switzerland AG 2019
C. D. Yoo et al. (Eds.): IWDW 2018, LNCS 11378, pp. 124–136, 2019.
https://doi.org/10.1007/978-3-030-11389-6_10

After two decades of the development, digital audio watermarking has been a fruitful research area [1]. A lot of audio watermarking methods have been proposed, such as spread spectrum (SS) [2–7], echo-hiding [8,9], patchwork [10,11] and etc. Among these methods, spread spectrum has several important advantages including strong robustness, high security, etc. However, due to the host signal interference, the PN sequences used in traditional spread spectrum methods are usually sufficient long, which will result in low embedding capacity.

Xiang et al. [4] proposed a spread spectrum-based watermarking method for audio signals, which has high embedding capacity. Their method embeds watermarks into DCT coefficients of the host audio signal within a certain frequency range by the multiplicative spread spectrum method. To increase the embedding capacity, they represent multiple watermark bits one to one by a series of near-orthogonal pseudonoise (PN) sequences which are formed by circularly shifting a random seed PN sequence. In the embedding process, the PN sequence representing multiple watermark bits is inserted into one segment of selected DCT coefficients. Furthermore, to reduce the host signal interference, they divide adjacent DCT coefficients of one audio segment into a pair of fragments with equal length. And then they add a proportion of the corresponding PN sequence into the first fragment, while subtract the same amount from the second one in a multiplicative manner. Compared with three newly SS-based watermarking methods [3,6,7], their method can obtain larger embedding rates, meanwhile ensuring high imperceptibility and strong robustness.

Note that the method in [4] heavily relies on the near-orthogonal property of the PN sequences. However, in practice, it is hard to ensure that a randomly generated seed PN sequence has sufficiently small cross-relations with a large number of its cyclic shifts, since the length of PN sequences is limited. Therefore, it is possible to use orthogonal sequences instead of cyclic shifted PN sequences to improve the performance of [4].

In fact, the idea of using orthogonal sequences to embed several watermark patterns that encoded M-ary symbols is already used in digital watermarking [5,12,13]. This method is routinely referred to as "CDMA watermarking". The common used "orthogonal" sequences include Gold sequences, Kasami sequences, Hadamard sequences, etc. More simply, one could rely on Gram-Schmidt procedure to orthogonalize a collection of spreading sequences. Among these sequences, Hadamard sequences have the advantages of being exactly orthogonal to each other, while Gold sequences and Kasami sequences are in fact near-orthogonal (have relatively small cross-relations), and being simple to implement, whose elements are either +1 or −1.

In this paper, we make two improvements of the method in [4]. Firstly, we replace cyclic shifted PN sequences by Hadamard sequences, which are randomly chosen from the rows of a Hadamard matrix. Different from cyclic shifted PN sequences, Hadamard sequences are strictly orthogonal to each other. Therefore, the usage of Hadamard sequences will improve the method of [4] in principle. Secondly, by interchanging the sign of Hadamard sequences during the watermark embedding process, we can further improve the embedding capacity. In details, if the lowest bit (LB) of multiple watermark bits is 0, similar to [4], we embed the other higher watermark bits into one audio segment by adding a proportion of the corresponding Hadamard sequence into the first fragment and simultaneously subtracting the same amount from the second fragment in a multiplicative manner. Otherwise, if the LB of multiple watermark bits is 1, to embed the other higher watermark bits, we subtract a proportion of the corresponding Hadamard sequence from the first fragment and add the same amount into the second fragment multiplicatively. Compared to [4], our method can embed one more bit per segment. In practice, this usually increases the embedding capacity at least by 10 percents. Experimental results show that under the same conditions, the watermarked signals by our method have a much better perceptual quality statistically than those by the method in [4]. Meanwhile, the average detection rates of two methods under conventional attacks are almost the same. Therefore, compared to [4], our method achieves a better perceptual quality and a higher embedding capacity while maintaining almost the same robustness.

Different from PN sequences, which are randomly generated and hence have good security performance, hadamard sequences are sophiscatedly designed. The direct use of hadamard sequences will cause potential security problem. In the paper, we solve this problem by adding a private key only known to both sides of communication. The private key is actually a random permutation of columns of a public Hadamard matrix. We provide a detailed theoretical analysis in subsection III. D to illustrate the of the good security performance of the proposed method.

The rest of the paper is organized as follows. The preliminaries of Hadamard matrices are reviewed in Sect. 2. The proposed SS-based audio watermarking method is presented in Sect. 3 and the experimental results are shown in Sect. 4. Section 5 concludes the paper.

2   Preliminaries of Hadamard Matrices

In mathematics, a Hadamard matrix, named after the French mathematician Jacques Hadamard, is a square matrix H whose entries are either $+1$ or -1 and whose rows are mutually orthogonal, i.e.,

$$HH^T = nI$$

where n is the order of H, I is the identity matrix and H^T is the transpose of H. In combinatorial terms, it means that each pair of rows in a Hadamard matrix has matching entries in exactly half of their columns and mismatched entries in the remaining columns. Hadamard matrices are widely used in many areas, such as error-correcting codes (Hadamard code), statistics (balanced repeated replication), compressed sensing and etc.

The order of a Hadamard matrix must be 1, 2, or a multiple of 4. Examples of Hadamard matrices were actually first constructed by James Joseph Sylvester in 1867. Let H be a Hadamard matrix of order n. Then the partitioned matrix

$$\begin{bmatrix} H & H \\ H & -H \end{bmatrix}$$

is a Hadamard matrix of order $2n$. This observation can be applied repeatedly and leads to large Hadamard matrices of order $2^k n$ from small Hadamard matrix H of order n. For more constructions of Hadamard matrices, see [14] and [15].

The Hadamard conjecture proposes that a Hadamard matrix of order $4k$ exists for every positive integer k. From [14], for $k \leq 500$, there are only 13 numbers k such that no Hadamard matrix of order $4k$ is known. These $4k$ are: 668, 716, 892, 1004, 1132, 1244, 1388, 1436, 1676, 1772, 1916, 1948, and 1964. In practice, those known Hadamard matrices are enough to use for our purpose.

3   Proposed Method

In this section, the watermark embedding and extraction processes of our method will be illustrated at length. Then, the selection of the key watermarking parameter β, which balances the imperceptibility and the robustness of watermarked audio signals, will be explained and shown by diagram. At the end of the section, the security of the proposed watermarking algorithm will be discussed, and then summarized.

3.1   Watermark Embedding Process

The watermark embedding process is composed of three parts: correspondence between multiple watermark bits and Hadamard sequences, DCT operation and segmentation, and embedding of watermark bits.

Correspondence Between Multiple Watermark Bits and Hadamard Sequences. Assume that the number of watermark bits to be embedded into one audio segment is $n_b + 1$. In our method, we embed higher n_b watermark bits by inserting the corresponding Hadamard sequence into the audio segment. Meanwhile, the lowest watermark bit (LB) is embedded by interchanging the sign of the Hadamard sequence, during the inserting process.

Viewing higher n_b watermark bits as a binary number, its numerical value m gives an integer between 0 and $2^{n_b} - 1$. For example, if $n_b = 2$, the binary numbers of 2 watermark bits 00, 01, 10 and 11 are $0 \times 2 + 0$, $0 \times 2 + 1$, $1 \times 2 + 0$ and $1 \times 2 + 1$, respectively.

Let $N > 2^{n_b}$ be an integer divisible by 4. Choose a public $N \times N$ Hadamard matrix H_0. Let SK_1 be a random permutation of $\{1, 2, ..., N\}$, which acts as a private key only known to both sides of communication. Using SK_1 to permute the columns of H_0, we still get a Hadamard matrix H. Randomly pick up 2^{n_b} distinct rows from H by the seed SK_2 and index them as $\mathbf{h}_0, \mathbf{h}_1, \cdots, \mathbf{h}_{N_h-1}$, where $N_h = 2^{n_b}$. We call $\mathbf{h}_0, \mathbf{h}_1, \cdots, \mathbf{h}_{N_h-1}$ Hadamard sequences. From the properties of Hadamard matrices, the elements of $\mathbf{h}_0, \mathbf{h}_1, \cdots, \mathbf{h}_{N_h-1}$ are ± 1 and $\mathbf{h}_i$ is orthogonal to $\mathbf{h}_j$ if $i \neq j$. We use $\mathbf{h}_m$ to represent higher n_b watermark bits whose corresponding binary number equals to m. Clearly this correspondence is one-to-one.

Hadamard sequences are orthogonal to each other, while the cyclic shifted PN sequences used in [4] are near-orthogonal. The orthogonal property of the sequences is vital to watermark extraction. This explains the reason we use Hadamard sequences.

DCT Operation and Segmentation. Let $x(n)$ be the host audio signal consisting of K samples. Apply DCT to the whole signal $x(n)$ and denote its DCT coefficients by $X(k)$, where $k = 0, 1, \cdots, K$. Since very low and high frequency components are sensitive to attacks, similar to [4], we only select DCT coefficients $X(k)$ corresponding to a certain frequency range $[f_l, f_h]$ for watermark embedding, where f_l and f_h are determined experimentally.

Split the selected DCT coefficients into N_s segments of length $2N$, and denote the ith segment as

$$X_i(k) = [X_i(0), X_i(1), \cdots, X_i(2N - 1)] \tag{1}$$

where $i = 1, 2, \cdots, N_s$. Then, split each $X_i(k)$ into a pair of fragments $\mathbf{x}_{i,1}$ and $\mathbf{x}_{i,2}$ with length N, according to the parity of k:

$$\begin{cases} \mathbf{x}_{i,1} = [X_i(0), X_i(2), \cdots, X_i(2N - 2)] \\ \mathbf{x}_{i,2} = [X_i(1), X_i(3), \cdots, X_i(2N - 1)]. \end{cases} \tag{2}$$

We call $\mathbf{x}_{i,1}$ and $\mathbf{x}_{i,2}$, the first fragment of $X_i(k)$ and the second fragment of $X_i(k)$, respectively.

Embedding of Watermark Bits. Given $n_b + 1$ watermark bits, let LB be its lowest bit and m be the binary number of the other higher n_b bits. Clearly, $0 \le m \le 2^{n_b} - 1$. To embed the $n_b + 1$ watermark bits into the ith segment $X_i(k)$, pick up $\mathbf{h}_m$, the Hadamard sequence corresponding to the higher n_b bits first. Then perform the following operation:

$$\begin{cases} \widetilde{\mathbf{x}}_{i,1} = (\mathbf{1} + \beta \mathbf{h}_m) \circ \mathbf{x}_{i,1} \\ \widetilde{\mathbf{x}}_{i,2} = (\mathbf{1} - \beta \mathbf{h}_m) \circ \mathbf{x}_{i,2} \end{cases} \tag{3}$$

if $LB = 0$ and

$$\begin{cases} \widetilde{\mathbf{x}}_{i,1} = (\mathbf{1} - \beta \mathbf{h}_m) \circ \mathbf{x}_{i,1} \\ \widetilde{\mathbf{x}}_{i,2} = (\mathbf{1} + \beta \mathbf{h}_m) \circ \mathbf{x}_{i,2} \end{cases} \tag{4}$$

otherwise, where $\mathbf{1}$ is a length-N row vector whose elements are all one, $\beta \in (0, 1)$ is a small parameter and "$\circ$" stands for the Hadamard product (i.e., the element-wise product).

Then arrange watermarked fragments $\widetilde{\mathbf{x}}_{i,1}$ and $\widetilde{\mathbf{x}}_{i,2}$ into one segment $\widetilde{X}_i(k)$ by the same order. Explicitly,

$$\widetilde{X}_i(k) = [\widetilde{X}_i(0), \widetilde{X}_i(1), \cdots, \widetilde{X}_i(2N - 1)] \tag{5}$$

where

$$\begin{cases} \widetilde{\mathbf{x}}_{i,1} = [\widetilde{X}_i(0), \widetilde{X}_i(2), \cdots, \widetilde{X}_i(2N-2)] \\ \widetilde{\mathbf{x}}_{i,2} = [\widetilde{X}_i(1), \widetilde{X}_i(3), \cdots, \widetilde{X}_i(2N-1)]. \end{cases} \tag{6}$$

After obtaining all watermarked segments $\widetilde{X}_i(k)$, $i = 1, 2, \cdots, N_s$, the watermarked signal $\widetilde{x}(n)$ is constructed by inverse discrete cosine transform (IDCT).

The parameter β in (3) and (4), which balances the perceptual quality and the robustness of watermarked signal $\widetilde{x}(n)$, is vital to our method. Its selection will be discussed detailedly in Sect. 3.3.

3.2   Watermark Extraction Process

Let $y(n)$ be the post-attack counterpart of the watermarked audio signal $\widetilde{x}(n)$. Clearly, $y(n) = \widetilde{x}(n)$ without attacks. In this subsection, we will describe the watermark extraction process from the received signal $y(n)$ by the known Hadamard sequences $\mathbf{h}_0, \mathbf{h}_1, \cdots, \mathbf{h}_{N_h-1}$, which are obtained from the public Hadamard matrix H_0 using private keys SK_1 and SK_2. Then we discuss the validity of the proposed method.

Extraction of Watermark Bits from $y(n)$. The DCT coefficients $Y(k)$ are computed by applying DCT to the received audio signal $y(n)$. Select the DCT coefficients corresponding to the frequency region $[f_l, f_h]$ and split them into length-$2N$ segments $Y_i(k)$, $i = 1, 2, \cdots, N_s$. Afterwards, these segments are further partitioned into pairs of length-N fragments $\mathbf{y}_{i,1}$ and $\mathbf{y}_{i,2}$, $i = 1, 2, \cdots, N_s$. Clearly, under no attack, $\mathbf{y}_{i,1} = \widetilde{\mathbf{x}}_{i,1}$ and $\mathbf{y}_{i,2} = \widetilde{\mathbf{x}}_{i,2}$.

Define

$$\mathbf{y}_{i,d} = |\mathbf{y}_{i,1}| - |\mathbf{y}_{i,2}| \tag{7}$$

where $|\cdot|$ stands for the element-wise absolute value. Since the elements of $(1 + \beta\mathbf{h}_m)$ and $(1 - \beta\mathbf{h}_m)$ are positive, by (3) and (4),

$$\mathbf{y}_{i,d} = (|\mathbf{x}_{i,1}| - |\mathbf{x}_{i,2}|) \pm \beta\mathbf{h}_m \circ (|\mathbf{x}_{i,1}| + |\mathbf{x}_{i,2}|) \tag{8}$$

where "$\pm$" is "$+$" if $LB = 0$ and "$-$" otherwise.

The decision process of $n_b + 1$ watermark bits is divided into two steps. Firstly, find

$$\widehat{m} = \underset{j \in \{0,1,\cdots,N_h-1\}}{\mathrm{argmax}} |\mathbf{y}_{i,d}\mathbf{h}_j^T| \tag{9}$$

where $\mathrm{argmax}(\cdot)$ returns the j value such that the absolute value of $\mathbf{y}_{i,d}\mathbf{h}_j^T$ yields maximum. The binary expansion of $\widehat{m}$ leads to the extracted higher n_b watermark bits. Secondly, the lowest bit LB is determined by the sign of $\mathbf{y}_{i,d}\mathbf{h}_{\widehat{m}}^T$. Explicitly,

$$\widehat{LB} = \begin{cases} 0 & \text{if } \mathbf{y}_{i,d}\mathbf{h}_{\widehat{m}}^T > 0 \\ 1 & \text{otherwise.} \end{cases} \tag{10}$$

Discussion about the validity of (9) **and** (10). From (8), it holds that

$$\mathbf{y}_{i,d}\mathbf{h}_j^T = (|\mathbf{x}_{i,1}| - |\mathbf{x}_{i,2}|)\mathbf{h}_j^T \pm \beta(|\mathbf{x}_{i,1}| + |\mathbf{x}_{i,2}|)(\mathbf{h}_m \circ \mathbf{h}_j)^T \qquad (11)$$

where "$\pm$" is "$+$" if $LB = 0$ and "$-$" otherwise.

The first term on the right-hand side acts as the host audio signal interference which has negative impact on watermark extraction. Since the Hadamard sequences are independent of the host signal, $(|\mathbf{x}_{i,1}| - |\mathbf{x}_{i,2}|)\mathbf{h}_j^T$ are statistically comparable for different j.

For the second term, if $j = m$, $\mathbf{h}_m \circ \mathbf{h}_j = \mathbf{1}$ is an all-one vector. Otherwise, $\mathbf{h}_m \circ \mathbf{h}_j$ has exactly half entries being $+1$ and nearly half entries being -1. Therefore, $(|\mathbf{x}_{i,1}| + |\mathbf{x}_{i,2}|)(\mathbf{h}_m \circ \mathbf{h}_j)^T$ reaches the peak when $j = m$.

As a result, for $LB = 0$, when β increases, $\mathbf{y}_{i,d}\mathbf{h}_m^T$ increases much more rapidly than $\mathbf{y}_{i,d}\mathbf{h}_{\bar{j}}^T$, where $\bar{j} = 0, 1, \cdots, m - 1, m + 1, \cdots, N_h - 1$. Similarly, for $LB = 1$, when β increases, $\mathbf{y}_{i,d}\mathbf{h}_m^T$ decreases much more rapidly than $\mathbf{y}_{i,d}\mathbf{h}_{\bar{j}}^T$, where $\bar{j} = 0, 1, \cdots, m - 1, m + 1, \cdots, N_h - 1$. Therefore, for suitable small β, the absolute value of $\mathbf{y}_{i,d}\mathbf{h}_m^T$ is likely to be larger than the absolute value of $\mathbf{y}_{i,d}\mathbf{h}_{\bar{j}}^T$ for $\bar{j} \neq m$ and the sign of $\mathbf{y}_{i,d}\mathbf{h}_m^T$ probably agrees with the sign of the second term $\pm\beta(|\mathbf{x}_{i,1}| + |\mathbf{x}_{i,2}|)\mathbf{1}$ in (11). This verifies (9) and (10) theoretically.

3.3   Selection of the Parameter β

The parameter β in (3) and (4) balances the imperceptibility and the robustness of watermarked audio signals. Large β will enhance the robustness but weaken the perceptual quality, and vice versa. So it is important to select a suitable β.

For the watermarks to be detectable, $\mathbf{y}_{i,d}\mathbf{h}_m^T$ should be positive (negative, respectively) if $LB = 0$ ($LB = 1$, respectively), and $|\mathbf{y}_{i,d}\mathbf{h}_m^T|$ should at least be greater than all $|\mathbf{y}_{i,d}\mathbf{h}_{\bar{j}}^T|$ with $\bar{j} \neq m$. From (11), β must satisfy

$$(|\mathbf{x}_{i,1}| - |\mathbf{x}_{i,2}|)\mathbf{h}_m^T + \beta(|\mathbf{x}_{i,1}| + |\mathbf{x}_{i,2}|)\mathbf{1}^T > 0,$$

$$(|\mathbf{x}_{i,1}| - |\mathbf{x}_{i,2}|)\mathbf{h}_m^T + \beta(|\mathbf{x}_{i,1}| + |\mathbf{x}_{i,2}|)\mathbf{1}^T > \qquad (12)$$

$$\pm\left((|\mathbf{x}_{i,1}| - |\mathbf{x}_{i,2}|)\mathbf{h}_{\bar{j}}^T + \beta(|\mathbf{x}_{i,1}| + |\mathbf{x}_{i,2}|)(\mathbf{h}_m \circ \mathbf{h}_{\bar{j}})^T\right)$$

if $LB = 0$ and

$$(|\mathbf{x}_{i,1}| - |\mathbf{x}_{i,2}|)\mathbf{h}_m^T - \beta(|\mathbf{x}_{i,1}| + |\mathbf{x}_{i,2}|)\mathbf{1}^T < 0,$$

$$-(|\mathbf{x}_{i,1}| - |\mathbf{x}_{i,2}|)\mathbf{h}_m^T + \beta(|\mathbf{x}_{i,1}| + |\mathbf{x}_{i,2}|)\mathbf{1}^T > \qquad (13)$$

$$\pm\left((|\mathbf{x}_{i,1}| - |\mathbf{x}_{i,2}|)\mathbf{h}_{\bar{j}}^T - \beta(|\mathbf{x}_{i,1}| + |\mathbf{x}_{i,2}|)(\mathbf{h}_m \circ \mathbf{h}_{\bar{j}})^T\right)$$

if $LB = 1$. In practice, the watermarking method should be robust to conventional attacks. Therefore, we require that β satisfy

$$\begin{cases} \mathbf{y}_{i,d}\mathbf{h}_m^T > 0 \text{ if } LB = 0, \\ \mathbf{y}_{i,d}\mathbf{h}_m^T < 0 \text{ otherwise.} \end{cases} \qquad (14)$$

Table 1. An algorithm for selecting β

Step 1: Set initial β to $\beta = \beta_{min}$ and construct $\overline{\mathbf{h}}^T$ by (16).

Step 2: If $LB = 0$, compute
$$\mathbf{d} = (|\mathbf{x}_{i,1}| - |\mathbf{x}_{i,2}|) + \beta\mathbf{h}_m \circ (|\mathbf{x}_{i,1}| + |\mathbf{x}_{i,2}|).$$
Otherwise, compute
$$\mathbf{d} = (|\mathbf{x}_{i,1}| - |\mathbf{x}_{i,2}|) - \beta\mathbf{h}_m \circ (|\mathbf{x}_{i,1}| + |\mathbf{x}_{i,2}|).$$

Step 3: Compute
$$u_1 = \mathbf{dh}_m^T$$
$$u_2 = \max|\mathbf{d}\overline{\mathbf{h}}^T|.$$

Step 4: If $LB = 0$ and $u_1 > 0$, go to Step 5.
Else if $LB = 1$ and $u_1 < 0$, set $u_1 = -u_1$, go to Step 5.
Otherwise, go to Step 7.

Step 5: If $\gamma_1 u_1 > \gamma_2$, set $v = \gamma_1 u_1$.
Otherwise, set $v = \gamma_2$.

Step 6: If $u_1 \leq u_2 + v$, go to Step 7.
Otherwise, end.

Step 7: Increase β to $\beta + \Delta\beta$. If $\beta \leq \beta_{max} - \Delta\beta$, go to Step 2.
Otherwise, end.

---

and
$$\begin{cases} |\mathbf{y}_{i,d}\mathbf{h}_m^T| > \max(|\mathbf{y}_{i,d}\overline{\mathbf{h}}^T|) + \gamma_1|\mathbf{y}_{i,d}\mathbf{h}_m^T| \\ |\mathbf{y}_{i,d}\mathbf{h}_m^T| > \max(|\mathbf{y}_{i,d}\overline{\mathbf{h}}^T|) + \gamma_2 \end{cases} \tag{15}$$

where
$$\overline{\mathbf{h}}^T = [\mathbf{h}_0^T, \cdots, \mathbf{h}_{m-1}^T, \mathbf{h}_{m+1}^T, \cdots, \mathbf{h}_{N_h-1}^T], \tag{16}$$

$|\cdot|$ stands for the element-wise absolute value, and γ_1, γ_2 are constants such that $0 < \gamma_1 < 1$ and $\gamma_2 > \gamma_1$. To maintain high imperceptibility, we choose the smallest β within the range $[\beta_{min}, \beta_{max}]$ satisfying (14) and (15).

The actual β is selected by an incremental search with the step size $\Delta\beta$ such that $0 < \Delta\beta \ll \beta_{max}$. We list the algorithm for selecting β in Table 1. The parameters $\gamma_1, \gamma_2, \beta_{min}, \beta_{max}$ and $\Delta\beta$ are determined experimentally.

3.4   Discussion of the Security

By the Kerckhoff's principle in cryptography, the security of the watermarking algorithm should depend on the key. In the following, we will show the security of our method by proving that the space of private keys SK_1 is very large and the probability that two different keys SK_1 and SK_1' have a collision is extremely low.

For the first point, since SK_1 is a random permutation of $\{1, 2, ..., N\}$, the total numbers of SK_1 is equal to $N!$. In practice, $N!$ is always a very large number. For example, in our experimental setting, $N = 768$, which implies $N! > 10^{768}$.

For the second point, we say that two different keys SK_1 and SK'_1 have a collision if and only if the Hadamard matrices H and H', obtained by permuting columns of H_0 according to keys SK_1 and SK'_1 respectively, have at least two common rows. The motivation of this concept comes from the fact that if H and H' have two many common rows, then an attacker, who knows Hadamard matrix H' by randomly guessing a key SK'_1, can perform correlation with all rows of H' to find the possible Hadamard sequences that are used, and therefore erase the embedded watermarks. The following lemma proves that the probability that a key SK'_1 has a collision with the key SK_1 is extremely low.

For simplicity of the proof, we assume that the public Hadamard matrix H_0 has an all-one row vector $\mathbf{1}_N$. In practice, this can always be achieved through multiplying some columns of H_0 by -1. Also, for security, we need to exclude the row $\mathbf{1}_N$ out of watermark embedding sequences in this case.

Lemma 1: Let H_0 be an $N \times N$ Hadamard matrix with $\mathbf{1}_N$ as its row vector. Let SK_1 be a fixed permutation of $\{1, 2, ..., N\}$. The random permutation SK'_1 has a collision with SK_1 with probability less than $N^3/2^N$.

Proof: Let H and H' be the Hadamard matrices obtained by permuting columns of H_0 according to keys SK_1 and SK'_1, respectively. Assume SK'_1 has a collision with SK_1.

Firstly, we will prove that the number of such permutations SK'_1s is no bigger than $(N-1)^2((N/2)!)^2$. By the definition of collision, H and H' have another common row vector $\mathbf{h}_c$ besides $\mathbf{1}_N$. Let $\mathbf{h}_b$ be a row vector of H_0 such that after column permutation of H_0 by SK'_1, $\mathbf{h}_b$ becomes to $\mathbf{h}_c$. Since $\mathbf{h}_b$ is orthogonal to $\mathbf{1}_N$, $\mathbf{h}_b$ has $N/2$ elements being $+1$ and $N/2$ elements being -1. The permutation SK'_1 should map the elements $+1$ (-1, respectively) of $\mathbf{h}_b$ to the elements $+1$ (-1, respectively) of $\mathbf{h}_c$. Therefore, for fixed $\mathbf{h}_b$ and $\mathbf{h}_c$, there are $((N/2)!)^2$ choices of such permutations SK'_1. Since $\mathbf{h}_b$ ($\mathbf{h}_c$, respectively) is a row of H_0 (H, respectively) distinct from $\mathbf{1}_N$, the total choices of $\mathbf{h}_b$ and $\mathbf{h}_c$ have $(N-1)^2$ possibilities. Therefore, the number of SK'_1 having a collision with SK_1 is $\leq (N-1)^2((N/2)!)^2$.

Secondly, since the total number of permutations of $\{1, 2, ..., N\}$ is equal to $N!$, the probability of random permutation SK'_1 having a collision with SK_1 is no bigger than $(N-1)^2((N/2)!)^2/N!$. Finally, the desired result follows from the rough estimation

$$N!/((N/2)!)^2 \geq 2^N/(N+1)$$

which can be easily shown by the binomial theorem.

The probability $N^3/2^N$ is a extremely small number for large N. For example, in our experimental setting, $N = 768$ which implies $N^3/2^N = 27/2^{734} < 1/2^{729}$.

Summing up, the proposed method via the design of private key SK_1 has a good performance of security. It is impossible for an attacker to find the possible used Hadamard sequences by randomly guessing a key SK'_1 and performing correlation with all rows of H'. So it is hard for an attacker to erase the embedded watermarks.

3.5 Summary of the Proposed Method

At the end, the proposed watermarking algorithm is summarized as follows:

Watermarking embedding

1. Choose a Hadamard matrix H_0 known to the public. Permute the columns of H_0 to get the Hadamard matrix H according to the private key SK_1. Randomly pick up N_h distinct rows from H by the seed SK_2 and index them as $\mathbf{h}_0, \mathbf{h}_1, \cdots, \mathbf{h}_{N_h-1}$.
2. Apply DCT to $x(n)$, select those DCT coefficients corresponding to the frequency range $[f_l, f_h]$, and segment them to obtain $X_i(k)$, $i = 1, 2, ..., N_s$.
3. Separate the ith DCT segment $X_i(k)$ into the fragments $\mathbf{x}_{i,1}$ and $\mathbf{x}_{i,2}$ by (1) and (2), respectively.
4. Use the algorithm shown in Table 1 to select β.
5. Insert the Hadamard sequence $\mathbf{h}_m$ into $\mathbf{x}_{i,1}$ and $\mathbf{x}_{i,2}$ by (3) or (4).
6. Construct the watermarked DCT segment $\widetilde{X}_i(k)$ by (5) and (6).
7. After obtaining all $\widetilde{X}_i(k)$, $i = 1, 2, ..., N_s$, construct the watermarked signal $\widetilde{x}(n)$ by applying IDCT.

Watermark extraction

1. From the public Hadamard matrix H_0 and the private key SK_1 to obtain the Hadamard matrix H. And then construct the Hadamard sequences $\mathbf{h}_0, \mathbf{h}_1, \cdots, \mathbf{h}_{N_h-1}$ from H by the seed SK_2.
2. Similar to Steps 2 and 3 in the watermark embedding part, construct $\mathbf{y}_{i,1}$ and $\mathbf{y}_{i,2}$ from the received audio signal $y(n)$, where $i = 1, 2, ..., N_s$.
3. Compute $\mathbf{y}_{i,d}$ by (7) and then find the index $\hat{m}$ and $\widehat{LB}$ by (9) and (10), respectively. Compute the binary expansion of $\hat{m}$, which is the higher n_b watermark bits. Put $\widehat{LB}$ behind the higher n_b watermark bits. Thus the $n_b + 1$ watermark bits are extracted
4. List all extracted $n_b + 1$ watermark bits successively. Then the whole embedded watermark is recovered.

4 Experimental Results

In this section, the experiments are performed to evaluate the proposed method. The method of [4] is compared with our method. In the experiments, a total of 320 randomly selected music clips (including 40 eastern classical music clips, 40 eastern folk music clips, 40 western country music clips, 40 western pop music clips, 40 rock music clips, 40 speech clips, 40 piano clips, and 40 violin clips) are used as host signals. Each audio clip is 10 s long, sampled at 44.1 kHz, and quantized with 16 bits.

The PEAQ algorithm [16] is used to evaluate the perceptual quality of the two methods. The PEAQ algorithm returns a value called objective difference grade (ODG) ranging between -4 and 0, where ODG $= 0$ means no degradation and ODG = −4 means a very annoying distortion. The detection rate (DR), defined as

$$DR = \left(\frac{\text{Number of watermarks correctly extracted}}{\text{Number of watermarks embedded}}\right) \times 100\%$$

is used to measure the robustness. It should be noted that we count number of symbols correctly extracted instead of number of bits correctly extracted in the calculation of DR. The following common attacks are used in the evaluation of robustness:

- closed-loop attack (no attack),
- re-quantization (8-bit),
- noise attack (20 dB white Gaussian noise added),
- amplitude attack (amplitudes scaled by 1.2 and 1.8),
- MP3 compression (128 kbps and 96 kbps MP3 compression),
- HPF (High-pass filtering with 50 Hz and 100 Hz cut-off frequencies),
- LPF (Low-pass filtering with 12 kHz and 8 kHz cut-off frequencies).

For the sake of fairness, the experimental parameters of our method and those of [4] are the same. The value of parameters are: $n_b = 8$, $N = 768$, $\gamma_1 = 0.1$, $\gamma_2 = 2$, $\beta_{min} = 0.001$, $\beta_{max} = 0.2$ and $\Delta\beta = 0.005$. Under these settings, the embedding rates of two methods are shown in Table 2. From Table 2, the embedding capacity of the proposed method is larger than that of [4] by 12.5%.

Table 2. Embedding rates of two methods

	Method in [4]	Proposed method
Embedding rate	84 bps	94.5 bps

Table 3. Average ODGs of two methods

Imperceptibility	Method in [4]	Proposed method
ODG	−1.1623	−0.6175

Firstly, we compare the imperceptibility of the two methods. Table 3 shows average ODGs of 320 watermarked audio clips by the two methods. From Table 3, it can be seen that the proposed method achieves a higher perceptual quality with average ODG = −0.6175 and outperforms the method in [4] (average ODG = −1.1623) by a large margin. The reason that our proposed method yields a much better perceptual quality than the method in [4] is due to the use of Hadamard sequences instead of cyclic shifted PN sequences. Since Hadamard sequences are strictly orthogonal to each other while cyclic shifted PN sequences are nearly orthogonal to each other, our parameter β, selected by the algorithm shown in Table 1, is usually much smaller than that of [4].

Secondly, we compare the robustness of two methods. The results of detection rates of two methods under general attacks are displayed in Table 4. It can be seen that the proposed method achieves more than 99.9% detection rates under closed-loop attack, amplitude attack scaled by 1.2, MP3 attack with 128 kbps compression bit rate, and filtering attacks. It also performs well under the other attacks. Note that the detection rates of [4] are slightly higher than those of our method in all cases. But the differences are very small: less than 1.6% for the case of noise attack (20 dB), less than 0.8% for the case of amplitude attack scaled by 1.8, less than 0.4% for the case of MP3 attack with 96 kbps compression bit rate, and less than 0.07% for the other attacks. The reason is still due to that our parameter β is much smaller than that of [4].

Table 4. Average detection rates of two methods

Attacks	DR(%)	
	Method in [4]	Proposed method
Closed-loop	99.9816	99.9602
Re-quantization (8 bit)	99.4700	99.4087
Noise (20 dB)	96.5165	94.9571
Amplitude (1.2)	99.9816	99.9602
Amplitude (1.8)	99.9786	99.1850
MP3 (128 kbps)	99.9816	99.9203
MP3 (96 kbps)	99.9786	99.6752
HPF (50 Hz)	99.9816	99.9602
HPF (100 Hz)	99.9816	99.9387
LPF (50 Hz)	99.9816	99.9602
LPF (100 Hz)	99.9816	99.9449

5 Conclusion

In this paper, we propose a high embedding capacity spread spectrum-based audio watermarking method by exploiting the orthogonality of Hadamard sequences and a technique of sign change. Experimental results show that, compared to the method of [4], our method achieves a better perceptual quality and a higher embedding capacity while maintaining almost equal strong robustness.

Acknowledgments. This work was supported by the National Natural Science Foundation of China (Grant No. U1536121, 61872368).

References

1. Hua, G., Huang, J., Shi, Y.Q., Goh, J., Thing, V.L.: Twenty years of digital audio watermarking—a comprehensive review. Signal Process. **128**, 222–242 (2016). https://doi.org/10.1016/j.sigpro.2016.04.005. http://www.sciencedirect.com/science/article/pii/S0165168416300263
2. Malvar, H.S., Florencio, D.A.F.: Improved spread spectrum: a new modulation technique for robust watermarking. IEEE Trans. Signal Process. **51**(4), 898–905 (2003). https://doi.org/10.1109/TSP.2003.809385
3. Valizadeh, A., Wang, Z.J.: Correlation-and-bit-aware spread spectrum embedding for data hiding. IEEE Trans. Inf. Forensics Secur. **6**(2), 267–282 (2011). https://doi.org/10.1109/TIFS.2010.2103061
4. Xiang, Y., Natgunanathan, I., Rong, Y., Guo, S.: Spread spectrum-based high embedding capacity watermarking method for audio signals. IEEE/ACM Trans. Audio Speech Lang. Process. **23**(12), 2228–2237 (2015). https://doi.org/10.1109/TASLP.2015.2476755
5. Tafreshi, H.F., Shakeri, R., Khattab, T.: Capacious spread spectrum watermarking utilizing hadamard matrix. In: 2016 International Wireless Communications and Mobile Computing Conference (IWCMC), pp. 570–575, September 2016. https://doi.org/10.1109/IWCMC.2016.7577120
6. Zhang, X., Wang, Z.J.: Correlation-and-bit-aware multiplicative spread spectrum embedding for data hiding. In: 2013 IEEE International Workshop on Information Forensics and Security (WIFS), pp. 186–190, November 2013. https://doi.org/10.1109/WIFS.2013.6707816
7. Zhang, P., Xu, S.Z., Yang, H.Z.: Robust audio watermarking based on extended improved spread spectrum with perceptual masking. Int. J. Fuzzy Syst. **14**(2), 289–295 (2012)
8. Ko, B.S., Nishimura, R., Suzuki, Y.: Time-spread echo method for digital audio watermarking. IEEE Trans. Multimed. **7**(2), 212–221 (2005). https://doi.org/10.1109/TMM.2005.843366
9. Xiang, Y., Natgunanathan, I., Peng, D., Zhou, W., Yu, S.: A dual-channel time-spread echo method for audio watermarking. IEEE Trans. Inf. Forensics Secur. **7**(2), 383–392 (2012). https://doi.org/10.1109/TIFS.2011.2173678
10. Kalantari, N.K., Akhaee, M.A., Ahadi, S.M., Amindavar, H.: Robust multiplicative patchwork method for audio watermarking. IEEE Trans. Audio Speech Lang. Process. **17**(6), 1133–1141 (2009). https://doi.org/10.1109/TASL.2009.2019259
11. Kang, H., Yamaguchi, K., Kurkoski, B., Yamaguchi, K., Kobayashi, K.: Full-index-embedding patchwork algorithm for audio watermarking. IEICE - Trans. Inf. Syst. **E91-D**(11), 2731–2734 (2008)
12. Maity, S.P., Kundu, M.K., Das, T.S.: Robust ss watermarking with improved capacity. Pattern Recognit. Lett. **28**(3), 350–356 (2007). https://doi.org/10.1016/j.patrec.2006.04.004. http://www.sciencedirect.com/science/article/pii/S0167865506000869. Advances in Visual information Processing
13. Rosa, L.: High capacity wavelet watermarking using CDMA multilevel codes. Via Paolo della Cella **3**, 10139 (2009)
14. Doković, D.Ž.: Hadamard matrices of order 764 exist. Combinatorica **28**(4), 487–489 (2008)
15. Hedayat, A., Wallis, W.D., et al.: Hadamard matrices and their applications. Annals Stat. **6**(6), 1184–1238 (1978)
16. Itu-R, B.S.: Method for objective measurements of perceived audio quality (2001)

DWT and QR Code Based Watermarking for Document DRM

Nicolò Cardamone and Fabrizio d'Amore[✉]

Sapienza University of Rome, Rome, Italy
damore@diag.uniroma1.it

Abstract. This paper presents a digital rights protection scheme for every type of document presented as an image, by using steps that use cryptography and watermarking. The entities involved in this process are two: the owner of the document that owns its digital rights and a generic user who can download or view a watermarked version of the original document. The watermarked version contains a QR code that is repeatedly inserted, and scrambled, by the document rights owner, into the frequency components of the image, thus producing the watermarked image. The QR code contains a signed ID that uniquely identifies every users using the system. The schema, a non-blind type, achieves good perceptive quality and fair robustness using the third level of the Discrete Wavelet Transform. The experimental results show that by inserting several occurrences of a scrambled QR code we get an approach that is quite resistant to JPEG compression, rotation, cropping, and salt and pepper noise.

Keywords: Watermarking · Steganography · DWT

1 Introduction

In a big company data protection is a critical requirement, due to the fact that data leaks about company strategies, assets or every other types of confidential data could destroy the business of the entire company and its economic value. For this reason is useful to mark documents that are given to employees or third party in order to know who is the responsible of the possible leak. Secure content manager systems (CMSes), like virtual data rooms, define another typical scenario where documents typically need to be watermarked for the correct accounting of the access operations made by authorised users.

There exists an approach [6] that relies on DWT and QR code based watermarking applied to coloured or black and white images, that are photos or pictures. In this paper we extend the approach to the case of images describing documents and we show that the use of DWT, QR code and cryptography assures good imperceptibility, watermark extraction performance and robustness against most common image manipulations, like JPEG compression, rotation, cropping and additive noise. In particular, each page of a document can be seen as an image and a straightforward question is "can we successfully apply the

C. D. Yoo et al. (Eds.): IWDW 2018, LNCS 11378, pp. 137–150, 2019.
https://doi.org/10.1007/978-3-030-11389-6_11

methodology presented in [6] to this new type of image?". We show that some changes are needed with respect to the original approach, because a document is made up mainly of black and white components, without shades of grey (if it has no pictures inside); in some cases however, for example coloured slides with background, documents look very similar to classic pictures and the approach [6] works with no issues. The main idea is to embed data into the image's lower frequency of the 3rd level Discrete Wavelet components; these data are encrypted and uniquely identify a subject, and if the document will be leaked we are able to extract this information, even if some modifications are made in the document, and understand who is the responsible of the leak. Data are encoded into a QR code that is inserted as watermark [5]; we choose a QR code because of its error correction capability. In order to improve imperceptibility and extraction performances, we insert it into the host image multiple times, in a key-scrambled version. This is a non-blind schema (see next section), hence to extract the watermark is necessary to provide the original image.

Related Work QR code has seen a variety of applications in information security area: it can be used for secret sharing, authentication, transaction verification and for e-voting authentication. Researchers have also proposed different schemes for using the QR code in the area of data hiding and steganography. In addition, QR codes have been used in a number of recent digital watermarking schemes. Among the works carried out in this area, Panyavaraporn et al. [11] proposed a data embedding approach using blind watermarking algorithm by means of two-level DWT for hiding a small watermark image in a QR code. A similar approach was proposed by Nishane and Umale [10]: in their method the watermark can be an image or a QR code that is embedded in the third level DWT of the image and the watermark is encrypted with random matrix. It works under various noise attacks. Chow et al. [7] proposed an approach that involves the use of a hybrid DWT-DCT technique in conjunction with the error correction mechanism; this is inherent as part of the QR code structure.

2   Preliminaries

Watermarking techniques can be classified [1] into different categories according to the type of domain in which data embedding takes place and the type of information that is needed to extract the watermark. There are mainly two domain types: space and frequency. When we want an invisible watermark we usually use steganography techniques because we want to hide some payload inside a document. In this way a user without a thorough analysis cannot distinguish between a watermarked document and a non-watermarked one; in the other case the watermark is visible, and this makes it a possible target for a removal. Of course mixed/hybrid approaches can be adopted.

Regarding what is needed to extract a watermark from an image, we can divide the cases into blind, semi-blind and non-blind schemes. A blind watermark, or public watermarking algorithm, requires neither the original image nor the embedded watermark to extract it from the watermarked image; a semi-blind, or semi-private scheme, requires only the watermark; a non-blind scheme requires at least the cover image. In this paper we will use a non-blind schema and only the cover image is needed to recover the original QR code inserted. Spatial image watermarking techniques are commonly used in steganographic contexts because, hiding data into the least significant bits of an image can allow to embed a large quantity of data. However, the watermark will not be robust to common manipulations, e.g., JPEG compression.

In the frequency domain there are two main techniques: the Discrete Cosine Transform (DCT) and the Discrete Wavelet Transform (DWT). The first one is not resistant to rotation, translation and image cropping, due to the block divide algorithm, while the second one assures good robustness against the most popular image manipulations [14]. Digital images rights can be better expressed through a wavelet transform since the frequency components are quickly varying around the image area. Through the wavelet decomposition the original signal can be represented by its coefficients which contain the spatial information. Each level of a DWT produces four types of coefficients: LL, or approximation coefficients, that represent the low frequency part of the image (most of information) and the details coefficients LH, HL and HH (vertical, horizontal and diagonal). In every level the decomposition is obtained on the LL component of the previous level. The original signal can be completely reconstructed performing the Inverse Wavelet Transformation on these coefficients. In order to achieve a good visual imperceptibility, according to the spectral sensitivity of human eye, the blue component of a colour image is most suitable for hiding data and this component will be used in our approach. Data hiding system performances [3] are described in terms of imperceptibility, embedding capacity and robustness. For digital watermarking the most important are imperceptibility and robustness. Some measures will be made on the final image to measure visual imperceptibility between the original image and the watermarked one, that are Mean Squared Error (MSE), Peak Signal to Noise Ratio (PSNR) and Structural Similarity [13]:

$$\text{MSE} = \frac{1}{m \times n} \sum_{i=1}^{m} \sum_{j=1}^{n} (X(i,j) - X'(i,j))^2$$

$$\text{PSNR} = 10 \log_{10} \frac{\text{MAX}_i^2}{\text{MSE}}$$

$$\text{SSIM} = \frac{(2\mu_i\mu_j + C_1)(2\sigma_{ij} + C_2)}{(\mu_i^2 + \mu_j^2 + C_1)(\sigma_i^2 + \sigma_j^2 + C_2)}$$

where m and n are the number of rows and columns of the image expressed in pixel, $X(i,j)$ is the value of the pixel at row i and column j of the original image, $X'(i,j)$ is the value of the pixel at row i and column j of the watermarked image, MAX_i is the biggest value of a pixel, μ, σ, σ_{ij} are, respectively, mean, standard deviation and correlation, and C_1, C_2 are constants (Fig. 1).

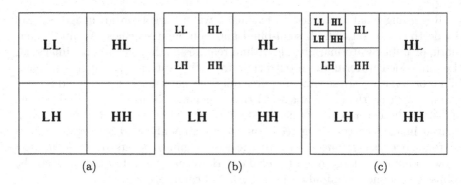

Fig. 1. (a) DWT single level decomposition, (b) two level decomposition, and (c) three level decomposition.

The payload is contained in a QR code (Quick Response Code [4]), that is the trademark for a type of matrix barcode first designed in 1994 for the automotive industry in Japan. A QR code consists of black squares arranged in a square grid on a white background, which can be read by an imaging device such as a camera, and processed using ReedSolomon error correction until the image can be appropriately interpreted. The required data is then extracted from patterns that are present in both horizontal and vertical components of the image.

3   Approach

In this section we describe the process of watermarking a given document and extracting a QR code from the watermarked image. Suppose all the documents that will be watermarked come from a single entity, a pair of public/private keys is given, and a message containing the ID of the user that will get the confidential document is digitally signed by the entity by its private key. This differs from the approach in [6] because in this case there is no collaboration between two subjects that sign a contract: in fact a central authority signs and distributes documents without any interaction among users of the system.

Starting from the original image and the signed message, the entity produces the watermarked document for the user by the following steps:

1. Convert each page of the document into an image and repeat the following steps for each image.
2. Compute the approximation coefficients of level 3 (AC_{LL3}) by performing a third-level decomposition of the image using a wavelet (blue component in case of colour image).
3. Generate a QR code encoding the hmac-sha256 of the signed message using its private key.

4. Derives a scrambling key from a hmac-sha256 of a password and use it to scramble the QR code repetitions necessary to fit the size of the AC_{LL3} (N × M) of the image obtaining WIM like in Fig. 2b.
5. Insert the watermark into the approximation coefficients of level 3 of the watermarked image $WAC_{LL3}(i,j) = AC_{LL3}(i,j) + k × WIM(i,j)$, $i = 1, 2, \ldots, N$ and $j = 1, 2, \ldots, M$, with $k = 20000$ for colour images and $k = 15000$ for black and white ones.
6. Obtain the watermarked image by performing the inverse discrete wavelet transform.
7. Reconstruct the document, starting from the watermarked images.

To extract the QR code starting from the original image (Fig. 6) and the watermarked image (Fig. 7a) it is necessary to:

1. Convert each page of the document into an image.
2. Compute the approximation coefficients of level 3 by performing a third-level decomposition of the image using a wavelet, blue component in case of colour image, for both original (AC_{LL3}) and watermarked image (WAC_{LL3}).
3. Reconstruct WIM:

$$f(x) = \begin{cases} 1 & \text{if } WAC_{LL3}(i,j) - AC_{LL3}(i,j) \geq t \\ 0 & \text{otherwise} \end{cases}$$

for $i = 1, 2, \ldots, N$ and $j = 1, 2, \ldots, M$, with $t = 40$ for colour images and $t = 22.5$ for black and white ones, obtaining a scrambled watermarked image.
4. Descramble by using the key derived from the hmac-sha256 of the previously generated password in the third step of watermark insertion.
5. Compute hmac-sha256 of the message using entity private key.
6. Recover the QR code from the single QR code repetitions occurring in the descrambled image (Fig. 7b) and verify if the decoded value is equal to the hmac-sha256 of the message, for payload extraction is used either each single extracted repetition of a QR code either a reconstructed QR code based on majority pixel value matching, upon 1 to the maximum value of them.

In the above steps, more sophisticated techniques for deriving a key from a password could be usefully employed.

The watermark extraction procedure can be done only by the entity because it needs its private key and the unscrambling password. If an attacker finds the password he cannot generate another document watermarked with another ID because the private key of the entity is unknown to him; if he is able to obtain public and private keys of the entity, he can not once again generate another document because he can generate an unscrambled watermarked version of the document like Fig. 7a but he cannot scramble QR code like Fig. 7b.

4   Applications

We implemented this technique in MATLAB using as original images the ones represented in Figs. 6, 8a and 11a. We used the open-source library `libqrencode` [9] for QR code generation and the `quirc` library [2] for QR code decoding. All images were tested with the first 20 wavelets of the Daubechies family [8,12]. In this we apply the procedure to three class of documents:

- Black and white text document;
- Text document with modified background;
- Slides with background.

(a)   (b)

Fig. 2. Unscrambled (a) and Scrambled (b) QR code.

4.1   Black and White Text Document

Black and white document needs preprocessing otherwise some information of QR code will be lost during image reconstruction from the wavelet transform. As we can see in Fig. 3a and b, the extracted QR code repetitions present noise in the white area and this results into a bad extraction of the QR code (see Fig. 4), even if changes have been made to the values of k and t. The QR code in Fig. 4 is different from the original one in Fig. 10b and presents errors but the information inside is not damaged and can be correctly obtained thanks to the error correction of QR code. In order to bypass the problem, the background is made slightly darker as we can see in Figs. 5 and 6. In this way payload is inserted in the background of the document too and no information is lost as we can see in Fig. 7a, where we can see the final result of the watermark insertion algorithm that produces an image with visible artefacts in the background. This is an example of visible watermark and a user that receives a document in this state can read it but understands that some extra information may have been added (Fig. 9).

4.2   Text Document with Modified Background

In Fig. 8 we can see the final result of the watermark insertion algorithm and the original image side by side, in this case the watermark is invisible because it is visually imperceptible and is very difficult to notice differences between the two images.

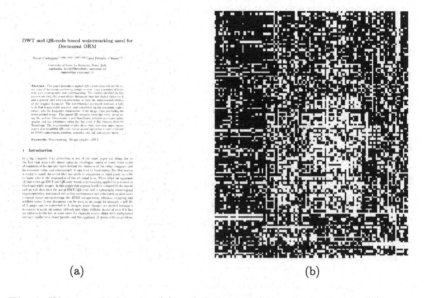

(a)   (b)

Fig. 3. Watermarked image (a) and Extracted QR code repetitions (b).

Fig. 4. QR code extraction failure.

4.3   Slides with Background

In Fig. 11 we can see the final result of the watermark insertion algorithm and the original image one above the other. In this case the watermark is slightly visible because the colours used in the slide are lighter than the example before and we can observe some background noise in the image.

4.4   Results

Results of the three test cases above are very good and the QR code is extracted without error as we can see from Fig. 10. In Table 1 we can find the MSE, PSNR, SSIM results for the three types of document.

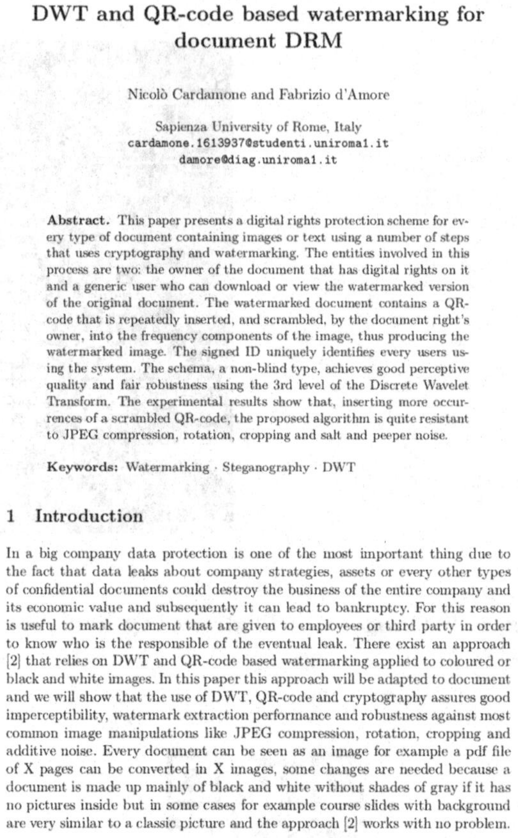

DWT and QR-code based watermarking for document DRM

Nicolò Cardamone and Fabrizio d'Amore

Sapienza University of Rome, Italy
cardamone.1613937@studenti.uniroma1.it
damore@diag.uniroma1.it

Abstract. This paper presents a digital rights protection scheme for every type of document containing images or text using a number of steps that uses cryptography and watermarking. The entities involved in this process are two: the owner of the document that has digital rights on it and a generic user who can download or view the watermarked version of the original document. The watermarked document contains a QR-code that is repeatedly inserted, and scrambled, by the document right's owner, into the frequency components of the image, thus producing the watermarked image. The signed ID uniquely identifies every users using the system. The schema, a non-blind type, achieves good perceptive quality and fair robustness using the 3rd level of the Discrete Wavelet Transform. The experimental results show that, inserting more occurrences of a scrambled QR-code, the proposed algorithm is quite resistant to JPEG compression, rotation, cropping and salt and peeper noise.

Keywords: Watermarking · Steganography · DWT

1   Introduction

In a big company data protection is one of the most important thing due to the fact that data leaks about company strategies, assets or every other types of confidential documents could destroy the business of the entire company and its economic value and subsequently it can lead to bankruptcy. For this reason is useful to mark document that are given to employees or third party in order to know who is the responsible of the eventual leak. There exist an approach [2] that relies on DWT and QR-code based watermarking applied to coloured or black and white images. In this paper this approach will be adapted to document and we will show that the use of DWT, QR-code and cryptography assures good imperceptibility, watermark extraction performance and robustness against most common image manipulations like JPEG compression, rotation, cropping and additive noise. Every document can be seen as an image for example a pdf file of X pages can be converted in X images, some changes are needed because a document is made up mainly of black and white without shades of gray if it has no pictures inside but in some cases for example course slides with background are very similar to a classic picture and the approach [2] works with no problem.

Fig. 5. Black and White preprocessed text example.

4.5   Possible Attacks

There are some image manipulation attacks that can be performed on the watermarked image depending on the different types of document. In the black and white document case an attacker can simply analyze the document pixel by pixel: if a pixel is black or white no modification is necessary, otherwise converts the pixels into white ones obtaining a result like that shown in Fig. 5. In the slides case an attacker can do a similar thing like converting all the shades of a particular colour, in the example mainly red and blue, in an unique colour

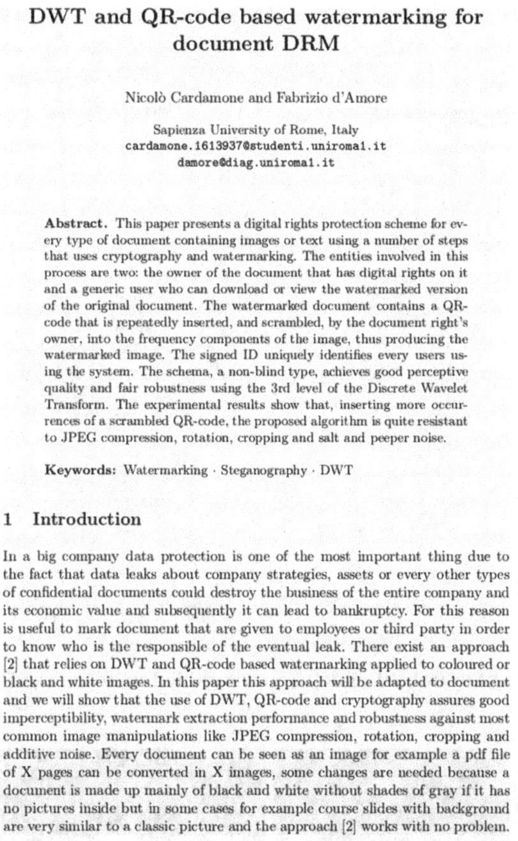

DWT and QR-code based watermarking for document DRM

Nicolò Cardamone and Fabrizio d'Amore

Sapienza University of Rome, Italy
cardamone.1613937@studenti.uniroma1.it
damore@diag.uniroma1.it

Abstract. This paper presents a digital rights protection scheme for every type of document containing images or text using a number of steps that uses cryptography and watermarking. The entities involved in this process are two: the owner of the document that has digital rights on it and a generic user who can download or view the watermarked version of the original document. The watermarked document contains a QR-code that is repeatedly inserted, and scrambled, by the document right's owner, into the frequency components of the image, thus producing the watermarked image. The signed ID uniquely identifies every users using the system. The schema, a non-blind type, achieves good perceptive quality and fair robustness using the 3rd level of the Discrete Wavelet Transform. The experimental results show that, inserting more occurrences of a scrambled QR-code, the proposed algorithm is quite resistant to JPEG compression, rotation, cropping and salt and peeper noise.

Keywords: Watermarking · Steganography · DWT

1 Introduction

In a big company data protection is one of the most important thing due to the fact that data leaks about company strategies, assets or every other types of confidential documents could destroy the business of the entire company and its economic value and subsequently it can lead to bankruptcy. For this reason is useful to mark document that are given to employees or third party in order to know who is the responsible of the eventual leak. There exist an approach [2] that relies on DWT and QR-code based watermarking applied to coloured or black and white images. In this paper this approach will be adapted to document and we will show that the use of DWT, QR-code and cryptography assures good imperceptibility, watermark extraction performance and robustness against most common image manipulations like JPEG compression, rotation, cropping and additive noise. Every document can be seen as an image for example a pdf file of X pages can be converted in X images, some changes are needed because a document is made up mainly of black and white without shades of gray if it has no pictures inside but in some cases for example course slides with background are very similar to a classic picture and the approach [2] works with no problem.

Fig. 6. Black and White postprocessed text example.

and this will result in a failure during watermark extraction. This method is robust against compression attack thanks to the redundancy of QR code in the images and QR code error correction feature that is implemented by adding a Reed-Solomon code to the original data. Experiments have proven that it is possible to compress the image up to 50% of the original quality, as we can see in Fig. 12a, and extract the QR code correctly. Salt and pepper noise attacks it is not effective, experiments have proven that it is still possible to extract the QR code even in presence of noise like in Fig. 12b. It is also possible to apply a function on the image, before extraction phase, that performs median filtering, where each output pixel contains the median value in the 3-by-3 neighborhood around the corresponding pixel in the input image in order to remove the noise. This method it is robust against geometric modification like cropping and rotation, in the experiments corners of the document were cropped (Fig. 13a) and a rotation of 45 degrees was applied (Fig. 13b) but the extraction phase was successful.

(a)   (b)

Fig. 7. (a) Scrambled and (b) unscrambled watermarked image.

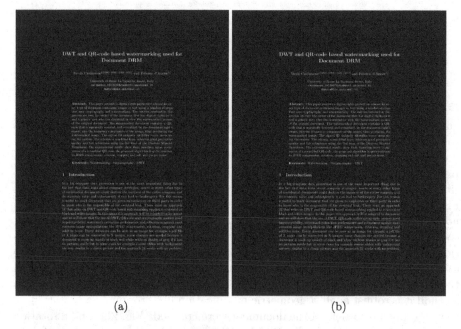

(a)   (b)

Fig. 8. Side by side comparison between (a) the original image, and (b) the water-marked one (b).

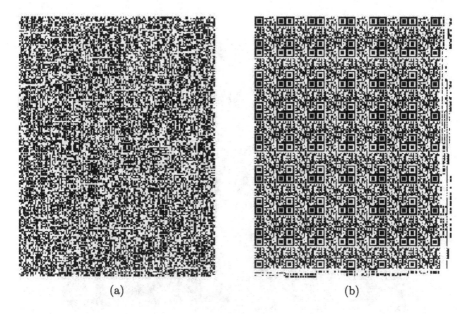

Fig. 9. (a) Scrambled and (b) unscrambled extracted QR codes.

Fig. 10. QR code: (a) inserted into the image; (b) extracted side by side.

Table 1. MSE PSNR SSIM results.

Document type	MSE	PSNR	SSIM
Black and White text document	22.75	79.58	0.9215
Text document with modified background	47.83	72.15	0.8208
Slides with background	47.73	72.17	0.9392

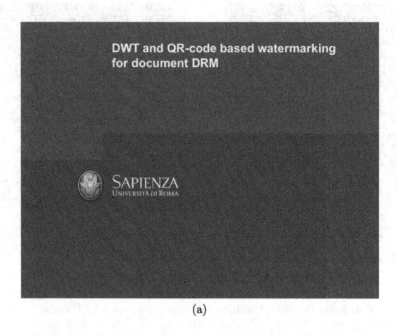

(a)

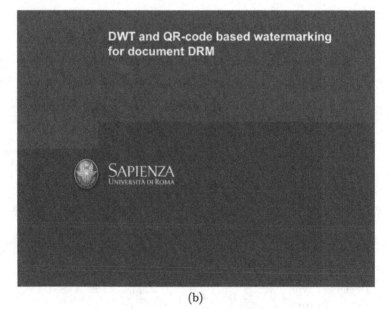

(b)

Fig. 11. (a) The original slide; (b) the watermarked slide.

(a)   (b)

Fig. 12. (a) 50% jpeg compression and (b) text with salt and pepper noise.

(a)   (b)

Fig. 13. (a) Cropped and (b) rotated text example.

5   Final Remarks and Future Works

Through these steps we can embed scrambled individual references within a document with almost no effects on its quality. Experimental results show that such a schema provides quite good quality and robustness and the results show that the algorithm performs fairly good in terms of imperceptibility. Further analysis could be done by searching for new possibilities to insert information in a document for examples using fonts modification or introducing errors following a certain pattern.

References

1. Altaay, A.A.J., Sahib, S.B., Zamani, M.: An introduction to image steganography techniques. In: 2012 International Conference on Advanced Computer Science Applications and Technologies (ACSAT). pp. 122–126, November 2012. https://doi.org/10.1109/ACSAT.2012.25
2. Beer, D.: Quirc. https://github.com/dlbeer/quirc
3. Beram, F.G.: Effective parameters of image steganography techniques. Int. J. Comput. Appl. Technol. Res. **3**(6), 361–363 (2014)
4. BSI: Information technology. Automatic identification and data capture techniques. QR Code bar code symbology specification. BSI, London, 3 March 2015, Standard Number BS ISO/IEC 18004:2015
5. Chen, J.H., Chen, W.Y., Chen, C.H.: Identification recovery scheme using Quick Response (QR) code and watermarking technique (2013)
6. Chiavarelli, S., d'Amore, F.: A novel approach to image DRM relying on DWT and QR-code based watermarking. In: Multidisciplinary Symposium on ICT Research in Russian Federation and Europe on "Integrating Research Agendas and Devising Joint Challenges" (REMS 2018), October 2018
7. Chow, Y.W., Susilo, W., Tonien, J., Zong, W.: A QR code watermarking approach based on the dwt-dct technique. In: Pieprzyk, J., Suriadi, S. (eds.) Information Security and Privacy, pp. 314–331. Springer International Publishing, Cham (2017)
8. Daubechies, I.: The wavelet transform, time-frequency localization and signal analysis. IEEE Trans. Inf. Theory **36**(5), 961–1005 (1990). https://doi.org/10.1109/18.57199
9. Fukuchi, K.: libqrencode. https://fukuchi.org/works/qrencode
10. Nishane, S., Umale, V.M.: Digital image watermarking based on DWT using QR code. Int. J. Curr. Eng. and Technol. (2015)
11. Panyavaraporn, J., Horkaew, P., Wongtrairat, W.: QR code watermarking algorithm based on wavelet transform. In: 2013 13th International Symposium on Communications and Information Technologies (ISCIT), pp. 791–796, September 2013. https://doi.org/10.1109/ISCIT.2013.6645969
12. Ramchandran, K., Vetterli, M., Herley, C.: Wavelets, subband coding, and best bases. Proc. IEEE **84**(4), 541–560 (1996). https://doi.org/10.1109/5.488699
13. Wang, Z., Bovik, A.C., Sheikh, H.R., Simoncelli, E.P.: Image quality assessment: from error visibility to structural similarity. IEEE Trans. Image Process. **13**(4), 600–612 (2004). https://doi.org/10.1109/TIP.2003.819861
14. Xu, J., Sung, A.H., Shi, P., Liu, Q.: Jpeg compression immune steganography using wavelet transform. In: Proceedingsof the International Conference on Information Technology: Coding and Computing, 2004, ITCC 2004. vol. 2, pp. 704–708, April 2004. https://doi.org/10.1109/ITCC.2004.1286737

Dynamic Watermarking-Based Integrity Protection of Homomorphically Encrypted Databases – Application to Outsourced Genetic Data

David Niyitegeka[1(✉)], Gouenou Coatrieux[1,3], Reda Bellafqira[1],
Emmanuelle Genin[2], and Javier Franco-Contreras[3]

[1] IMT Atlantique, Unité INSERM UMR 1101 LaTIM, Brest, France
`david.niyitegeka@imt-atlantique.fr`
[2] Unité INSERM UMR 1078, Brest, France
[3] WaToo, Brest, France

Abstract. In this paper, we propose a dynamic database crypto-watermarking scheme that enables a cloud service provider (CSP) to verify the integrity of encrypted databases outsourced by different users. This scheme takes advantage of the semantic security property most homomorphic cryptosystems have, so as to embed a watermark into encrypted data without altering users' data. The incorrect detection of the watermark, not only informs the CSP the database has been illegally modified but also indicates which data have been altered. In addition, the proposed scheme is dynamic in the sense the watermarking and integrity verification processes can be conducted along the database lifecycle, i.e. even when the database owner updates his or her data (i.e. addition, suppression or modification of database elements). Experimental results carried out with the Paillier cryptosystem on a genetic database demonstrate that our method can efficiently detect different illegal data tamper with a high location precision.

Keywords: Confidentiality · Data outsourcing · Database watermarking ·
Genetic data · Homomorphic encryption · Integrity

1 Introduction

Nowadays, cloud computing allows data owners to flexibly store and process large amounts of data remotely, without a need to purchase and maintain their own infrastructure. Despite these benefits, such a data outsourcing induces critical security issues especially in terms of data confidentiality and integrity. Indeed, users lose the control over the data they outsource. Among available security mechanisms, encryption ensures the confidentiality of data. In cloud environment, homomorphic encryption has recently gained in interest due to the fact that it allows performing linear operations (e.g. "+", "×") onto encrypted data with the guarantee that the decrypted result equals the one carried out onto unencrypted data [1]. Information can thus be processed without accessing it in a clear form. In this work, we are interested in giving to the

© Springer Nature Switzerland AG 2019
C. D. Yoo et al. (Eds.): IWDW 2018, LNCS 11378, pp. 151–166, 2019.
https://doi.org/10.1007/978-3-030-11389-6_12

cloud service provider the capacity to verify the integrity of databases outsourced homomorphically encrypted by their owners with the help of watermarking, under the constraint that users can update their data (i.e. modify, suppress or add data).

Different tools can be used so as to verify the integrity of a database such as: digital signatures (DS) [2], message authentication code (MAC) [3] or, more recently, watermarking. DS and MAC are common solutions exploited in database management systems (DBMS). However, they introduce additional pieces of information into the database. On the contrary, watermarking relies on the imperceptible insertion of a message into the data by modifying them based on the principle of controlled distortion. As defined, watermarking leaves access to the data while maintaining them protected by the message. Depending on the relationship between the message and the host data, one can ensure various security services like integrity control, in particular.

The first database watermarking method was introduced by Agrawal *et al.* [4]. As most database watermarking schemes, this one focuses on copyright protection or traitor tracing applications where the message corresponds to the buyer or user identifier [5, 6]. Embedding is conducted in a robust way so as to be able to retrieve the identifier even if the watermarked database has been modified. Some watermarking methods have been especially designed in order to verify the integrity of databases. Contrarily to the previous schemes, these ones embed a "fragile" watermark that will not survive any database modifications [7–11]. Sometimes, such schemes provide the capability to identify which database elements have been altered [9]. These methods are either distortion-free or reversible. Distortion-free methods do not modify the values of the database elements. The database is watermarked: by introducing new data, like some "virtual" attributes where the watermark is dissimulated [8] or by modulating the organization of the database elements (i.e. tuples or attributes [7]). Regarding reversible methods, they ensure it is possible to invert the insertion process and to remove the watermark distortion restoring thus the original attribute values of the database. They are well adapted for verifying the integrity. In particular, one can insert a digital signature of the database itself. At the verification stage, the digital signature is extracted and compared with the one computed on the restored database. Such an approach has been proposed either for numerical data [10] or categorical data [11], applying reversible histogram shifting or difference expansion modulations. It is important to notice that the above methods have several limitations. All of them work on static databases i.e. on databases that are not updated. Moreover, they consider tuple additions, suppressions or modifications as non-authorized modifications. Distortion-free methods can localize modifications but without a really good precision (i.e. tuple level at best). On their side, reversible methods only indicate whether a database has been modified. There is thus a need for a watermarking scheme capable to protect database integrity in a dynamic way with also good localization performance while being also compliant with data encryption. Several crypto-watermarking methods, i.e. solutions that combine encryption and watermarking, have been proposed. Most of them focus on multimedia data (e.g. image, video) in order to ensure at the same time data confidentiality and copyright protection in their distribution [12] or watermarking-based integrity and authenticity services from decrypted/encrypted data [13]. Crypto-watermarking schemes can be differentiated depending on whether the embedded message is available in the clear domain, in the encryption domain, or in both domains [14]. To the best of our knowledge, the method proposed by Xiang et al. [15] is the first that combines watermarking and encryption for the protection of databases. It is based on Order Preserving Encryption (OPE), whose encryption function preserves numerical ordering of the plain-texts, and Discrete Cosine Transformation (DCT). To embed the watermark, the encrypted database is divided into groups, and for each group, DCT coefficients (i.e. DC and AC coefficients) are calculated. AC coefficients are used to generate the watermark bits which are then embedded into the DC coefficients by using quantization index modulation (QIM) [16]. After that, the encrypted and watermarked database can be obtained after executing inverse DCT operations. At the verification stage, integrity of the database can be verified by matching the hash value of AC coefficients and the extracted watermark information from DC coefficients. If this method allows verifying the integrity of an encrypted database, it does not consider update operations. Beyond, it relies on OPE which has several security limitations due to some of its deterministic properties [17].

In this paper, we propose a watermarking method that allows a Cloud Service Provider (CSP) to verify the integrity of homomorphically encrypted databases that are outsourced, handled or updated by their owners remotely. The objective is to detect and localize non-authorized database modifications. To do so, we take advantage of the semantic security property of some homomorphic cryptosystems so as to embed a watermark, a binary message, into encrypted data without altering users' data. As we will see, being available from the hash of subset of attribute values, this message, if not detected properly, not only informs CSP that the database has been modified but also indicates which data have been altered. Contrarily to all the above schemes, the proposed solution is dynamic in the sense the watermarking and integrity verification processes can be conducted along the database lifecycle.

The rest of this paper is organized as follows. In Sect. 2, we come back on some homomorphic encryption preliminaries as well as on the database outsourcing scenario we consider. Section 3 provides the details of the proposed solution while experimental results and performance and security analysis are given in Sect. 4. Conclusions and some perspectives are drawn in Sect. 5.

2 Homomorphic Encryption Preliminaries and Data Outsourcing Scenario

2.1 Homomorphic Encryption: Paillier Cryptosystem

In this work, we opted for the well-known asymmetric Paillier cryptosystem because of its additive homomorphic properties and its simplicity of use [18]. Its principles are as follows. Let p and q be two large prime numbers, the user public key is given by $K_p = pq$. Let $Z^*_{K_p^2}$ denotes the set of integers in $Z_{K_p^2} = \left\{0, 1, .., K_p^2 - 1\right\}$ that have multiplicative inverses modulo K_p^2, and select $g \in Z^*_{K_p^2}$ such that $gcd\left(L\left(g^{K_s} \bmod K_p^2\right), K_p\right) = 1$, where: $gcd(.)$ is the greatest common divisor function, $L(s) = (s - 1)/K_p$ and $K_s = lcm(p - 1, q - 1)$ defines the user private key with $lcm(.)$ the least common multiple function. The cipher-text of the clear message $m \in Z_{K_p}$ is derived as

$$c = E[m, r] = g^m r^{K_p} \, mod \, K_p^2 \tag{1}$$

where $E[.]$ is the encryption function and $r \in Z_{K_p}^*$ is a random integer that ensures the Paillier cryptosystem satisfies the so-called "semantic security". More clearly, the same plain-text has different cipher-texts depending on the value of r. The decryption of the cipher-text c is based on the decryption function $D[.]$ such that

$$m = D[c, K_s] = L(c^{K_s} \, mod \, K_p^2)/L\left(g^{K_s} \, mod \, K_p^2\right) mod \, K_p \tag{2}$$

This cryptosystem has additive homomorphic properties. Considering two plain-texts m_1 and m_2, we have

$$E[m_1, r_1] * E[m_2, r_2] = E[m_1 + m_2, r_1 r_2] \tag{3}$$

$$E[m_1, r_1]^{m_2} = E\left[m_1 m_2, r_1^{m_2}\right] \tag{4}$$

As we will see in Sect. 3, both semantic security and additive homomorphic properties of the Paillier cryptosystem will be of importance in our scheme.

2.2   Data Outsourcing Scenario and Database Model

The scenario we consider is given in Fig. 1, where a data owner securely outsources his database into the cloud after independently homomorphically encrypting its elements. By doing so, the owner can ask the cloud service provider (CSP) to process his data while preserving their confidentiality. Herein, the CSP honestly stores and processes encrypted data uploaded based on the owners' requests (processing, updating data). The CSP is not malicious and will not try to alter owners' data. At least, it can be curious, aiming at inferring user data. These privacy issues are however out of the scope of this work where we focus on the verification by CSP of the integrity of the encrypted data under his responsibility. Notice that CSP that is authorized to store users' data with the help of sub-contracted service providers that can be malicious.

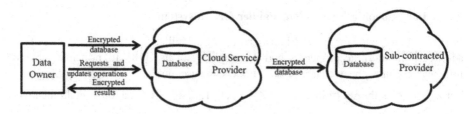

Fig. 1. The considered data outsourcing scenario

In the sequel, we consider the relational database model. A database DB is composed of a finite set of tables $\{T_i\}_{i=1,...,N}$. From here on and for sake of simplicity, we use a database constituted of one single table of u tuples $\{t_i\}_{i=1,...,u}$, where each tuple has m attributes $\{A_1, A_2, ..., A_m\}$. The attribute A_j takes its values within an attribute domain and $t_i.A_j$ refers to the value of the jth attribute of the ith tuple. In a database, each tuple is uniquely identified by either one attribute or a set of attributes which is called primary key, noted $t_i.PK$. The encrypted version DB_e of DB is obtained by independently encrypting the values $\{t_i.A_j\}_{i=1,...,u,j=1,...,m}$ using Eq. (1)

$$E\left[t_i.A_j, r_{ij}\right] = g^{t_i.A_j} r_{ij}^{K_p} \bmod K_p^2 \tag{5}$$

where K_p is the public key of the database owner and $r_{ij} \in Z_{K_p}^*$ is a random integer.

The objective we pursue in this work is to allow the Cloud Service Provider to protect DB_e in terms of integrity using watermarking under the constraint not altering the owners' data and that data can be updated during time. To do so, and as we will see, we will take advantage of the semantic security property of homomorphic encryption. It is important to notice that all modifications conducted at the request of one data owner, i.e. deletion, addition or modification of tuples or attributes, are authorized. Modifications resulting from system errors (e.g. transmission or storage errors) or from malicious actions, by an intruder for instance, should be detected.

3 Watermarking of Homomorphically Encrypted Database

In this section, we first present our watermarking method for protecting the integrity of homomorphically encrypted databases in the case of "static" databases, before extending it to "dynamic" databases, i.e. when data are remotely updated by their owners.

3.1 Watermarking of Static Homomorphically Encrypted Database

The general architecture and principles of our system are illustrated in Fig. 2. It is based on two main processes: database protection and database integrity verification. The protection process (see Fig. 2a), takes as input an encrypted database DB_e in order to embed a message M that will be available in the encrypted domain. This process stands on three steps: a preprocessing step the purpose of which is to secretly reorganize the database DB_e into DB_e^r based on the secret watermarking key K_w, followed by the insertion of M in DB_e^r to produce DB_e^{wr}, and the back reorganization of DB_e^{wr} into the watermarked encrypted database DB_e^w. The verification process works in a similar way (see Fig. 2b). Considering a protected database $\widehat{DB_e^w}$, based on the secret watermarking key K_w, it first secretly reorganizes $\widehat{DB_e^w}$, elements; the message $\widehat{M}$ is extracted and compared to the message M. Any differences between these two messages will: (i) alert the CSP of the database integrity loss; (ii) identify which attribute values have been altered. We detail these different steps in the sequel.

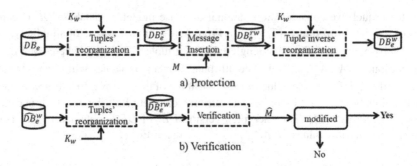

Fig. 2. General architecture of the proposed system. M, $\widehat{M}$ and K_w are the embedded message, extracted message and the secret watermarking key, respectively.

Data Protection. This process is constituted of three main steps:

Preprocessing – Secret Database Reorganization. The purpose of this step is to ensure that a non-authorized user cannot access to M. It basically consists in secretly reorganizing the database DB_e into the database DB_e^r based on the secret watermarking key K_w. In this work, we reorganize the database tuples in the ascending order of the cryptographic hash values: $hash(t_i) = hash(K_w||E[t_i.PK, r_{iPK}])$, where: '$||$' represents the concatenation operator, $t_i.PK$ is the primary key of the tuple t_i and $hash$ is the cryptographic Secure Hash Algorithm-2(SHA-2). The security of this procedure thus relies on the one of SHA-2 and, in particular, on its collision and diffusion properties [19], as well on the knowledge of the watermarking key K_w.

Message Embedding for Integrity Control. The basic idea of this process stands in the embedding of one bit of the message M into the hash value of a subset of encrypted attribute values of the database. Assuming the database is constituted of k subsets, M is thus a sequence of k uniformly distributed bits ($M = \{b_l\}_{l=1..k}$, $b_l \in \{0, 1\}$) secretly generated based on the watermarking key K_w. The integrity of the database will be verified by checking the presence of M into the subset hash values. Working with subsets provides the capacity to identify which parts or attributes of the database have been altered. This insertion step relies on two sub-steps:

i. *Database partitioning in subsets* – As illustrated in Fig. 3, the secretly reorganized encrypted database DB_e^r is partitioned into k overlapping 'subsets' $\{B_l\}_{l=1...k}$ of 3×3 elements.

ii. *Insertion of one bit b_l of M in an attribute subset B_l* – B_l is watermarked into B_l^w such that $b_l = hash\left(B_l^w\right)_v = s_v$, where s_v represents the vth bit of the cryptographic S hash of B_l^w, *i.e.* $S = hash\left(B_l^w\right)$. The choice of the value of v depends on the watermarking key K_w. Based on the fact it is not possible to predict the SHA-2 output for a given input, we use an iterative procedure so as to watermark B_l into B_l^w. The center element of a subset (e.g. $E\left[t_i.A_j, r_{ij}\right]$ of the subset B_l in Fig. 3) is modified taking advantage of the homomorphic and semantic properties of the Paillier cryptosystem as follows

$$B_l^w = B_l \ ;$$
While $b_l \neq hash(B_l^w)_v$
$\quad \alpha = rand(.);$
$\quad E[t_i.A_j, r_{ij}\alpha] = E[t_i.A_j, r_{ij}]E[0,\alpha];$ % $E[t_i.A_j, r_{ij}]$ center ele-
$\qquad\qquad\qquad\qquad\qquad$ % ment of B_l^w
$\quad$ End

where *rand(.)* is a uniform random function in $Z_{K_p}^*$. Due to the "strength" of SHA-2, there is half a chance to get the correct value of s_v at each iteration.

Back Reorganization of the Watermarked Database DB_e^{rw}. Once all subsets watermarked, the database DB_e^{wr} is reorganized back so as to give access to the encrypted watermarked database DB_e^w.

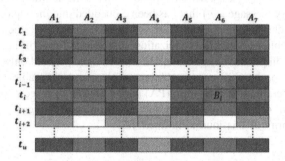

Fig. 3. Partitioning of DB_e^r into subsets. Blue areas represent subsets in the database and hatched areas represent the intersection between blue subsets and grey subsets. Note that standalone attribute values are regrouped into independent subsets. (Color figure online)

Message Extraction and Database Integrity Verification. The integrity verification of a protected database works in a similar way as the database protection. Let us consider a suspicious database $\widehat{DB_e^w}$. Based on the secret watermarking key K_w, $\widehat{DB_e^w}$ is secretly reorganized into $\widehat{DB_e^{rw}}$ and partitioned into subsets. The cryptographic hash value of each subset is computed and the bits of the message $\widehat{M}$ are extracted from these hashes. Any differences in between $\widehat{M}$ and the a priori known or original embedded message M will indicate the database has been altered. It is also possible to identify/localize which subsets have been modified. As we will see in the experimental section, this protection allows detecting different attacks like tuple suppression, tuple addition or modification of encrypted attribute value.

3.2 Watermarking of Updatable Homomorphically Encrypted Database

In this scenario, the user is allowed to remotely update the database. Database tuples can be added, suppressed or modified. Being requested by an authorized owner, such an update should not be at the origin of an alarm. We want to detect unauthorized modifications like addition, suppression or modification of tuples by an intruder, for instance.

Rather than re-watermarking the whole database using the previous scheme, we propose a dynamic watermarking method which allows protecting the database integrity on the fly with the capability to localize data modifications as before. To do so, our scheme takes advantage of a journal table J_t that contains some pieces of information such as the historical details of all added or suppressed tuples. Beyond, the protection and verification processes of this scheme are similar to those depicted in Sect. 3.1.

To give an idea about how our solution works, let us consider an already protected database DB_e^w along its journal J_t. As shown in Table 1, one record of J_t is associated to one tuple of DB_e^w. Its components correspond to: the tuple identifier (e.g. the encrypted primary key $E[t_i.PK, r_{iPK}]$), the action applied to this tuple: addition (A) or suppression (S); and the binary message (m_i) that has been embedded into the tuple. J_t is organized according to the chronological order database elements have been updated. As we will see in the rest of this section, this organization will be used for verifying the integrity of the database. It is important to notice that the elements of J_t should only be known from the CSP. To do so, the CSP encrypts J_t record elements (see Table 1) and permutes records using a permutation algorithm (PA) parameterized by a secret permutation key K_π. PA is used in order to hide the chronological order of J_t records. We will come back on the security of this journal in Sect. 4.3.

Table 1. A sample view of the journal table J_t.

Added(A)/Suppressed(S)	Identifier (Id_i)	Embedded message (m_i)
$E[A, r_{1a}]$	$E[Id_1, r_1]$	$E[m_1, r_{m_1}]$
$E[A, r_{2a}]$	$E[Id_2, r_2]$	$E[m_2, r_{m_2}]$
$E[S, r_{3s}]$	$E[Id_3, r_3]$	$E[m_3, r_{m_3}]$

In the following, we go into the details of our scheme. For the sake of simplicity, we first present how it works when new tuples are added, before presenting its principles when considering tuple suppression and authorized attribute value modification.

Protection on the Fly When Adding One New Tuple. To illustrate this process, let us consider an encrypted watermarked database DB_e^w constituted of only two tuples as shown in Fig. 4a. When a new homomorphically encrypted tuple indexed by t_i is added by a user, the CSP conducts the following steps:

1- The CSP decrypts J_t and reorganizes the records of J_t in their chronological order using the permutation algorithm parameterized with the secret key K_π. Then the CSP looks for the two previous last added tuples (that is to say the two last lines of the database DB_e^w – see Fig. 4a) accordingly to J_t.

2- As exposed in Fig. 4b, the CSP concatenates the new tuple to the two previous ones and computes the relative attribute subset partitioning. This partition depends on the position of the tuple in the database and can be simply computed based on t_i; computation we cannot detail due to paper length limitation.

3- The cloud watermarks this set of tuples accordingly the two following sub-steps:

   a. Bits of the message M are extracted from pre-existing but incomplete sub-sets (i.e. subsets some attributes of which do not exist - e.g. B_1 in Fig. 4a) and are next re-inserted into these subsets once these ones completed with the attribute values of the new added tuple (see new version of B_1 on Fig. 4b).

   b. New subsets, created after the addition of the new tuple (e.g. B_4 in Fig. 4b), are watermarked. To do so, the CSP secretly generates a sequence of bits based on the watermarking key K_w, i.e. a sub-message m_i.

After watermarking, the CSP adds to J_t the record R_{t_i} such as $R_{t_i} = <A, Id_i = E[t_i.PK, r_{iPK}], m_i >$. J_t is next secretly permuted before is encrypted.

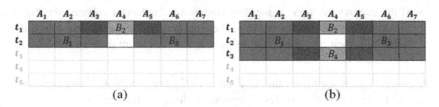

(a)   (b)

Fig. 4. (a) Initial protected database constituted of two tuples. Blue areas represent the uncomplete subsets B_1 and B_3 while grey areas represents the subset B_2. t_3, t_4 and t_5 correspond to empty positions where new tuples should be added. (b) The database after concatenation of new tuples to the two previous ones. Blue areas represent the subsets B_1 and B_3 completed. B_4 is a new subset created after the addition of new tuple in the database. (Color figure online)

Protection on the Fly When Modifying an Attribute Value. Let us consider a protected database DB_e^w. If an attribute value $E[t_i.A_j, r_{ij}]$ is updated by its user, the CSP renews the database protection as follows:

1- The CSP decrypts J_t and permutes its records based on K_π.

2- The database records are ordered accordingly the J_t and the CSP finds the position of the tuple t_i as well as the subset partition that corresponds to the attribute value that is updated by its owner.

3- The CSP extracts the message bit embedded from the corresponding subset and re-inserts it once attribute value updated.

Notice that as such an update does not remove or add a new tuple, J_t is not modified.

Protection on the Fly When Suppressing One Tuple. Let us now consider a protected database DB_e^w and that a user modifies it by suppressing the tuple t_i. To update the protection, the CSP proceeds as follows:

1- It decrypts J_t and reorganizes its records. Then, based on J_t, it reorganizes the database and finds the position of the tuple t_i in the database.

2- The CSP extracts the message from the subsets concerned by the suppression and replaces it by an "empty" tuple, that is to say a tuple the encrypted attribute values of which are set to zero or any other predefined value.

3- The CSP re-watermarks subsets using the extracted message while distinguishing two distinct cases:

   a. If the suppressed tuple contains the centers of some subsets, as illustrated in the Fig. 5a, where t_i contains the center of B_l^w, then these subsets are re-watermarked by re-inserting the bit of the message by modifying with the help of iterative procedure presented in Sect. 3.1, one of the encrypted attributes of the tuples t_{i-1} and t_{i+1} out of the intersection of two subsets (as for example one of the attributes identified in B_l^w by a red cross in Fig. 5a).

   b. If the suppressed tuple t_i does not contain the centers of subsets, see Fig. 5b, then the message is extracted from these subsets and re-embedded into them by modifying their center element using iterative procedure presented in Sect. 3.1.

After message embedding, the CSP adds to J_t, the record R_{t_i} associated to the suppressed tuple t_i, and J_t is secretly permuted before is encrypted.

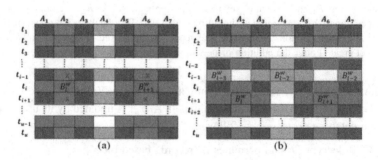

Fig. 5. (a) Update of the database protection in the case the suppressed tuple contains the centers of subsets. Red outlines represent subsets concerned by the suppression of the tuple t_i and red cross indicates encrypted attribute values to modify when re-watermarking the data subset. (b) Update of the database protection in the case the suppressed tuple do not contain centers of subsets. Red and green outlines represent subsets concerned by the suppression of the tuple t_i. (Color figure online)

Message Extraction and Integrity Verification. Let us consider a protected database $\widehat{DB_e^w}$ the CSP wants to verify the integrity. To do so, the CSP has to conduct following three steps:

1- The CSP decrypts and reorganizes J_t and accordingly reorganizes $\widehat{DB_e^w}$.
2- The CSP starts by verifying the latest tuple updated in the database. For each tuple t_i to verify, the CSP finds tuple's neighbors i.e. $\{t_{i-2}, t_{i-1}, t_{i+1}, t_{i+2}\}$.
3- The integrity verification is conducted according to the action applied to t_i and reported in J_t:
   a. If t_i has been added, only t_{i-1} and t_{i+1} are needed so as to compute the subset partition around to t_i. The CSP retrieves these tuples from J_t, identifies the subsets and extracts from them the message it next compares with the ones stored in J_t. Any difference will raise an alarm, indicating an unauthorized alteration of t_i, t_{i-1} or t_{i+1} and the position of the suspicious subsets.
   b. If t_i has been suppressed, the CSP adds an "empty" tuple so as to compute the subset partition. Two cases have to be considered depending on whether the suppressed tuple contains subset centers or not. In the former case, the CSP has to retrieve the tuples t_{i-1} and t_{i+1} (see Fig. 5a) while in second, it needs to access the tuples t_{i-2}, t_{i-1}, t_{i+1} and t_{i+2} (See Fig. 5b). Once subsets constituted, the CSP extract the message bits and compare them to the ones stored in J_t.

It is important to notice that the above procedure allows detecting the tampering of encrypted attributes. Other non-authorized modifications such as addition or suppression of tuples will be identified with the help of J_t. Indeed, added tuple will not be reorganized and will appear as extra data, while suppressed tuples will not be retrieved $\widehat{DB_e^w}$.

4 Experimental Results and Discussion

The proposed watermarking scheme was experimented on a relational database constituted of one table of 10 000 tuples issued from a real genetic database containing pieces of information related to genetic variants of 57 individuals. Each tuple or line containing information about a position in the genome. As shown in Table 2, each tuple is represented by eight attributes that are chromosome (*#chrom*), position (*pos*), identifier (*id*), reference (*ref*), alternative base(s) (*alt*), quality (*qual*), filter status (*filter*) and additional information (*info*). In the sequel, the attribute *pos*, or more clearly its encrypted version, is considered as the primary key as it uniquely identify one tuple.

Table 2. Sample view of the genetic database used in these experiments. One tuple containing information about a position in the genome

#chrom	*pos*	*id*	*ref*	*alt*	*qual*	*filter*	*Info*
21	9825790	.	C	CT, G	1130.64	PASS	CSQ=G
21	9825796	.	C	CGCGT	1179.35	PASS	CSQ=GCGT
21	9825809	.	G	A	1079.59	PASS	CSQ=A

This database was encrypted using Paillier cryptosystem with a public key encoded in 2048 bits so as to ensure a high level of security. In the case of static database watermarking, this table was divided into 11 390 subsets where a uniformly distributed binary message of 11 390 bits was inserted (see Sect. 3.1). The permutation of the journal table J_t records was conducted using the permutation technique based on indices vectors and described in [20]. In the sequel, we evaluate the performance of our scheme in terms of: computation complexity, modification detection and localization precision.

4.1   Computation Complexity

As shown in Sects. 2 and 3, message embedding and integrity verification processes are performed by the CSP on encrypted databases. Whatever the scheme, static or dynamic, message embedding consists in the insertion of one message bit into one subset of encrypted attributes. To do so, an iterative procedure is applied (see Sect. 3.1) such that the vth bit of the hash value corresponds to the bit of the message. At each iteration, the center of the subset (a Paillier encrypted attribute) is multiplied by the Paillier encrypted version of the value zero with a different random value (see iterative procedure in Sect. 3.1). Since the encryption of zero is of higher complexity than a modular multiplication, the computation complexity when watermarking one subset is bounded by $O(L)$ encryptions where L represents the number of iterations. Based on the fact, at each iteration there is one chance out of two that the bit hash value corresponds to the message bit, we thus have in average $L = 2$ with as consequence a watermarking computation complexity bounded by $O(2)$. Considering a static or dynamic database of n subsets, the computation complexity is thus bounded by $O(2n)$ encryptions. Regarding the verification process, its computation complexity mainly depends on the calculation of the subset hash values. However, such computation remains negligible compared to the homomorphic encryption operations. Table 3 provides the computation time for the

Table 3. Computation time for message insertion and integrity verification in the case of the protection of our test database.

Watermarking scheme	Computation step	Computation time
Watermarking of a static encrypted database	Database encryption	24 min 43 s
	Message embedding in the database	7 min 14 s
	Database integrity verification	8 s
Watermarking of a dynamic encrypted database	Message embedding if one tuple is added	0.1 s
	Message embedding if one tuple is suppressed	0.1 s
	Integrity verification for one added tuple	0.07 s
	Integrity verification for one suppressed tuple	0.09 s

message embedding and the integrity verification of our test database. Notice that our method was implemented in C/C++ with GMP library and all experiments were conducted using a machine equipped with 8 GB RAM running on Ubuntu 18.04 LTS.

4.2 Dynamic Database Watermarking and Attack Detection

As stated in Sect. 3.1, three kinds of attacks have to be considered: *"tuple suppression attack"*, *"tuple addition attack"* and *"Encrypted attribute value modification attack"*. They can be the result of an intrusion in the system or of transmission errors.

"Tuple suppression" **and** *"tuple addition"* **Attacks.** For sake of simplicity, let us consider the simple case where a hacker suppresses or adds one tuple in the database DB_e^w. As seen in Sect. 3.2, the integrity verification process relies on pieces information stored in the journal table J_t. In the case of an added tuple, the CSP will not find its identifier in J_t (see Table 1, Sect. 3.2) and will consequently raise an alarm. In the case of a suppressed tuple, the CSP will not be able to retrieve it in the database and will raise an alarm. In this case, in order to pursue the integrity verification of the whole database, the CSP just has to add an empty tuple in $\widehat{DB_e^w}$ (i.e. attacked version of DB_e^w). Based on the tuple identifiers stored in J_t, the detection rate of such attacks is of 100%.

"Encrypted attribute value modification attack". In this attack a non-authorized user conducts homomorphic operations so as to damage or falsify some database elements. Indeed, due to the fact data are homomorphically encrypted with the user public key; he/she can make some operations so as to modify the database attribute values.

One can distinguish different integrity level checking: the subset level and the database level. At the subset level, depending on the subset partitioning (Sect. 3.2 – Fig. 4), if the altered attribute value is not at the intersection of two subsets, the probability of not detecting such a modification is ½ due to the fact there is a half chance that the message bit inserted in the hash subset changes (see Sect. 3.1 – performance detection of SHA-2). If now the modified attribute belongs to two subsets then the probability of non-detection is ¼. In any case, the probability of non-detection in one subset is bounded by ½. At the database level, if a hacker modifies k subsets of DB_e^w, the probability of detection is bounded by $1 - (1/2)^k$ which converges rapidly to 1 with the increase of k.

To experimentally evaluate the performance of our method against this attack, a given percentage of attributes of our protected database DB_e^w were randomly modified: 0.001% (that is to say one attribute value has been modified in the database), 0.003% (three attribute values modified), 25%, 50%, 75%, and 100%. As it can be seen in Fig. 6 the successful detection of a tampered database depends on the number of modified attribute values. For instance, if a hacker only modifies one attribute value we have detection rate of 70%. We also compare in Fig. 6, the experimental detection rate with the theoretical limit. Experimental results provide better performance.

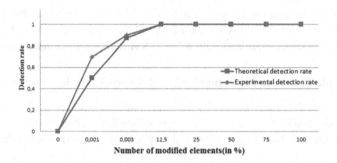

Fig. 6. Theoretical and experimental detection rates of our scheme in the case of the attribute modification attack. Experimental results are given in average.

4.3 Security Analysis

The proposed watermarking scheme allows the CSP to control the integrity of encrypted databases outsourced by different users. In the following, we discuss its security in terms of data confidentiality and data integrity. We first start by analyzing our scheme considering cryptographic attacks, which aims at breaking the data confidentiality, and then focus on watermarking attacks which aims at breaking the integrity protection of the database.

Encryption operations are performed using Paillier cryptosystem. The security analysis of this cryptosystem has been investigated in [18]. Because we only exploit its semantic security and homomorphic properties, there is no access to private parameters like user's data and private key. Even though, a hacker knows some watermarking parameters (e.g. K_w, partitioning), this gives him no additional information about the security parameters of the Paillier cryptosystem. Furthermore, the message embedding does not modify the clear data thanks to properties of homomorphic encryption. Therefore, the decryption operation is not compromised.

Regarding the integrity of the database, there are different attacks that a hacker can perform over the database. For a static database, the message embedding in DB_e and the integrity verification of DB_e^w depend on the watermarking key K_w. Without the knowledge of K_w, it is extremely difficult for an attacker to identify and reorganize the database subsets and find the location of the watermark. In fact, the partitioning and the location of the bits of the message M within the hash of the watermarked subset depend on K_w. Without this key, a hacker cannot distinguish the bits of M from the others. Even though he knows the structure of the message M (the way it is generated), he can only try an exhaustive search until he finds a valid message.

The security of dynamic database watermarking depends on the secret watermarking key K_w and on the security of the journal J_t. To ensure the confidentiality of J_t, this one is encrypted by the CSP which has to keep secret the encryption keys. Notice that if J_t is encrypted using a deterministic cryptosystem, some cipher-texts may leak information about the plain-texts. That will be the case of the first column of the J_t which indicates if a tuple has been added or suppressed. Such an information leak can support chosen plain-text attacks. Beyond, our scheme relies on a secret permutation algorithm of the records of J_t using a secret permutation key K_π so as to mask the chronological order of users' operations. Without K_π, it should be extremely difficult for an attacker to identify the chronological order of records in J_t and of the tuples in the database neither. In this work we use the algorithm issued from [20] the security analysis of which has been established. Anyway, even though a hacker knows the secret permutation key K_π, he cannot permute J_t because it is encrypted. Similarly, even if a hacker knows the secret decryption key being able to decrypt the J_t, without K_π he cannot conduct the inverse permutation operations and reorganize DB_e^w. He will thus not be able to modify the database while ensuring the correct detection of the watermark. As conclusion, in order to break the integrity of the journal table, a hacker should dispose of both the secret permutation key K_π and the secret journal decryption key of the CSP.

5 Conclusion

In this paper, we have proposed the first watermarking scheme which allows verifying the integrity of homomorphically encrypted databases taking advantage of the homomorphic and semantic security properties of such cryptosystems. Another main originality of this scheme is that it is dynamic, making possible to protect databases that are updated by their owners (e.g. tuple additions, tuple suppressions and encrypted attribute value modifications). Experimental results conducted on a genetic database show that the proposed scheme provides very high detection and localization performance capabilities; better alteration localization performance than watermarking schemes for clear data. Future works will focus on adapting our method on genetic data so as to ensure data integrity control when processing data.

Acknowledgements. This work has received a French government support granted to the Labex CominLabs and managed by the ANR in the "Investing for the future" program under reference ANR-10-LABX-07-01, and to the Labex GenMed, ANR-10-LABX-0013, through the project PrivGen.

References

1. Bellafqira, R., Coatrieux, G., Bouslimi, D., Quellec, G.: Content-based image retrieval in homomorphic encryption domain. In: 37th Annual International Conference of the IEEE Engineering in Medicine and Biology Society, pp. 2944–2947 (2015)
2. Mykletun, E., Narasimha, M., Tsudik, G.: Authentication and integrity in outsourced databases. ACM Trans. Storage **2**(2), 107–138 (2006)
3. Almulla, S.A., Yeun, C.Y.: Cloud computing security management. In: 2nd International Conference on Engineering Systems Management and Its Applications, pp. 1–7 (2010)
4. Agrawal, R., Kiernan, J.: Watermarking relational databases. In: Proceedings of the 28th International Conference on Very Large Data Bases (VLDB 2002), pp. 155–166 (2002)
5. Franco-Contreras, J., Coatrieux, G., Cuppens, F., Cuppens-Boulahia, N., Roux, C.: Robust lossless watermarking of relational databases based on circular histogram modulation. IEEE Trans. Inf. Forensics Secur. **9**(3), 397–410 (2014)

6. Wang, C., Wang, J., Zhou, M., Chen, G., Li, D.: ATBaM: an Arnold transform based method on watermarking relational data. In: International Conference on Multimedia and Ubiquitous Engineering, pp. 263–270. IEEE (2008)
7. Kamel, I., Kamel, K.: Toward protecting the integrity of relational databases. In: World Congress on Internet Security, pp. 258–261. IEEE (2011)
8. Prasannakumari, V.: A robust tamperproof watermarking for data integrity in relational databases. Res. J. Inf. Technol. 1(3), 115–121 (2009)
9. Guo, H., Li, Y., Liu, A., Jajodia, S.: A fragile watermarking scheme for detecting malicious modifications of database relations. Inf. Sci. 176, 1350–1378 (2006)
10. Chang, J.N, Wu, H.C.: Reversible fragile database watermarking technology using difference expansion based on SVR prediction. In: International Symposium on Computer, Consumer and Control, pp. 690–693 (2012)
11. Coatrieux, G, Chazard, E., Beuscart, R., Roux, C.: Lossless watermarking of categorical attributes for verifying medical data base integrity. In: 33rd IEEE Annual International Conference of the Engineering in Medicine and Biology Society, pp. 8195–8198 (2011)
12. Memon, N., Wong, P.: A buyer–seller watermarking protocol. IEEE Trans. Image Process. Image 10, 643–649 (2001)
13. Bouslimi, D., Coatrieux, G., Roux, C.: A joint watermarking/encryption algorithm for verifying medical image integrity and authenticity in both encrypted and spatial domains. In: IEEE Annual International Conference of the Engineering in Medicine and Biology Society, pp. 8066–8069 (2011)
14. Bouslimi, D., Bellafqira, R., Coatrieux, G.: Data hiding in homomorphically encrypted medical images for verifying their reliability in both encrypted and spatial domains. In: Engineering in Medicine and Biology Society. pp. 2496–2499. IEEE (2016)
15. Xiang, S., He, J.: Database authentication watermarking scheme in encrypted domain. IET Inf. Secur. 12(1), 42–51 (2017)
16. Chen, B., Wornell, G.W.: Quantization index modulation: a class of provably good methods for digital watermarking and information embedding. IEEE Trans. Inf. Theory 47, 1423–1443 (2001)
17. Xiao, L., Yen, I.L.: Security analysis for order preserving encryption schemes. In: 46th Annual Conference on Information Sciences and Systems (CISS), pp. 1–6 (2012)
18. Paillier, P.: Public-Key Cryptosystems Based on Composite Degree Residuosity Classes. In: Stern, Jacques (ed.) EUROCRYPT 1999. LNCS, vol. 1592, pp. 223–238. Springer, Heidelberg (1999). https://doi.org/10.1007/3-540-48910-X_16
19. Bakhtiari, S., Safavi-Naini, R., Pieprzyk, J.: Cryptographic hash functions: a survey, Technical report 95–09, Department of Computer Science, University of Wollongong (1995)
20. Radwan, A.G., AbdElHaleem, S.H., AbdElHafiz, S.K.: Symmetric encryption algorithms using chaotic and non-chaotic generators: a review. J. Adv. Res. 7(2), 193–208 (2016)

Reversible Data Hiding

Pixel-Value-Ordering Based Reversible Data Hiding with Adaptive Texture Classification and Modification

Bo Ou[1](✉), Xiaolong Li[2], Wei Li[3], and Yun-Qing Shi[4]

[1] College of Computer Science and Electronic Engineering, Hunan University,
Changsha 410082, China
oubo@hnu.edu.cn
[2] Institute of Information Science, Beijing Jiaotong University, Beijing 100044, China
[3] School of Mathematical Sciences, Capital Normal University, Beijing 100048, China
[4] Department of Electrical and Computer Engineering,
New Jersey Institute of Technology, Newark, USA

Abstract. Pixel-value-ordering (PVO) is a new technique for the high-fidelity reversible data hiding (RDH). It contains a process of sorting the pixels of a block by their values at first and then embedding into data bits into the maximum or minimum pixels of a block. In this paper, we propose to modify the pixel blocks differently according to how smooth they are, and embed the adequate number of bits into different types of blocks. The pixel blocks are first classified into five types based on the local complexity. The maximum pixels of the most smooth block will be embedded at most four bits, and the less smooth ones are embedded with a lower number of bits. The block classification is dynamically adjusted to achieve the adaptive embedding with the best trade-off between the capacity and the embedding distortion. Experimental results show that the proposed method can give a better performance over the previous PVO-based methods.

Keywords: Reversible data hiding · Block classification ·
Adaptive embedding

1 Introduction

Multimedia content protection becomes a hot topic since the 21th century, because the enormous exchange of information without protection may easily lead to the privacy leakage in the digital age. It includes several research issues such as copyright protection, covert communication and authentication and so on. One special technique designed for the image protection is reversible data hiding (RDH) [1,2]. Different from the conventional watermarking, RDH can not only extract the secret data and also losslessly recover the original medium. As such, it can be used for the sensitive image processing in the military, medical and judicial fields, in which the recovery of the original medium is desired as well as the hidden data.

C. D. Yoo et al. (Eds.): IWDW 2018, LNCS 11378, pp. 169–179, 2019.
https://doi.org/10.1007/978-3-030-11389-6_13

There are many algorithms that can be used to achieve a RDH process, including lossless compression [3, 4], difference expansion (DE) [5–9], histogram shifting (HS) [10–19], prediction-error expansion (PEE) [20–32] and integer-to-integer transform [33–35]. The key problem in RDH is to minimize the embedding distortion on the original image for a given capacity, in order to preserve a better visual quality of the marked image. The peak-signal-noise-ratio (PNSR) is used to measure the extent to which the marked image is similar to the original one. Usually, a high-fidelity marked image causes less attention from the malicious attackers and makes the data hiding more safe as a result. For this reason, many efforts are made in the research of high-fidelity RDH. For RDH, the "high-fidelity" means that a pixel is added or substracted by 1 at most, and the PSNR of the marked image is 48.13 dB at least.

Recently, a RDH technique based on pixel-value-ordering (PVO) is proposed in [36] to make high-fidelity embedding more efficient. In contrast with the previous RDH methods, the PVO-based method [36] modifies the image in a block-wise manner and predicts a maximum or a minimum pixel by the second largest or smallest pixels in the block. The prediction is determined by the intensity similarity between two pixels, but not dependent on their spatial distance. Specifically, the maximum (minimum) pixel of a block is predicted to derive a prediction-error, and then will be either increased (decreased) or unchanged to hide one bit. The prediction-error 0 should be kept unused, and the value 1 is employed to hide a bit. Because the marked maximum/minimum pixels will be larger/smaller than the original values after embedding, the sorting result of pixels in terms of the intensity can be invariant. This is the basis of PVO to guarantee the reversible extraction and recovery. After that, Peng *et al.* [37] proposed to utilize the spatial order between the pixels, and allow the prediction-error -1 be used for embedding. Ou *et al.* [38] proposed to modify k maximum- and minimum-valued pixels together to embed a bit. Qu *et al.* [39] proposed to use the sorted context for the pixel prediction and therefore developed the pixel-wise PVO. For the PVO-based methods, the most merit is the high-fidelity embedding performance yet a very simple computational complexity.

However, the PVO embedding has not been fully exploited by the exiting methods, because the smooth and the rough pixels are equally treated and embedded with the same amount of bits. For the most smooth block, there usually exist multiple maximum pixels. But in the previous work, they are either kept unchanged or modified together to embed only one bit. In fact, the multiple maximum pixels can be embedded with multiple bits, such that the performance can be enhanced. In this paper, we propose to first classify the blocks into five types and embed different amount of bits into blocks. Four noise level thresholds are employed to classify the blocks with their smoothness, and the multiple maximum/minimum pixels will be separately embedded with a bit. In this way, at most four bits will be embedded into the maximum/minmum pixels of a block, and the derived capacity is much higher than that of the conventional PVO methods [36–38]. To ensure the accurate recovery, both the intensity and spatial orders between pixels are utilized. Moreover, the adaptive modification is achieved by dynamically adjusting the four thresholds in order to achieve the minimum distortion-versus-capacity value. The experimental results demonstrate that the proposed method is better than some of the state-of-the-art methods [22, 36–38].

The rest of paper is organized as follows. Section 2 describes the proposed method, and Sect. 3 gives the experimental results to verify the superiority of the proposed method. Section 4 concludes this paper.

2   Proposed Method

In this section, the proposed PVO-based method is presented. We first describe the basic embedding/extraction modification on a block, and then give the dynamical threshold selection to achieve the adaptive embedding.

2.1   Data Embedding and Extraction on the Maximum Pixels

Unlike the conventional predictors which determine the similarity of two pixels by their spatial distance, PVO-based prediction measures the similarity by their intensities. The PVO-based prediction defines the optimal context pixel only by the intensity, and can obtain a better prediction for various cases. Similar to the other PVO-based methods, we use the maximum and the minimum pixels for data embedding. As the modifications are similar for the maximum and the minimum pixels, we first describe the dynamical data embedding on the maximum pixels of different blocks for simplicity. The detailed data embedding is given as follows.

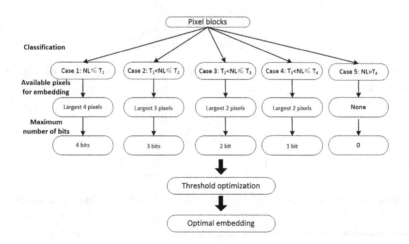

Fig. 1. The proposed block classification and the corresponding modification manner for each category.

Suppose the cover image I is partitioned into the non-overlapped blocks $\{B_1, ..., B_N\}$ with the size of $a \times b$, and the pixels of a block are scanned in a given spatial order as $(p_1, ..., p_n)$, where $n = a \times b$. To obtain the PVO of these pixels, they are sorted by the intensity in an ascending order as $(x_{\sigma(1)}, ..., x_{\sigma(n)})$, where $\sigma : \{1, ..., n\} \rightarrow \{1, ..., n\}$ is the unique one-to-one mapping such that $x_{\sigma(1)} \leq \cdots \leq x_{\sigma(n)}$, $\sigma(i) < \sigma(j)$ if $x_{\sigma(i)} = x_{\sigma(j)}$ and $i < j$. Then, we have

$$x_{\sigma(1)} \leq x_{\sigma(2)} \leq \cdots \leq x_{\sigma(n)} \tag{1}$$

Suppose the noise level of the block B_k is NL_k, where the noise level is calculated as the sum of the vertical and horizontal absolute differences in the local context. The detail computation could be referred to [38]. Then, we employ four noise level thresholds, namely, $\{T_1, T_2, T_3, T_4\}$ ($T_1 \leq T_2 \leq T_3 \leq T_4$) to classify the modification on a block into four cases as shown in Fig. 1, and each case will be differently treated. For a block B_k, the modification manner on the maximum pixels is determined as below.

- Case 1: If $NL_k \leq T_1$, we use the largest four pixels (i.e., $x_{\sigma(n)}, ..., x_{\sigma(n-3)}$) for data embedding and compute three prediction-errors $(d_{max}^1, ..., d_{max}^4)$ as

$$\begin{cases} d_{max}^1 = x_u - x_{\sigma(n-4)} \\ d_{max}^2 = x_v - x_{\sigma(n-4)} \\ d_{max}^3 = x_w - x_{\sigma(n-4)} \\ d_{max}^4 = x_z - x_{\sigma(n-4)} \end{cases} \tag{2}$$

where $u, v, w, z \in \{\sigma(n-3), \sigma(n-2), \sigma(n-1), \sigma(n))\}$ and $u \geq v \geq w \geq z$. The marked prediction-error $\tilde{d}_{max}^h$ is calculated as

$$\tilde{d}_{max}^h = \begin{cases} d_{max}^h, & \text{if } d_{max}^h = 0 \\ d_{max}^h + b, & \text{if } d_{max}^h = 1 \\ d_{max}^h + 1, & \text{if } d_{max}^h > 1 \end{cases} \tag{3}$$

where the index $h \in \{1, ..., 4\}$ and $b \in \{0, 1\}$ is a binary bit. Consequently, the marked maximum pixel i.e., $\tilde{x}_{\sigma(n)}$ is accordingly changed to

$$\begin{cases} \tilde{x}_u = x_{\sigma(n-4)} + \tilde{d}_{max}^1 \\ \tilde{x}_v = x_{\sigma(n-4)} + \tilde{d}_{max}^2 \\ \tilde{x}_w = x_{\sigma(n-4)} + \tilde{d}_{max}^3 \\ \tilde{x}_z = x_{\sigma(n-4)} + \tilde{d}_{max}^4 \end{cases} \tag{4}$$

In this case, at most four bits can be embedded into the maximum pixels.
- Case 2: If $T_1 < NL_k \leq T_2$, we use the largest three pixels (i.e., $x_{\sigma(n)}, x_{\sigma(n-1)}, x_{\sigma(n-2)}$) for data embedding and compute three prediction-errors $(d_{max}^1, d_{max}^2, d_{max}^3)$ as

$$\begin{cases} d_{max}^1 = x_u - x_{\sigma(n-3)} \\ d_{max}^2 = x_v - x_{\sigma(n-3)} \\ d_{max}^3 = x_w - x_{\sigma(n-3)} \end{cases} \tag{5}$$

where
$$\begin{cases} u = \max(\sigma(n-2), \sigma(n-1), \sigma(n)) \\ v = \min(\sigma(n-2), \sigma(n-1), \sigma(n)) \\ w = \mathrm{med}(\sigma(n-2), \sigma(n-1), \sigma(n)) \end{cases} \tag{6}$$

and $\max(\cdot)$, $\min(\cdot)$ and $\mathrm{med}(\cdot)$ return the maximum, medium and minimum values in the set, respectively. The marked prediction-error $\hat{d}^h_{max}$ is calculated using (11), where the index $h \in \{1, 2, 3\}$. Consequently, the marked maximum pixel *i.e.*, $\tilde{x}_{\sigma(n)}$ is accordingly changed to

$$\begin{cases} \tilde{x}_u = x_{\sigma(n-3)} + \tilde{d}^1_{\max} \\ \tilde{x}_v = x_{\sigma(n-3)} + \tilde{d}^2_{\max} \\ \tilde{x}_w = x_{\sigma(n-3)} + \tilde{d}^3_{\max} \end{cases} . \tag{7}$$

In this case, at most three bits can be embedded into the maximum pixels.
- Case 3: If $T_2 < NL_k \leq T_3$, the largest two pixels (i.e., $x_{\sigma(n)}, x_{\sigma(n-1)}$) are considered for data embedding, and the prediction-errors are calculated as

$$\begin{cases} d^1_{\max} = x_u - x_{\sigma(n-2)} \\ d^2_{\max} = x_v - x_{\sigma(n-2)} \end{cases} \tag{8}$$

The marked prediction-error is obtained using (11), with $h \in \{1, 2\}$. The marked pixels are given as

$$\begin{cases} \tilde{x}_u = x_{\sigma(n-2)} + \tilde{d}^1_{\max} \\ \tilde{x}_v = x_{\sigma(n-2)} + \tilde{d}^2_{\max} \end{cases} . \tag{9}$$

- Case 4: If $T_3 < NL_k \leq T_4$, only the maximum pixel is used, and this case is the same to the conventional PVO [36]. For simplicity, we omit the description for simplicity.
- Case 5: If $NL_k > T_4$, the block is regarded as "rough" and will be kept unmodified during the embedding.

The data embedding on the multiple minimum pixels in a block is similar to the case of maximum pixels. We simply take the case of modifying three pixels for illustration. For the three smallest pixels be $(x_{\sigma(1)}, x_{\sigma(2)}, x_{\sigma(3)})$, the prediction-errors are calculated as

$$\begin{cases} d^1_{\min} = x_u - x_{\sigma(4)} \\ d^2_{\min} = x_v - x_{\sigma(4)} \\ d^3_{\min} = x_w - x_{\sigma(4)} \end{cases} \tag{10}$$

and the marked ones are modified as

$$\tilde{d}^h_{\min} = \begin{cases} d^h_{\min}, & \text{if } d^h_{\min} = 0 \\ d^h_{\min} - b, & \text{if } d^h_{\min} = -1 \\ d^h_{\min} - 1, & \text{if } d^h_{\min} < -1 \end{cases} \tag{11}$$

The blocks are modified one by one according to the above modification, until the capacity is fulfilled.

At decoders, by using the same thresholds $\{T_1, T_2, T_3, T_4\}$, one can retrieve the same classification, and recover the original pixels and the hidden data correctly. The recovery process on a block is inverse to that of data embedding. We take the **Case 2** of maximum pixels for example. We select the largest three marked pixels (i.e., $\tilde{x}_{\sigma(n)}, \tilde{x}_{\sigma(n-1)}, \tilde{x}_{\sigma(n-2)}$), and sort them by their local spatial order by using (6). Note that the ranking result of the marked values $(\tilde{x}_u, \tilde{x}_v, \tilde{x}_w)$ is the same to (x_u, x_v, x_w) for each block. Then, calculate the prediction-errors and one data bit is extracted as 0 and 1 for the cases of $\tilde{d}^h_{\min} = 1$ and $\tilde{d}^h_{\min} = 2$, respectively. The original pixels are obtained using the d^h_{max}.

2.2   Parameter Selection

In our method, the optimal block size $a \times b$ and the optimal thresholds should be determined according to the capacity and the image content. Generally, the larger block size produces a higher PSNR but a lower capacity. So, the embedding distortion can be tuned by adjusting the block size. It is allowed to trade off the capacity for the embedding distortion reduction. However, the relation between the block classification and the embedding performance is not implicit. So, to solve the optimization, for each block size, we exhaustively check all the candidate combinations of $(T_1, ..., T_4)$ and select the best one. The optimal parameter set $(T_1^*, T_2^*, T_3^*, T_4^*)$ is the one that minimizes the distortion while satisfying a given capacity EC, and is determined as

$$
\begin{cases}
(T_1^*, T_2^*, T_3^*, T_4^*) = \underset{T_1, T_2, T_3, T_4}{\arg\min} \ D_1(T_1) + D_2(T_1, T_2) + D_3(T_2, T_3) + D_4(T_3, T_4) \\
\text{subject to} \ \ C_1(T_1) + C_2(T_1, T_2) + C_3(T_2, T_3) + C_4(T_3, T_4) \geq EC
\end{cases}
$$
$$(12)$$

where the functions of $D_1(T_1)$, $D_2(T_1, T_2)$, $D_3(T_2, T_3)$ and $D_4(T_3, T_4)$ estimate respectively the distortion on the blocks with $NL \leq T_1$, $T_1 < NL \leq T_2$, $T_2 < NL \leq T_3$ and $T_3 < NL \leq T_4$, and the function $C_1, ...C_4$ estimate the corresponding capacities.

3   Experimental Results

In this section, we compare the embedding performance of the proposed method with four state-of-the-art methods of Sachnev et al. [22], Li et al. [36], Peng et al. [37] and Ou et al. [38]. We mainly focus on the PSNR comparison of low capacity embedding as the PVO-based methods usually yield a higher visual quality but provide a limited capacity. Among the four methods, [22] is a classical PEE-based method, and modifies the pixels individually to achieve a high capacity. The methods [36–38] are the conventional PVO-based algorithms, and can guarantee the high-fidelity data embedding for low capacity cases. The experimental comparisons are tested on the eight standard gray-scale images, including Lena, Baboon, Airplane, Barbara, Elaine, Boat, Lake and Peppers images, each of which has the size of 512×512. The pixel block size of our method is set as $a \times b$ with $a, b \in \{2, 3, 4, 5\}$. So, there are 15 block sizes, and the number of pixels ranges from 4 to 25.

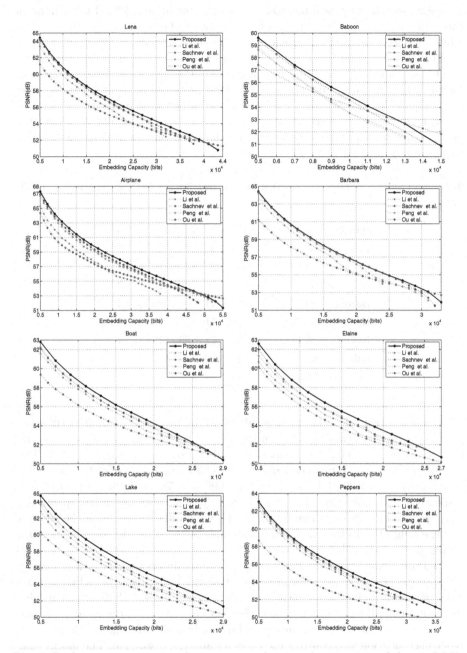

Fig. 2. Performance comparison between our scheme and some state-of-the-art RDH works.

The performance comparison of distortion-capacity curve is given in Fig. 2. It is seen that the proposed method can provide the highest PSNR value in most cases. In addition, because the maximum capacity of a block can be increased to 4 bits, the proposed method provides a larger capacity than the compared PVO-based methods. Since the PVO prediction cannot work well in edge area, the PVO-based method usually performs worse on the image consisted of complex textures. For instance, on Baboon image, the proposed method is less effective than [22] for the capacities of 14,000 and 15,000 bits. Compared with the conventional PVO-based methods [36–38], the proposed method usually gives a better performance for the relatively larger capacity. The biggest PSNR gain can be found on the medium range of the curve.

Table 1. Optimal parameter selection on the test images for the capacity of 10,000 bits.

Images	PSNR (dB)	T_1	T_2	T_3	T_4	n_1	n_2
Lena	60.82	34	48	73	98	5	3
Baboon	54.83	151	232	247	616	4	3
Airplane	63.68	17	19	21	29	3	3
Barbara	60.72	29	41	64	86	3	4
Boat	58.75	69	71	97	160	3	4
Elaine	58.11	57	62	89	142	3	3
Lake	60.10	41	56	62	101	3	3
Peppers	59.37	49	73	107	149	5	3

To demonstrate the adaptive embedding of the proposed method, we observe the parameters selection for different capacities and the images. Particularly, the first comparison is done for a capacity of 10,000 bits as shown in Table 1. The average PSNRs of the proposed method is 59.55, and the results for the PVO-based methods of [36,37] and Ou *et al.* [38] are 58.30, 58.88 and 59.17 dB, respectively. The average gain of ours are 1.25, 0.67 and 0.38 dB, respectively. The performance gains is mainly due to that we differently utilize the smooth and the rough blocks for embedding, and implement a more flexible modification on image than the other methods.

In Table 2, we investigate how the optimal parameters vary with the capacity. For our method, the best performance trade-off is achieved by adjusting the block size and the block classification. We can see in Table 2 that as the capacity increases, a small block size is chosen. For low capacity case, the large block size makes the prediction more accurate, and thus a better performance. Besides, the block classification also controls the capacity and the distortion. The blocks that are labeled as "smooth" will be averagely embedded more bits per block than the rough ones. So, including more blocks as the smooth category will increase the capacity. However, the average distortion is also increased, especially for a high capacity embedding, most of blocks have to undertake the maximum capacity.

Table 2. Optimal parameters of the proposed method from the capacity of 10,000 to 40,000 bits, where the test image is Lena.

Capacity (bits)	PSNR (dB)	T_1	T_2	T_3	T_4	n_1	n_2
10,000	60.82	34	48	73	98	5	3
20,000	56.94	38	55	75	107	5	2
30,000	54.28	67	69	97	180	5	2
40,000	51.81	85	85	154	254	3	3

4   Conclusions

In this paper, we propose a new pixel-value-ordering (PVO) based method to dynamically embedding data bits into the multiple largest and smallest pixels in a block according its smoothness. By separately modifying the largest/smallest pixels, a smooth block can be at most embedded with eight bits. The smoother a block is, the more bits are embedded into it. Four thresholds are employed to classify the blocks into four categories and each category adopts a different modification manner. Since a more flexible modification is designed, the overall embedding performance can be further enhanced. Experimental results on the standard images verify the proposed method is better than the previous PVO-based methods [36–38] as well as one other classical method [22].

Acknowledgement. This work was supported by the National Science Foundation of China (No. 61502160), the Hunan Provincial Natural Science Foundation of China under grant No. 2018JJ3078 and the Fundamental Research Funds for the Central Universities.

References

1. Caldelli, R., Filippini, F., Becarelli, R.: Reversible watermarking techniques: an overview and a classification. EURASIP J. Inf. Secur. **2010**, 2 (2010)
2. Li, B., He, J., Huang, J., Shi, Y.Q.: A survey on image steganography and steganalysis. J. Inf. Hiding Multimedia Signal Process. **2**(2), 142–172 (2011)
3. Fridrich, J., Goljan, M., Du, R.: Lossless data embedding - new paradigm in digital watermarking. EURASIP J. Appli. Signal Process. **2002**(2), 185–196 (2002)
4. Celik, M.U., Sharma, G., Tekalp, A.M.: Lossless watermarking for image authentication: A new framework and an implementation. IEEE Trans. Image Process. **15**(4), 1042–1049 (2006)
5. Tian, J.: Reversible data embedding using a difference expansion. IEEE Trans. Circuits Syst. Video Technol. **13**(8), 890–896 (2003)
6. Alattar, A.M.: Reversible watermark using the difference expansion of a generalized integer transform. IEEE Trans. Image Process. **13**(8), 1147–1156 (2004)
7. Tai, W.L., Yeh, C.M., Chang, C.C.: Reversible data hiding based on histogram modification of pixel differences. IEEE Trans. Circuits Syst. Video Technol. **19**(6), 906–910 (2009)

8. Hu, Y., Lee, H.K., Li, J.: DE-based reversible data hiding with improved overflow location map. IEEE Trans. Circuits Syst. Video Technol. **19**(2), 250–260 (2009)
9. Li, X., Zhang, W., Gui, X., Yang, B.: A novel reversible data hiding scheme based on two-dimensional difference-histogram modification. IEEE Trans. Inf. Forens. Secur. **8**(7), 1091–1100 (2013)
10. Ni, Z., Shi, Y.Q., Ansari, N., Su, W.: Reversible data hiding. IEEE Trans. Circuits Syst. Video Technol. **16**(3), 354–362 (2006)
11. Lee, S.K.: Suh, Y.H., Ho, Y.S.: Reversible image authentication based on watermarking. In: IEEE International Conference on Multimedia and Expo, pp. 1321–1324 (2006)
12. Fallahpour, M.: Reversible image data hiding based on gradient adjusted prediction. IEICE Electron. Express **5**(20), 870–876 (2008)
13. Luo, L., Chen, Z., Chen, M., Zeng, X., Xiong, Z.: Reversible image watermarking using interpolation technique. IEEE Trans. Inf. Forens. Secur. **5**(1), 187–193 (2010)
14. Li, Y.C., Yeh, C.M., Chang, C.C.: Data hiding based on the similarity between neighboring pixels with reversibility. Digital Signal Process. **20**(4), 1116–1128 (2010)
15. Wu, H.T., Huang, J.: Reversible image watermarking on prediction errors by efficient histogram modification. Signal Process. **92**(12), 3000–3009 (2012)
16. Tsai, Y.Y., Tsai, D.S., Liu, C.L.: Reversible data hiding scheme based on neighboring pixel differences. Digital Signal Process. **23**(3), 919–927 (2013)
17. Li, X., Li, B., Yang, B., Zeng, T.: General framework to histogram-shifting-based reversible data hiding. IEEE Trans. Image Process. **22**(6), 2181–2191 (2013)
18. Pan, Z., Hu, S., Ma, X., Wang, L.: Reversible data hiding based on local histogram shifting with multilayer embedding. J. Vis. Commun. Image Represent. **31**, 64–74 (2015)
19. Wu, H.T., Huang, J., Shi, Y.Q.: A reversible data hiding method with contrast enhancement for medical images. J. Vis. Commun. Image Represent. **31**, 146–153 (2015)
20. Thodi, D.M., Rodriguez, J.J.: Expansion embedding techniques for reversible watermarking. IEEE Trans. Image Process. **16**(3), 721–730 (2007)
21. Hong, W., Chen, T.S., Shiu, C.W.: Reversible data hiding for high quality images using modification of prediction errors. J. Syst. Softw. **82**(11), 1833–1842 (2009)
22. Sachnev, V., Kim, H.J., Nam, J., Suresh, S., Shi, Y.Q.: Reversible watermarking algorithm using sorting and prediction. IEEE Trans. Circuits Syst. Video Technol. **19**(7), 989–999 (2009)
23. Gao, X., An, L., Yuan, Y., Tao, D., Li, X.: Lossless data embedding using generalized statistical quantity histogram. IEEE Trans. Circuits Syst. Video Technol. **21**(8), 1061–1070 (2011)
24. Li, X., Yang, B., Zeng, T.: Efficient reversible watermarking based on adaptive prediction-error expansion and pixel selection. IEEE Trans. Image Process. **20**(12), 3524–3533 (2011)
25. Coltuc, D.: Improved embedding for prediction-based reversible watermarking. IEEE Trans. Inf. Forens. Secur. **6**(3), 873–882 (2011)
26. Lin, Y.C.: Reversible data-hiding for progressive image transmission. Signal Process. Image Commun. **26**(10), 628–645 (2011)
27. Hong, W.: Adaptive reversible data hiding method based on error energy control and histogram shifting. Optics Commun. **285**(2), 101–108 (2012)
28. Ou, B., Li, X., Zhao, Y., Ni, R.: Reversible data hiding based on PDE predictor. J. Syst. Softw. **86**(10), 2700–2709 (2013)

29. Coatrieux, G., Pan, W., Cuppens-Boulahia, N., Cuppens, F., Roux, C.: Reversible watermarking based on invariant image classification and dynamic histogram shifting. IEEE Trans. Inf. Forens. Secur. **8**(1), 111–120 (2013)

30. Qin, C., Chang, C.C., Huang, Y.H., Liao, L.T.: An inpainting-assisted reversible steganographic scheme using histogram shifting mechanism. IEEE Trans. Circuits Syst. Video Techn. **23**(7), 1109–1118 (2013)

31. Ou, B., Li, X., Zhao, Y., Ni, R., Shi, Y.Q.: Pairwise prediction-error expansion for efficient reversible data hiding. IEEE Trans. Image Process. **22**(12), 5010–5021 (2013)

32. Li, X., Zhang, W., Gui, X., Yang, B.: Efficient reversible data hiding based on multiple histograms modification. IEEE Trans. Inf. Forens. Secur. **10**(9), 2016–2027 (2015)

33. Coltuc, D., Chassery, J.M.: Very fast watermarking by reversible contrast mapping. IEEE Signal Process. Lett. **14**(4), 255–258 (2007)

34. Wang, X., Li, X., Yang, B., Guo, Z.: Efficient generalized integer transform for reversible watermarking. IEEE Signal Process. Lett. **17**(6), 567–570 (2010)

35. Coltuc, D.: Low distortion transform for reversible watermarking. IEEE Trans. Image Process. **21**(1), 412–417 (2012)

36. Li, X., Li, J., Li, B., Yang, B.: High-fidelity reversible data hiding scheme based on pixel-value-ordering and prediction-error expansion. Signal Process. **93**(1), 198–205 (2013)

37. Peng, F., Li, X., Yang, B.: Improved pvo-based reversible data hiding. Digital Signal Process. **25**, 255–265 (2014)

38. Ou, B., Li, X., Zhao, Y., Ni, R.: Reversible data hiding using invariant pixel-value-ordering and prediction-error expansion. Signal Process. Image Commun. **29**(7), 760–772 (2014)

39. Qu, X., Kim, H.J.: Pixel-based pixel value ordering predictor for high-fidelity reversible data hiding. Signal Process. **111**, 249–260 (2015)

Reversible Data Hiding in Encrypted Images Based on Image Partition and Spatial Correlation

Chang Song[1]([✉]), Yifeng Zhang[1,2,3], and Guojun Lu[4]

[1] School of Information Science and Engineering, Southeast University,
Nanjing 210096, People's Republic of China
songchangseu@163.com, yfz@seu.edu.cn
[2] Nanjing Institute of Communications Technologies,
Nanjing 211100, People's Republic of China
[3] State Key Laboratory for Novel Software Technology, Nanjing University,
Nanjing 210093, People's Republic of China
[4] Faculty of Science and Technology, Federation University Australia,
Melbourne, Australia
guojun.lu@federation.edu.au

Abstract. Recently, more and more attention is paid to reversible data hiding (RDH) in encrypted images because of its better protection of privacy compared with traditional RDH methods directly operated in original images. In several RDH algorithms, prediction-error expansion (PEE) is proved to be superior to other methods in terms of embedding capacity and distortion of marked image and multiple histograms modification (MHM) can realize adaptive selection of expansion bins which depends on image content in the modification of a sequence of histograms. Therefore, in this paper, we propose an efficient RDH method in encrypted images by combining PEE and MHM, and design corresponding mode of image partition. We first divide the image into three parts: W (for embedding secret data), B (for embedding the least significant bit(LSB) of W) and G (for generating prediction-error histograms). Then, we apply PEE and MHM to embed the LSB of W to reserve space for secret data. Next, we encrypt the image and change the LSB of W to realize the embedding of secret data. In the process of extraction, the reversibility of image and secret data can be guaranteed. The utilization of correlation between neighbor pixels and embedded order decided by the smoothness of pixel in part W contribute to the performance of our method. Compared to the existing algorithms, experimental results show that the proposed method can reduce distortion to the image at given embedding capacity especially at low embedding capacity.

Keywords: Reversible data hiding · Encrypted images ·
Prediction-error expansion · Multiple histograms modification

© Springer Nature Switzerland AG 2019
C. D. Yoo et al. (Eds.): IWDW 2018, LNCS 11378, pp. 180–194, 2019.
https://doi.org/10.1007/978-3-030-11389-6_14

1   Introduction

The reversible data hiding is an emerging technology that uses the redundancy of the carrier to embed secret information and ensures the reversibility of the carrier and hidden information. Nowadays, digital images are used in reversible data hiding which has a wide range of applications in the field of military images, medical images and court certification.

In the past decades, a plenty of RDH algorithms have been proposed. These techniques can be roughly divided into three categories: lossless compression appending scheme [1,2], difference expansion [3] and histogram modification [4]. Among them, the histogram-based ones have been widely investigated because of its high embedding capacity and low degree of distortion. This type of methods can control the embedding distortion and has a sufficient embedding capacity. The method called PEE was first proposed by Thodi and Rodriguez [5], which can contribute a more sharply prediction-error histogram and higher PSNR value because of the more peak points for embedding and less shifted points for the guarantee of reversibility. Then, some attempts on PEE have been made and realize higher embedding capacity and lower distortion of original image [6–8].

Generally, these RDH methods are useful for embedding secret data into images that are open to the data-hider. However, in some application, the image owner may be unwilling to disclose the image content to the data-hider. For example, the private information of patient must not be revealed to the person who embeds data into medical images, while the original image contain information of patient must be perfectly recovered and the embedded data completely extracted on the receiver end. In this case, the channel provider has to append additional data to the encrypted version of the original image.

Many RDH method in encrypted images have been proposed in recent years. In [9], Zhang first proposed a RDH algorithm in encrypted image: the original image is encrypted by a stream cipher, then one bit of the secret data is embedded into an image block by flipping the 3 least signification bits of half pixels within the block. Data extraction and image recovering are accomplished by a smoothness measurement function of the recovered image. In [10], an improved measurement of smoothness is proposed to make full use of all pixels in the image, and a side match scheme is proposed to further decrease the error rate of extracted bits, both of which have improve the embedding capacity of the basic data hiding scheme in the encrypted image proposed in [9]. In [11], Li et al. improve the algorithm by using a full embedding strategy to achieve a large embedding rate. These methods both rely on the spatial correlation of original image to extract secret data, which mean that the encrypted image should be decrypted first before data extraction. For solving this problem, separable RDH method in encrypted images was proposed. Zhang improved his own method in [12], emptied out space for data embedding following the idea of compressing encrypted images. Furthermore, in [13], Ma et al. proposed a new framework different from previous method by vacating room before encryption. To do this, LSB of some pixels are first embedded into other pixels using a tradition RDH method [14], and the image is then encrypted. As a result, position of these LSB in the encrypted image can be used for embedding information with the data-hider.

The algorithm in [13] is a creative one which combine traditional RDH method with the encrypted domain of image. By using traditional RDH method, the performance of RDH method in encrypted image will not only be increase in embedding capacity, but also have a large promotion in the quality of marked images. In several traditional RDH methods, PEE has become the most effective method because the local correlation of a larger neighborhood is exploited. Moreover, in [8], Li et al. proposed a new embedding mechanism called multiple histograms modification based on complexity measurement which can adaptively select expansion bins in each histogram considering the image content. For each pixel, its prediction value and complexity measurement are computed according to its context, and multiple histograms are generated for different complexity levels. That is to say, the pixels with a given complexity are collected together to generate a prediction-error histogram, and by varying the complexity measurement to cover the whole image, a sequence of histograms can be derived. The key of this method is that based on an estimation of embedding distortion, the expansion bins can be effectively determined such that the distortion is minimized which will contribute to the improvement of PSNR. Inspired by the framework in [13] and the advantage of PEE and MHM, we design a new RDH method in encrypted image which can further improve PSNR of marked decrypted image by combining PEE and MHM, at the same time, give a new way of image partition so that can ensure the reversibility of algorithm.

The rest of paper is organized as follows. Section 2 briefly introduces the previous method proposed in [13]. The novel method is presented in Sect. 3 followed by Sect. 4 on experimental results. Some conclusions are drawn in Sect. 5.

2   Previous Work

In [13], Ma et al. proposed a new reversible data hiding framework in encrypted images. In this framework, the content owner first reserves enough space on original image and then converts the image into its encrypted version with the encrypted key. Now, the data embedding process in encrypted images is reversible because the data hider only need to embed the secret data in the

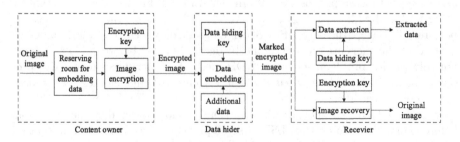

Fig. 1. New framework proposed in [13]

spare space previous emptied out. The data extraction and image recovery are identical to that of traditional framework. This new framework is shown in Fig. 1.

In [13], the main idea of reversing space for embedding is to divide the image into two part A and B. Then, the LSB of part A are reversibly embedded into part B with a standard RDH algorithm in [14] so that the LSB of part A can be used for accommodating messages. At last, the arranged image is encrypted to generate its final version. The goal of image partition is to construct a smoother area B so that the RDH algorithms can achieve a better performance. According to the size of the to-be-embedded data l, compute first-order smoothness of every several rows with a smoothness evaluated function to get the value f. Highest f relates to blocks which contain relatively more complex textures. The content owner select the block with highest f to be part A, and put it to the front of the image concatenated by the rest part B with fewer textured areas as shown in Fig. 2.

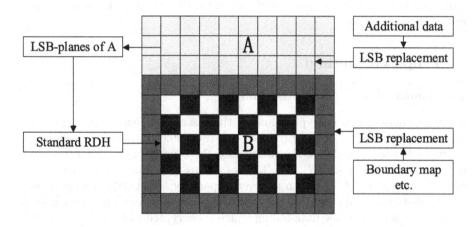

Fig. 2. Illustration of image partition and embedding process in [13]

In the process of reversing space, the algorithm in [13] is utilized which is based on the prediction-error expansion and double-pairs histogram modification. After rearranged self-embedded image, the encrypted image E can be calculated through exclusive-or operation.

Once the data hider get the encrypted image E, he can embed data into part A by replace the LSB of this part and further encrypted additional data according to data hiding key to formulate marked encrypted image denoted by E'. Since data extraction is completely independent from image decryption, receiver can extract data from encrypted images or decrypted images which depend on practical applications.

According to [13], in the process of choosing the LSB of some pixels, the smoothness of image block is utilized. However, there are two disadvantage in this method:

1. Only through the exchange of specified block and remaining part can the algorithm be reversible. The receiver can not acquire the marked decrypted image directly to extract additional data from part A only if he knows the start row and end row of part A where this two parameters are embedded in the marginal area of B.
2. The spatial correlation between specified block and remaining part is neglected. Ma et al. treat these two different parts as disconnected parts. Although part A contains a more complex textures, but synthetic relationship between part A and B is not clear in the process of embedding. On the other hand, by utilizing the traditional RDH method in [14], on account of that part B is consist of two separated part from original image, the spatial correlation will certainly not be better utilized.

In next section, we take the integrality of the image as starting point and divide the image into several interlaced parts, which can make better use of spatial correlation between pixels and reduce the distortion in the process of self reversible data hiding.

3   Proposed Method

3.1   Generation of Encrypted Image

For the generation of encrypted image, three steps are executed to generate the encrypted image: image partition, self-reversible data hiding and image encryption. First, we divide the image into three part: black part (B), white part (W) and gray part (G). The LSB of W are reversibly embedded into B with a standard RDH algorithm to reverse space for secret data. The gray part is regarded as a predicted area for B in the process of reversible data hiding. At last, the self-reversible-data-hiding image is encrypted to its to-be-embedded version.

Image Partition. According to this new mode of image partition, we can better utilize the correlation between neighbor pixels, which can reduce the distortion in the process of reversing space for secret data and improve PSNR of the marked decrypted image.

In the state-of-arts RDH methods, PEE has a better performance than some traditional algorithms such as HM and PD. The key of PEE methods is the generation of histograms. In [6], Sachnev proposed a new RDH framework: double layer RDH and rhombus prediction to acquire a more sharply distributed histogram with higher peak point. Inspired by this algorithm, except for the last row and last column, we first divide the image into two parts: white pixels with their indices satisfying $mod(i + j, 2) = 0$ and gray pixels with their indices satisfying $mod(i + j, 2) = 1$. For the integrality of the process of image recovery, the neighbor pixels of to-be-predicted pixel should be same to those in the process of generating histogram. Therefore, we divide the white part in two parts: the pixels in even-numbered rows (B) as to-be-predicted pixels and the pixels in odd-numbered rows (W), as shown in Fig. 3. The gray part in the original image (G) is used for the prediction of B.

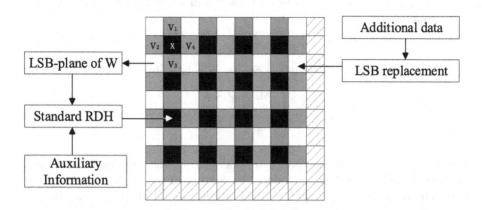

Fig. 3. Illustration of image partition and embedding process

Self-reversible Data Hiding to Reserve Space. The goal of self-reversible embedding is to embed the LSB of part W to part B by employing traditional RDH algorithm. In this part, we mainly employ the method combined with PEE and MHM to show the process of self-embedding.

Rhombus Prediction and Prediction-Error Expansion. Let x from part B be the to-be-predicted pixel value, v_1, v_2, v_3, v_4 from part G be the four neighbor pixels of pixel x, as illustrated in Fig. 3. The predicted value of x is

$$\hat{x} = \lfloor \frac{v_1 + v_2 + v_3 + v_4}{4} \rfloor \tag{1}$$

The prediction error of rhombus prediction e is defined as

$$e = x - \hat{x} \tag{2}$$

According to the embedding capacity, we assume that a and b are two to-be-expanded bins selected from the prediction-error. Without loss of generality, we assume that $a < b$ and the zero value points on both sides of the histogram is two minimum points. Let m be the data bit. The prediction-error after modification e' can be defined as

$$e' = \begin{cases} e - 1 & e < b \\ e - m & e = b \\ e & a < e < b \\ e + m & e = a \\ e + 1 & e > a \end{cases} \tag{3}$$

Then, the pixel value of the secret image x' is

$$x' = x + (e' - e) \tag{4}$$

In the receiver, data bit can be extracted from secret image x' and the value of a and b by

$$m = \begin{cases} 1 & e' = a - 1 \quad or \quad b + 1 \\ 0 & e' = a \quad or \quad b \end{cases} \tag{5}$$

The pixel value of original image can be calculated by

$$x = \begin{cases} x' - 1 & e' > b \\ x' & a \le e' \le b \\ x' + 1 & e' < a \end{cases} \tag{6}$$

Generating Multiple Histogram. After calculating the predicted value and prediction-error of pixel, we introduce the concept of complexity measurement. It is defined as the sum of both vertical and horizontal absolute differences of the neighbor pixels of x. CM_i is computed as

$$CM_i = |v_1 - v_3| + |v_2 - v_4| \tag{7}$$

In order to reduce the number of histogram, CM_i will be scaled to M values for a relatively small M. We first select $M - 1$ thresholds as

$$s_j = \min_n \{ \frac{\sharp 1 \le i \le N : CM_i < CM}{N} \ge \frac{j+1}{M} \}, \forall j \in 0, 1, \cdots, M - 2 \tag{8}$$

Then, we divide CM_i into M intervals $I_0 = [0, s_0], I_1 = [s_0 + 1, s_1], \cdots$, $I_{M-2} = [s_{M-3} + 1, s_{M-2}], I_{M-1} = [s_{M-2} + 1, +\infty)$. CM_i will be updated to j if CM_i belongs to jth interval. Finally, we get M prediction-error histograms. For each histogram, embed data according to rhombus prediction and prediction-error expansion.

In our experiment, the number of histogram in every image is 4. As an example, the histograms for the image Lena, are shown in Fig. 4. One can see from that, as expected, the histogram with a smaller complexity level has a higher peak with more rapid two-sided decay.

Determination of Parameters. In the process of embedding, the selection of to-be-expanded bins a and b has an impact on the PSNR value of the marked decrypted image. According to [8], the condition of the optimization of distortion as to multiple histograms is

$$\begin{cases} min(\dfrac{\sum\limits_{n=0}^{M-1}(\sum\limits_{e < a_n} h_n(e) + \sum\limits_{e < b_n} h_n(e))}{\sum\limits_{n=0}^{M-1}(h_a(a_n)) + h_a(b_n)}) \\ subject\ to \quad \sum\limits_{n=0}^{M-1}(h_a(a_n)) + h_a(b_n)) \end{cases} \tag{9}$$

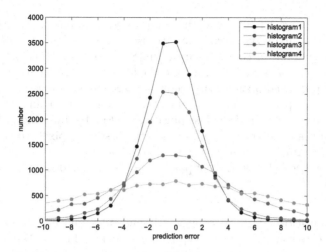

Fig. 4. Multiple histograms of image Lena

In order to reduce the complexity, we determine the $2M$ parameters (a_n, b_n), $0 \leq n \leq M - 1$ by utilizing exhaustive search. The conditions on the parameters are

1. For each $n \in \{0, 1, \cdots, M - 1\}, a_n = -b_n - 1$
2. For each $n \in \{0, 1, \cdots, M - 1\}, b_n \in \{0, 1, 7, \infty\}$
3. $b_0 \leq b_1 \leq b_2 \leq \cdots \leq b_{M-1}$

The first condition is heuristic such that the expansion bins are symmetrically selected in each histogram. The second condition is based on the fact that the histogram has rapid two-sided decay especially for small n. Thus only some informative bins are exploited for expansion. For the third condition, we try to embed more data into histogram with smaller n. By this condition, the data will be priorly embedded into smooth pixels.

Auxiliary Information. The same with other RDH algorithms, overflow/underflow problems cannot be prevented when the pixels change from 0 to -1 or from 255 to 256. Here, to avoid overflow or underflow, the pixels valued 0 will be changed to 1, and the pixels valued 255 will be changed to 254. Meanwhile, a location map will be established to record these problematic locations. The location map is a binary sequence sized N and it will be losslessly compressed to reduce its size. In our implementation, arithmetic coding is used for lossless compression. As a result, each x is ranged from 1 to 254, and it can be freely increased or decreased by 1 without overflow or underflow.

In order to realize the reversibility of data embedding and image recovery, some auxiliary information should be embedded into the original image. The necessary auxiliary information includes b_n for $n \in 0, 1, , M - 1(4M$ bits), s_n for $n \in 0, 1, , M - 2(10(M - 1)$ bits), the index of the last embedded pixel $N_{end}(\lceil log_2 N \rceil$ bits), the length of location map used for prevent overflow and underflow $LM(\lceil log_2 N \rceil$ bits) and the compressed location map (LM bits). In the front of the auxiliary information, we use 8 bits to represent the length of auxiliary information in coded binary form. Supposed that the total length of auxiliary information is S_{aux} bits. After embedding the LSB of part W, supposed that the last processed pixel for the secret message embedding is $x_{N'}$, record the LSB of first S_{aux} pixels to form a sequence S_{LSB} and embed this sequence into the unprocessed pixels until the last pixel $x_{N_{end}}$. Finally, by using LSB replacement, embed the auxiliary information into the first S_{aux} pixels to generate the marked image. After reserving space, the part B becomes a new part denoted as B' which is embedded with LSB of part W. A new image denoted as I' consists of part B', W, G.

Image Encryption. After rearranged self-embedded image I' is generated, we can encrypt I' to construct the encrypted image, denoted by E. Assume that the image after reserving space I' is an 8 bits gray-scale image with its size $W \times L$ and pixels ${X_{i,j}}' \in [0, 255]$, $1 \leq i \leq W$, $1 \leq j \leq L$. The encrypted bits $E_{i,j}(k)$ can be calculated through exclusive-or operation

$$E_{i,j}(k) = X'_{i,j}(k) \oplus r_{i,j}(k) \tag{10}$$

where $r_{i,j}(k)$ is generated by a standard stream cipher determined by the encryption key, $X'_{i,j}(k)$ is the binary bits of $X'_{i,j}$ calculated by:

$$X'_{i,j}(k) = \left\lfloor \frac{X'_{i,j}}{2} \right\rfloor mod \quad 2, k = 0, 1,, 7 \tag{11}$$

After image encryption, part B', W, G become part B'', W', G'. Finally, we embed 16 bits information into LSB of first 16 pixels in encrypted version of part W' to tell data hider the number of bit in part W' he can embed into. After image encryption, the data hider or any other the third party cannot access the content of the original image with encryption key. Therefore, the privacy of the content owner can be guaranteed.

3.2   Data Hiding in Encrypted Image

When the data hider acquires the encrypted image E, he can embed some data into it. It is easy for the data hider to read first 16 bits information in LSB of first 16 pixels in part W'. After knowing how many bits he can modify, the data hider simply adopts LSB replacement to change the available bit with additional data m and part W' becomes part W''. There is obvious that the first 7 bits of part W' are same with those of W''. Finally, the data hider sets a label following m to point out the end position of embedding process. Furthermore, the data hider can encrypts m according to data hiding key to formulate marked encrypted image consists of part B'', W'', G' denoted as E'. Therefore, anyone who does not know the data hiding key could not acquire the additional data even he know the principle of data extraction.

3.3   Data Extraction and Image Recovery

In this method, data extraction and image decryption are independent from each other. As a result, the order of them implies two different applications.

Extracting Data from Encrypted Image. In order to better protection of image content, when the marked encrypted image come to database manager, the order of data extraction before image encryption appear to be more important. When someone gets the data hiding key, he can decrypt the LSB of W, which can also be seen as W'', and extract the additional data m by directly reading the decrypted version. As the whole process is operated on encrypted version, it avoids the leakage of the image content.

Extracting Data from Decrypted Image. In the discussion above, both embedding and extracting are operated in the encrypted domain. However, there is a different situation that the image is decrypted firstly and then the data is extracted from the decrypted image. The process of extracting additional data from decrypted image will be discussed in next part.

Generating the Marked Decrypted Image. With the encryption key r, the content owner decrypts the image except the LSB of part W'' by xor $E'_{i,j}(k)$ and $r_{i,j}(k)$ to form the $I''_{i,j}(k)$ where $E'_{i,j}(k)$ and $I''_{i,j}(k)$ are the binary bits of $E'_{i,j}$ and $I''_{i,j}$, obtained via (11) respectively. Finally, we get the marked decrypted image I'' via (12).

$$I''_{i,j} = \sum_{k=0}^{7} I''_{i,j}(k) \times 2^k \tag{12}$$

After that, the part B'', G' in marked encrypted image E' will become B', G as same with the parts in the image after reserving space which denoted as I', the $W''_{i,j}(k), k = 0, 1, 2, 3, 4, 5, 6$ in part W'' will be same with $W_{i,j}(k), k = 0, 1, 2, 3, 4, 5, 6$ in part W. Therefore, the distortion in marked decrypted image is introduced by the embedding of additional data to the LSB of part W and self-reversible embedding process by embedding the LSB of W into B. The whole process of changing in three parts is shown in Fig. 5.

Data Extraction and Image Restoration. After generating the marked decrypted image, the content owner can further extract the additional data and recover original image. The steps are described as follow:

Step 1: Record and decrypted the LSB of part W to obtain the additional data m according to the data hiding key; extract the data until the end label is reached.

Step 2: Determine the auxiliary information by reading LSB of the first S_{aux} pixels.

Step 3: In the reverse scanning order, extract the sequence S_{LSB} from $x_{N'}$ to $x_{N_{end}}$ according to self-reversible extraction method, and meanwhile realize restoration for these pixels, replace LSB of the first S_{aux} pixels by S_{LSB}.

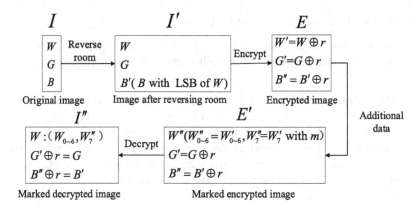

Fig. 5. Process of extracting data from decrypted image

Step 4: In the reverse scanning order, extract the LSB of part W from the first N' pixels and meanwhile realize restoration for these pixels.

Step 5: Determine the overflow and underflow locations by decompressing LM. For each overflow and underflow pixel, update its value as 255 if it is 254 or 0 if it is 1.

Step 6: Replace marked LSB of part W with its original bits extracted from part B to get original image I.

Of particular note is that in Step 4, the part G is same with the part in image I. From the (7), it is obvious that CM is computed by v_1, v_2, v_3 and v_4 from part G. In this way, the same complexity measurement can be obtained by receiver. According to (5) and (6), original part B and W can be recovered without distortion.

4   Experimental Results

In this section, several experiments are conducted to demonstrate the performance of the proposed method. Six standard $512*512$ sized gray-scale images [15] including Lena, Baboon, Peppers, Airplane, Barbara and Boat are used in our experiments.

Lena image is taken to demonstrate the feasibility of our method. With the result of which shown in Fig. 6, the embedding capacity is 10000 bits. Figure 6(a) is the image after self-reversible data hiding. Figure 6(b) is the image after encryption. The objective criteria PSNR is employed to evaluate the quality of marked decrypted image just as Fig. 6(c). Figure 6(d) depicts the recovery version which is identical to original image.

Some classic RDH methods in encrypted images were proposed such as [9] which first presented the possibility of RDH in encrypted images, [10] which improved the method in [9] by side match, [11] which proved the step of decryption and extraction are exchangeable in the dissertation. All of above methods were proved that the performance of them were inferior to the method in [13]. Therefore, we only compare our method with [13], which first proposed the framework mentioned in Sect. 2.

Table 1. Ultimate embedding capacity of six images

Image	e	h_1	h_2	h_3	h_4	EC(bits)
Lena	−1	3224	2282	1942	1084	17191
	0	3330	2264	1973	1092	
Baboon	−1	1227	786	437	267	5530
	0	1236	827	462	288	
Pepper	−1	1614	1795	1111	877	10898
	0	1715	1745	1127	914	
Airplane	−1	6265	1454	394	2208	26430
	0	10264	699	2920	2226	
Barbara	−1	2993	1824	1027	458	12961
	0	3181	1878	1103	497	
Boat	−1	3492	2538	1292	726	16156
	0	3519	2508	1292	789	

   (a)   (b)   (c)   (d)

Fig. 6. (a) image after reversing space (b) encrypted image (c) marked decrypted image (d) recovery version

Ultimate embedding capacity of every image is shown in Table 1. h_1, h_2, h_3 and h_4 represent four histograms of every image. For unartificial images, the two peak points in prediction-error histogram are generally −1 and 0. Therefore, the ultimate embedding capacity of image is the sum of the number of prediction error which are equal to −1 and 0.

The quality of marked decrypted images is compared in the term of PSNR. Figure 7 plots the PSNR results of different marked decrypted images under given embedding capacity. From the Fig. 7, it can be observed that almost over all range of embedding capacity except higher embedding capacity in image Peppers and Boat, our approach outperforms RDH algorithm in encrypted images in [13].

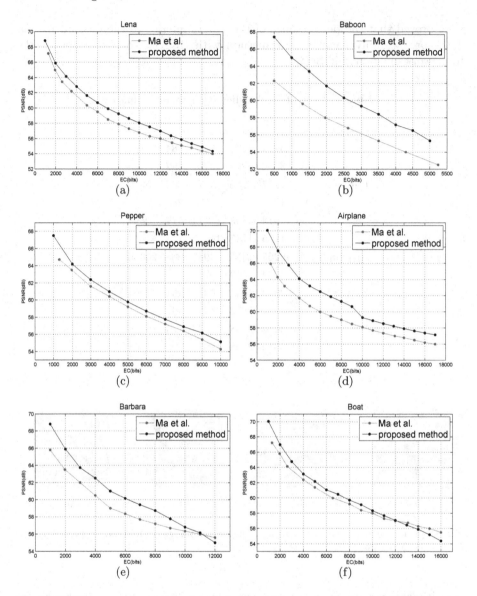

Fig. 7. PSNR comparison with the methods of Ma et al. (a) Lena (b) Baboon (c) Pepper (d) Airplane (e) Barbara (f) Boat

As to the a given embedding capacity, higher PSNR value means the lower degree of the distortion of images. The gain in terms of PSNR under ultimate embedding capacity is obvious in all range. The PSNR value of our method and the method in [13] when the embedding capacity is 5000 bits and 10000 bits are shown in Table 2. Referring to Table 2, for a capacity of 5000 bits, our method outperform [13] with an average increase of PSNR by 1.58 dB, for a capacity of

Table 2. Comparison PSNR (in dB) between the proposed method and the method of Ma et al. [13]

EC(bits)	5000 bits			10000 bits		
Image	[13]	Proposed	Gain	[13]	Proposed	Gain
Lena	60.34	61.63	1.29	56.79	58.05	1.26
Baboon	52.89	55.31	2.42	/	/	/
Pepper	59.23	59.76	0.53	54.32	55.16	0.84
Airplane	60.71	63.22	2.51	58.13	59.28	1.15
Barbara	59.06	61.01	1.95	56.35	56.81	0.46
Boat	61.42	62.17	0.75	58.04	58.35	0.31
Average	**58.94**	**60.52**	**1.58**	**56.73**	**57.53**	**0.80**

10000 bits, our method outperform [13] with an average increase of PSNR by 0.80 dB.

In conclusion, compare with the work in [13], the superiority of proposed method is experimentally verified. It demonstrates the effectiveness of the proposed algorithm.

5   Conclusion

In this paper, we proposed a new reversible data hiding method in encrypted images by dividing the grey images into three parts and reserving space for embedding. Part B is used for embedding the LSB of part W and part W is used for embedding additional data. In the process of embedding the LSB of part W, a RDH method based on prediction-error expansion and multiple histograms modification is utilized. Part G is used to generate prediction-error histograms. Actually, the mode of image partition is decided by the RDH method used for reversing space. Under the framework of [13], we design the detailed procedures of our algorithm and realize the reversibility of both original image and additional data. The result of comparative experiments prove the superiority of the proposed method in reducing the distortion of image. Furthermore, this novel method realizes the independence of the process of additional data extraction and image decryption.

Acknowledgments. This work was supported in part by the Natural Science Foundation of Jiangsu Province under Grant BK20151102, in part by the Ministry of Education Key Laboratory of Machine Perception, Peking University under Grant K-2016-03, in part by the Open Project Program of the Ministry of Education Key Laboratory of Underwater Acoustic Signal Processing, Southeast University under Grant UASP1502, and in part by the Natural Science Foundation of China under Grant 61673108.

References

1. Fridrich, J., Goljan, M., Du, R.: Lossless data embedding for all image formats. In: Ei SPIE Security and Watermarking of Multimedia Contents IV, vol. 4675, pp. 572–583 (2002)
2. Celik, M.U., Sharma, G., Tekalp, A.M., Saber, E.: Lossless generalized-LSB data embedding. IEEE Trans. Image Process. **14**(2), 253–266 (2005)
3. Tian, J.: Reversible data embedding using a difference expansion. IEEE Trans. Circuits Syst. Video Technol. **13**(8), 890–896 (2003)
4. Ni, Z., Shi, Y.Q., Ansari, N., Su, W.: Reversible data hiding. IEEE Trans. Circuits Syst. Video Technol. **16**(3), 354–362 (2006)
5. Thodi, D.M., Rodriguez, J.J.: Expansion embedding techniques for reversible watermarking. IEEE Trans. Image Process. **16**(3), 721–730 (2007)
6. Sachnev, V., Kim, H.J., Nam, J., Suresh, S., Shi, Y.Q.: Reversible watermarking algorithm using sorting and prediction. IEEE Trans. Circuits Syst. Video Technol. **19**(7), 989–999 (2009)
7. Tsai, P., Hu, Y.C., Yeh, H.L.: Reversible image hiding scheme using predictive coding and histogram shifting. Signal Process. **89**, 1129–1143 (2009)
8. Li, X., Zhang, W., Gui, X.: Efficient reversible data hiding based on multiple histograms modification. IEEE Trans. Inf. Forensics Secur. **10**(9), 2016–2027 (2015)
9. Zhang, X.: Reversible data hiding in encrypted image. IEEE Signal Process. Lett. **18**(4), 255–258 (2011)
10. Hong, W., Chen, T.S., Wu, H.Y.: An improved reversible data hiding in encrypted images using side match. IEEE Signal Process. Lett. **19**(4), 199–202 (2012)
11. Li, M., Xiao, D., Kulsoom, A.: Improved reversible data hiding for encrypted images using full embedding strategy. Electron. Lett. **51**(9), 690–691 (2015)
12. Zhang, X.: Separable reversible data hiding in encrypted image. IEEE Trans. Inf. Forensics Secur. **7**(2), 826–832 (2012)
13. Ma, K., Zhang, W., Zhao, X., Yu, N., Li, F.: Reversible data hiding in encrypted images by reserving space before encryption. IEEE Trans. Inf. Forensics Secur. **8**(3), 553–562 (2013)
14. Luo, L.: Reversible image watermarking using interpolation technique. IEEE Trans. Inf. Forensics Secur. **5**(1), 187–193 (2010)
15. Miscelaneous Gray Level Images. http://decsai.ugr.es/cvg/dbimagenes/g512.php. Accessed 13 Mar 2014

A Multiple Linear Regression Based High-Accuracy Error Prediction Algorithm for Reversible Data Hiding

Bin Ma[1], Xiaoyu Wang[1(✉)], Bing Li[1], and Yun-Qing Shi[2]

[1] School of Information Science, Qilu University of Technology
(Shandong Academic of Science), Jinan 250300 China
qluwxy@163.com
[2] New Jersey Institute of Technology, Newark, NJ 07102, USA

Abstract. In reversible data hiding, the higher embedding capacity and lower distortion are simultaneously expected. Hence, the precise and efficient error-prediction algorithm is essential and crucial. In this paper, a high-performance error-prediction method based on Multiple Linear Regression (MLR) algorithm is proposed to improve the performance of Reversible Data Hiding (RDH). The MLR matrix function that indicates the inner correlations between the pixels and their neighbors is established adaptively according to the consistency of pixels in local area of a natural image, and thus the targeted pixel is predicted accurately with the achieved MLR function that satisfies the consistency of the neighboring pixels. Compared with conventional methods that only predict the targeted pixel with fixed predictors through simple arithmetic combination of its surroundings pixel, the proposed method can provide a sparser prediction-error image for data embedding, and thus improves the performance of RDH. Experimental results have shown that the proposed method outperform the state-of-the-art error prediction algorithms.

Keywords: Reversible data hiding · Error prediction ·
Multiple linear regression · Embedded capacity

1 Introduction

RDH enables the embedding of secret message into a host image without loss of any original information. It considers not only extracting the hidden message correctly, but also recovering the original image exactly after data extraction [1]. It is mainly used in sensitive images that can not tolerate any mistake such as military, medical and remote sensing images.

At present, RDH based on difference expansion and RDH based on histogram shifting are two kinds of most prevalent methods being widely employed. Tian [2] presented the first difference expansion based RDH scheme. The secret messages are embedded by multiplying the difference between the targeted pixel and its predicted value (prediction error). The RDH scheme based on histogram shifting is proposed by Ni *et al.* [3]. The method achieves data embedding by translating the largest number of prediction errors.

C. D. Yoo et al. (Eds.): IWDW 2018, LNCS 11378, pp. 195–205, 2019.
https://doi.org/10.1007/978-3-030-11389-6_15

As the secret messages are hidden into the redundant information of the host image, accurate error prediction algorithm can obtain small prediction errors and thus the histogram distributes steeper around "0", causing the data embedding capacity is enhanced at the same marked image quality. Therefore, the study of high performance error predictor to improve the prediction accuracy of targeted pixel attracts more and more attentions. Thodi and Rodríguez [4] firstly provided the prediction-error expansion based RDH scheme. This new technique exploited the inherent correlations between the targeted pixel and its neighbors better than Tian's difference-expansion scheme. Therefore, the prediction-error expansion method can reduced the image distortion at low embedding capacity and mitigate the capacity control problem. Fallahpour *et al.* [5] illustrated a lossless data hiding method based on the technique of gradient-adjusted prediction (GAP), in which the prediction-errors are computed and slightly modified with histogram shifting method, so as to hided more secret message at high PSNR. Yang and Tsai [6] provided an interleaving error prediction method, in which the amount of predictive values is as many as the pixels, and all prediction-errors are transformed into image histogram to create higher peak bins to improve the embedding capacity. Sachnev *et al.* [7] proposed the rhombus error prediction method to embed secret message into an image, and a sorting technique is employed to record the prediction-errors according to the magnitude of its local variance. Rhombus predictor has the best performance among fixed predictor. Therefore, many paper implemented embedding algorithm based on rhombus predictor [8–11].

Dragoi and Coltuc [12] presented a local error prediction method and evaluated it with difference expansion based RDH scheme. For each pixel, a least square predictor is established from a square block centered on the pixel, and thus the smaller corresponding prediction-errors are obtained. Lee *et al.* [13] proposed a novel piecewise 2D auto-regression (P2AR) predictor that is based on a rhombus-embedding scheme is used. The predictor utilizes six critical full-context SPs through the pixels in the TS, enabling an identification of the shape of the region around the TP and the proper coefficients. Thus, the method has a tendency that significant improvement happens in high embedding capacity. Hwang *et al.* [14] presented an enhanced predictor by using LASSO approach over normal LS predictor with rhombus-shaped two-stage embedding scheme. It enables finding out the shape of region around the targeted pixel and the proper weight coefficients. Therefore, the tendency of the method significantly improves the embedding capacity, especially regarding highly variative images.

In this paper, we proposed a machine learning method for multiple linear regression algorithm to adaptively estimate the targeted pixels. Unlike the conventional methods just employing the fixed parameters algorithm to estimate the targeted pixel through simple arithmetical combinations of its neighbors, the proposed method explores the inner correlations among the targeted pixel and its neighborhoods. The method adaptively studies the inner relations among the targeted pixel and its neighbors, and then predicts the targeted pixel with the MLR function achieved from its nearest neighboring pixels. According to the local consistency of the natural image, the prediction accuracy is highly improved and the prediction errors are minimized, which enable the image prediction errors to distribute around "0" closely and the histogram distribute steep. And thus, the performance of RDH scheme based on the proposed prediction-error image outperforms those state-of-the-art schemes clearly.

The outline of the paper is as follows. The principle of MLR algorithm is introduced in Sect. 2. The error prediction method based on MLR algorithm for RDH is presented in Sect. 3. The experimental results of error prediction based on MLR algorithm are shown in 4. In Sect. 5, the comparisons of RDH performance based on the proposed prediction-error image and images from other state-of-the-art algorithms are demonstrated. Finally, conclusions are drawn in Sect. 6.

2 MLR Algorithm

MLR is a linear approach for modeling the relationship between a scalar dependent variable Y and independent variables denoted by X. The relationships are modeled with the linear predictor whose unknown model parameters are estimated from the data, and such models are called linear models. The basic purpose of MLR is utilizing the independent variables to estimate another dependent variable and its variability.

The general model of multiple linear regression is

$$Y = \beta_0 + \beta_1 x_{i1} + \beta_2 x_{i2} + \cdots + \beta_k x_{ik} + \varepsilon \tag{1}$$

Where, $\beta_0, \beta_1, \beta_2, \ldots, \beta_k$ are $k+1$ unknown parameters, β_0 is regression constant, $\beta_1, \beta_2, \ldots, \beta_k$ are called regression coefficients and $x_1, x_2, \ldots, x_k$ are variables that can be accurately measured, and ε is random error.

In a multiple variable estimated system, where the variables comply with the same mapping regular, the MLR function can be expressed in matrix format as

$$Y = \beta X + \varepsilon \tag{2}$$

Where, Y, β, X are as follows

$$Y = \begin{bmatrix} y_1 \\ y_2 \\ \vdots \\ y_n \end{bmatrix} \quad \beta = \begin{bmatrix} \beta_0 \\ \beta_1 \\ \vdots \\ \beta_n \end{bmatrix} \quad \varepsilon = \begin{bmatrix} \varepsilon_1 \\ \varepsilon_2 \\ \vdots \\ \varepsilon_n \end{bmatrix} \quad X = \begin{bmatrix} 1 & x_{11} & x_{12} & \cdots & x_{1k} \\ 1 & x_{21} & x_{22} & \cdots & x_{2k} \\ \vdots & \vdots & \vdots & \cdots & \vdots \\ 1 & x_{n1} & x_{n2} & \cdots & x_{nk} \end{bmatrix} \tag{3}$$

The above matrix equation can be solved with the Least-Square (LS) method, so that the MLR function is constructed with respect to the known and unknown variables, which enables the sum of the squared deviations between the estimated and observed values of the model is as small as possible, i.e. the sum of squared residuals is smallest. At last, the value of the regression coefficients β is calculated as formula (4), and the prediction of the targeted variables is achieved effectively.

$$\beta = (X^T X)^{-1} X^T Y \tag{4}$$

3   MLR Algorithm Based Targeted Pixel Error Prediction

According to the consistency of pixels in local area of natural image, the neighboring pixels generally have similar values, and the neighboring pixels and the targeted pixel from same local area usually have close relation. Thus, the targeted pixel can be predicted by exploiting the inner relation among its neighboring pixels.

Suppose the targeted pixel to be predicted is $x_{m,n}$, its neighboring pixels are chosen as the prediction samples, and the prediction result is $x'_{m,n}$. The MLR predictor of the targeted pixel is calculated by the M neighboring pixels as follows:

$$x'_{m,n} = \sum_{k=1}^{M} \beta_k x_k \tag{5}$$

where, x_k are the neighbors of targeted pixel.

Considering the closely correlations of pixels distribute in local area of natural image, the targeted pixel and its neighbors usually comply with the same pixel prediction function, thus, the targeted pixel can be predicted with the same function of its neighboring pixels precisely. In the light of this principle, the targeted pixel is not predicted through simple arithmetical combinations with its neighboring pixels in our proposed scheme, but through the MLR function established from the neighboring pixels, and thus, the prediction accuracy of the targeted pixel is improved.

Let $x_{m,n}$ be the pixel to be predicted, choose N pixels around the targeted pixel as the prediction samples, at the same time, choose closest two neighboring pixels of each prediction sample as training samples. Construct the MLR matrix function with the training samples as variables X and the prediction samples as variable Y. The MLR coefficients that indicate the inner correlation of pixels in local area are obtained by least-square method. Then, the targeted pixel is predicted with the achieved MLR equation which indicates the consistency relations of neighboring pixels in local area. The prediction sample Y be denoted by an N × 1 column vector, as follow:

$$Y = [x_1, x_2, \cdots, x_N]^T \tag{6}$$

In the first stage, choose N pixels at the top left of the targeted pixel (shown as Fig. 1) as prediction samples Y, and every closest two pixels located on the top and left of each prediction pixel is chosen as the training sample X. Then, the MLR matrix function is established according to the relationship between the training samples and the training pixels, through which the parameters are obtained adaptively (shown as formula (7)).

$$\begin{bmatrix} x_1 \\ x_2 \\ \vdots \\ x_6 \end{bmatrix} = \begin{bmatrix} x_5 & x_2 \\ x_7 & x_8 \\ & \vdots \\ x_8 & x_9 \end{bmatrix} \begin{bmatrix} \beta_1 \\ \beta_2 \\ \vdots \\ \beta_6 \end{bmatrix} + \begin{bmatrix} \varepsilon_1 \\ \varepsilon_2 \\ \vdots \\ \varepsilon_6 \end{bmatrix} \tag{7}$$

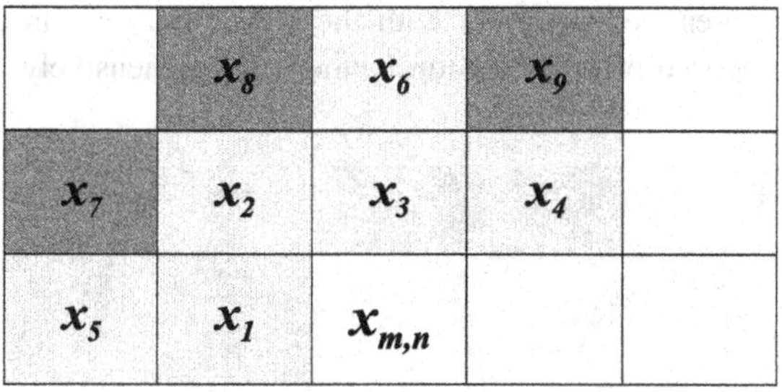

	x_8	x_6	x_9	
x_7	x_2	x_3	x_4	
x_5	x_1	$x_{m,n}$		

Fig. 1. Pixel chosen method.

The MLR coefficients are obtained with Least-Squares (*LS*) method (Eq. 4). As the optimal resolutions of MLR matrix function enable to minimize the sum of squared residuals (the residual is the difference between the estimated and original pixels), the optimal coefficients of a MLR function composed by the similar neighboring pixels are achieved.

In the following stage, the obtained MLR function and the four pixels located at the upper left corner of the targeted pixel are employed to predict the targeted pixel value according to the formula (8).

$$\hat{x}_{m,n} = \beta_1 x_1 + \beta_2 x_3 \tag{8}$$

Finally, the prediction-error is obtained with the formula (8), where, the original pixel value is subtracted by its predicted value.

$$e(i,j) = round(x(m,n) - \hat{x}(m,n)) \tag{9}$$

Apparently, the proposed method does not just rely on the simple arithmetical combination of pixels closely adjacent to the targeted pixel to predict the targeted pixel, but learns the inner correlations between the training samples and the prediction samples. According to the close relation of local pixels, the targeted pixel is predicted with the optimized MLR function established from its neighboring pixels. As the method adaptively learns the inner correlation of pixels distribute in local area, the accuracy of prediction is improved clearly compared with those coefficients fixed error prediction method.

4 Experimental Results

To evaluate the performance of the proposed MLR based error prediction method, four well known standard 512×512 test images (see Fig. 2) from image database of MISC are chosen to evaluate the performance of the proposed method. As image Lena and Tiffany have plenty of moderate frequency information, that is, it is moderate texture complexity; while image Baboon is high texture complexity, and image Airplane is with large uniform areas, experiments with these four images can evaluate the performance of the proposed error prediction method comprehensively.

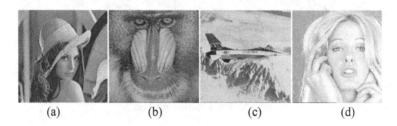

Fig. 2. Four standard test images: (a) Lena, (b) Baboon, (c) Airplane, (d) Tiffany

In the experiment, the targeted pixel is predicted by its closest two neighboring pixels locate on its top and left. It is supposed that the data embedding is from the lower right corner to the upper left corner, so that the value of the prediction samples are consistent before and after data embedding, accordingly, high accurate pixel prediction is achieved. The prediction samples on the upper left corner of the targeted pixel and training samples of the prediction sample are employed to established the MLR function coefficients, and the targeted pixel is predicted with the established MLR function and the four prediction samples.

Moreover, to enable the correct extraction of the embedded message and the lossless recovery of the original image, the left two columns as well as the top two rows of the image are not involved in the reversible data hiding process, however, they are reserved for additional information saving or other specific application. Therefore, the net amount of the pixels involved for RDH is 508 × 508 actually.

The effect of the prediction samples N for the MLR prediction is important. The greater number of prediction samples, the better result in MLR method. Figure 2 shows that we adopted prediction samples of different size (N = 2, 4, 6) to carry out. It is obvious that the effect of prediction samples N = 6 and N = 4 outperforms the effect of N = 2 and significant gap exists in the result. We can also see that prediction error of N = 6 slightly exceeds prediction error of N = 4. Conclusion, predicted effect of N = 6 produces the best result, better than N = 4 and N = 2.

Meanwhile, we compare the proposed error prediction method with other state-of-the-art error prediction methods such as Yang et al.'s method and Sachnev et al's method. Yang et al. proposed the interleaving prediction methods, in which the number of prediction-errors are as many as the pixels, Sachnev et al. presented the rhombus error prediction method for RDH. They all have achieved excellent experimental results in the process of targeted pixel error prediction. The experimental results show that the performance of the proposed predictor outperforms other state-of-art predictor clearly. Figure 2 shows that the distribution of the prediction errors range −10 to 10 with our proposed scheme is more constrained than with other schemes.

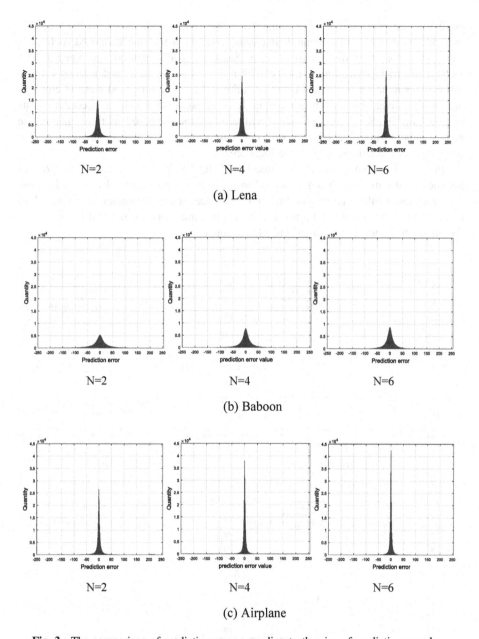

Fig. 3. The comparison of prediction error according to the size of prediction samples.

The result of the comparisons with the state-of-the-art scheme of Sachnev et al. method, Yang et al. method, are shown in Fig. 2. It is manifested that the proposed method outperforms Sachnev et al's and Yang et al's method in four images. It is well known that Sachnev et al's method was achieved highest performance among the fixed predictor, the proposed method outperform the other methods of Sachnev et al's method and Yang et al's method. It can be concluded that the proposed method is superior to the other three algorithms of Sachnev et al's method and Yang et al's method in large embedding capacity. The reason why the proposed method outperforms other methods are summarized as follows. First, the proposed method employs the multiple linear regression in machine learning adaptively to learn according to its neighboring pixels of the local area. Furthermore, the proposed method only utilize nearest neighboring pixel of the pixel to increase accuracy of the LS computation, take advantage of the consistency of the local area.

Figure 4 has shown that the proposed predictor has higher accuracy than those of Sachnev et al's method, Yang's method in prediction error range −10 to 10. Because the proposed method results in higher occurrence of small prediction error values compared to other methods. Figure 4 confirms that the proposed method is superior to the other three methods in large embedding capacity.

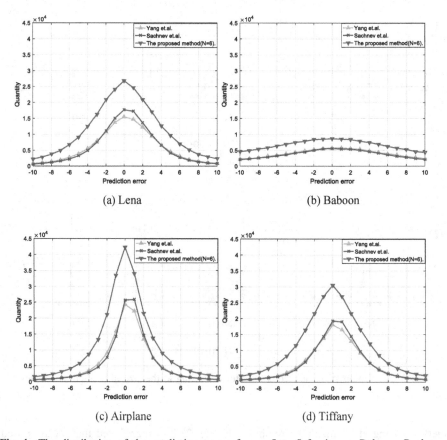

(a) Lena   (b) Baboon

(c) Airplane   (d) Tiffany

Fig. 4. The distribution of the prediction errors from −5 to 5 for image *Baboon, Barbara, Sailboat, Boat*.

5 Comparison of RDH on Different Prediction-Error Image

To further verify the superiority of the MLR based error prediction method, we compare the performance of difference expansion based RDH scheme on different prediction-error image formulated with Sachnev et al.'s method, Yang et al.'s method, Dragoi et al's method and the proposed methods. Here, we choose difference expansion based RDH scheme, as it is a kind of simple but effective approach for data embedding. The comparison results on four classical images are shown in Fig. 3.

The PSNR comparison results with other schemes are shown in Fig. 5. It is ensured that the proposed method outperforms state-of-the-art methods such as Sachnev et al's method, Dragoi et al's method, Yang et al's method. Figure 5 also shows that the proposed scheme achieves higher performance than others at moderate to high data embedding capacity, that is, when the data embedding capacity is low, all kinds of error prediction algorithms can provide sufficient prediction-errors "0" for data embedding,

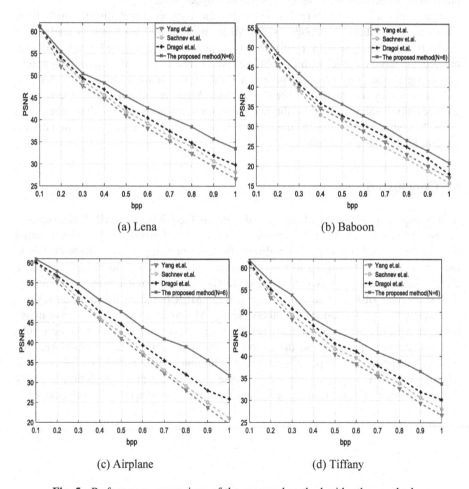

(a) Lena

(b) Baboon

(c) Airplane

(d) Tiffany

Fig. 5. Performance comparison of the proposed method with other methods

but with the embedding capacity increase, the error image with less prediction errors "0" brings more image distortion than others. The better the error prediction algorithm is, the more accuracy the error prediction would be, and the higher the RDH performance is achieved.

The reason of the experimental results can be interpreted as follows. Both the two methods of Yang et al.'s and Sachnev et al.'s employed fixed coefficient function to estimate the targeted pixel value. The Yang et al.'s method employed the two pixels at the left and right of the targeted pixel, and Sachnev et al.'s method employs the four pixels at the four directions of the targeted pixels(left, right, up and down) for targeted pixel error prediction. As the pixels distribute differently from one region to another in a natural image, the targeted pixel prediction accuracy different from one area to another. The more texture the host image has, the lower the prediction accuracy would be. Although Drogia et al.'s method predict the targeted pixel adaptively with pixels distribute in a local area, the marked and the original pixels are both involved for error prediction, its prediction accuracy is decreased apparently.

Our proposed scheme not just estimates the targeted pixel directly with fixed parameters algorithm, it establishes the MLR function and deciding its coefficients firstly from the neighboring pixels closely adjacent to the targeted pixel, and then predicts the targeted pixel with the achieved MLR function and its surrounding pixels. According to the consistency of pixels in local area of natural image, the error prediction accuracy is improved effectively. The MLR algorithm can achieve more accuracy pixel value prediction, the prediction-error image is sparser than others (has more "0" elements) and thus the marked image maintains high quality even after quite a lot data having been embedded.

6 Conclusion

In this paper, a new kind of error prediction method based on MLR algorithm is presented. The targeted pixel is predicted with MLR function and its neighboring pixels, where, the MLR is established from the neighboring pixels distribute closely to the targeted pixel. According to the consistency of the pixels in local area of natural image, the targeted pixel is predicted accurately. The experimental results compared with some state-of-the-art schemes show that the MLR based error prediction scheme achieves higher performance than others clearly. Moreover, the prediction-error image achieves with the proposed method also has been employed for RDH, and the results demonstrate that the RDH on the proposed prediction-error image outperforms the counterparts apparently, especially for image with much texture areas. The MLR based adaptive error prediction method can increase the targeted pixel prediction accuracy (minimize the prediction error) largely and then improve image RDH performance in great extent.

References

1. Shi, Y.Q., Li, X., Zhang, X., et al.: Reversible data hiding: advances in the past two decades. IEEE Access **4**, 3210–3237 (2016)
2. Tian, J.: Reversible data embedding using a difference expansion. IEEE Trans. Circuits Syst. Video Technol. **13**(8), 890–896 (2003)
3. Ni, Z., Shi, Y.Q., Ansari, N., et al.: Reversible data hiding. IEEE Trans. Circuits Syst. Video Technol. **16**(3), 354–362 (2006)
4. Thodi, D.M., Rodriguez, J.J.: Prediction-error based reversible watermarking. In: 2004 International Conference on Image Processing. ICIP 2004, vol. 3, pp. 1549–1552. IEEE (2004)
5. Fallahpour, M.: Reversible image data hiding based on gradient adjusted prediction. IEICE Electron. Express **5**(20), 870–876 (2008)
6. Yang, C.H., Yang, M.H.: Improving histogram-based reversible data hiding by interleaving prediction. Iet Image Process. **4**(4), 223–234 (2010)
7. Sachnev, V., Kim, H.J., Nam, J., et al.: Reversible watermarking algorithm using sorting and prediction. IEEE Trans. Circuits Syst. Video Technol. **19**(7), 989–999 (2009)
8. Luo, L., Chen, Z., Chen, M., et al.: Reversible image watermarking using interpolation technique. IEEE Trans. Inf. Forensics Secur. **5**(1), 187–193 (2010)
9. Hwang, H.J., Kim, H.J., Sachnev, V., et al.: Reversible watermarking method using optimal histogram pair shifting based on prediction and sorting. TIIS **4**(4), 655–670 (2010)
10. Kang, S., Hwang, H.J., Kim, H.J.: Reversible watermark using an accurate predictor and sorter based on payload balancing. ETRI J. **34**(3), 410–420 (2010)
11. Feng, G., Qian, Z., Dai, N.: Reversible watermarking via extreme learning machine prediction. Neurocomputing **2012**(82), 62–68 (2012)
12. Dragoi, I.C., Coltuc, D.: Local-prediction-based difference expansion reversible watermarking. IEEE Trans. Image Process. **23**(4), 1779 (2014). A Publication of the IEEE Signal Processing Society
13. Lee, B.Y., Hwang, H.J., Kim, H.J.: Reversible data hiding using a piecewise autoregressive predictor based on two-stage embedding. J. Electr. Eng. Technol. **11**(4), 974–986 (2016)
14. Hwang, H.J., Kim, S.H., Kim, H.J.: Reversible data hiding using least square predictor via the LASSO. EURASIP J. Image Video Process. **2016**(1), 42 (2016)

A Strategy of Distinguishing Texture Feature for Reversible Data Hiding Based on Histogram Shifting

Yinyin Peng[1] and Zhaoxia Yin[1,2(✉)]

[1] Key Laboratory of Intelligent Computing and Signal Processing,
Ministry of Education, Anhui University, Hefei 230601, People's Republic of China
`yinzhaoxia@ahu.edu.cn`
[2] Department of Computer Science, Purdue University,
West lafayette 47906, USA

Abstract. Reversible data hiding has received growing attention, which not only protects the secret information but also can recover the cover image accurately. Many algorithms have aimed at embedding capacity and rarely consider the texture features of spatial images. In this paper, to better improve the image quality, a novel strategy of distinguishing texture feature for reversible data hiding based on histogram shifting is proposed. Firstly, the cover image is separated into blocks of the equal size, and the texture feature value of blocks is calculated. Then, the relatively smooth blocks are selected for information embedding. Experimental results show that our method can improve image quality effectively.

Keywords: Reversible data hiding · Image texture · Image quality

1 Introduction

In recent years, the protection of privacy has received more and more attention due to the frequent occurrence of privacy leakage. Reversible data hiding not only protects the secret information but also can recover the cover image accurately. Therefore, it is widely utilized in various applications, e.g., image authentication [1], medical and military image processing [2], and stereo image coding [3], etc.

Since Barton [4] proposed the first reversible data hiding scheme in 1997, reversible data hiding has had a lot of improved algorithms. Lossless compression [5,6], difference expansion [7,8], and histogram shifting [9–11] are three main methods of data hiding. Histogram shiftings main idea is to select a pair of peak and zero bins and move the pixels between peak and zero bins. When 0 is embedded, the peak points remain unchanged; when 1 is embedded, the peak points are incremented or decremented by 1.

Linear prediction error histogram was proposed by Tsai et al. [12] in 2009. Firstly, the cover image is divided into sized $n \times n$ blocks and the center pixel of

© Springer Nature Switzerland AG 2019
C. D. Yoo et al. (Eds.): IWDW 2018, LNCS 11378, pp. 206–215, 2019.
https://doi.org/10.1007/978-3-030-11389-6_16

each block is selected as the baseline. The pixels in each block minus the central pixel to obtain an error value table e, and the central pixel value is discarded. The correlation between pixel values is strengthened in this method. A higher hiding capacity is obtained and a good quality stego-image is preserved. In 2013, Chen et al. [13] made improvements based on the method of Tsai et al. [12]. Embedding in the first layer, firstly, the cover image is divided into sized 2×2 blocks and the pixel in the lower right is selected as the baseline. Then, the pixels in each 2×2 block minus the baseline, and three error values e_1, e_2, and e_3 can be obtained. Finally, the maximum prediction error $Max(e_1, e_2, e_3)$ is selected as the error value of the pixel which is the baseline. Embedding in the second layer, the minimum predictive error $Min(e_1, e_2, e_3)$ is selected in the same way for information embedding. This method improves prediction accuracy and improves visual effect. In 2016, asymmetric-histogram based reversible data hiding scheme using edge sensitivity detection is utilized by Lu et al. [14]. In [14], the pixels of the cover image I is divided into two parts: blank and shadow. Taking blank as an example, first calculate the edge sensitivity coefficients of four pixels adjacent to the $I(p, q)$ position and normalize it, and then calculate the prediction value and error value of the $I(p, q)$ position. This method not only strengthens the correlation between adjacent pixels, but also reduces the distribution of error values and improves the prediction accuracy. In 2017, high-fidelity reversible data hiding using directionally enclosed prediction was implemented by Chen et al. [15]. The error values of each pixel include the horizontal direction e_h and the vertical direction e_v, and the smaller of the absolute values of the two is selected as the prediction error of x in [15]. Jung [16] implied a high-capacity reversible data hiding scheme based on sorting and prediction in digital images in 2017. The proposed method could embed two bits of the secret data in each 3×1 sub-block at maximum by grouping into the max and min groups. It further improves the embedding capacity in the same embedded capacity.

Because the texture feature of the image is not fully considered in the previous papers, a strategy of distinguishing texture feature for reversible data hiding based on histogram shifting is proposed in this paper. In this paper, firstly, the cover image is separated into blocks of equal size and the block texture information is described by five parameters of mean square error, homogeneity, entropy, contrast, energy. Then, the relative smooth blocks are selected for information embedding. Experimental results show that the proposed strategy can improve the image visual effect and make full use of the correlation between pixels.

The rest of the paper is organized as follows. Section 2 presents the proposed method. The experimental results are followed in Sect. 3. Finally, the conclusions are summarized in Sect. 4.

2   Proposed Method

In order to achieve better image quality under the same embedding capacity, a strategy of distinguishing texture feature for reversible data hiding based on histogram shifting is proposed in this paper. Our method mainly includes four sections: calculation of texture features of image blocks, weight optimization, threshold optimization, embedding and extraction process.

2.1   Calculation of Texture Features of Image Blocks

The method proposed in this paper employs a cover image I to implement reversible data hiding. Firstly, the cover image is separated into sized $s_1 \times s_2$ blocks, and the texture feature value of blocks is computed. The block texture information is described by five parameters: mean square error, homogeneity, entropy, contrast, and energy in the proposed method. The meaning and calculation formula of the five parameters will be introduced below. Let i represent the gray value of the current pixel ($0 \leq i \leq 255$), j represent the neighborhood gray mean ($0 \leq j \leq 255$), and (i, j) constitutes the co-occurrence matrix M. $f(i, j)$) is the frequency at which the feature two-tuples (i, j) appears, and N is the scale of the image. Then the probability of each two-tuples is as follows:

$$P_{i,j} = \frac{f(i, j)}{N^2} \tag{1}$$

Entropy is used to describe the amount of information contained in the image. The larger the entropy value, the finer the texture; the smaller the entropy, the smoother the image. Entropy can be obtained:

$$H_{m,n} = \sum_{t=1}^{s_1} \sum_{k=1}^{s_2} P_{i,j} log P_{i,j} \tag{2}$$

Energy is utilized to reflect the distribution of image grayscale uniformity. The greater the energy, the more uniform the grayscale distribution of the image. Energy is calculated by (3):

$$J_{m,n} = \sum_{t=1}^{s_1} \sum_{k=1}^{s_2} P_{i,j}^2 \tag{3}$$

Contrast can describe the clarity of the image, that is, the clarity of the texture. The greater the difference between adjacent grayscale pixel pairs, the greater the contrast. Contrast can be computed by (4):

$$G_{m,n} = \sum_{t=1}^{s_1} \sum_{k=1}^{s_2} P_{i,j} (i - j)^2 \tag{4}$$

The local variation of image texture is described by homogeneity. If the image texture has less variation between different domains and the locality is very uniform, homogeneity is larger. Homogeneity is defined as:

$$Q_{m,n} = \sum_{t=1}^{s_1} \sum_{k=1}^{s_2} \frac{P_{i,j}}{\left(1 + (i-j)^2\right)} \tag{5}$$

Mean square error indicates the discrete degree of adjacent pixels. The larger the mean square error, the greater the difference between adjacent gray pixel pairs. Mean square error can be estimated by:

$$COV_{m,n} = \sum_{t=1}^{s_1} \sum_{k=1}^{s_2} \left(i - \frac{\sum_{t=1}^{s_1} \sum_{k=1}^{s_2} i}{s_1 \cdot s_2} \right) \tag{6}$$

Finally, the texture information of each block can be described by using the above five parameters together, as shown in formula (7). Since each parameter reflection degree to the texture of the block is different, the method assigns weights to entropy, energy, contrast, homogeneity, and mean square error, which are represented by w_1, w_2, w_3, w_4, and w_5, respectively.

$$C_{m,n} = w_1 \cdot H_{m,n} + w_2 \cdot J_{m,n} + w_3 \cdot G_{m,n} + w_4 \cdot Q_{m,n} + w_5 \cdot COV_{m,n} \tag{7}$$

Where $C_{m,n}$ represents the texture feature value of the blocks.

2.2 Weight Optimization

Take Lena as the example, the weights of entropy, energy, contrast, homogeneity, and mean square error in the texture feature are shown in Table 1 which is optimal in the experiment. The threshold optimization of different images is calculated in the same way as Lena. The method for finding the approximate optimal of Lena weight is as follows:

Step 1: The initial weight of entropy, energy, contrast, homogeneity and mean square error is set as 1.0;
Step 2: Maintain the weight of energy, contrast, homogeneity, and the mean square error, increase or decrease the weight of the entropy, and compare the PSNR of images before and after weight changes. Retain a set of weight values with higher PSNR. Gradually reduce the range of weight changes, specifically: ±0.8, ±0.4, ±0.2, ±0.1;
Step 3: The operation of step 2 is performed on the other four weights;
Step 4: Repeat steps 2 and 3 until performance is no longer improved;
Step 5: The five weights obtained are normalized.

Table 1. The approximate optimal weight of Lena.

Weight	w_1	w_2	w_3	w_4	w_5
Value	−0.1812	0.2373	0.2514	−0.0926	0.2375

2.3   Threshold Optimization

The threshold T is closely related to the embedded capacity. When the threshold T is too small, the embedding capacity cant be fulfilled, and when the threshold T is too large, the improvement in image quality is not significant. In the special case, when $T > max\,(C_{m,n})$, all blocks will be deemed to the smooth blocks, and the image quality is not improved. Therefore, an optimal threshold T^* should be found, which can adaptively satisfy the embedding capacity and optimize the image quality. In our method, information embedding can only be performed at the peak of the prediction error in the smooth blocks, so the optimal threshold T^* should satisfy:

$$T^* = \underset{C_{m,n} \geq T}{argmin}\,\{sum\,(count\,(P_{m,n})) \geq data\} \qquad (8)$$

Where $C_{m,n} \leq T$ represents the blocks whose texture feature values are less than the threshold T, $count\,(P_{m,n})$ denotes the number of the peak bins of prediction errors histogram in a single smooth block and $sum\,(count\,(P_{m,n}))$ is the number of the peak bins of prediction errors histogram in all smoothing blocks. $data$ is the length of secret information.

2.4   Embedding and Extraction Process

In this section, the embedding process is exhibited in Sect. 2.4.1 and the extraction process is introduced in Sect. 2.4.2.

Embedding. The cover image I is separated into sized $s_1 \times s_2$ blocks. Pixels are processed in raster-scanning order starting from the upper left corner. The embedding procedure is as follow:

Step 1: Calculate prediction value x_p according to [12–14], [16];
Step 2: Compute the prediction error such as $e = x - x_p$;
Step 3: Estimate texture feature information of blocks;
  (a) Generate a co-occurrence matrix M;
  (b) Compute the frequency $f\,(i,j)$ of the feature two-tuples (i,j);
  (c) Evaluate the entropy, energy, contrast, homogeneity, and mean square error respectively;
  (d) Calculate the optimal weights for the five parameters separately, then get the texture feature information of the final block;
Step 4: Select the blocks according to the threshold value;
Step 5: Embedding secret information in blocks that satisfy conditions by combining existing reversible data hiding methods.

After data embedding, the smooth block selected according to the threshold will be changed. Therefore, we use a matrix X to record which block is embedded with secret information. The smooth blocks are denoted as 1 and the texture blocks are denoted as 0 before embedding the secret information. Then, the matrix X is compressed and sent to the receiver as auxiliary information. When extracting information, the secret information can be accurately extracted and the cover image can be restored by the receiver according to the matrix X.

Extraction. The stego-image I' is divided into sized $s_1 \times s_2$ blocks. Pixels are processed in the same order as Sect. 2.4.1. The extraction procedure shows following:

Step 1: Obtain matrix X and embedding capacity from auxiliary information;
Step 2: Compute the prediction error such as $e' = x' - x'_p$;
Step 3: Extract the secret information and recover the image.

3   Experimental Results

We implement the reversible data hiding algorithms of Tsai et al. [12], Chen et al. [13], Lu et al. [14], Jung [16], and the proposed method using MATLAB. The proposed method is evaluated by four images of size 512×512, including: Lena, Boat, Plane, Tiffany, as shown in Fig. 1. For reversible data hiding, the image quality of the stego-image and the embedded capacity ER are important criteria for judging an algorithm. PSNR (peak signal to noise ratio) is a widely used measurement for evaluating the quality of data hiding algorithms.

(a)   (b)

(c)   (d)

Fig. 1. Standard test images: Lena, Boat, Plane, Tiffany.

3.1 A Detailed Example for the Proposed Method

Since the proposed strategy combines with the method in [12–14] and [16] respectively, the proposed strategy compares with their performance. Take Lena, Boats, Plane, Tiffany as the example: vertical coordinate is PSNR and horizontal coordinate is payload, as shown in Fig. 2. The threshold is uniformly set to 100 and the image is separated into sized 4×4 blocks. In the same embedding capacity, PSNR of the method [12–14], [16] is improved by combining with the proposed method, as shown in Fig. 2. In high embedding capacity, the image quality of the proposed method is improved obviously; in low embedding capacity, the image quality of the proposed method is similar to that of the method [12–14], [16]. As an example, when the embedding capacity is 7000 bits, the proposed method respectively improves the PSNR by 0.31 dB, 0.20 dB compared to that of Lu et al. [14] and Jung [16]; when the embedding capacity is 25000 bits, the proposed method enhance s the PSNR by 0.87 dB, 1.44 dB, as shown in Fig. 2(a).

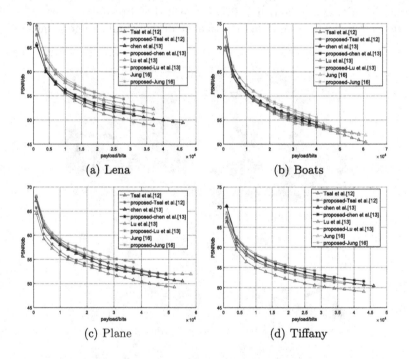

(a) Lena

(b) Boats

(c) Plane

(d) Tiffany

Fig. 2. PSNR-ER comparison.

3.2 Impact of Block Size

In this section, the impact of block size on image quality will be analyzed. In order to get the optimal block size, the threshold is uniformly set to 100, and the cover image is divided into smaller size $s_1 \times s_2$. The experiment tests the PSNR of the image in different block size and the same payload. Taking an example of Lena, when the block size is 4 × 4, 5 × 5, 6 × 6, and 7 × 7 respectively, the PSNR of the proposed method is higher than the method of [12–14], [16], as shown in Fig. 3. With the increase in block size, the PSNR increases, but the embedding capacity decreases. When the embedding capacity is 22000 bits, as shown in Fig. 3(c), the 5 × 5 size block improves the PSNR by 0.33 compared to the 4 × 4 size block, but the embedded capacity cannot be satisfied. Therefore, according to the embedding capacity, the block should be selected, which not only satisfies the embedding capacity but also optimizes the image quality.

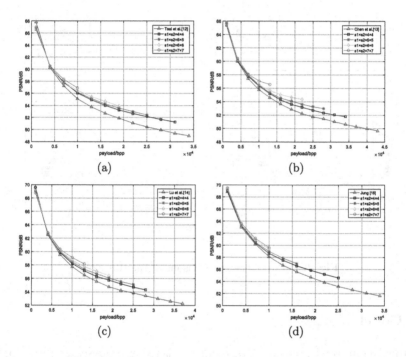

Fig. 3. Performance comparisons of the block size.

3.3 Impact of the Threshold

Under the premise of satisfying the embedding capacity, the optimal threshold should be selected to ensure the optimal image quality. The proposed strategy also combines with the method in [12–14] and [16] respectively. Taking Lena as an example, in the case of the same block and threshold, the image quality with embedding capacity 10000 bits is superior to image quality with embedding capacity 20000 bits. Furthermore, the PSNR keeps decreasing and tends to be flat, as shown in Fig. 4. Under the same block conditions, the embedding capacity decreases with the decrease of the threshold value. The embedding capacity is less than 20000 bits when the block size is 5 × 5 and the threshold is 40, 50 respectively, as shown in Fig. 4(a) and (b). At the same capacity, the image quality of the 5×5 size block shows much better performance than the image quality of the 4×4 size block, and the PSNR also keeps decreasing and tends to be flat. Therefore, with the decrease of the threshold value, the embedding capacity of the image is also reduced, but the PSNR increases with the same embedding capacity.

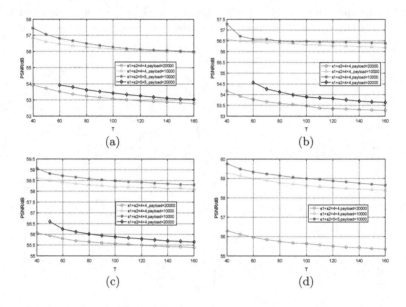

Fig. 4. Performance comparisons of the threshold.

4   Conclusions

In order to improve the stego-image quality, this paper proposes a strategy of distinguishing texture feature for reversible data hiding based on histogram shifting. After calculating the texture feature value of each block, we select the optimal threshold value which can achieve the optimal image quality according to the embedding capacity. Finally, the information is embedded at the point where the condition is satisfied. Experimental results show that the selection of block size and threshold is closely related to the embedding capacity and the image. Our method can improve image quality effectively.

Acknowledgements. This research work is partly supported by National Natural Science Foundation of China (61502009, 61872003, U1536109), Foundation of China Scholarship Council (201706505004).

References

1. Honsinger, C.W., Jones, P.W., Rabbani, M., Stoffel, J.C.: Lossless recovery of an original image containing embedded data. US Patent 6,278,791, 21 August 2001
2. Coatrieux, C., Le Guillou, C., Cauvin, J.M., Roux, C.: Reversible watermarking for knowledge digest embedding and reliability control in medical images. IEEE Trans. Inf. Technol. Biomed. Publ. IEEE Eng. Med. Biol. Soc. **13**(2), 158–165 (2009)
3. Tong, X., Shen, G., Xuan, G., Li, S., Yang, Z., Li, J., Shi, Y.-Q.: Stereo image coding with histogram-pair based reversible data hiding. In: Shi, Y.-Q., Kim, H.J., Pérez-González, F., Yang, C.-N. (eds.) IWDW 2014. LNCS, vol. 9023, pp. 201–214. Springer, Cham (2015). https://doi.org/10.1007/978-3-319-19321-2_15
4. Barton, J.M.: Method and apparatus for embedding authentication information within digital data. US Patent 5,646,997, 8 July 1997
5. Celik, M.U., Sharma, G., Tekalp, A.M., Saber, E.: Reversible data hiding. In: Proceedings of the International Conference on Image Processing, vol. 2, pp. II-157–II-160 (2002)
6. Celik, M.U.: Lossless watermarking for image authentication: a new framework and an implementation. IEEE Trans. Image Process. **15**(4), 1042–1049 (2006)
7. Hong, W.: Adaptive reversible data hiding method based on error energy control and histogram shifting. Opt. Commun. **285**(2), 101–108 (2011)
8. Xiang, S., Wang, Y.: Non-integer expansion embedding techniques for reversible image watermarking. Eurasip J. Adv. Signal Process. **2015**(1), 56 (2015)
9. Ni, Z., Shi, Y.Q., Ansari, N., Su, W.: Reversible data hiding. In: International Workshop on Digital Watermarking, pp. 1–12 (2004)
10. Wang, J., Ni, J., Zhang, X., Shi, Y.Q.: Rate and distortion optimization for reversible data hiding using multiple histogram shifting. IEEE Trans. Cybern. **47**(2), 315 (2017)
11. Ma, X., Pan, Z., Hu, S., Wang, L.: High-fidelity reversible data hiding scheme based on multi-predictor sorting and selecting mechanism. J. Vis. Commun. Image Represent. **28**, 71–82 (2015)
12. Tsai, P., Hu, Y.C., Yeh, H.L.: Reversible image hiding scheme using predictive coding and histogram shifting. Signal Process. **89**(6), 1129–1143 (2009)
13. Chen, X., Sun, X., Sun, H., Zhou, Z., Zhang, J.: Reversible watermarking method based on asymmetric-histogram shifting of prediction errors. J. Syst. Softw. **86**(10), 2620–2626 (2013)
14. Lu, T.C., Tseng, C.Y., Wu, J.H.: Asymmetric-histogram based reversible information hiding scheme using edge sensitivity detection. J. Syst. Softw. **116**, 2–21 (2016)
15. Chen, H., Ni, J., Hong, W., Chen, T.S.: High-fidelity reversible data hiding using directionally enclosed prediction. IEEE Signal Process. Lett. **24**(5), 574–578 (2017)
16. Jung, K.H.: A high-capacity reversible data hiding scheme based on sorting and prediction in digital images. Multimedia Tools Appl. **76**, 13127–13137 (2017)

Reversible Data Hiding Scheme in Encrypted-Image Based on Prediction and Compression Coding

Fan Chen[1], Yuan Yuan[1], Yuyu Chen[2], Hongjie He[1(✉)], and Lingfeng Qu[1]

[1] School of Information Science and Technology, Southwest Jiaotong University, Chengdu 611756, China
hjhe@swjtu.com
[2] Mao Yisheng Honors College, Southwest Jiaotong University, Chengdu 611756, China

Abstract. For cloud storage management and security of images, more and more attention is paid to reversible data hiding in encrypted images (RDH-EI). This work proposes a RDH-EI method based on a novel compression coding that can vacate more space for data hiding. To improve the embedding capacity, several most significant bits (MSB) of an original image are firstly predicted in turn to generate the corresponding prediction bit-planes, and then the XOR operation and a shorter variable-length coding are designed to further decrease the coding length of the prediction bit-planes. The proposed scheme can achieve a larger embedding capacity and real reversibility and lossless decryption. Experimental results demonstrate that the performance of the proposed method outperforms other RDH-EI schemes, including embedding capacity, reversibility and the ability against the cipher-only attack.

Keywords: Reversible data hiding · Image encryption · Cloud storage · Compression coding

1 Introduction

With the development of information technology, the growth in cloud computing has led to serious security problems. Hackers or other illegal person threaten the confidentiality, authentication and integrity of information [1]. The malicious use of information by these illegal people makes the information security of people and even the country not guaranteed. Therefore, owners need to consider reliable storage and secure transmission of digital images. Jolfaei et al. [2] point out that encryption is an effective and popular solution to maintain confidentiality and privacy of data since it converts the original and meaningful image content to

This work is supported by National Natural Science Foundation of China (NSFC) under grants (61872303, 61461047), and Technology Innovation Talent Program of Science & Technology Department of Sichuan Province (2018RZ0143).

incomprehensible and noise-like one. That is, the analysis and processing of the encrypted image is performed without knowledge of the original content during storage or archiving. It is inevitable that people pay more and more attention in reversible data hiding in encrypted images (RDH-EI) [3].

In the encryption process of the RDH-EI technology, the cloud manager can embed and losslessly extract additional data for assisting in processing and protecting the encrypted image in the cloud without knowing the original content of the image. At the receiving end, a legitimate user must rely on an encrypted image containing additional data, also known as a marked-encrypted image, if he wants to fully restore the original image. In recent years, researchers have proposed many RDH-EI methods which can be classified into two categories: VRAE (vacating room after encryption) and VRBE (vacating room before encryption) [3]. VRAE framework vacates embedding room from the encrypted images directly, and the additional data are embedded by modifying some bits of the encrypted pixels [4–6]. VRAE framework is simple for content owner since it does not require to perform an extra pre-processing before image encryption. However, it is difficult to make space from the encrypted image because the encrypted image is already completely close to the noise image, and the pixel correlation is lower than the original image. As a result, the VRAE-based RDHEI methods only achieve small payloads or generate decrypted image with poor quality for larger payload [7]. Taking Qian's algorithm [6] as an example, the maximum embedding payload can be achieve 0.3 bpp, and PSNRs of decrypted images are between 25 dB and 35 dB for different images.

On the contrary, The VRBE framework vacates the room to embed additional data in the plaintext domain. Thus, the content owner needs to process the plaintext image before encryption to vacate room for embedding. It is worth to increase the burden on the content owner because it makes RDH-EI achieve real reversibility, and makes data hiding/extracting process effortless [7]. Moreover, the embedded payload has also been greatly improved owing to the local correlation of natural images. Ma et al. [7] first proposed the VRBE framework to vacate the room by embedding least significant bits (LSBs) of some pixels into other pixels with a traditional RDH method, so the positions of the corresponding LSBs could be used to embed data. The data hider can make data hiding process effortless and lossless due to the extra space vacated out by the content owner. The embedding rate can be increased to about to 0.5 bpp with the traditional method of reversible data hiding. The decrypted image is slightly altered when compared to the original one (PSNR $\approx$ 40 dB). In order to further increase the embedding capacity, researchers proposed a variety of VRBE-based RDH-EI schemes using the different strategies. For example, Xu et al. [8] proposed a RDH-EI by adopting the interpolation prediction errors coding combined with traditional RDH, in which a specific encryption mode was designed to encrypt the interpolation error. Cao et al. [9] adopted a patch-level sparse representation to increase the embedding payload to close to 1 bpp. However the time complexity of Cao et al. [9] since the preprocessing operations before encryption included the block sparse coding and traditional reversible data hiding.

To further improved the embedding capacity, the MSB-inversion prediction-based RDH-EI methods were proposed by Puteaux et al. [1] and Chen et al. [10], respectively. Their time complexity was reduced. Moreover, Chen et al. [10] reduced the difficulty of key management and broadens the scope of use of the RDH-EI technique. Because the decrypted image of [10], which is identical to the original one, can be obtained only by the encryption key.

From the perspective of cloud storage security, it is noted that most existing RDH-EI methods [1,4–9] generate the encrypted images by stream cipher before data hiding. Although the stream cipher is faster and provides greater flexibility, it is vulnerable to the Ciphertext-Only-Attack (COA) proposed by Khelifi [11]. In this case, the data hider can break the security of the encryption system and consequently disclose the visual content of encrypted images. Therefore, the researchers have pro-posed the scrambling encryption including block scram-bling [12], pixel classification scrambling [13] and bit scrambling [14,15] to improve the security of encrypted images. The embedded capacity of some RDH-EI algorithms such as [14] and [15] has exceeded 2 bpp by using the correlation of high significant bit planes. About $\frac{1}{4}$ of the space is vacated to hide additional information in such an encrypted images. However, they do not make good use of the relevance of natural images.

In this paper, we propose a reversible data hiding scheme in encrypted image based on prediction and compression coding. Main contribution of this paper includes three aspects as follows. (1) An efficient prediction method is proposed to make the bit planes smoother; (2) These smooth bit planes are compressed with more flexible coding to make room for embedded information; (3) The security of images in the cloud is effectively improved because the stream cipher and bit-wise scrambling encryptions are used to generate the encrypted images.

The remainder of this paper is organized as follows. Section 2 introduces the detail of proposed RDH-EI method. In Sect. 3, we present and analyze the experimental results. Finally, conclusions are provided in Sect. 4.

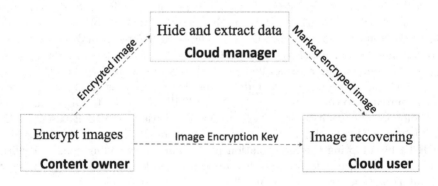

Fig. 1. RDH-EI model for cloud storage

2   Proposed RDH-EI Scheme

The process of RDH-EI cloud storage model is shown in Fig. 1. The existing re-versible data hiding algorithm has been able to achieve a large embedding rate, and cloud managers can extract data losslessly. Moreover, if cloud users have an image encryption key, they can obtain the decrypted images with high quality and even fully recover original images. As is well known, the embedding capacity is an important indicator of RDH-EI technology. According to the model shown in Fig. 1, it can be seen that both the content owners uploading the encrypted image and the users downloading the marked-encrypted image require network bandwidth. Moreover, saving and managing encrypted images in the cloud require storage space. Therefore, the goal of this paper is to increase the embedding capacity and improve the Cloud storage security (such as the ability to resist COA attacks). On this basis, it also provides the possibility to reduce the size of encrypted images. Next, the algorithm proposed in this paper is introduced in detail.

2.1   Image Encryption

The proposed algorithm uses the method of vacating the space before encryption since the correlation of natural images is well which are easy to compress. This frame of the encryption process is shown in Fig. 2.

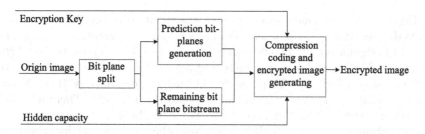

Fig. 2. A framework of the encryption process of the proposed algorithm

In order to enable the multi-MSB planes compressed well, the content owner first predicts and XORs the multi-MSB planes of the original image I whose size is M × N × 8, and then reconstructs an image that is not larger than the original image I according to the data D that the cloud manager needs to embed. To ensure its security, the reconstructed image is encrypted by the stream cipher and scrambling. Each bit plane data of I is I_i ($1 \leq i \leq 8$), where I_1 is the most significant bit (MSB) planes and I_8 is the least significant bit (LSB) planes. Divide the original image I into two parts according to the bit plane k which we choose to compress: I_H (high significant k bit planes), I_L (low significant 8-k bit planes). The I_L is bit-scanned into a one-dimensional matrix.

Prediction Bit-Planes Generation. In the prediction phase, only the first row and first column of the image are preserved. The prediction starts from the second row and second column. The original pixel value p is derived from Eq. (1) based on the predicted bit-plane t ($1 \leq t \leq k$), where p' is the pixel value after p is flipped by the most significant bit. As shown in Eq. (2), the predicted value x is the average of three pixels known around. By comparing the sizes of $|p(i,j) - x(i,j)|$ and $|p'(i,j) - x(i,j)|$ to obtain the t_{th} bit plane value H_t (i,j),($1<i\leq M, 1<j\leq N$) in Eq. (3).

$$p(i,j) = \sum_{u=t}^{8} I_u(i,j) \times 2^{8-u} \tag{1}$$

$$x(i,j) = \frac{p(i,j-1) + p(i-1,j) + p(i-1,j-1)}{3} \tag{2}$$

$$H_t(i,j) = \begin{cases} 0, & if \ |p(i,j) - x(i,j)| < |p'(i,j) - x(i,j)| \\ 1, & if \ |p(i,j) - x(i,j)| > |p'(i,j) - x(i,j)| \\ \lfloor \frac{p(i,j)}{2^{8-t}} \rfloor, & if \ |p(i,j) - x(i,j)| = |p'(i,j) - x(i,j)| \end{cases} \tag{3}$$

In Eqs. (1) to (3), $1 < i \leq M, 1 < j \leq N$. The k bit planes H_i ($1 < i \leq k$) for H are XORed from the MSB plane since the predicted neighboring bit planes also have a correlation. H_i is obtained by

$$H_{i+1} = H_i \oplus H_{i+1} \tag{4}$$

Taking the House image as an example, the result of the predicted planes and the XOR operation of the adjacent bit planes is analyzed. Figure 3(a)–(c) are the three high significant bit planes binary images, Fig. 3(d)–(f) are the predicted bit planes of Fig. 3(a)–(c), respectively, Fig. 3(g)–(h) are the bit planes after the XOR operation of adjacent bit planes of Fig. 3(d)–(f), respectively. It can be seen that the value of the predicted bit plane is mostly 0 (black). There are many similarities between Fig. 3(e) and (f), so the new third high significant plane Fig. 3(h) obtained after the XOR becomes smoother than the original third high significant plane Fig. 3(f) and is more favorable to compression.

Compression Coding and Encrypted Image Generating. Since the high significant bit planes of vacated image is similar to Fig. 3(d) having a large number of black areas (value 0), there are only a small number of completely white blocks or blocks with many white pixels, so the block type identifiers are shown in Table 1. The block will be divided into three categories: all-zero block G-Imost of the blocks are 0 G-IImost pixels in the block with value of 1 or exceeding the threshold are Bad blocks. Each predicted multi-MSBs planes H is divided into $m \times n$ blocks of size $s \times s$.

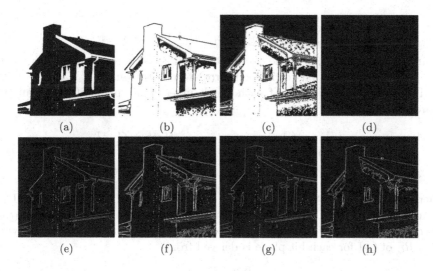

Fig. 3. Bit planes of House ((a)–(c) is the three high significant bit planes of the original image (d)–(f) is the three predicted high significant bit planes of original image; (g) The second high significant bit plane after prediction and XOR; (h) The third high significant bit plane after prediction and XOR.).

Table 1. Block classification identification.

Condition	Block type	Block-labeling bits
$f = n1 = 0$	G-I	0
$1 \leq f \leq na, n1 < n0$	G-II	1 0
Other cases	Bad	1 1

In Table 1, n_0 is the number of pixel values of 0, n_1 is the number of pixel values of 1, $f = min\{n_0, n_1\}$. n_a is the threshold for classification, which is derived from

$$n_a = \arg\max_{x}\{h - 2 - max\{\lceil \log_2 x \rceil\}, 1\} - x\lceil \log_2 h \rceil\} \geq 0 \quad 1 \leq x \leq \lceil 0.16 \times h \rceil,$$

(5)

where $h = s \times s$.

The G-I block only needs to record the block-labeling bits. The Bad block needs to record all the original data in addition to the block-labeling bits. A block of type G-II needs to record a few pixel positions as structural information in addition to the block-labeling bits. The space occupied by a few pixels g in G-II is $p = max\{\lceil \log_2 na \rceil, 1\}$. The relative positions with each pixels value of 1 is given by Eq. (6). The space occupied by the relative positions is obtained by Eq. (7).

$$t_i = \begin{cases} z_i & , i = 1 \\ z_i - z_{i-1} & , 2 \leq i \leq n \end{cases}$$

(6)

$$q_i = \begin{cases} \lceil log_2 h \rceil & , \quad i = 1 \\ max\{\lceil log_2(h - z_{i-1}) \rceil, 1\} & , \quad 2 \leq i \leq n \end{cases} \quad (7)$$

In Eqs. (6) and (7), z_i is the one-dimensional coordinate of pixels with value of 1 in the block from left to right and from top to bottom.

The compression length of each block in each bit plane $l(i, j, t)$ can be expressed as

$$l(i, j, t) = \begin{cases} 1 & , \quad blcok \ is \ G - I \\ 2 + p + \sum_{i=1}^{f} q_i & , \quad blcok \ is \ G - II \\ 2 + s \times s & , \quad blcok \ is \ Bad \end{cases} \quad (8)$$

where $1 \leq i \leq m, 1 \leq j \leq n, 1 \leq t \leq k$. Then the predicted bit planes H is compressed into the One-dimensional matrix H. As can be seen from Eq. (8), the compression length of the block of type G-I is the shortest. The block type ratio R_G of G-I for each bit plane is derived from

$$R_{G_i} = \frac{n_{g_i}}{m \times n} \quad 1 \leq i \leq k. \quad (9)$$

Where n_{g_i} is the number of G-I blocks per bit plane.

Table 2. The proportion of good block types.

Condition	R_{G_1}	R_{G_2}	R_{G_3}
Original bit plane	0.92	0.83	0.71
Predicted bit plane	0.98	0.89	0.80
Predicted and XOR bit plane	0.98	0.90	0.83

Table 2 shows the proportion of the good blocks of the three bit planes in different cases in Fig. 3. The ratio of the first row is the block ratio of the pixel value of all 0s and all 1s. The second and third rows are predicted and the bit planes after the adjacent bit planes are XORed. Since most pixels are 0, the good block ratio is the block ratio where the pixel value is all 0s.

It can be seen from Table 2 that the prediction greatly improves the good block ratio of the MSB plane, and the block ratio R_{G_3} of the predicted bit plane with the adjacent bit plane XOR operation (as shown in Fig. 3(h)) is larger than the predicted only bit plane (as shown in Fig. 3(f)). Therefore, prediction and XOR operations are necessary for bit plane compression. To get the number of actually compressed bit planes k', we compare the length of each bit plane compression with the original image size. k' is obtained by Eq. (10). The embedding rate of each bit planes is calculated from Eq. (11). The total embedding rate is calculated from Eq. (12).

$$k' = \arg\min_{t}(\lfloor \sum_{i=1}^{m} \sum_{j=1}^{n} \frac{l(i,j,t)}{M \times N} \rfloor = 1) - 1 \quad 1 \leq t \leq k \quad (10)$$

$$r_i = \frac{m \times n - \sum_{i=1}^{m} \sum_{j=1}^{n} l(i,j,t)}{M \times N} \qquad 1 \le t \le k' \tag{11}$$

$$R = \sum_{t=1}^{k'} r_t \tag{12}$$

Convert each bit planes of original image I into a one-dimensional matrix. According to k', the high k bit planes can be divided into two parts: $C1 = [H_1'|| \ldots ||H_{k'}']$, $C2 = [I_{k'+1}|| \ldots ||I_k]$. The length of the compressed bitstream C of the original image I is l_c. $C = [C1||C2||I_L]$, where $[||]$ is a matrix connection.

It is assumed that the column of the compressed encrypted image coincides with the original image as N. In order to facilitate the restoration of the image, some parameters P need to be stored in the image, here P includes: 3 bits of k, 3 bits of k', 20 bits of M, The total length of P is 26 bits.

The maximum embedding capacity Max is derived from the Eq. (13). Cloud Manager embedded capacity $D \le Max$.

$$Max = M \times N \times 8 - 26 \tag{13}$$

When generating an encrypted image, the bit C compressed by the original image is first scrambled by the encryption key K_E to generate an encrypted bit stream Z. Then, Z is combined with the embedded information D_A to form a one-dimensional bit stream $B = [Z, D_A, P]$, where D_A are the bits initialized to all 0s. Finally, the encrypted bit stream E_b is obtained by encrypting B with the encryption key K_E. Then divide E_b into eight bit-planes of size $M \times N$, and an encrypted image E of size $M \times N$ is generated.

Content owner uploaded encrypted image E to the cloud, the cloud manager can embeds D bits data in E to obtain the marked-encrypted image X. The cloud manager can extract the embedded information from X, and if the cloud users hold the encryption key, they can download the image from the cloud and decrypt it to obtain the original image.

2.2   Decrypt Image

The image decryption operations can be described as follows: (1) decrypting the bit stream; (2) restoring the original low significant bit planes; (3) restoring the original multi-MSB planes; (4) restoring the adjacent bit planes; (5) recovering multi-MSB planes predictions.

(1) Decrypt the bit stream. For the encrypted image X containing the hidden information, its bit-plane bits are scanned into a one-dimensional matrix D_b. Utilizing the key K_E to decrypt D_b, and the parameters are extracted: the number of Multi-MSB planes for prediction and XOR operation, $\overline{k}$, the number of compressed high significant bit planes, $\overline{k}'$, the number of original image row $\overline{M}$. The K_E is used to recovery the bits other than the bitstream of the parameter and embedding information in D_b which is decrypted by scrambling. The decrypted bit stream is Q.

(2) Restore the original low significant bit. The bits other than the parameters in Q are denoted by Q'. The last $\bar{l}$ bits in Q' are the data of the recovered low $(8 - \bar{k}')$ bit planes,Re_L. The bits in Q' other than Re_L are the compressed high significant bitstream, Re_H. The low significant bit plane$RL_i(8 - \bar{k}' < i \leq 8)$ of the restored images are obtained by dividing the Re_L into $(8 - \bar{k}')$ bit planes of size $\overline{M}' \times N$.

$$\bar{l} = \overline{M} \times N \times (8 - \bar{k}') \tag{14}$$

(3) Restore the original multi-MSB planes. The block type is determined based on the identification information. Scan $Re_H$to recovery the block $B'_i(1 \leq i \leq \frac{Re_H \times N \times \bar{k}'}{s \times s}$ based on the block type. If the block type is G-II, the position of the pixel with a value of 1 in the block is obtained by the Eqs. (15) and (16).

$$q'_i = \begin{cases} \lceil log_2 s \times s \rceil & , i = 1 \\ max\{\lceil log_2(s \times s - z'_{i-1})\rceil, 1 & , 2 \leq i \leq f \end{cases} \tag{15}$$

$$z'_i = \begin{cases} t'_i & , i = 1 \\ t'_i + t'_{i-1} & , 2 \leq i \leq n \end{cases} \tag{16}$$

Dividing B'_i into $\bar{k}'$ bit-planes of size $\frac{\overline{M} \times N}{s \times s}$ to obtain the high-level bitmap of the recovered image $Re_{H_i}(1 \leq i \leq \bar{k}')$.

(4) Restore adjacent bit planes. Re_{H_i} and Re_{L_i} are used as the 8 bit planes of the image to compose a image R' of size $M \times N$. The adjacent bit plane of the high $\bar{k}$ bit plane of the image R' is recovered as

$$R'_{\bar{k}-i} = R'_{\bar{k}-i} \oplus R'_{\bar{k}-i-1} \quad , 0 \leq i < \bar{k} - 1. \tag{17}$$

(5) Restore multi-MSB predictions. The value of the original bit plane is restored from the $\bar{k}^{th}$ bit plane. The original pixels $\bar{p}$, the predicted pixels value $\bar{x}$, and the flipped pixels value $\bar{p}'l$ are still derived from the Eqs. (1) and (2). Denote the $t^{th}(1 \leq t \leq \bar{k})$ bit plane is $\overline{H}_t(i, j)$. When $\overline{H}_t(i, j) = 0$, the original bit is restored by the Eq. (18); When $\overline{H}_t(i, j) = 1$, the original bit is restored by the Eq. (19). In both cases, if the original pixel $\bar{p}(i, j)$ is equal to the flipped pixel $\bar{p}'(i, j)$, the original bit is restored by the Eq. (20).

$$R'_t(i, j) = \begin{cases} \lfloor \frac{\bar{p}(i,j)}{2^{8-t}} \rfloor, & if \ |\bar{p}(i, j) - \bar{x}(i, j)| < |\bar{p}'(i, j) - \bar{x}(i, j)| \\ \lfloor \frac{\bar{p}'(i,j)}{2^{8-t}} \rfloor, & if \ |\bar{p}(i, j) - \bar{x}(i, j)| > |\bar{p}'(i, j) - \bar{x}(i, j)| \end{cases} \tag{18}$$

$$R'_t(i, j) = \begin{cases} \lfloor \frac{\bar{p}(i,j)}{2^{8-t}} \rfloor, & if \ |\bar{p}(i, j) - \bar{x}(i, j)| > |\bar{p}'(i, j) - \bar{x}(i, j)| \\ \lfloor \frac{\bar{p}'(i,j)}{2^{8-t}} \rfloor, & if \ |\bar{p}(i, j) - \bar{x}(i, j)| < |\bar{p}'(i, j) - \bar{x}(i, j)| \end{cases} \tag{19}$$

$$R'_t(i, j) = \lfloor \frac{\bar{p}(i, j)}{2^{8-t}} \rfloor, \quad if \ |\bar{p}(i, j) - \bar{x}(i, j)| = |\bar{p}'(i, j) - \bar{x}(i, j)| \tag{20}$$

Where $1 < i \leq \overline{M}, 1 < j \leq N$. The decrypted image R is obtained by combining the $\bar{k}$ high significant bit planes with the rest low significant bits.

Fig. 4. Test images applied on the proposed algorithm. (a)–(c) are the original images of Lena, Airplane and House respectively; (d)–(f) are the marked-encrypted images of Lena, Airplane and House with the total embedding capacity when embedding in three bit planes respectively; (g)–(i) is decrypted images of Lena, Airplane and House respectively.

3   Experimental Results

In the following experiment, all the test images were gray-scale images of size 512×512. The parameters used in the experiment were the bit planes for prediction and XOR operation $k = 3$, the block size $s = 4$. First, the embedding capacity of the high k significant bit planes of the four images of Lena, Baboon, Airplane, and House are tested. Then, the embedding rate of 100 images was tested. In order to show the advantages of the algorithm in cloud storage, the ratio of the size of the encrypted image to the original image at $D = 10000$ bits was tested. Finally, the security of the proposed algorithm is analyzed.

Lena, Airplane, and House, shown in Fig. 4, are used as examples in the proposed algorithm. When we chose three bit planes to embed additional data, the embedded capacity for these images are 2.23, 2.21, 2.54 bpp, respectively. The decrypted images Fig. 4(g)–(i) is same as Fig. 4(a)–(c).

3.1 Maximum Embedding Rate

In order to illustrate the proposed algorithm can vacate more space to embed additional data, the Lena, Airplane and House as the test images to discuss the total embedding rate for 3 bit planes. The result is shown in Table 3.

Table 3. The embedding rate for 3 bit planes.

RDH-EI methods	Lena	Airplane	House	Average
Yi et al. [14]	1.68	1.81	2.16	1.88
Liu et al. [15]	1.58	1.72	2.04	1.78
Puteaux et al. [1]	0.99	0.99	0.99	0.99
Proposed	2.23	2.21	2.54	2.33

In Table 3, the Algorithms [14, 15] are based on bit-plane block compression. None of them changed the relevance of natural images. The proposed algorithm vacates larger space than [14, 15] because we uses the Multi-MSB prediction and the XOR operation of adjacent bit plans to smooth the multi-MSB planes of the natural image. The embedding rate of the proposed algorithm is larger than [1] since the proposed algorithm uses Multi-MSB prediction and [1] only predicted the MSB plane.

Figure 5 shows the embedding rates of [1, 14, 15] and the proposed algorithm in the case that 100 images are compressed the highest 3 bit planes and the block size is 4. As we can see, the embedded rate of proposed method is better than [14] and [15]. This is because the compressible coding method of [14] is better than [15], but the time complexity of [15] is lower. The reference [1] predicts the MSB of an image and vacates it for embedding information. The degree of embedded information is not much correlated with the texture degree of the image. The information embedded in the reference [14, 15] and the proposed algorithm has a great relationship with the texture degree of the image. The more texture the image is embedded, the less data is embedded. The three texture images with the lowest embedding rate in Fig. 5 are shown in Fig. 6. The embedding rate of the three images of Fig. 6 is as shown in Table 4. We can find that the proposed algorithm has higher average embedding rate for images with more complex textures than [1, 14, 15]. The average embedded capacity of [1, 14, 15] and the proposed algorithm for 100 images is 0.996 bpp, 1.59 bpp, and 1.51 bpp, 2.15 bpp respectively. The embedding rate of the proposed algorithm is 0.56 bpp higher than [14], 0.64 bpp higher than [15], and 1.16 bpp higher than [1].

In general, the proposed algorithm has higher embedding capacity than [1,14,15], which shows the applicability of the proposed algorithm for images with different textures.

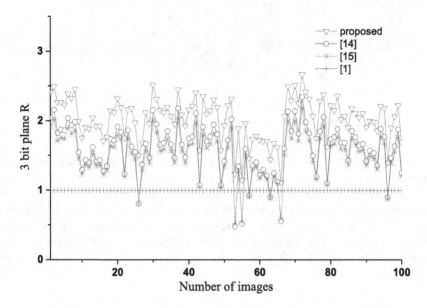

Fig. 5. Comparison of embedding capacity for 100 images

Table 4. The embedding rate of texture images for 3 bit planes.

RDH-EI methods	Baboon	Texture1	Texture2	Average
Yi et al. [14]	0.48	0.55	0.52	0.52
Liu et al. [15]	0.52	0.59	0.55	0.55
Puteaux et al. [1]	0.99	0.99	0.99	0.99
Proposed	1.18	1.21	1.25	1.21

3.2 Security Analysis

As people pay more and more attention to privacy, the issue of cloud security has also become a concern for many researchers. The PSNR of the encrypted images of [1] and the proposed algorithm attacking by [11] is as shown in Fig. 7. It can be seen from Fig. 7 that the PSNR of the encrypted image of [1] attacking by COA is about 33, and there is a certain degree of image content leakage, because only the

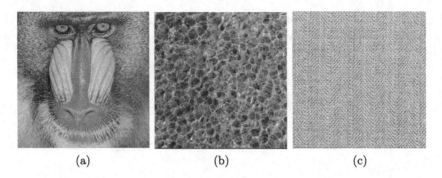

(a)   (b)   (c)

Fig. 6. Texture images. (a) Baboon; (b) Texture1; (c) Texture2.

stream cipher encryption is used in [1]. The proposed algorithm combines stream cipher and scrambling encryption. Our encryption method not only changes the position of the pixel, but also changes the value of the pixel. In summary, the image uploaded to the cloud has better security. The high significant bit planes of [14] are used to compress, and the remaining lower significant bits are used to embed data. The encryption effect of [14] is similar to the algorithm proposed in this paper. The image in [15] is encrypted by scrambling, so it can resist COA attacks.

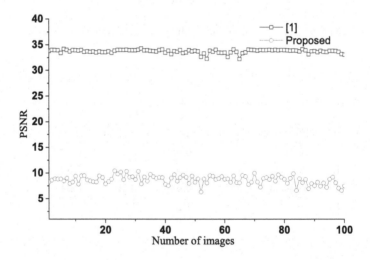

Fig. 7. PSNR of decrypted image and original image after attack with [11].

4   Conclusion

Many existing reversible data hiding algorithms can achieve a large embedding rate and reversible recovery of images while ensuring security. However, it is also possible to further increase the embedding rate by utilizing the correlation of natural images. So this paper proposes an algorithm for reversible data Hiding scheme in encrypted-image based on prediction and compression coding. The experimental results show that the algorithm of this paper make full use of the image correlation to obtain a larger embedding space. The embedding rate of the proposed algorithm is about 0.6 bpp higher than the literature [14, 15] and 1.16 bpp higher than [1]. Moreover, the encrypted image uploaded to the cloud is changed by the value of the pixel and the position of the pixel, and the security is further improved. In addition, the embedded information can be extracted without loss, and the decrypted image consistent with the original image can be obtained.

References

1. Puteaux, P., Puech, W.: An efficient MSB prediction-based method for high-capacity reversible data hiding in encrypted images. IEEE Trans. Inf. Forensics Secur. **13**(7), 1670–1681 (2018)
2. Jolfaei, A., Wu, X.W., Muthukkumarasamy, V.: On the security of permutation-only im-age encryption schemes. IEEE Trans. Inf. Forensics Secur. **11**(2), 235–246 (2016)
3. Shi, Y.Q., Li, X., Zhang, X., Wu, H.T., Ma, B.: Reversible data hiding: advances in the past two decades. IEEE Access **4**, 705–720 (2016)
4. Zhang, X.: Separable reversible data hiding in encrypted image. IEEE Trans. Inf. Forensics Secur. **7**(2), 826–832 (2012)
5. Zhou, J., Sun, W., Dong, L., et al.: Secure reversible image data hiding over encrypted domain via key modulation. IEEE Trans. Circuits Syst. Video Technol. **26**(3), 441–452 (2016)
6. Qian, Z., Zhang, X.: Reversible data hiding in encrypted images with distributed source encoding. IEEE Trans. Circuits Syst. Video Technol. **26**(4), 636–646 (2016)
7. Ma, K., Zhang, W., Zhao, X., et al.: Reversible data hiding in encrypted images by reserving room before encryption. IEEE Trans. Inf. Forensics Secur. **8**(3), 553–562 (2013)
8. Xu, D., Wang, R.: Separable and error-free reversible data hiding in encrypted images. Signal Proc. **123**, 9–21 (2016)
9. Cao, X., Du, L., Wei, X., et al.: High capacity reversible data hiding in encrypted images by patch-level sparse representation. IEEE Trans. Cybern. **46**(5), 1132–1143 (2016)
10. Chen, Y., Yan, S., He, H., et al.: Secure reversible data hiding in encrypted images based on MSB-flip prediction. Patent No: 201810174576.8, 02 March 2018
11. Khelifi, F.: On the security of a stream cipher in reversible data hiding schemes operating in the encrypted domain. Signal Proc. **143**, 336–345 (2018)
12. Huang, F., Huang, J., Shi, Y.Q.: New framework for reversible data hiding in encrypted domain. IEEE Trans. Inf. Forensics Secur. **11**(12), 2777–2789 (2016)
13. Chen, F., He, H., Ma, T., et al.: Reversible data hiding in classification-scrambling encrypted-image based on iterative recovery. In: International Conference on Cloud Computing and Security, pp. 162–174 (2018)
14. Yi, S., Zhou, Y.: Binary-block embedding for reversible data hiding in encrypted images. Signal Proc. **133**, 40–51 (2017)
15. Liu, Z.L., Pun, C.M.: Reversible data-hiding in encrypted images by redundant space transfer. Inf. Sci. **433–434**, 188–203 (2018)

Steganographic Algorithms

A High Capacity HEVC Steganographic Algorithm Using Intra Prediction Modes in Multi-sized Prediction Blocks

Yi Dong[1], Tanfeng Sun[1,2], and Xinghao Jiang[1,2(✉)]

[1] School of Electronic Information and Electrical Engineering,
Shanghai Jiao Tong University, Shanghai, China
xhjiang@sjtu.edu.cn
[2] National Engineering Lab on Information Content Analysis Techniques,
Shanghai GT036001, China

Abstract. The existing video steganographic schemes based on intra prediction modes for video coding standards H.264/AVC and HEVC all use single-sized blocks to embed the secret payload. Thus, the steganographic properties of HEVC multi-sized tree-structured intra partition still need exploration. In this paper, a novel video steganographic algorithm is presented. Base on the fact that visual quality degradation caused by steganography is basically the same for both large-sized Prediction Blocks (PBs) and small-sized PBs, this algorithm tries to exploit intra prediction modes in multi-sized PBs in each Coding Tree Units (CTU). The innovation of this paper includes: (1) Improvement in capacity without introducing great degradation in visual quality. (2) High coding efficiency maintained by defining cost function based on rate distortion. (3) A new indicator to measure Bit Increase Ratio(BIR) under different capacity. The Experimental results show that this algorithm outperforms the latest intra prediction modes based HEVC steganographic algorithm in both capacity and perceptibility while preserving coding efficiency as well.

Keywords: HEVC · Intra prediction modes · Video steganography

1 Introduction

With the development of broadband network and mobile Internet technology, the transmission and service based on video media are booming. Video media in HEVC format, because of its high resolution and small file size, are very suitable as carrier of secret communication, with the possibility of large capacity communication provided. On the other hand, unlike image steganography, HEVC video steganography can naturally conceal that the communication is occurring from user behavior [1, 2]. While HEVC video steganography can ensure the rationality of the user's behavior and reduce the risk of exposing the hidden communication.

Many works have been done in both H.264/AVC and HEVC [3, 4]. Hu et al. [5] proposed a steganographic algorithm based on intra prediction mode in H.264/AVC. Yang et al. [6] have improved Hu's method by matrix coding. Bouchama [7] divided the intra prediction modes in H.264/AVC into four groups according to their prediction

© Springer Nature Switzerland AG 2019
C. D. Yoo et al. (Eds.): IWDW 2018, LNCS 11378, pp. 233–247, 2019.
https://doi.org/10.1007/978-3-030-11389-6_18

direction, the result shows a better video quality while ensuring high capacity. Zhang et al. [8] analyzed the texture of the video, and proposed a high security adaptive embedding algorithm using STC. Wang et al. [9] proposed intra prediction mode based method for HEVC, a mapping between angle difference and secret message was established to embed data. Dong et al. [10] further proposed the prediction mode steganography technology under the HEVC standard, and made a breakthrough in the capacity limitation of the previous HEVC intra prediction mode based algorithm, while also improving the security.

As far as selection of intra prediction modes is concerned, previous steganographic methods in H.264/AVC all choose to use intra prediction modes in 4×4 macroblock to embed the secret message. This selection rule is reasonable in H.264/AVC since the capacity of embedding into 16×16 macroblock is low, and this kind of macroblock usually concern homogeneous areas for which the Human Visual System (HVS) is more sensitive to small degradations. Thus, in the previous HEVC steganographic schemes, authors in [9, 10] still use the PB of 4×4 size as the embedding cover. However, this selection rule ignores some objective conditions in HEVC: (1) HEVC partitioning is achieved using tree structures. It supports variable-sized PBs selected according to needs of encoders in terms of video content and resolution. (2) Previous H.264/AVC steganography schemes are all tested under low resolution video dataset. But in high resolution dataset for HEVC, larger size PBs occur more frequently. Using only small size PBs will limit capacity to a great extent. In short, the capacity of previous HEVC steganographic schemes is limited since unique techniques in HEVC are not considered sufficiently.

In order to solve the problem mentioned above, and make full use of new features introduced by HEVC, an extension of our previous work in [10] is made. The innovation of this paper includes: (1) Improvement in capacity without introducing great degradation in visual quality. (2) High coding efficiency maintained by defining cost function based on rate distortion. (3) A new indicator to measure BIR under different capacity.

The rest of this paper is organized as follows. In Sect. 2, detailed analysis on why large-sized PBs can be modified without introducing great degradation in visual quality is presented. Section 3 describes the proposed HEVC steganographic algorithm. In Sect. 4, experiments and analysis on multi-resolution dataset are presented. Finally, conclusion is drawn in Sect. 5.

2 Analysis of HEVC Intra Coding Scheme

In this section, the HEVC intra coding scheme will be first described, with which analysis of visual quality degradation in HEVC intra steganographic algorithm can be thoroughly introduced next.

2.1 HEVC Intra Coding Scheme

The HEVC standard introduces CTU and Coding Tree Block (CTB) structure to intra coding scheme. Each frame in a video is first split into block-shaped CTUs, which each contain luma CTBs and chroma CTBs. The blocks specified as CTBs can either be directly used as Coding Blocks (CBs) or be further partitioned into multiple CBs. As shown in Fig. 1, Partitioning is achieved using tree structures. An intra predicted CB of size $M \times M$ may have one of the two types of PB partitions referred to as PART-$2N \times 2N$ and PART-$N \times N$, the first of which indicates that the CB is not split and the second indicates that the CB is split into four equal-sized PBs.

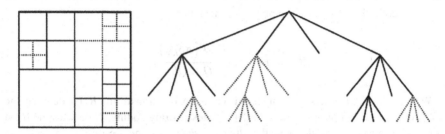

Fig. 1. HEVC tree structured partitioning

The PB size, which is the block size at which the intra prediction mode is established is the same as the CB size except for the smallest CB size (usually 8×8) is allowed in the bitstream. For the latter case, a flag is present that indicates whether the CB is split into four PB quadrants, each PB with their own intra prediction mode. The actual region size at which the intra prediction operates depends on the residual coding partitioning.

For residual coding, a CB can be recursively partitioned into Transform Blocks (TBs). The partitioning is signaled by a residual quadtree. Intra prediction operates based on the TB size, and previously decoded boundary samples from spatially neighboring TBs are used to form the prediction signal. Directional prediction with 33 different directional orientations is defined for (square) TB sizes from 4×4 to 32×32.

2.2   Analysis of Visual Quality Degradation

According to the HEVC intra coding scheme, this subsection will present the analysis of visual quality degradation caused by HEVC steganography, in order to illustrate the reason why large-sized PBs can be modified without introducing significant visual distortion.

Spatial-domain intra prediction has previously been successfully used in H.264/AVC. The intra prediction of HEVC operates similarly in the spatial domain, but is extended significantly—compared to the eight prediction directions of H.264/AVC, HEVC supports a total of 33 angular prediction directions with DC and Planar mode.

The residual signal of the intra prediction, which is the difference between the original block and its prediction, is transformed by a linear spatial transform. The coefficients are then scaled, quantized, entropy coded, and transmitted together with the prediction information. When the prediction mode m_1 of ith N × N size PB is modified to m_2. The original residual of this PB, denoted as $RS_{i,N}^o$, can be expressed as:

$$RS_{i,N}^o = P_{i,N}^o - Pre_{i,N}^o \tag{1}$$

Where $P_{i,N}^o$ denotes the original pixel value in the ith PB, and $Pre_{i,N}^o$ denotes the prediction value calculated by original mode m_1. After obtaining the $RS_{i,N}^o$, the bits $B_{i,N}^o$ used to encode this PB can be expressed as follows:

$$B_{i,N}^o = Ent(RT(\frac{DCT\left(RS_{i,N}^o\right)}{Q \times QS})) \tag{2}$$

Where $DCT(.)$ denotes the integer discrete cosine transform, $RT(.)$ denotes the rounding and truncating operations, $Ent(.)$ denotes entropy coding, Q denotes the fixed quantization matrix, QS denotes the quartier scale. In the decoding process, the reconstruction residual $RSR_{i,N}^o$ can be calculated as:

$$RSR_{i,N}^o = IDCT\left(IEnt\left(B_{i,N}^o\right) \times Q \times QS\right) \tag{3}$$

Where $IDCT(.)$ denotes the inverse integer discrete cosine transform, $IEnt(.)$ denotes the inverse entropy coding, and decoded pixel value $PR_{i,N}^o$ can be expressed as:

$$PR_{i,N}^o = FTR(RSR_{i,N}^o + Pre_{i,N}^o) \approx P_{i,N}^o \tag{4}$$

Where $FTR(.)$ denotes deblocking filter and Sample Adaptive Offset (SAO) operations. Equation (4) shows that the difference between decoded pixel value and original value is mostly depended on quantization. For the next M × M sized PB, its prediction value is determined as:

$$Pre_{i+1,M}^o = SF_N(PR_{i,N}^o) \tag{5}$$

$SF_N(.)$ denotes the intra estimation, prediction and smoothing operation applied by HEVC according to the block size. It shows that as long as we keep the size of candidate PB unchanged, the prediction value of next PB will not be affected significantly. After modifying the prediction modes to m_2, the sum of modified prediction value and its residual is still equal to the true pixel value. So, after processing the modified residual value with same parameters as the original, following equation can be obtained:

$$PR_{i,N}^m = FTR(RSR_{i,N}^m + Pre_{i,N}^m) \approx P_{i,N}^o \tag{6}$$

Where $PR_{i,N}^m$ denotes the modified reconstruction value and $RSR_{i,N}^m$ denotes the modified reconstruction residual. Thus, the conclusion can be drawn:

$$PR_{i,N}^m \approx P_{i,N}^o \approx PR_{i,N}^o \qquad (7)$$

From Eq. (7), it shows that visual quality of videos generated by this kind of steganographic algorithms will not degrade significantly. Another conclusion can be drawn that the difference among values in Eqs. (4–7) is mainly caused by the choice of Q and QS. Thus, the degradation of visual quality will be mainly caused by the increment of QP, not increment of embedded bits. Intra mode steganography has more potential capacity with multi-sized PBs.

To summarize, the visual quality of generated video file won't be affected by changes in the HEVC intra coding process. Thus, improving capacity by utilizing angular intra prediction modes in multi-sized PBs is viable in theory.

3 The Proposed HEVC Steganographic Algorithm

In this section, based on the above analysis, large-sized PBs can be modified without introducing great degradation in visual quality. The remaining problem is to keep the coding efficiency during the process of embedding secret message. The framework of the proposed algorithm is shown in Fig. 2.

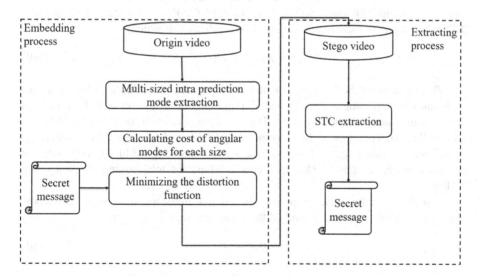

Fig. 2. The framework of the proposed algorithm

3.1 Selection Rule of Intra Prediction Mode

According to the recursive procedure of block partition in HEVC, when QP increases, the number of small blocks decreases. Utilizing large-size PBs will improve the steganography capacity in videos with high QP.

Based the 35 intra prediction directions used in HEVC, it is noticeable that unlike the prediction directions in H.264/AVC, modes of HEVC have a regular pattern. In HEVC, two number-adjacent directions have similar prediction direction. The common way to modify the intra prediction mode is to replace it with a mode that is similar in prediction direction. In this case, these modes are grouped as follows:

$$\left\{ (M_i, M_j) | 2 | M_i = 2 | M_j, \quad i, j \in (0, 34) \right\} \tag{8}$$

Where the $|$ symbol means exact division, M_i means that the current PB prediction mode has the ith prediction direction. One element in the group denotes the bit 0, another denotes the bit 1. According to Eq. (8), the final grouping is $\{(0, 1), (2, 3)...\}$. However, changing mode 0 and mode 1 will significantly affect coding efficiency since they are usually used to encode homogeneous areas. Thus, the first group (0, 1) is removed here. Finally, all the qualified prediction modes of PBs in I frames are extracted, and taken as cover sequence.

3.2 Rate Control Method

However, according to the analysis in the above section, if the best mode is altered, then the coding efficiency will suffer. In HEVC, Rate Distortion Optimization (RDO) technique is used to achieve the best prediction direction:

$$J = D + \lambda R \tag{9}$$

Where J denotes the RD cost, λ denotes the Lagrangian multiplier which depends on quantization parameter QP, D and R represent the distortion and the estimated bitrate of the current PB respectively. The best intra prediction mode is judged by the lowest RD cost. Therefore, if the corresponding RD cost of the current PB is increases, which means residual signal of stego block is larger than original block, the number of bits used to encode this block will increase. Thus, the total coding efficiency will decline.

In order to reduce the proposed algorithm's influence on coding efficiency. The STC method is utilized to embed the secret message into cover:

$$Hx^T = m \tag{10}$$

Where H denotes the parity check matrix generated by STC algorithm, m is the secret message and x is the modified cover sequence. Detail description and implementation of STC can be found in [11]. According to the selection rule of Intra prediction mode, one prediction mode has one candidate mode that can replace it. Thus, this is a binary STC problem. After grouping these prediction modes, the following equation is used to map them into binary sequence:

$$c_i = m_i \bmod 2 \tag{11}$$

Where c_i denotes the binary cover and m_i denotes the original cover.

From Eq. (9), each RD cost is calculated through estimated bitrate and distortion of each PB. Thus, difference in RD cost can represent the coding efficiency reduction caused by changing the prediction mode of the current PB. The cost of changing one PB is defined as:

$$\varphi_i = |J_i - J_j|, \ i,j \ is \ from \ the \ same \ group \tag{12}$$

Where φ_i is the cost of changing the ith PB and J_i is the RD cost of the prediction mode with the ith prediction direction. The difference of RD cost between two prediction modes is used in the same group as the cost for changing one to another. The total distortion D_c is present as:

$$D_c = \sum_{k=1}^{n} \varphi_k \tag{13}$$

Where n presents the total number of all qualified PBs in the video file. Finally, the secret data can be embedded into a video with little distortion.

Finally, the secret payload can be hidden into the video with little rate distortion and high capacity while preserving high coding efficiency.

4 Experiments and Analysis

Since the proposed algorithm is the first intra prediction modes based algorithm using multi-sized PB designed specifically for HEVC, previous single-sized PB based algorithms in [9, 10] are selected for comparison. Performance comparisons between the proposed steganographic algorithm and the previous one are made in terms of embedding capacity, SSIM, and bitrate. Moreover, the effect of introducing large-sized PBs on visual quality and effect of different QPs will also being analyzed in this section.

4.1 Experiment Setup

Dataset and Development Environment. The proposed steganographic algorithm has been implemented in an open source software X265. HEVC is the state-of-art video codec standard, designed for high definition videos aiming to achieve higher coding efficiency. For this reason, the proposed algorithm was tested on HEVC standard test dataset with multi-resolution. In these experiments, pseudo random binary sequences are generated as secret data, and payload is set to $\alpha = 0.5$, in order to produce the stego sets. The GOP size is 10 and coding structure is IPPP. The video coding platform for

HEVC decoding is HM16. The algorithm is developed with Visual C++ 2013. The details of experiment dataset in listed in Table 1.

Table 1. Details of the dataset.

Video name	Resolution	Frame number
Traffic	2560 × 1600	150
PeopleOnStreet	2560 × 1600	150
ParkScene	1920 × 1080	240
BasketballDrive	1920 × 1080	501
Johnny	1280 × 720	600
FourPeople	1280 × 720	600

Indicators. In this section, several indicators are used to measure the performance of the proposed algorithm and other algorithm. Capacity, SSIM, BIR and Bit Increase Ratio with Normalized Capacity (BIR-NC). BIR is defined as:

$$BIR = \frac{TB_{steg} - TB_{ori}}{TB_{ori}} \times 100\% \tag{14}$$

Where TB_{steg} is the total bits of modified video and TB_{ori} is the total bits of original video.

Because the original cover length is different for these two algorithms, a new indicator is proposed to measure the capacity under different BIR. BIR is normalized with 1 Kbits to show the coding efficiency reduction, named as BIR-NC. The physical meaning of BIR-NC is the bit increase ratio using secret payload of the same size. This is very common in real application. The definition of BIR-NC is:

$$BIR - NC = BIR/Capacity \tag{15}$$

4.2   Comparison Experiments

In this section, the proposed steganographic algorithm will be compared with previous algorithms [9, 10] on a different dataset, because algorithm [9] only design a mapping rule between secret message and cover, while proposed an individual dataset. For objective comparison, comparison experiment of [9] is performed under the same setup in [9]. Moreover, for algorithm [10], it also includes the distortion control method as the proposed one, so this algorithm is performed on the above dataset.

As far as the embedding payload is concerned, the capacity of our algorithm is 240% larger than algorithm [10] in average. Even if algorithm [10] embed less payload, the SSIM still 0.8% lower than ours. The reason for this phenomenon may be that in our algorithm, all the block partitioning is exactly the same as in the original video, but in algorithm [10], only the position of 4 × 4 PBs is preserved. As shown in Eq. (5), different smoothing filter (usually stronger) may apply to other PBs, which leads to the degradation in SSIM. This result proves that utilizing large-sized PBs will not cause severe visual degradation but providing high capacity.

From Table 2, it shows that our algorithm is inferior to the algorithm [10] in terms of BIR. The average BIR of algorithm [10] is 54.5% smaller than the proposed algorithm. However, considering capacity and BIR at the same time, our algorithm can achieve smaller BIR at the same capacity, as shown by BIR-NC. For videos in all resolutions, our algorithm has better BIR-NCs, which are 15.6%, 10.9%, 23.1%, 1.8%, 3.9% and 11.9% smaller than algorithm [10]. The average BIR-NCs of the proposed algorithm are 86.7% of the algorithm [10] on 2K videos, 87.6% on 1080P videos and 92.1% on 720P video. This result draws the conclusion that our algorithm is better on preserving coding efficiency.

Table 2. Comparison results with algorithm [10]

Sequences	Algorithms	QP	Resolution	SSIM	Capacity (Kbits)	BIR	BIR-NC (%/Kbits)
Traffic	Proposed	40	2560 × 1600	**0.9577**	**155.037**	0.0519	**0.0335**
	[10]	40	2560 × 1600	0.9433	60.418	0.0240	0.0397
PeopleOnStreet	Proposed	40	2560 × 1600	**0.9318**	**254.517**	0.0291	**0.0114**
	[10]	40	2560 × 1600	0.9288	122.208	0.0157	0.0128
ParkScene	Proposed	40	1920 × 1080	**0.9481**	**815.81**	0.0340	**0.0417**
	[10]	40	1920 × 1080	0.9303	310.06	0.0168	0.0542
BasketballDrive	Proposed	40	1920 × 1080	**0.9431**	**215.051**	0.0702	**0.0326**
	[10]	40	1920 × 1080	0.9394	732.22	0.0243	0.0332
Johnny	Proposed	40	1280 × 720	**0.9784**	**105.433**	0.0911	**0.0864**
	[10]	40	1280 × 720	0.9746	440.05	0.0396	0.0899
FourPeople	Proposed	40	1280 × 720	**0.9547**	**173.580**	0.0758	**0.0437**
	[10]	40	1280 × 720	0.9363	798.65	0.0396	0.0496

It can be also observed that BIR-NC can differ even when the resolutions of video are the same, such as 0.0035 for 2K video *Traffic* or 0.0014 for *PeopleonStreet*. Several tools were used to analyze the difference among these videos. It shows that TBs with complex texture often has a higher residual signal. This kind of TBs can tolerate more bit changes than other blocks. In addition, in a high-resolution video, larger sized PBs also often occurs in texture-rich area. As shown in Table 2 and Fig. 3, the conclusion is drawn that under the same resolution, videos with lower BIR-NC always has more complex texture. Thus, a texture-rich video is more suitable for our algorithm than plain video in terms of preserving coding efficiency.

Next, Wang's work [9] is compared with our algorithm. Algorithm [9] designs a mapping rule between difference of intra directions and secret message, but do not consider the distortion of HEVC intra prediction mode. Five videos named as video1, video2, video3, video4 and video 5, which are originally used in [9], are tested in this section. The experiment setup is the same as it in their work [9]. Comparison results in capacity, BIR and difference in PSNR is shown in Table 3. PSNR and this dataset are used here solely since they are originally used in [9] to illustrate the performance.

(a) (b)

Fig. 3. (a) Content of *Fourpeople* in 720P. (b) Content of *Johnny* in 720P. *Johnny* has more homogeneous areas than *Fourpeople*. Texture-rich video always has a lower BIR-NC.

In Table 3, it shows that the average capacity of the proposed algorithm is 327313, which is about 32 times larger than the average capacity of algorithm [9], 10069. In theory, algorithm [9] only use a few 4 × 4 PBs to embed the secret message while our algorithm using all size of PBs. In terms of preserving coding efficiency, our algorithm has better BIR-NCs, which are 89.9%, 52.4%, 87.5%, 85.9%, and 90.6% smaller than algorithm [9]. The average BIR-NCs of the proposed algorithm are 18.7% of the algorithm [9] on their dataset. Furthermore, our algorithm has less difference in PSNR, which is −0.024 dB in average. These results prove that the proposed algorithm outperforms algorithm [9] in both capacity, perceptibility and coding efficiency.

Conclusion can be drawn that, first, our algorithm outperforms the existing HEVC intra prediction mode algorithm with higher capacity and better coding efficiency. Second, utilizing large-sized PBs will not cause severe visual degradation but providing

Table 3. Comparison results with algorithm [9]

Sequences	Algorithms	QP	Resolution	ΔPSNR (dB)	Capacity (Kbits)	BIR	BIR-NC (%/Kbits)
Video1	Proposed	22	832 × 480	**−0.02**	**357.688**	0.0354	**0.0099**
	[9]	22	832 × 480	−0.06	161.82	0.0158	0.098
Video2	Proposed	22	832 × 480	**−0.02**	**313.863**	0.0255	**0.0081**
	[9]	22	832 × 480	−0.06	110.70	0.0190	0.017
Video3	Proposed	22	1280 × 720	**−0.02**	**331.941**	0.0339	**0.010**
	[9]	22	1280 × 720	−0.04	9.534	0.0076	0.080
Video4	Proposed	22	1280 × 720	**−0.01**	**322.784**	0.0255	**0.0079**
	[9]	22	1280 × 720	−0.01	8.058	0.0045	0.056
Video5	Proposed	22	1280 × 720	**−0.01**	**310.289**	0.0244	**0.0079**
	[9]	22	1280 × 720	−0.03	5.502	0.0046	0.084

high capacity. Third, a texture-rich high-resolution video is more suitable for our algorithm in terms of preserving coding efficiency.

4.3 Analysis of the Influence on Performance with Different QPs

In this section, two algorithms will be performed and discussed to illustrate the influence on algorithm performance with different QPs. The first one is the proposed algorithm using multi-sized PBs, another is the algorithm exactly the same as the proposed one except for using smallest single-sized PBs.

Analysis of Visual Quality. As explained in Sect. 2, video quality of stego video will not dramatically degrade when larger size PBs are used. To prove this, SSIMs between original video and modified video are used to demonstrate the perceptibility and visual quality of the proposed HEVC algorithm. PSNR is not used here because SSIM can present visual quality better. The results are shown in Fig. 4.

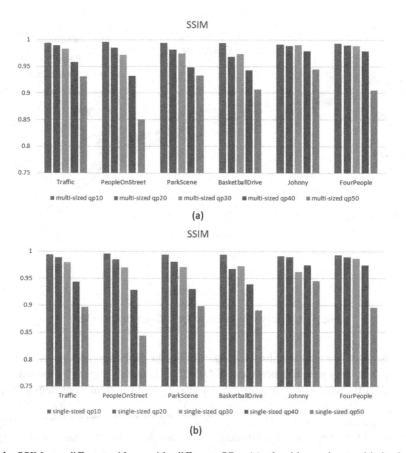

Fig. 4. SSIM on different videos with different QPs. (a) algorithm using multi-sized PBs (b) algorithm using single-sized PBs

It is shown that SSIMs between algorithm using multi-sized PBs and algorithm using single-sized PBs are similar under the same QP. The average SSIM of the proposed algorithm is 1.006 time higher than the algorithm using single-sized PBs. The decreasing of SSIM is mainly caused by the increment of QPs, not by the different sizes of PBs. The overall SSIM value ranges from 0.85 to 0.99 and decreases with the increase of QP. It shows that under the same resolution and QP, videos with more homogeneous areas have higher SSIM than texture-rich videos, such as *Johnny* and *Fourpeople*. The reason may be that although texture-rich areas can tolerate more bit changes, they also bring more pixel changes. Thus, it is totally safe to utilize larger-sized PBs in terms of perceptibility with different QPs.

Analysis of Capacity. Figure 5 demonstrates the influence of different QPs on capacity of proposed algorithm and algorithm using single-sized PBs. Red lines denote results of the proposed algorithm, and blue line denotes results of algorithm using single-sized PBs. For the sake of clear and succinct presentation, we have only drawn six curves of three videos in Figs. 5 and 6.

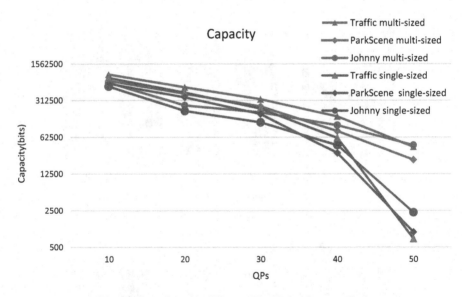

Fig. 5. Capacity with different QPs (Color figure online)

In Fig. 5, the vertical coordinate is logarithmic, the difference between red lines and blue lines increases with the increment of QPs. This is mainly caused by the number of larger size PBs increases with QPs, which also leads to a significant degradation in capacity for algorithm using single-sized PBs. For example, the capacity of the Traffic video using multi-sized PBs with QP50 is 40681, while reduced to 718 when using single-sized PBs. Moreover, the capacity decrease logarithmically with increment of QPs.

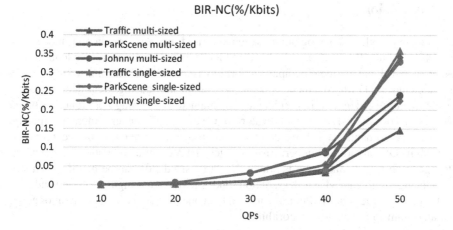

Fig. 6. BIR-NC on different videos with different QPs. (Color figure online)

When QP increases, more reconstruction pixels will be calculated with the same quantized value, which leads to a smaller RD cost for large partition mode. The sizes of PBs are exponential {4, 8, 16, and 32}, meaning the large-sized PBs exponentially merge the small-sized PBs during this process. This may be the reason for logarithmically decrement in capacity. These results prove that the bigger the QP, the bigger the advantage of the proposed algorithm using multi-sized PBs.

Analysis of Coding Efficiency. Figure 6 shows that the proposed algorithm has the advantage of preserving coding efficiency compared with algorithm using single-sized PBs when the payload is the same. The difference between red lines and blue lines increases with the increment of QPs. For example, the BIR-NC of the *Traffic* video using multi-sized PB with QP50 is 0.145, and raises to 0.358 when using single-sized PBs. Furthermore, with the increase of QPs, the proposed algorithm achieves better BIR-NC. The averaging BIR-NC of the proposed algorithm when QP equals to 40 is 89.3% of the algorithm using single-sized PBs, but reduces to 63.7% when QP equals to 50. The conclusion can be drawn that when QP increases, the advantage of using multi-sized PBs to embed the secret payload grows.

To summarize, first, our algorithm outperforms the existing HEVC intra prediction mode algorithm with higher capacity and better coding efficiency. Second, utilizing large-sized PBs will not cause severe visual degradation but providing high capacity. Third, a texture-rich high-resolution video is more suitable for our algorithm in terms of preserving coding efficiency. Fourth, our algorithm achieve better performance than others when QP is high. Some interesting phenomenon in the experiment results is discussed, which may be helpful to further improve the performance of the proposed steganographic algorithm.

5   Conclusion

The existing video steganographic schemes based on intra prediction modes for H.264/AVC and HEVC all use single-sized blocks to embed the secret payload. In this paper, a novel video steganographic algorithm is presented. The innovation of this paper includes: (1) Improvement in capacity without introducing great degradation in visual quality. (2) High coding efficiency maintained by defining cost function based on rate distortion. (3) A new indicator to measure BIR under different capacity. Detailed experiments have been conducted to prove the effeteness of the proposed algorithm. Our algorithm outperform the latest HEVC intra prediction mode based steganography. The conclusion is drawn that large-sized PBs can be modified without introducing significant visual degradation, and a texture-rich high-resolution video is preferred for our algorithm. Future work can be made in security improvement or adopt the algorithm to an adaptive algorithm.

Acknowledgement. This work is supported by the National Natural Science Foundation of China (No. 61572320, 61572321). Corresponding author is Professor Xinghao Jiang, any comments should be addressed to xhjiang@sjtu.edu.cn.

References

1. Aparna, R., Ajish, S.: A review on data hiding techniques in compressed video. Int. J. Comput. Appl. **134**(13), 1–4 (2016)
2. Sullivan, G.J., Ohm, J.R., Han, W.J., Wiegand, T.: Overview of the high efficiency video coding (HEVC) standard. IEEE Trans. Circ. Syst. Video Technol. **22**(12), 1649–1668 (2013)
3. Chang, P.C., Chung, K.L., Chen, J., Lin, C.H., Lin, T.J.: A DCT/DST-based error propagation-free data hiding algorithm for HEVC intra-coded frames. J. Vis. Commun. Image Represent. **25**(2), 239–253 (2014)
4. Tew, Y., Wong, K.S.: Information hiding in HEVC standard using adaptive coding block size decision. In: IEEE International Conference on Image Processing, pp. 5502–5506. IEEE (2015)
5. Hu, Y., Zhang, C., Su, Y.: Information hiding based on intra prediction modes for H. 264/AVC. In: 2007 IEEE International Conference on Multimedia and Expo, pp. 1231–1234. IEEE (2007)
6. Yang, G., Li, J., He, Y.: An information hiding algorithm based on intra-prediction modes and matrix coding for H.264/AVC video stream. Int. J. Electron. Commun. **65**(4), 331–337 (2011)
7. Bouchama, S., Hamami, L., Aliane, H.: H. 264/AVC data hiding based on intra prediction modes for real-time applications. In: Proceedings of the World Congress on Engineering and Computer Science, vol. 2200, no. 1, pp. 655–658 (2012)
8. Zhang, L., Zhao, X.: An adaptive video steganography based on intra-prediction mode and cost assignment. In: Shi, Y.Q., Kim, H.J., Perez-Gonzalez, F., Liu, F. (eds.) IWDW 2016. LNCS, vol. 10082, pp. 518–532. Springer, Cham (2017). https://doi.org/10.1007/978-3-319-53465-7_39

9. Wang, J., Wang, R., Xu, D., Li, W., Yan, D.: An information hiding algorithm for HEVC based on intra prediction modes. J. Softw. **10**(2), 213–221 (2015). https://go.galegroup.com/ps/i.do?p=AONE&sw=w&u=googlescholar&v=2.1&it=r&id=GALE%7CA461704620&sid=classroomWidget&asid=3346b4ef

10. Dong, Y., Jiang, X., Sun, T., Xu, D.: Coding efficiency preserving steganography based on HEVC steganographic channel model. In: Kraetzer, C., Shi, Y.-Q., Dittmann, J., Kim, H. J. (eds.) IWDW 2017. LNCS, vol. 10431, pp. 149–162. Springer, Cham (2017). https://doi.org/10.1007/978-3-319-64185-0_12

11. Filler, T., Judas, J., Fridrich, J.: Minimizing additive distortion in steganography using syndrome-trellis codes. IEEE Trans. Inf. Forensics Secur. **6**(3), 920–935 (2011)

Improving the Embedding Strategy
for Batch Adaptive Steganography

Xinzhi Yu, Kejiang Chen, Weiming Zhang$^{(\boxtimes)}$, Yaofei Wang, and Nenghai Yu

CAS Key Laboratory of Electromagnetic Space Information,
University of Science and Technology of China, Hefei, China
zhangwm@ustc.edu.cn

Abstract. Recent works have demonstrated that images with more texture regions should be selected as the sub-batch of covers to carry the total message when applying batch steganography to adaptive steganography and the core challenge of which is how to evaluate the texture complexity of image accurately according to the need of steganography security. In this paper, we first propose three methods for measuring the texture complexity of image to select images with highly textured content, then put forward our universal embedding strategy for batch adaptive steganography in both spatial and JPEG domain. To assess the security of embedding strategies for batch adaptive steganography, we use a pooling steganalysis method based majority decision for the omniscient Warden, who informed by the average payload, embedding algorithm and cover source. Given a batch of images, our proposed embedding strategy is to select images with largest residual values to carry the total message, which is named max-residual-greedy (MRG) strategy. Experimental results show that the proposed embedding strategy outperforms the previous ones for batch adaptive steganography.

Keywords: Batch adaptive steganography · Embedding strategy · Texture complexity

1 Introduction

Steganography is the art of covert communication, which aims to hide secret messages in ordinary objects such as digital images without drawing suspicion from steganalysis [1,2]. It is challenging to design steganographic algorithms due to the lack of accurate models. Currently, the most successful approach is minimal additive distortion model and the practical message embedding is usually realized by syndrome-trellis codes (STCs) [3], which can approach the theoretical bound of embedding distortion.

Content-adaptive steganography based on minimal additive distortion model has developed greatly in both spatial and JPEG domain. HUGO (Highly Undetectable steGO) [4] is the first method based on additive distortion model, which

This work was supported in part by the National Natural Science Foundation of China under Grant U1636201 and 61572452.

computes the weighted sum of difference between feature vectors extracted from a cover image and its corresponding stego version in SPAM (Subtractive Pixel Adjacency Matrix) [5] feature space. In this way, a pixel after modification which makes the feature vector deviate widely will be assigned a high cost. The embedding changes of HUGO will be made within texture regions and along edges. WOW (Wavelet Obtained Weights) [6] assigns high costs to pixels in areas that are easily to predict by directional filters. Thus the modifications will be suppressed in the clean edges, which improves the security performance when resisting the powerful steganalysis with both SRM [7] and its select-channel-aware version maxSRMd2 [8]. S-UNIWARD (Spatial UNIversal WAvelet Relative Distortion) [9] has a slightly modified cost function which can be extended to an arbitrary domain, thus WOW and S-UNIWARD have similar performance. HILL (HIgh-pass, Low-pass and Low-pass) [10] improves WOW significantly by spreading the costs with a low-pass filter and makes more modifications cluster in complex regions. Similar to the spatial steganography, the modifications of the JPEG steganography is also gathered in the texture areas, such as UERD [11], HDS [12], RBV [13].

When applying steganography to the real-world, a sender usually has multiple images and a long message, the problem faced by this sender becomes how to allocate message among multiple images to be the least detectable, which is the main research issue of batch steganography. For the traditional steganography, Ker et al. have proposed five embedding strategies in [14] and demonstrated that the max-greedy strategy and the max-random strategy are more secure than the linear strategy, the even strategy and the sqroot strategy when resisting the universal blind steganalysis. The former two strategies try to use as few covers as possible, while the latter three want to distribute the message into all available covers. Although the max-greedy strategy has the most secure performance, it needs to estimate the capacity of images in advance.

When batch steganography is applied to adaptive steganography, the capacity of image depends on the coding scheme and the specific steganographic algorithm, for instance, UERD [11] and RBV [13] can modify all types of DCT coefficients (including the DC and zero AC coefficients) while UED [15] can only modify the non-zero AC coefficients, thus the capacity of image is small when it embedded by UED. The essence of adaptive steganography is to cluster as many modifications as possible in the texture areas. When embedded the same message, images with more texture areas will have higher security. As mentioned before, the max-greedy strategy is not adapted when it comes to batch adaptive steganography, meaning that images with highest texture complexity should be selected orderly to be fitted candidate. Therefore, the core challenge of batch adaptive steganography is how to measure the texture complexity of image, which has been explored in [16,17]. In [16] Zhao et al. have proposed a method to measure the complexity of image in spatial domain based on the relation between distortion and payload. Further onwards, they improve the selecting strategy by employing histogram equilibrium to measure the complexity of image in [17]. However, both methods measure the complexity of image roughly and indirectly. Therefore, it is imperative to propose a finer and more direct method for measuring the complexity of image for batch adaptive steganography.

In this paper, we propose a universal embedding strategy for batch adaptive steganography in both spatial and JPEG domain. To select the most complex images, we put forward three methods for measuring the texture complexity of image: image residual, image energy and image fluctuation, which are extensions of block residual [13], block energy [11] and block fluctuation [12], respectively. We use image residual, which proved to be the securest image selection method in Subsect. 4.2, to select the most complex images to carry the total message and name our embedding strategy as max-residual-greedy (abbreviated as MRG) strategy. We also propose a pooling steganalysis method based majority decision for the omniscient Warden to evaluate the security of embedding strategies.

The rest of this paper is organized as follows. In Sect. 2, we briefly introduce the minimal additive distortion model and the related work. The proposed batch adaptive steganography embedding strategy is presented in Sect. 3 and the experimental results are elaborated in Sect. 4. Conclusion and future work are given in Sect. 5.

2   Preliminaries and Related Work

2.1   Notations

Throughout the paper, matrices, vectors and sets are written in bold face. The cover image (of size $n_1 \times n_2$) is represented by $\mathbf{X} = (x_{i,j}) \in \{\zeta\}^{n_1 \times n_2}$, where ζ is the pixel or DCT coefficient dynamic range of image. For example, $\zeta = \{0, ..., 255\}$ for 8-bit grayscale image and $\zeta = \{-1024, ..., 1024\}$ for JPEG image. $\mathbf{Y} = (y_{i,j}) \in \{\zeta\}^{n_1 \times n_2}$ represents the stego image. The embedding operation on $x_{i,j}$ is formulated by the range I. An embedding operation is called binary if $|I| = 2$ and ternary if $|I| = 3$ for all i, j. For example, the ± 1 embedding operation is ternary embedding with $I_{i,j} = \{min(x_{i,j} - 1, 0), x_{i,j}, max(x_{i,j} + 1, 255)\}$, where "0" denotes no modification.

2.2   Minimal Additive Distortion Model

In the model established in [3], the cover $\mathbf{X}$ is assumed to be fixed, so the distortion of changing an element $x_{i,j}$ to $y_{i,j}$ can be simply denoted by $\rho_{i,j}(\mathbf{X}, y_{i,j})$. It's assumed that $\rho_{i,j}(\mathbf{X}, x_{i,j}) = 0$ and $\rho_{i,j}(\mathbf{X}, y_{i,j} - 1) = \rho_{i,j}(\mathbf{X}, y_{i,j} + 1) = \rho_{i,j} \in [0, \infty)$. The additive distortion function of the image can be calculated as follows:

$$D(\mathbf{X}, \mathbf{Y}) = \sum_{i=1}^{n_1} \sum_{j=1}^{n_2} \rho_{i,j}(\mathbf{X}, y_{i,j}) |x_{i,j} - y_{i,j}|. \tag{1}$$

Supposed that the flipping probability of $x_{i,j}$ to $y_{i,j}$ is $\pi_{i,j}$, and thus the sender can send up to $H(\pi)$ bits of message on average with average distortion $E_\pi(D)$ such that

$$H(\pi) = -\sum_{i=1}^{n_1} \sum_{j=1}^{n_2} \pi_{i,j} \log \pi_{i,j}, \tag{2}$$

$$E_\pi(D) = \sum_{i=1}^{n_1} \sum_{j=1}^{n_2} \pi_{i,j} \rho_{i,j}(\mathbf{X}, y_{i,j}). \tag{3}$$

For a given message m, the sender wants to minimize the average distortion, which can be formulated as the following optimization problems:

$$\min_\pi E_\pi(D), \tag{4}$$

$$\text{subject to } H(\pi) = m. \tag{5}$$

Following the maximum entropy principle, we can calculate the flipping probability via

$$\pi_{i,j} = \frac{exp(-\lambda \rho_{i,j}(\mathbf{X}, y_{i,j}))}{\sum_{y_{i,j} \in I_{i,j}} exp(-\lambda \rho_{i,j}(\mathbf{X}, y_{i,j}))}. \tag{6}$$

Where the scalar parameter $\lambda > 0$ can be determined by the payload constraint (5). In fact, as proven in [18], the entropy in (5) is monotone decreasing in λ, so for a given m, λ can be fast calculated by binary search.

2.3 Review of the Related Work

Before introducing the proposed embedding strategy, we will first review the related work. Since ESBAS [16] only applies to spatial domain and has been improved by UES [17] which can be used in both spatial and JPEG domain, we will only present the latter.

The embedding strategy UES contains two rules: Size-First Rule and Histogram Equilibrium-First Rule, when embedding, images with larger "size" and more equilibrated histogram are selected as sub-batch and set a high priority to carry the message. The key point of the first rules is to calculate the "size" which means the number of pixels for spatial image or the number of non-zero AC coefficients for JPEG image. The reader can also associate it with the "Square Root Law" [19], which indicates that the secure capacity of a cover is proportional to the square root of its size. The essence of the second rule is the measurement of histogram equilibrium that we will introduce in detail.

Whether spatial or JPEG image, the essence is still pixels, JPEG image saves storage space merely by combining with DCT transform and quantization encoding. UES has mentioned that the more gray levels an image occupies, the higher texture complexity it has. Once an image is given, histogram of pixels can be easily obtained. Let $\mathbf{P} = \{p_i | 1 \leq i \leq n\}$ represent the statistical probability of pixels, n is the number of gray levels. Then the value of pixel x in this image meets the distribution of the statistical probability. Assuming all pixels in different location are independent and identically distributed, then the information entropy of pixel x can be represented as

$$E(x) = -\sum_{i=1}^{n} p_i \log p_i, \tag{7}$$

and the standard deviation of statistical probability can be represented as

$$S(x) = \sqrt{\frac{1}{n}\sum_{i=1}^{n}|p_i - \overline{p_i}|^2}.$$ (8)

The above formulas (7) (8) indicate that information entropy has a positive correlation with the complexity of image, while standard deviation has a negative correlation. Although the standard deviation and information entropy contain the overlapping information, which is regarded as the fundamental information of histogram for image and kept repetitively by UES. The histogram equilibrium is defined as

$$H(x) = \frac{E(x)}{\tau + \gamma \cdot S(x)},$$ (9)

where τ and γ are parameters avoiding the value of denominator tending to zero.

3   Proposed Embedding Strategy

3.1   Methods of Measuring Image Complexity

The texture complexity of an image determines its security capacity. Images with higher complexity will have bigger security capacity, and vice versa. Motivated by the JPEG steganographic algorithms that contain the methods of measuring the complexity of image block, such as RBV [13], HDS [12] and UERD [11], we propose the following three methods for measuring the complexity of image.

Image Residual. Here, we use a wavelet filter bank to filter image to obtain directional residual matrices and define the image residual as the sum of all absolute residual values in the corresponding directional residual matrices. The detailed procedures are described as follows.

(1) Given an image, we first decompressed it from DCT domain to spatial domain if it is a JPEG image, without quantizing the pixel values to $\{0, ..., 255\}$ to avoid any loss of information.
(2) As the wavelet filter shows admirable performance in steganography [6,13], we generate a 2-D wavelet filter bank consisting of three high-pass filters from the wavelet's 1-D low-pass decomposition filter $\mathbf{h}$ and a high-pass decomposition filter $\mathbf{g}$. Generally, a filter bank $\mathbf{B} = \{\mathbf{K}^{(1)}, ..., \mathbf{K}^{(n)}\}$ consists of n multiple directional high-pass filters represented by their kernels normalized so that all L_2-norms $||\mathbf{K}^{(k)}||_2$ are the same. We want to evaluate the texture complexity of image along horizontal, vertical and diagonal directions by directional residuals. Therefore, the filter bank $\mathbf{B} = \{\mathbf{K}^{(1)}, \mathbf{K}^{(2)}, \mathbf{K}^{(3)}\}$ can be computed as follows.

$$\mathbf{K}^{(1)} = \mathbf{h} \cdot \mathbf{g}^{(T)}, \ \ \mathbf{K}^{(2)} = \mathbf{g} \cdot \mathbf{h}^{(T)}, \ \ \mathbf{K}^{(3)} = \mathbf{g} \cdot \mathbf{g}^{(T)},$$ (10)

where the vector $\mathbf{h}$ and $\mathbf{g}$ denote the coefficients of decomposition low-pass filter and high-pass filter, respectively. The matrices $\mathbf{K}^{(k)}, k \in \{1,2,3\}$ represent high-pass filters in 2-D wavelet filter bank. In fact, any kind of wavelet families, such as Haar, Daubechies and Symlets can be selected to construct the 2-D wavelet filter bank. We adopted the Daubechies 8-tap wavelets in here due to its highest security performance for WOW [6] and RBV [13].

(3) Let $\mathbf{X} = (x_{i,j}) \in \{\zeta\}^{n_1 \times n_2}$ represent the spatial image or the decompressed image from JPEG domain. The k-th residual $\mathbf{R}^{(k)}, k \in \{1,2,3\}$ is computed as $\mathbf{R}^{(k)} = \mathbf{K}^{(k)} * \mathbf{X}$, where '$*$' is a convolution mirror-padded so that $\mathbf{R}^{(k)}$ has again the same number of elements with $\mathbf{X}$.

(4) In terms of a pixel, it has three directional residuals and if the sum of absolute values of those is large, it means the texture is complex around the pixel. Similarly, for the entire image, if the sum of all absolute values of its corresponding directional residuals is large, the texture is complex as well. Therefore, we define the image residual as follows.

$$R = \sum_{k=1}^{3} \sum_{i=1}^{n_1} \sum_{j=1}^{n_2} |r_{i,j}^{(k)}|, \tag{11}$$

where the $r_{i,j}^{(k)}$ represents the residual value of pixel $x_{i,j}$ in the residual matrix $\mathbf{R}^{(k)}$.

Image Energy. The energy function of the DCT block for JPEG image was first proposed in UERD [11], which can measure the distortion of the corresponding DCT block. From the distortion function of UERD, we can conclude that the larger the energy of a DCT block, the smaller the costs of DCT coefficients within the block. In other words, the texture of the image block is complex when the corresponding DCT block has large energy. Similarly, the texture of the entire image is complex when the image has large energy.

Given a JPEG image $\mathbf{X}$ with size $n_1 \times n_2$ (assuming that the size of $\mathbf{X}$ is a multiple of 8), let $x_{i,j}$ $(i,j \in \{1,...,8\})$ be a DCT coefficient in position (i,j) of a 8×8 DCT block in position (m,n) and $q_{i,j}$ represent its corresponding quantization step, the energy of mn^{th} block is defined as

$$e_{m,n} = \sum_{i=1}^{8} \sum_{j=1}^{8} |x_{i,j}| \cdot q_{i,j}, \tag{12}$$

where $x_{1,1} = 0$ to avoid the influence of the DC coefficient. The image energy is defined as

$$E = \sum_{m=1}^{n_1/8} \sum_{n=1}^{n_2/8} e_{m,n}. \tag{13}$$

Although the concept of energy block was initially proposed for JPEG image, we can still calculate the image energy of a spatial image by (12) (13) after transforming it to JPEG domain. We do not demonstrate the results of image energy in spatial domain in Sect. 4.2 due to the similar performance trends of those in JPEG domain.

Image Fluctuation. The most direct assessment of the complexity of image is the difference between adjacent pixels, which has been considered in [12,20]. Since the definition of block texture [20] and block fluctuation [12] are similar, and the former is more direct and concise, we do not use the method in [12] but adopt another proposed in [20].

Given an image $\mathbf{X}$ sized $n_1 \times n_2$, we should first process it if it is a JPEG image, just like we do for image residual described above, and then compute the mean absolute value of differences between a pixel $x_{i,j}$ and its eight neighbors as the complexity value of the pixel $x_{i,j}$:

$$f_{i,j} = \frac{1}{8} \sum_{m=-1}^{1} \sum_{n=-1}^{1} |x_{i,j} - x_{i+m,j+n}|, \tag{14}$$

at last, calculate the sum value of them within the whole image as the image fluctuation of the image:

$$F = \sum_{i=2}^{n_1-1} \sum_{j=2}^{n_2-1} f_{i,j}. \tag{15}$$

It is obvious that images with larger image fluctuation values will be more complex.

3.2 Proposed Embedding Strategy (MRG)

When applying batch adaptive steganography to practical application, we should first calculate the texture complexity of images within a batch of covers according to the image residual method proposed above and verified to be the most superior image selection method in Subsect. 4.2, then select images with largest residual values orderly from the batch of images, following the concept of "greedy", to embed message until reach their maximum capacity. Due to the capacity of image determined by the coding scheme and the specific steganographic algorithm, which has been mentioned in Introduction, we should set the maximun capacity of image practically. For instance, we set the maximum embedding rate to 1.0 bpp (or bpnzac) for WOW (or RBV) in Subsect. 4.3.

Taking into account the receiver's message extraction, the auxiliary information, such as the message-embedded images, the embedding message length and the encoding key, are necessities for the receiver. In this paper, we pay more attention to the secure performance of our proposed embedding strategy and regardless of the auxiliary information because this information can be embedded in these pixels determined by the secret key for each image. To further clarify the scheme of our proposed embedding strategy, we provide a pseudo-code in Algorithm 1.

Algorithm 1. Proposed embedding strategy (MRG)

Input: the batch of covers $\mathbf{X}$ (with N images); L bits of message $\mathbf{m}$; Distortion function FUNC and the coding scheme (STCs).

Output: the batch of stegos $\mathbf{Y}$ (Partially embedded message).

1: Decompress the covers $\mathbf{X}$ into spatial domain if necessary.
2: Use the image residual method in subsection 3.1 to calculate the complexity of all covers in $\mathbf{X}$ and sort them in descending order.
3: Set the maximum capacity of image according to the coding scheme (STCs) and FUNC.
4: Select images with largest residual values orderly from $\mathbf{X}$ to embed fully, until the message is completely embedded.
5: Combine the message-carried images with other covers and then scramble them to obtain $\mathbf{Y}$.

4 Experimental Results

4.1 Setups

All experiments in this section are conducted on BOSSbase 1.01 [21] containing 10000 grayscale images sized 512×512. Since the proposed strategy is universal to both spatial and JPEG domain, we compress all of the images to JPEG domain with quality factor 75. We use the optimal embedding simulator as default for all experiments. To verify the superiority of our proposed strategy, we use the state-of-the-art distortion functions and steganalysis features, such as WOW [6] and HILL [10] in spatial domain, J-UNIWARD [9] and RBV [13] in JPEG domain. In the aspect of steganalysis, we select SRM [7] and its variant maxSRMd2 [8] in spatial domain, DCTR [22] and GFR [23] in JPEG domain.

4.2 Effectiveness of the Image Selection Methods

Since our experiments in this subsection are just to verify the effectiveness of our proposed image selection methods, which use the methods in Subsect. 3.1 to select highly textured images, with the methods in [17] in both spatial and JPEG domain. When selecting images from the BOSSbase 1.01 we just set it as 5000 like [17]. Then a number of 2500 images are randomly selected for training, and the rest 2500 images are used for testing. The detectors are trained as binary classifiers implemented using the FLD ensemble [24] with default settings. The ensemble by default minimizes the total classification error rate under equal priors $P_E = min_{P_{FA}} \frac{1}{2}(P_{FA} + P_{MD})$, where P_{FA} and P_{MD} are the false-alarm rate and the missed-detection rate respectively. The ultimate security is qualified by average error rate $\overline{P_E}$ averaged over ten 2500/2500 selected images splits, and large $\overline{P_E}$ means stronger security.

Effectiveness of the Image Selection Methods in Spatial Domain. Here, we compare our proposed image selection methods with the histogram equi-librium [17] (called "histeq") and random (select images randomly) in spatial domain. We assume that all images with the same size and the relative payload rate from 0.05 to 0.5 bpp (bits per pixel). The performance of those four methods are shown in Figs. 1 and 2. It is obvious that the proposed methods perform better than histeq and random all the time and the image residual has the securest performance. When the payload is 0.05 bpp, the image residual improves the histeq about 0.8% on average, but when the payload is bigger than 0.2 bpp, the improvement is higher 2.0–4.7% for both WOW and HILL, especially for HILL against SRM, the improvement is almost higher than 4.5%.

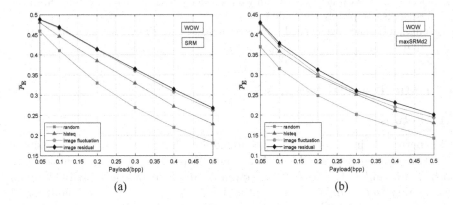

Fig. 1. Steganalytic performance of random, histeq, image residual and image fluctuation for WOW under SRM (a) and maxSRMd2 (b) detection.

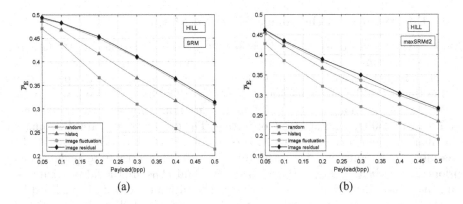

Fig. 2. Steganalytic performance of random, histeq, image residual and image fluctuation for HILL under SRM (a) and maxSRMd2 (b) detection.

Effectiveness of the Image Selection Methods in JPEG Domain. To demonstrate the universality of our proposed image selection methods, comparison of performance has been made among the proposed three methods, random, histeq and the "size-first method" [17] (called "nzac") which selects images with big number of non-zero AC DCT coefficients in JPEG domain. We also assume that all images with the same size and the relative payload rate from 0.05 to 0.5 bpnzac (bits per non-zero AC DCT coefficient). As shown in Figs. 3 and 4, the proposed three methods have comparable performance but all of them perform better than the others and among these methods image residual has a clear superiority too. When the payload is smaller than 0.2 bpnzac, image residual improves the nzac 0.3% on average, but when the payload is bigger than 0.2 bpnzac, the improvement is about 0.8–1.5% for both J-UNIWARD and RBV.

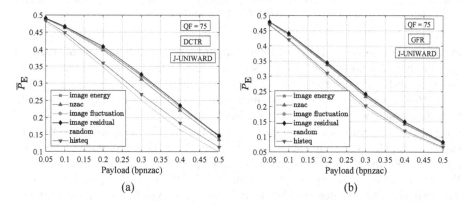

Fig. 3. Steganalytic performance of random, histeq, nzac, image energy, image residual and image fluctuation for J-UNIWARD under DCTR (a) and GFR (b) detection.

4.3 The Performance of MRG

In Subsect. 4.2, experimental results have shown that our proposed three image selection methods all perform better than the methods proposed in [17] and among them the image residual method always has a clear superiority in both spatial and JPEG domain. Therefore, we just use image residual as our image selection method. Since our proposed embedding strategy for batch adaptive steganography is to select images with largest residual values within a batch of covers to carry the total message, we call our embedding strategy max-residual-greedy (MRG) strategy.

To evaluate the performance of different embedding strategies, we put forward a pooling steganalysis method based majority decision for the omniscient Warden, under the assumption that the Warden knows the average payload, embedding method and cover source used by the users. During detecting, the Warden just need to count the number of stegos of the batch of images judged

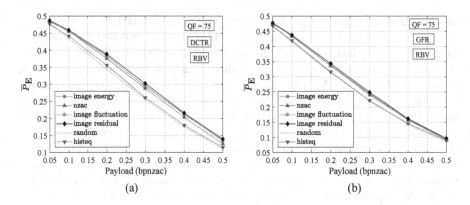

Fig. 4. Steganalytic performance of random, histeq, nzac, image energy, image residual and image fluctuation for RBV under DCTR (a) and GFR (b) detection.

by the pre-trained classifier, and then compare whether the number of stegos is greater than the threshold, which is set according to the number of stegos of the innocent and guilty users.

In this experiment, we first randomly select 5000 images from BOSSbase 1.01 to train classifiers with the average payload and embedding method used by the users, then randomly select 100 images from the rest 5000 images each time to embed using the embedding strategies. We repeat 400 times for each embedding strategy, 200 times for innocent users and 200 times for guilty users, respectively. We set the maximum payload to 1.0 bpp for WOW and 1.0 bpnzac for RBV. The experimental results are shown in Fig. 5, from which we can see that the proposed embedding strategy always has the best secure performance in both spatial and JPEG domain.

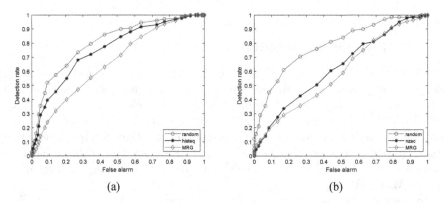

Fig. 5. Image (a) is the pooling steganalytic performance of three embedding strategies named random, histeq and proposed MRG using ROC curves for WOW against SRM at $\overline{R} = 0.1$ bpp. Image (b) is the pooling steganalytic performance of three embedding strategies named random, nzac and proposed MRG using ROC curves for RBV against DCTR at $\overline{R} = 0.1$ bpnzac.

5   Conclusions

Batch adaptive steganography has a wide range of applications in practice and the key of which is to select images with highest texture complexity. In this paper, we first propose three methods for measuring the texture complexity of image to select images with highly textured content, then propose our universal embedding strategy for batch adaptive steganography in both spatial and JPEG domain. To evaluate the security of different embedding strategies, We also propose a majority decision pooling steganalysis method designed specifically for the omniscient Warden. From the experimental results we can see that our proposed embedding strategy MRG always has the best secure performance under any condition.

Since image selection methods vary greatly, we will try to explore the effectiveness of other methods. In addition, the secure capacity of image is very important for batch steganography and has not attracted much attention, we will try to study it in our future work.

References

1. Fridrich, J.: Steganography in Digital Media: Principles, Algorithms, and Applications. Cambridge University Press, Cambridge (2009)
2. Pevný, T., Fridrich, J.: Benchmarking for steganography. In: Solanki, K., Sullivan, K., Madhow, U. (eds.) IH 2008. LNCS, vol. 5284, pp. 251–267. Springer, Heidelberg (2008). https://doi.org/10.1007/978-3-540-88961-8_18
3. Filler, T., Judas, J., Fridrich, J.: Minimizing additive distortion in steganography using syndrome-trellis codes. IEEE Trans. Inf. Forensics Secur. **6**(3), 920–935 (2011)
4. Pevný, T., Filler, T., Bas, P.: Using high-dimensional image models to perform highly undetectable steganography. In: Böhme, R., Fong, P.W.L., Safavi-Naini, R. (eds.) IH 2010. LNCS, vol. 6387, pp. 161–177. Springer, Heidelberg (2010). https://doi.org/10.1007/978-3-642-16435-4_13
5. Pevny, T., Bas, P., Fridrich, J.: Steganalysis by subtractive pixel adjacency matrix. IEEE Trans. Inf. Forensics Secur. **5**(2), 215–224 (2010)
6. Holub, V., Fridrich, J.: Designing steganographic distortion using directional filters. In: 2012 IEEE International Workshop on Information Forensics and Security (WIFS), pp. 234–239. IEEE (2012)
7. Fridrich, J., Kodovsky, J.: Rich models for steganalysis of digital images. IEEE Trans. Inf. Forensics Secur. **7**(3), 868–882 (2012)
8. Denemark, T., Sedighi, V., Holub, V, Cogranne, R., Fridrich, J.: Selection-channel-aware rich model for steganalysis of digital images. In: 2014 IEEE International Workshop on Information Forensics and Security (WIFS), pp. 48–53. IEEE (2014)
9. Holub, V., Fridrich, J., Denemark, T.: Universal distortion function for steganography in an arbitrary domain. EURASIP J. Inf. Secur. **2014**(1), 1–13 (2014)
10. Li, B., Wang, M., Huang, J., Li, X.: A new cost function for spatial image steganography. In: 2014 IEEE International Conference on Image Processing (ICIP), pp. 4206–4210. IEEE (2014)
11. Guo, L., Ni, J., Su, W., Tang, C., Shi, Y.-Q.: Using statistical image model for JPEG steganography: uniform embedding revisited. IEEE Trans. Inf. Forensics Secur. **10**(12), 2669–2680 (2015)

12. Wang, Z., Zhang, X., Yin, Z.: Hybrid distortion function for JPEG steganography. J. Electron. Imaging **25**(5), 050501 (2016)
13. Wei, Q., Yin, Z., Wang, Z., Zhang, X.: Distortion function based on residual blocks for JPEG steganography. Multimed. Tools Appl. **77**, 1–14 (2017)
14. Ker, A.D., Pevny, T.: Batch steganography in the real world. In: Proceedings of the on Multimedia and Security, MM&Sec 2012, pp. 1–10. ACM, New York (2012)
15. Guo, L., Ni, J., Shi, Y.Q.: An efficient JPEG steganographic scheme using uniform embedding. In: 2012 IEEE International Workshop on Information Forensics and Security (WIFS), pp. 169–174. IEEE (2012)
16. Zhao, Z., Guan, Q., Zhao, X., Yu, H., Liu, C.: Embedding strategy for batch adaptive steganography. In: Shi, Y.Q., Kim, H.J., Perez-Gonzalez, F., Liu, F. (eds.) IWDW 2016. LNCS, vol. 10082, pp. 494–505. Springer, Cham (2017). https://doi.org/10.1007/978-3-319-53465-7_37
17. Zhao, Z., Guan, Q., Zhao, X., Yu, H., Liu, C.: Universal embedding strategy for batch adaptive steganography in both spatial and JPEG domain. Multimed. Tools Appl. **77**, 14093–14113 (2017)
18. Filler, T., Fridrich, J.: Gibbs construction in steganography. IEEE Trans. Inf. Forensics Secur. **5**(4), 705–720 (2010)
19. Ker, A.D., Pevný, T., Kodovský, J., Fridrich, J.: The square root law of steganographic capacity. In: Proceedings of the 10th ACM Workshop on Multimedia and Security, MM&Sec 2008, pp. 107–116. ACM, New York (2008)
20. Wang, R., Ping, X., Niu, S., Zhang, T.: Segmentation based steganalysis of spatial images using local linear transform. In: Shi, Y.Q., Kim, H.J., Perez-Gonzalez, F., Liu, F. (eds.) IWDW 2016. LNCS, vol. 10082, pp. 533–549. Springer, Cham (2017). https://doi.org/10.1007/978-3-319-53465-7_40
21. Bas, P., Filler, T., Pevný, T.: "Break our steganographic system": the ins and outs of organizing BOSS. In: Filler, T., Pevný, T., Craver, S., Ker, A. (eds.) IH 2011. LNCS, vol. 6958, pp. 59–70. Springer, Heidelberg (2011). https://doi.org/10.1007/978-3-642-24178-9_5
22. Holub, V., Fridrich, J.: Low-complexity features for JPEG steganalysis using undecimated DCT. IEEE Trans. Inf. Forensics Secur. **10**(2), 219–228 (2015)
23. Song, X., Liu, F., Yang, C., Luo, X., Zhang, Y.: Steganalysis of adaptive JPEG steganography using 2D gabor filters. In: Proceedings of the 3rd ACM Workshop on Information Hiding and Multimedia Security, pp. 15–23. ACM (2015)
24. Kodovsky, J., Fridrich, J., Holub, V.: Ensemble classifiers for steganalysis of digital media. IEEE Trans. Inf. Forensics Secur. **7**(2), 432–444 (2012)

Content-Adaptive Steganalysis via Augmented Utilization of Selection-Channel Information

Shijun Zhou[1], Weixuan Tang[1,2], Shunquan Tan[3], and Bin Li[1(✉)]

[1] Guangdong Key Laboratory of Intelligent Information Processing and Shenzhen
Key Laboratory of Media Security, College of Information Engineering,
Shenzhen University, Shenzhen 518060, China
libin@szu.edu.cn
[2] School of Information Science and Technology, Sun Yat-sen University,
Guangzhou 510275, China
[3] National Engineering Laboratory for Big Data System Computing Technology,
College of Computer Science and Software Engineering, Shenzhen University,
Shenzhen 518060, China

Abstract. Modern adaptive image steganographic schemes embed secret message into textural regions to make it difficult for steganalytic detection. To overcome the presented challenges, existing steganalytic methods incorporate selection-channel information into steganalytic features so as to improve detection capability. In this paper, we extended the maxSRM steganalytic scheme by better exploiting the selection-channel information in two aspects. On one hand, we processed the embedding change probabilities by highlighting the large probabilities to obtain the so called augmented coefficients. On the other hand, we used the augmented coefficients weighted by the approximated probabilities of occurrence of image residuals for computing co-occurrence matrix in steganalytic features. In this way, we further utilized the selection-channel information and make pixels with high embedding change probability contribute more to final steganalysis features. Experiments on BOSSBase image dateset showed that our proposed steganalytic method achieved the state-of-the-art performance against various steganographic schemes under different payloads.

Keywords: Content-adaptive steganography · Selection-channel · Steganalysis · Embedding change probability

1 Introduction

Image steganography is the technique of embedding secret information in digital images without being noticed [1,2]. On the contrary, steganalysis aims to uncover the existence of secret information. They are in a hunting and escaping game.

This work was supported in part by the NSFC (61572329, 61772349, U1636202), Shenzhen R&D Program (JCYJ20160328144421330). This work was also supported by Alibaba Group through Alibaba Innovative Research (AIR) Program.

© Springer Nature Switzerland AG 2019
C. D. Yoo et al. (Eds.): IWDW 2018, LNCS 11378, pp. 261–274, 2019.
https://doi.org/10.1007/978-3-030-11389-6_20

Modern steganography methods are designed under the framework of minimizing a distortion function [3], where effective embedding costs should be defined. For example, HUGO (Highly Undetectable steGO) [4] defines the cost by a weighted norm of the difference between the SPAM (Subtractive Pixel Adjacency Matrix) [5] vectors respectively extracted from cover images and candidate stego images. In WOW (Wavelet Obtained Weights) [6], wavelet-based directional filter banks are used to detect complex regions and then the filtered residuals are assembled to obtain embedding costs, while the residuals are aggregated from high frequency subbands in S-UNIWARD (Spatial UNIversal Wavelet Relative Distortion) [7]. Using a high-pass filter and two low-pass filters, HILL (HIgh-pass, Low-pass, and Low-pass) [8] assigns pixels in textural areas and their neighbors lower costs. MiPOD (Minimizing the Power of Optimal Detector) [9] employs the Generalized Gaussian distribution to model cover images, and uses the Neyman-Pearson criterion to optimize the embedding cost defined by Fisher Information between cover and stego. In MS (Micro-Scope) scheme [10], cover image is preprocessed with a high-pass filter to obtain costs. CPP (Controversial Pixels Prior) [11] combine several cost functions that have comparative security level and assign controversial pixels lower cost values. Both CMD (Clustering Modification Direction) [12] and Sync [13] assign lower costs to pixels with synchronized modifications.

A well-designed cost function usually ensures the embedding modifications content-adaptive. To counter such steganographic schemes, selection-channel-aware steganalysis is developed [14–17]. It is assumed that the embedding scheme is known and therefore the embedding costs can be estimated from the stego images. Incorporated such additional information in existing steganalytic schemes such as SRM (Spatial Rich Model) [18] and PSRM (Projected Spatial Rich Model) [19], steganalytic performance can be boosted. In tSRM (thresholded SRM) [14], a selection-channel-aware steganalysis scheme against WOW is proposed by means of extracting feature from the regions with high modification probabilities, which are located by the cost function of WOW. Similar to tSRM, maxSRM [15] makes great progress by involving the estimated maximum embedding change probabilities of consecutive image elements in computing co-occurrence features. At the same time, Tang et al. proposed to use the mean value instead of the maximum value of the embedding change probabilities [16]. Denemark et al. [17] proposed σmaxSRM and σspamPSRM by replacing the estimated embedding change probabilities of pixels with the expectation of distortion from filtered image residuals. Besides, Ye et al. [20] and Yang et al. [21] respectively proposed to incorporate the selection-channel information similar to maxSRM in their CNN designs.

In this paper, we proposed an effective steganalytic method by augmenting the utilization of selection-channel information. As pixels with higher embedding change probability provide more information of embedding traces, we utilized them in two ways. On one hand, we used a mapping function to strengthen the estimated embedding change probabilities so as to further highlight the traces in elements with large embedding probabilities. The processed probabilities are called augmented coefficients. On the other hand, the augmented coefficients weighted by the approximated probabilities of the quantized image residuals were used for computing the co-occurrence features. In this manner, pixels with high embedding change probabilities contribute more in steganalytic features, and resulting in improved steganalytic performance.

The rest part of this paper is organized as follows. In the next section, a brief overview of the SRM, maxSRM, and σmaxSRM is given. In Sect. 3, the proposed steganalytic method is described in details. In Sect. 4, experimental results are reported, and conclusions are drawn in Sect. 5.

2   Related Work

For better understanding the improvement made in our proposed method, we provide an overview of the SRM, maxSRM, and σmaxSRM in this section. Throughout the paper, we use capital letters in bold to represent matrices, and use lowercase letters for the corresponding matrix elements. Denote $n_1 \times n_2$ grayscale cover image and stego image as $X = (x_{i,j})^{n_1 \times n_2}$ and $Y = (y_{i,j})^{n_1 \times n_2}$ ($x_{i,j}, y_{i,j} \in \{0, \cdots, 255\}$), respectively. We assume ternary embedding is used for spatial images.

2.1   SRM

Four main steps are employed in computing SRM features [18]. Firstly, several linear and non-linear filters are utilized to suppress the image content and capture the subtle embedding noise. The filtered residual image is denoted as $Z = (z_{i,j})^{n_1 \times n_2}$. Secondly, the residuals are quantized and truncated to make features more compact, i.e.,

$$r_{i,j} = \mathrm{trunc}_T \left(\mathrm{round} \left(\frac{z_{i,j}}{q} \right) \right), \tag{1}$$

where q is the quantization step, $round(\cdot)$ is the rounding function, $\mathrm{trunc}_T(\cdot)$ is the truncation function, and T is the truncation threshold. The truncation is performed as follows:

$$\mathrm{trunc}_T(x) = \left\{ \begin{array}{ll} x, & x \in [-T, T], \\ T\mathrm{sign}(x), & \text{otherwise.} \end{array} \right. \tag{2}$$

Thirdly, image statistical features are extracted by using the four dimensional co-occurrence of the truncated and quantized residuals. For example, the horizontal co-occurrence for four horizontally neighbouring residuals is computed as

$$C_{d_0,d_1,d_2,d_3}^{\mathrm{SRM}} = \sum_{i=1}^{n_1} \sum_{j=1}^{n_2-3} [(r_{i,j}, r_{i,j+1}, r_{i,j+2}, r_{i,j+3}) = (d_0, d_1, d_2, d_3)], \tag{3}$$

where $[P]$ is the Iverson bracket, which is equal to 1 when the statement P is true and 0 otherwise. Finally, features are aggregated according to the symmetry properties.

2.2   maxSRM

The difference between maxSRM [15] and SRM is that selection-channel information is employed in computing the co-occurrence features. Take the horizontal fourth-order co-occurrences as example:

$$
C^{\text{maxSRM}}_{d_0,d_1,d_2,d_3} = \sum_{i=1}^{n_1} \sum_{j=1}^{n_2-3} \max\left(\beta_{i,j}, \beta_{i,j+1}, \beta_{i,j+2}, \beta_{i,j+3}\right) \times \left[(r_{i,j}, r_{i,j+1}, r_{i,j+2}, r_{i,j+3})\right.
$$
$$
\left. = (d_0, d_1, d_2, d_3)\right],
\tag{4}
$$

where $\beta_{i,j}$ is the estimated embedding change probability and can be computed by optimal simulator [16] with the cost values obtained from the image under scrutiny. It can be seen that the maximum value of the estimated embedding change probabilities of four consecutive pixels is used, so that only the highest change probability contributes in the feature.

2.3   σmaxSRM

σmaxSRM [17] is adapted from maxSRM by replacing the maximum value of the estimated embedding change probabilities with the expected difference in the filtered residual to compute the co-occurrence features. Take the horizontal fourth-order co-occurrences as example:

$$
C^{\sigma\text{maxSRM}}_{d_0,d_1,d_2,d_3} = \sum_{i=1}^{n_1} \sum_{j=1}^{n_2-3} \max\left(\sigma_{i,j}, \sigma_{i,j+1}, \sigma_{i,j+2}, \sigma_{i,j+3}\right) \times \left[(r_{i,j}, r_{i,j+1}, r_{i,j+2}, r_{i,j+3})\right.
$$
$$
\left. = (d_0, d_1, d_2, d_3)\right].
\tag{5}
$$

where $\sigma_{i,j}$ is an estimated value of the expected difference in the filtered residual, i.e.,

$$
\sigma_{ij} = E(|z_{ij}(\boldsymbol{Y}) - z_{ij}(\boldsymbol{X})|).
\tag{6}
$$

For linear filtered residual, it can be estimated by

$$
\sigma_{ij} = \sqrt{\sum_{k,l} w_{k,l}^2 \beta_{i-k,j-l}},
\tag{7}
$$

where $w_{k,l}$ is the weights of the linear filter. For non-linear filtered residual, it can be estimated by using Monte-Carlo simulation with repeated embedding, which is computational expensive.

3   The Proposed Steganalysis Scheme with Augmented Selection-Channel Information

The selection-channel-aware steganalysis schemes [15,17] show effectiveness in detecting content-adaptive steganography. It is expected that the better utilization of the selection-channel information, the more effective the steganalytic performance. In this paper, following the framework of maxSRM, we consider to make a better use of selection-channel information by strengthening the estimated embedding change probabilities to obtain augmented coefficients and forming co-occurrence features with augmented coefficients and processed residuals. The proposed steganalytic feature extraction process is illustrated in Fig. 1, where the two additional steps are highlighted.

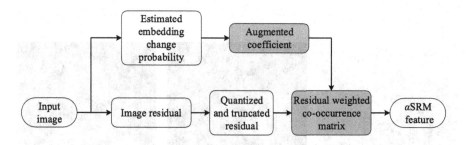

Fig. 1. Flowchart of the proposed feature extraction process

3.1 Strengthening the Embedding Change Probabilities

As shown in [15] and [17], it is reasonable to make pixels with high embedding change probabilities contribute more in steganalytic features. We follow such philosophy and strengthen the embedding change probabilities with a high-pass filter. Assume $\beta = (\beta_{i,j})^{n_1 \times n_2}$ is the matrix of the estimated change probabilities, and H is a high-pass filer. The high-pass filtered probabilities are computed as

$$\varepsilon \triangleq (\varepsilon_{i,j})^{n_1 \times n_2} = \beta \otimes H \tag{8}$$

where $\otimes$ is the convolution operation. We augment the embedding change probabilities by

$$\alpha_{i,j} = \beta_{i,j} + \lambda |\varepsilon_{i,j}|, \quad 1 \leq i \leq n_1, 1 \leq j \leq n_2 \tag{9}$$

where $\lambda > 0$ is the parameter to control the augmentation strength and symbol $|\cdot|$ is the operator of taking absolute value. In (9), since the $\varepsilon_{i,j}$ can be negative, we use an absolute operator to rectify the outputs, for the magnitude of negative $\varepsilon_{i,j}$ can also provide useful information. We call $\alpha_{i,j}$ *augmented coefficient*. In our implementation, we use the KV high-pass filter chosen from SRM filters as

$$H = \frac{1}{12} \begin{bmatrix} -1 & 2 & -2 & 2 & -1 \\ 2 & -6 & 8 & -6 & 2 \\ -2 & 8 & -12 & 8 & -2 \\ 2 & -6 & 8 & -6 & 2 \\ -1 & 2 & -2 & 2 & -1 \end{bmatrix} . \tag{10}$$

According to our trial experiments, the KV high-pass filter, which is central-symmetric and rotation invariant, has slightly better performance than other SRM filters. Since the augmented coefficient is intensively involved in the proposed steganalytic feature, we call our proposed feature extraction method as αSRM. Figure 2 shows an example of embedding change probability map and the corresponding augmented coefficient map. It can be observed that the amplitudes of the elements in texture regions of the augmented coefficient map are magnified.

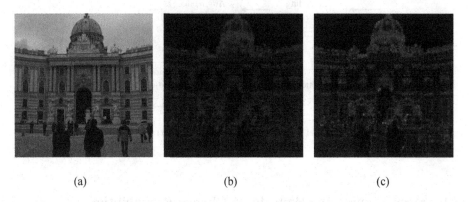

(a)   (b)   (c)

Fig. 2. Illustration of (a) cover image, (b) embedding change probability map of S-UNIWARD under 0.4 bpp payload, and (c) the augmented coefficient under $\lambda = 10$. For display purpose, we scale the estimated probability and augmented coefficient to the range of $[0, 255]$.

3.2 Forming Residual Weighted Co-occurrence Features

In order to make the co-occurrence matrix well-populated, quantization and truncation on image residuals are needed to perform. Following the quantization and truncation process as shown in (1), the resultant residual for z_{ij} is denoted as r_{ij}. We use $T = 2$ in our implementation according to extensive experimental trials.

In maxSRM, the maximum value of the embedding change probabilities of consecutive pixels is used in computing co-occurrence features, as shown in (3). Therefore, the selection-channel information is incorporated in the feature design. To further exploit the information, we take image residuals into account. The image residuals with high probabilities of occurrence should have larger contribution in the feature. Therefore, instead of using the augmented coefficients directly, we use the coefficients weighted by the probabilities of occurrence of image residuals. It is usually assumed that the image residuals follow a Laplacian distribution, in which small values have large probabilities. To simply the computation, we have done some experiments and approximate the distribution with a fixed non-parametric model as follows:

$$
p_{r_{ij}} = \begin{cases} 0.4, & r_{ij} = 0, \\ 0.2, & r_{ij} = \pm 1, \\ 0.1, & r_{ij} = \pm 2. \end{cases} \tag{11}
$$

The horizontal co-occurrence feature of the proposed αSRM is computed as

$$
\begin{aligned}
C_{d_0,d_1,d_2,d_3}^{\alpha\mathrm{SRM}} &= \sum_{i=1}^{n_1} \sum_{j=1}^{n_2-3} \left(\sum_{k=0}^{3} \alpha_{i,j+k}\, p_{r_{i,j+k}} \right) \times [(r_{i,j}, r_{i,j+1}, r_{i,j+2}, r_{i,j+3}) \\
&= (d_0, d_1, d_2, d_3)].
\end{aligned} \tag{12}
$$

Other co-occurrence features can be obtained correspondingly.

4   Experimental Results

We performed experiments to demonstrate the effectiveness of the proposed method. All experiments were carried out on 10,000 grayscale images of size 512×512 from BOSSBase ver. 1.01 dataset [22]. Six contend-adaptive steganographic methods, i.e. S-UNIWARD [7], HILL [8], MiPOD [9], CMD-S-UNIWARD [12], CMD-HILL [12] and CMD-MiPOD [12] were included for evaluation with the payload rate from 0.1 bpp (bit per pixel) to 0.5 bpp. SRM [18], maxSRM [15], and σmaxSRM [17] are used for comparison, and Fisher linear discriminant (FLD) based ensemble classifier [23] is used for classification. The cover image set is randomly split into a training set and a testing set, each consists of 5,000 images. The detection accuracy is evaluated by 10 times of random splits and denoted as $\bar{P}_E$.

We also employed the 5×2 *fold cross-validated pair t-test* [24] to validate if two methods for comparison have statistical difference in performance. All the image pairs were divided into two equal-sized image sets randomly for five times, denoted as $S_1(i)$ and $S_2(i)$ for the i-th division. For each time, on one hand, the classifier was trained on $S_1(i)$ and tested on $S_2(i)$ with method A and method B to get their testing errors, denoted as $p_A^{(1)}(i)$ and $p_B^{(1)}(i)$ respectively. On the other hand, the classifier was trained on $S_2(i)$ and tested on $S_1(i)$ with these two method to get another two testing errors, denoted as $p_A^{(2)}(i)$ and $p_B^{(2)}(i)$. As a result, a statistic $\tilde{t}$ was calculated as:

$$
\tilde{t} = \frac{p_A^{(1)}(1) - p_B^{(1)}(1)}{\sqrt{\sum_{i=1}^{5} \frac{(p_A^{(1)}(i) - p_B^{(1)}(i) + p_B^{(2)}(i) - p_A^{(2)}(i))^2}{10}}}. \tag{13}
$$

Here we chose a significant level of 0.95 with $t_{0.95} = 2.015$. When statistic $\tilde{t}$ is larger than $t_{0.95}$, we can say that there is a statistical significant difference between method A and B.

4.1 The Impact of Augmentation Parameter

As shown in Subsect. 3.1, the parameter λ is used for controlling the augmentation strength. We make a search on λ by testing its impact on detecting S-UNIWARD and HILL with 0.4 bpp. It can be seen from Fig. 3 that the performance with $\lambda > 0$ is better than the performance with $\lambda = 0$, implying that the augmentation takes effect. As λ increases, the trend for S-UNIWARD and that for HILL are different. Therefore, we choose $\lambda = 60$ in our experiments as it achieves satisfactory detection performance on both two steganographic schemes.

4.2 Comparisons to Prior Arts

In order to evaluate the performance of the proposed method, we perform three groups of experiments as follows.

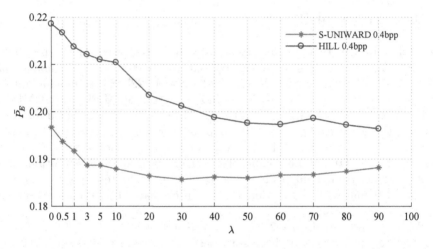

Fig. 3. Testing errors of the proposed αSRM scheme against two steganographic schemes under different λ when the embedding payload is 0.4 bpp

Comparison with SRM and maxSRM: In our first group of experiment, we compare our proposed method to SRM and maxSRM with features of 34,671-D. The steganographic algorithm and the embedding payload are assumed to be known in maxSRM and αSRM. The results are shown in Table 1. It can be observed that both maxSRM and αSRM outperform SRM since selection-channel information is used in these two schemes. In most of cases, αSRM performs the best. Moreover, note that for CMD-S-UNIWARD, CMD-HILL and CMD-MiPOD, the embedding change probabilities are estimated according to S-UNIWARD, HILL and MiPOD, respectively. It implies that the proposed method still works when the selection-channel information is not accurate.

Table 1. Detection errors of SRM, maxSRM, and αSRM on detecting four steganographic schemes under different payloads.

Steganographic scheme	Steganalytic feature	0.1 bpp	0.2 bpp	0.3 bpp	0.4 bpp	0.5 bpp
S-UNIWARD	SRM	0.4022	0.3208	0.2561	0.2068	0.1636
	maxSRM	0.3697	0.2990	0.2440	0.1989	0.1638
	αSRM	**0.3625**	**0.2869**	**0.2316**	**0.1866**	**0.1499**
HILL	SRM	0.4324	0.3608	0.3002	0.2492	0.2051
	maxSRM	0.3803	0.3167	0.2688	0.2253	0.1897
	αSRM	**0.3533**	**0.2875**	**0.2380**	**0.1973**	**0.1664**
MiPOD	SRM	0.4165	0.3459	0.2885	0.2388	0.1998
	maxSRM	0.4011	**0.3313**	0.2792	0.2330	0.1942
	αSRM	**0.4006**	0.3331	**0.2767**	**0.2276**	**0.1889**
CMD-S-UNIWARD	SRM	0.4251	0.3591	0.3026	0.2544	0.2135
	maxSRM	0.3822	0.3199	0.2730	0.2350	0.2027
	αSRM	**0.3678**	**0.3069**	**0.2611**	**0.2275**	**0.1956**
CMD-HILL	SRM	0.4544	0.3956	0.3427	0.2983	0.2552
	maxSRM	0.4016	0.3454	0.3048	0.2696	0.2361
	αSRM	**0.3663**	**0.3080**	**0.2613**	**0.2267**	**0.1961**
CMD-MiPOD	SRM	0.4434	0.3876	0.3379	0.2922	0.2516
	maxSRM	**0.4246**	0.3680	0.3201	0.2781	**0.2398**
	αSRM	0.4251	**0.3640**	**0.3177**	**0.2734**	0.2400

Table 2. The value of the statistic $\tilde{t}$ in detecting four steganographic schemes. The numerics are marked in bold fonts when αSRM performs statistically significant better than SRM or maxSRM.

Comparison schemes	Steganographic scheme	0.1 bpp	0.2 bpp	0.3 bpp	0.4 bpp	0.5 bpp
αSRM vs SRM	S-UNIWARD	**7.042**	**5.532**	**4.730**	**5.388**	**4.747**
	HILL	**16.182**	**13.717**	**6.445**	**9.152**	**6.120**
	MiPOD	**6.030**	1.600	**3.238**	**4.620**	**3.019**
	CMD-S-UNIWARD	**15.085**	**16.825**	**5.853**	**5.074**	**3.719**
	CMD-HILL	**9.677**	**9.989**	**13.467**	**13.365**	**11.512**
	CMD-MiPOD	**3.662**	**7.255**	**5.272**	**6.968**	1.655
αSRM vs maxSRM	S-UNIWARD	1.859	**2.503**	**2.528**	**3.814**	**3.806**
	HILL	**6.165**	**5.567**	**5.426**	**5.435**	**4.714**
	MiPOD	0.462	−0.049	1.941	0.306	**4.889**
	CMD-S-UNIWARD	**3.071**	**4.337**	**3.464**	1.489	1.594
	CMD-HILL	**6.837**	**18.874**	**7.424**	**7.732**	**6.251**
	CMD-MiPOD	0.121	0.466	**2.759**	**3.769**	0.391

Table 3. Detection errors of three steganalytic features with non-linear mapping on detecting four steganographic schemes under different payloads.

Steganographic scheme	Steganalytic feature	0.1 bpp	0.2 bpp	0.3 bpp	0.4 bpp	0.5 bpp
S-UNIWARD	SRM(exp-Hellinger)	0.3920	03071	0.2401	0.1860	0.1422
	maxSRM(exp-Hellinger)	0.3663	0.2839	0.2262	0.1783	0.1391
	αSRM(exp-Hellinger)	**0.3589**	**0.2749**	**0.2146**	**0.1655**	**0.1286**
HILL	SRM(exp-Hellinger)	0.4066	0.3381	0.2786	0.2291	0.1853
	maxSRM(exp-Hellinger)	0.3698	0.3001	0.2489	0.2055	0.1679
	αSRM(exp-Hellinger)	**0.3484**	**0.2814**	**0.2309**	**0.1886**	**0.1545**
MiPOD	SRM(exp-Hellinger)	0.4007	0.3324	0.2727	0.2229	0.1837
	maxSRM(exp-Hellinger)	0.3955	**0.3206**	**0.2636**	0.2148	0.1784
	αSRM(exp-Hellinger)	**0.3937**	0.3239	0.2655	**0.2143**	**0.1763**
CMD-S-UNIWARD	SRM(exp-Hellinger)	0.4162	0.3460	0.2888	0.2400	0.1926
	maxSRM(exp-Hellinger)	0.3796	0.3134	0.2630	0.2189	0.1838
	αSRM(exp-Hellinger)	**0.3728**	**0.3008**	**0.2452**	**0.2018**	**0.1655**
CMD-HILL	SRM(exp-Hellinger)	0.4313	0.3720	0.3186	0.2748	0.2354
	maxSRM(exp-Hellinger)	0.3910	0.3359	0.2879	0.2495	0.2166
	αSRM(exp-Hellinger)	**0.3663**	**0.3020**	**0.2544**	**0.2204**	**0.1876**
CMD-MiPOD	SRM(exp-Hellinger)	0.4434	0.3875	0.3379	0.2921	0.2515
	maxSRM(exp-Hellinger)	0.4246	0.3680	0.3200	0.2780	0.2397
	αSRM(exp-Hellinger)	**0.4183**	**0.3553**	**0.3088**	**0.2621**	**0.2235**

Table 4. The value of the statistic $\tilde{t}$ under several steganographic schemes. The numerics are remarked in bold fonts when αSRM performs statistically significant better than its counterparts.

Comparison schemes	Steganographic scheme	0.1 bpp	0.2 bpp	0.3 bpp	0.4 bpp	0.5 bpp
αSRM(exp-Hellinger) vs SRM(exp-Hellinger)	S-UNIWARD	**6.475**	**8.578**	**8.348**	**7.705**	**11.963**
	HILL	**18.821**	**12.899**	**9.910**	**7.311**	**10.649**
	MiPOD	0.029	1.448	1.116	**8.408**	**2.553**
	CMD-S-UNIWARD	**11.532**	**12.057**	**12.114**	**10.189**	**12.238**
	CMD-HILL	**14.147**	**35.369**	**16.578**	**14.537**	**9.875**
	CMD-MiPOD	**7.832**	**3.300**	**6.306**	**5.042**	**4.238**
αSRM(exp-Hellinger) vs maxSRM(exp-Hellinger)	S-UNIWARD	0.805	**2.772**	**5.692**	**5.770**	**2.759**
	HILL	**6.642**	**7.466**	**6.667**	**6.548**	**2.619**
	MiPOD	0.345	−1.797	−0.493	**3.133**	1.764
	CMD-S-UNIWARD	0.277	**4.772**	**3.417**	**3.439**	**5.178**
	CMD-HILL	**3.887**	**13.425**	**10.847**	**9.818**	**10.256**
	CMD-MiPOD	0.054	**2.233**	**2.281**	**2.742**	**2.569**

The results of statistic $\tilde{t}$ are listed in Table 2, comparing αSRM with SRM and with maxSRM, respectively. The results in Table 2 show that αSRM performs statistically significant better than SRM in all cases except for MiPOD with 0.2 bpp and CMD-MiPOD with 0.5 bpp embedding rates. For S-UNIWARD with 0.1 bpp embedding rate, CMD-HILL with 0.4 bpp and 0.5 bpp embedding rates

Content-Adaptive Steganalysis   271

Table 5. Comparison between "spam" part of σmaxSRM and αSRM on detecting steganographic schemes under different payloads.

Steganographic scheme	Steganalytic feature	0.1 bpp	0.2 bpp	0.3 bpp	0.4 bpp	0.5 bpp
S-UNIWARD	σmaxSRM("spam")	0.4113	0.3406	0.2975	0.2347	0.2010
	αSRM("spam")	**0.3879**	**0.3142**	**0.2559**	**0.2134**	**0.1733**
HILL	σmaxSRM("spam")	0.4173	0.3557	0.3075	0.2640	0.2249
	αSRM("spam")	**0.3763**	**0.3070**	**0.2594**	**0.2209**	**0.1877**
MiPOD	σmaxSRM("spam")	0.4185	0.3587	0.3062	0.2619	0.2230
	αSRM("spam")	**0.4122**	**0.3428**	**0.2898**	**0.2440**	**0.2021**
CMD-S-UNIWARD	σmaxSRM("spam")	0.4373	0.3753	0.3124	0.2856	0.2431
	αSRM("spam")	**0.4032**	**0.3388**	**0.2876**	**0.2483**	**0.2120**
CMD-HILL	σmaxSRM("spam")	0.4475	0.3944	0.3387	0.3131	0.2745
	αSRM("spam")	**0.3960**	**0.3370**	**0.2923**	**0.2562**	**0.2230**
CMD-MiPOD	σmaxSRM("spam")	0.4466	0.3993	0.3544	0.3152	0.2806
	αSRM("spam")	**0.4339**	**0.3781**	**0.3311**	**0.2892**	**0.2523**

Table 6. The value of the statistic $\tilde{t}$ under several steganographic schemes. The numerics are remarked in bold fonts when αSRM performs statistically significant better than σmaxSRM.

Comparison Schemes	Steganographic Scheme	0.1 bpp	0.2 bpp	0.3 bpp	0.4 bpp	0.5 bpp
αSRM("spam") vs σmaxSRM("spam")	S-UNIWARD	**3.582**	**7.612**	**6.754**	**6.343**	**6.025**
	HILL	**12.994**	**18.836**	**10.370**	**11.826**	**12.796**
	MiPOD	**2.333**	**4.232**	**3.498**	**4.409**	**7.443**
	CMD-S-UNIWARD	**6.079**	**9.499**	**15.641**	**9.116**	**8.786**
	CMD-HILL	**8.415**	**8.504**	**8.451**	**8.662**	**9.147**
	CMD-MiPOD	1.399	**3.364**	**3.210**	**10.315**	**13.147**

and majority payloads for MiPOD and CMD-MiPOD, αSRM performs as good as maxSRM. In other cases, αSRM performs significantly better than maxSRM.

The Performance with Non-linear Feature Mapping: It has been shown in [25,26] that non-linear mapping can boost feature performance. To investigate whether the proposed features can be benefited from the non-linear mapping, we perform experiments by using the exponential-Hellinger kernel mapping [25] on steganalytic features. The experimental results are shown in Tables 3. It can be observed that the detection performance can be further improved by the non-linear mapping for all three steganalytic schemes. αSRM with exp-Hellinger mapping performs the best under majority circumstances, especially for HILL and CMD-HILL. Taking HILL as an example, αSRM with exp-Hellinger mapping increases the performance ranges from 3.08% to 5.82% compared with SRM

Table 7. Testing errors of each procedure combined with maxSRM on detecting four steganographic scheme under 0.4 bpp.

Steganalytic feature	S-UNIWARD	HILL	CMD-S-UNIWARD	CMD-HILL
maxSRM	0.1989	0.2253	0.2350	0.2696
maxSRM-S	0.1949	0.2036	**0.2271**	0.2302
maxSRM-W	0.1967	0.2186	0.2316	0.2648
αSRM	**0.1866**	**0.1973**	0.2275	**0.2267**

with exp-Hellinger mapping from 0.1 to 0.5 bpp. For steganalytic method with exp-Hellinger mapping, the results of statistic $\tilde{t}$ are listed in Table 4. αSRM performs statistically significant better than SRM and maxSRM under many cases.

Comparison with σmaxSRM: We compare the proposed method with σmaxSRM [17]. Due to the fact that computing non-linear residual features is time consuming, we adopted the implementation of [17] by using the linear residual features ("spam" type) for detecting steganographic schemes. For fair comparison, we also use "spam" part of the features in our scheme. The results shown in Table 5 indicate that the "spam" part of our proposed αSRM performs better than that of σmaxSRM. Furthermore, considering that αSRM has only marginal increasement of computation cost due to the two additional steps over maxSRM, it is more efficient than σmaxSRM, especially for the non-linear residual feature part. The values of statistic $\tilde{t}$ are shown in Table 6. All the statistic $\tilde{t}$ are larger than $t_{0.95}$ except for CMD-MiPOD with 0.1 bpp embedding rate, which verify that the "spam" part of αSRM is statistically performs better than that of σmaxSRM in majority cases.

4.3   The Effectiveness of Selection-Channel Information Utilization in Each Procedure

In our proposed method, we improve maxSRM with two additional steps. These two procedures work together to achieve good results. In this part, we investigate the effectiveness of each procedure. The two procedures are abbreviated by S (strengthening embedding change probability) and W (residual weighted co-occurrence), respectively. We use these abbreviations as suffix of maxSRM to denote the corresponding applied procedures. For instance, maxSRM-S means that the augmented coefficients are used to replace the embedding change probability in maxSRM.

The experimental results on 0.4 bpp are shown in Table 7. The lowest testing error for each steganographic scheme are in bold. The second best results are highlighted with underlines. The results show that both the two procedures play positive roles in improving in detection capability. Strengthening the embedding change probability can boost the detection performance more.

5   Concluding Remarks

Content-adaptive steganalysis prioritizes image pixels based on selection-channel information. In this paper, we propose a content-adaptive steganalysis strategy that utilizes selection-channel information in two novel ways. Considering that pixels with high embedding change probability can provide more useful information, more attention should be paid on those pixels. We firstly augment the information by a mapping function, and then incorporate the augmented information with co-occurrence formation to highlight pixels with high embedding change probability. The experimental results show that the proposed αSRM achieves better performance against modern state-of-art steganographic schemes compared with former steganalysis features. It is also demonstrated that the two proposed improved techniques, strengthening embedding change probability and utilizing weighted augment coefficients are both effective. We should note that an "overly content-adaptive" steganalytic scheme, which relies much on the selection channel information, might end up in the steganographer using a "less content-adaptive" embedding scheme and thus evading the content-adaptive method. In this case, we may resort to game theory in future for addressing this cat-and-mouse-race.

References

1. Li, B., He, J., Huang, J., Shi, Y.Q.: A survey on image steganography and steganalysis. Dep. Comput. **2**(3), 288–289 (2011)
2. Ker, A.D., Bas, P., Craver, S., Fridrich, J.: Moving steganography and steganalysis from the laboratory into the real world. In: ACM Workshop on Information Hiding and Multimedia Security, pp. 45–58 (2013)
3. Huang, F., Zhong, Y., Huang, J.: Improved algorithm of edge adaptive image steganography based on LSB matching revisited algorithm. In: Shi, Y.Q., Kim, H.-J., Pérez-González, F. (eds.) IWDW 2013. LNCS, vol. 8389, pp. 19–31. Springer, Heidelberg (2014). https://doi.org/10.1007/978-3-662-43886-2_2
4. Pevný, T., Filler, T., Bas, P.: Using high-dimensional image models to perform highly undetectable steganography. In: Böhme, R., Fong, P.W.L., Safavi-Naini, R. (eds.) IH 2010. LNCS, vol. 6387, pp. 161–177. Springer, Heidelberg (2010). https://doi.org/10.1007/978-3-642-16435-4_13
5. Pevný, T., Bas, P., Fridrich, J.: Steganalysis by subtractive pixel adjacency matrix. In: ACM Workshop on Multimedia and Security, pp. 75–84 (2009)
6. Holub, V., Fridrich, J.: Designing steganographic distortion using directional filters. In: IEEE International Workshop on Information Forensics and Security, pp. 234–239 (2012)
7. Holub, V., Fridrich, J., Denemark, T.: Universal distortion function for steganography in an arbitrary domain. Eurasip J. Inf. Secur. **2014**(1), 1 (2014)
8. Li, B., Wang, M., Huang, J., Li, X.: A new cost function for spatial image steganography. In: IEEE International Conference on Image Processing. pp. 4206–4210 (2015)
9. Sedighi, V., Cogranne, R., Fridrich, J.: Content-adaptive steganography by minimizing statistical detectability. IEEE Trans. Inf. Forensics Secur. **11**(2), 221–234 (2015)

10. Chen, K., Zhang, W., Zhou, H., Yu, N., Feng, G.: Defining cost functions for adaptive steganography at the microscale. In: IEEE International Workshop on Information Forensics and Security, pp. 1–6 (2017)
11. Zhou, W., Zhang, W., Yu, N.: A new rule for cost reassignment in adaptive steganography. IEEE Trans. Inf. Forensics Secur. **12**(11), 2654–2667 (2017)
12. Li, B., Wang, M., Li, X., Tan, S., Huang, J.: A strategy of clustering modification directions in spatial image steganography. IEEE Trans. Inf. Forensics Secur. **10**(9), 1905–1917 (2015)
13. Denemark, T., Fridrich, J.: Improving steganographic security by synchronizing the selection channel. In: Proceedings of the 3rd ACM Workshop on Information Hiding and Multimedia Security, pp. 5–14. ACM (2015)
14. Tang, W., Li, H., Luo, W., Huang, J.: Adaptive steganalysis against WOW embedding algorithm. In: Proceedings of the 2nd ACM workshop on Information hiding and multimedia security. ACM (2014)
15. Denemark, T., Sedighi, V., Holub, V., Cogranne, R., Fridrich, J.: Selection-channel-aware rich model for steganalysis of digital images. In: IEEE International Workshop on Information Forensics and Security, pp. 48–53 (2014)
16. Tang, W., Li, H., Luo, W., Huang, J.: Adaptive steganalysis based on embedding probabilities of pixels. IEEE Trans. Inf. Forensics Secur. **11**(4), 734–745 (2016)
17. Denemark, T., Fridrich, J., Comesaña-Alfaro, P.: Improving selection-channel-aware steganalysis features. Electron. Imaging **2016**(8), 1–8 (2016)
18. Fridrich, J., Kodovský, J.: Rich models for steganalysis of digital images. IEEE Trans. Inf. Forensics Secur. **7**(3), 868–882 (2012)
19. Holub, V., Fridrich, J.: Random projections of residuals for digital image steganalysis. IEEE Trans. Inf. Forensics Secur. **8**(12), 1996–2006 (2013)
20. Ye, J., Ni, J., Yi, Y.: Deep learning hierarchical representations for image steganalysis. IEEE Trans. Inf. Forensics Secur. **12**(11), 2545–2557 (2017)
21. Yang, J., Liu, K., Kang, X., Wong, E., Shi, Y.: Steganalysis based on awareness of selection-channel and deep learning. In: Kraetzer, C., Shi, Y.-Q., Dittmann, J., Kim, H.J. (eds.) IWDW 2017. LNCS, vol. 10431, pp. 263–272. Springer, Cham (2017). https://doi.org/10.1007/978-3-319-64185-0_20
22. Bas, P., Filler, T., Pevný, T.: "Break our steganographic system": the ins and outs of organizing BOSS. In: Filler, T., Pevný, T., Craver, S., Ker, A. (eds.) IH 2011. LNCS, vol. 6958, pp. 59–70. Springer, Heidelberg (2011). https://doi.org/10.1007/978-3-642-24178-9_5
23. Kodovský, J., Fridrich, J., Holub, V.: Ensemble classifiers for steganalysis of digital media. IEEE Trans. Inf. Forensics Secur. **7**(2), 432–444 (2012)
24. Dietterich, T.G.: Approximate Statistical Tests for Comparing Supervised Classification Learning Algorithms. MIT Press, Cambridge (1998)
25. Boroumand, M., Fridrich, J.: Boosting steganalysis with explicit feature maps. In: ACM Workshop on Information Hiding and Multimedia Security, pp. 149–157 (2016)
26. Li, B., Li, Z., Zhou, S., Tan, S., Zhang, X.: New steganalytic features for spatial image steganography based on derivative filters and threshold LBP operator. IEEE Trans. Inf. Forensics Secur. **13**(5), 1242–1257 (2018)

Pitch Delay Based Adaptive Steganography for AMR Speech Stream

Chen Gong[1,2], Xiaowei Yi[1,2(✉)], and Xianfeng Zhao[1,2]

[1] State Key Laboratory of Information Security, Institute of Information Engineering, Chinese Academy of Sciences, Beijing 100093, China
yixiaowei@iie.ac.cn
[2] School of Cyber Security, University of Chinese Academy of Sciences, Beijing 100049, China

Abstract. Most existing speech steganography breaks the continuity of adjacent pitch delay, which obviously degrades their statistically undetectability. This paper presents a novel steganographic scheme for low bit-rate speech stream against pitch delay steganalysis. Three measures are adopted to enhance steganographic security. First, the short-term stability of pitch delay and the statistical distribution of adjacent subframe are considered for designing a distortion function. Second, syndrome-trellis codes (STCs) is utilized to minimize the overall embedding impact based on the defined distortion function. Third, the suboptimal pitch delay is searched to maintain speech quality. Experimental results demonstrate that our scheme achieves higher level of security, especially in the case of low embedding rate. When the relative embedding rate is 0.2 for 10.2 kbit/s AMR stream, the test error rate of our method rises by 12.44% compared with the existing algorithm.

Keywords: Adaptive steganography · Speech steganography · ACELP · Pitch delay · Adaptive multi-rate

1 Introduction

Steganography is a kind of covert technology. It conceals secret messages to be conveyed under the camouflage of common and innocent cover media in order to reduce the suspicion. In contrast, the goal of steganalysis is to detect the presence of hidden data in a cover object. In recent years, with the increased popularity of the social web, highly interactive multimedia such as image, video and speech are in great demand. In 1999 Adaptive Multi-Rate (AMR) was selected as the standard speech codec by the Third Generation Partnership Project (3GPP)

This work was supported by National Key Technology R&D Program under 2016YFB0801003 and 2016QY15Z2500, NSFC under U1636102, U1736214, 61872356 and 61802393, and Project of Beijing Municipal Science & Technology Commission under Z181100002718001.

C. D. Yoo et al. (Eds.): IWDW 2018, LNCS 11378, pp. 275–289, 2019.
https://doi.org/10.1007/978-3-030-11389-6_21

together with European Telecommunication Standards Institute (ETSI) for the mobile communication. Additionally, in 2002 AMR was adopted by International Telecommunication UnionTelecommunication Sector (ITU-T) for wideband speech coding. The adoption by ITU-T marks the first time the same codec is adopted for both wireless and wireline services. Further more, many telephone handsets select AMR as their default file format for spoken audio storage. At the same time, AMR is extended to many popular mobile applications for voice chat audio, such as WeChat, QQ. Therefore, AMR audio codec could be regarded as an ideal carrier for secret message passing. Pitch delay (PD) has been utilized as the covert information carrier in a series of steganographic approaches [2,10,12,14–16,21,22]. Specifically, these PD-based schemes are typically integrated with speech encoding by modifying the codec parameters. Typically, PD describes the predicted value of pitch period which is almost inverse proportional with the fundamental frequency of an audio waveform [6,11]. Specifically, the determination of the pitch delay is made based on adaptive codebook search. Despite a variety of algorithms for pitch period prediction have been proposed, pitch period is still difficult to predict accurately in speech processing [6,8]. All in all, PD is a feasible embedding domain. Algorithm [2] modified such PDs as close to the change point. The principle of pitch prediction between Algebraic Code Excited Linear Prediction (ACELP) and Code Excited Line Prediction (CELP) codec is almost same, so the PD-based embedding schemes for G.723.1 and G.729 based on CELP is also can be applied to AMR. In [21], Wu et al. proposed an analysis-by-synthesis-based steganography by modifying the pitch delay of G.729. Liu et al. [14] took full advantage of both integer and fractional of pitch to embed secret messages by adjusting the pitch period search range. Huang et al. [10] implemented information hiding integrated into speech coding by modifying the search range during the closed-loop adaptive codebook search of G.723.1. Despite the pitch search range is adjusted, the encoder can find a suboptimal solutions whose values are be restricted to a specified range while introducing less embedding distortion and maintaining good imperceptibility. Yan et al. [22] only chose even subframes to embed messages. They exploited the characteristics of PD during the closed-loop and proposed a double-layer embedding algorithm for G.723.1. This method reduces the steganographic distortion to achieve high imperceptibility.

To detect PD-based AMR steganographic schemes, a few steganalytic studies have been carried out in the recent years [13,17,19]. In their views, existing PD-based embedding schemes destroy the statistics of pitch delay and the modified pitch delay is not the optimal. Consequently. The operation of modification leaves clues of data embedding. Among existing targeted attacks, Ren's method [17] (called MSDPD) performs better than the others. Specifically, the sequence of pitch period should be stable for a short time because of the quasi-periodic characteristic of voiced speech segments, so the difference of pitch delay which is sensitive to embedding is used as steganalytic feature. Consequently, Ren employs Markov transition probabilities to measure the change between the adjacent pitch delay. The experimental results show that this method can efficiently detect the two existing PD based steganography methods [10, 22], the former [10] performed a higher security than the latter [22].

This paper aims to enhance the steganographic security of PD-based schemes by resisting the attack of latest steganalytical algorithms. The main problems in the existing PD-based stegaography were analyzed. One problem ignored the changes in statistical property caused by the embedding. The second problem is that embedding schemes did not take the suboptimal pitch delay search into account. Motivated by the existing problems, we make two improvements. Firstly, we designed a distortion function which considered embedding influence from different aspects. Specifically, both the difference of pitch delay (DPD) related to steganalytic feature and the relation between adjacent subframe within one frame were considered into cost function. Secondly, the syndrome-trellis codes (STCs) [4] was used to locate suitable embedding regions, then the suboptimal pitch period of the subframe was searched according to search principle. Therefor, the proposed algorithm, pitch delay adaptive steganography (PDAS) is capable of resisting the current best PD steganalysis while keeping a higher speech quality.

The rest of paper is organized as follows. In Sect. 2, we briefly introduce the basic knowledge of AMR codec. The implementation of the proposed method is presented in Sect. 3, including the framework of distortion minimization for PD-based steganograpy and the definition of the distortion function. The results of comparative experiments are shown in Sect. 4. Finally, the conclusions and future work are given in Sect. 5.

2 Preliminaries

2.1 Principles of AMR Codec

AMR is based on the ACELP coding model. This technique results in more efficient codebook search algorithms. The encoder operates on frames of 20 ms, 8-kHz, 13-bit, PCM format each into a set of parameters, including Line Spectral Pair (LSP) , pitch delay, algebraic code index and gains. These parameters are transmitted as bit streams mode from 4.75 kbit/s to 12.2 kbit/s. The basic block diagram of the encoding process is depicted in Fig. 1. After preprocessing, LSP parameters analysis is aculeated every other 20 ms. The speech samples is divided into four subframes of 5 ms (40 samples). For each subframe, the excitation signal is reconstructed by searching appropriate adaptive codebooks and algebraic codebooks. The criteria of search is to minimize the mean square error of the perceptually weighted error between the original and synthesized speeches.

2.2 Analysis of AMR Pitch Delay

To facilitate the understanding, we take the 12.2 kbit/s mode as an example. The implementation of the PD is operated in a combination of open-loop and closed-loop. At the first stage, the open-loop pitch period (T_{OL}) is conducted for every

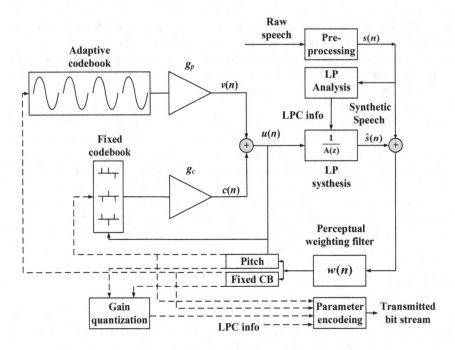

Fig. 1. Block diagram of the ACELP synthesis model

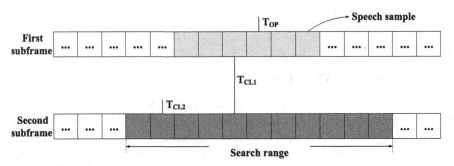

Fig. 2. Diagram of pitch delay search based on a two step procedure: open loop and closed loop analysis by a rigorous search strategy. The dark background indicates the search range.

two subframes in order to simplify the pitch analysis and avoid multiples of the pitch period. The search range is from 18 to 143 samples. At the second stage, the closed-loop pitch period (T_{CL}) which consist of integer pitch delay and fractional pitch delay is computed based on the T_{OL}. Specifically, the integer pitch delay (T) for the first and third subframe is computed in a small neighborhood around the T_{OL}, while the integer pitch delay for the second and fourth subframes are calculated as the difference from the integer pitch delay of previous subframe T. The corresponding diagram is illustrated in Fig. 2.

Once the optimal integer pitch delay has been determined, a fractional pitch delay is searched with resolutions of $\frac{1}{6}$ in the lower delay range $[7\frac{6}{3}, 9\frac{3}{6}]$. Integer resolution is searched only in the range $[95, 143]$. For the second and fourth subframes, a pitch with a resolution of $\frac{1}{6}$ is always used in the range $[T - 5\frac{3}{6}, T + 4\frac{3}{6}]$, where T is the integer part of the previous 1st or 3rd subframe, bounded by a given range $[18...143]$. This procedure is shown in Fig. 3.

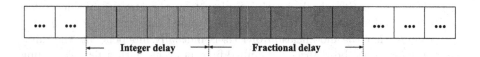

Fig. 3. Closed loop search consist of integer and fractional pitch delay.

3   Proposed Scheme

In this section, we describe the details of proposed hiding scheme which utilizes the PD as data carrier for AMR. The procedure is illustrated in Fig. 4.

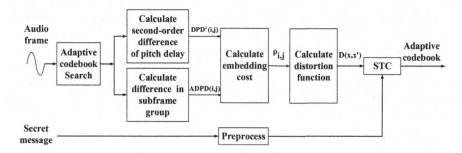

Fig. 4. The flow chart of adaptive steganographic algorithm. $DPD_{i,j}^2$ represents the second-order difference of pitch delay, $ADPD_{i,j}$ represents difference of the specified adjacent pitch delay in a frame, $\rho_{i,j}$ represents the cost function, $D(\mathbf{x}, \mathbf{y})$ is the additive distortion function.

3.1   Principle of Distortion Minimization

Minimizing the overall embedding distortion which stems from image steganography is an accepted approach to improve steganography security [7,9]. Different from operations on pixels in image steganography, PD-based steganographic approaches perform embedding during PD process. The specific framework of distortion-minimization is established as follows.

In PD-based embedding scenario, n PDs are obtained during speech compression, denoted by $\mathbf{p} = \{p_1, ..., p_n\}$. The cover vector $\mathbf{x} = \{x_1, ..., x_n\} = \{0, 1\}$ can be obtained by a binary mapping function $\mathcal{P}(p_i) = p_i \bmod 2$, $i = \{1, ..., n\}$. Given the embedding rate α, the $\alpha \cdot n$-length binary message $\mathbf{m}$ can be embedded by modifying $\mathbf{x}$ into $\mathbf{y} = \{y_1, ..., y_n\}$ using a variety of steganographic codes, which satisfies

$$\mathbf{Hy}^T = \mathbf{m} \tag{1}$$

where $\mathbf{H}$ is the parity check matrix employed by the steganographic codes. Finally, the modified PD $\mathbf{p}' = \{p'_1, ..., p'_n\}$ is obtained satisfying $\mathcal{P}(p'_i) = y$.

Assuming that the modification of PDs is mutually independent, the minimal distortion could be realized by embedding messages with a flexible coding method-STCs. The embedding and extraction are formulated respectively as:

$$\mathbf{y} = \text{Emb}(\mathbf{x}, \mathbf{m}) = \underset{y \subseteq \mathcal{C}(m)}{\arg\min} \ D(\mathbf{x}, \mathbf{y}) \tag{2}$$

$$\text{Ext}(\mathbf{y}) = \mathbf{Hy}^T = \mathbf{m} \tag{3}$$

where the overall distortion is computed by $D(\mathbf{x}, \mathbf{y})$, $\mathcal{C}(m)$ is the coset corresponding to syndrome $\mathbf{m}$, and $\mathbf{y}$ is the binary bit stream embedded with message. The details for the implementation of STCs can refer to [4]. The goal of syndrome coding process is to search the stego $\mathbf{y}$ which satisfy $\mathbf{Hy}^T = \mathbf{m}$ and have minimal distortion. Typically, once the stego objects are obtained, the message sequence can be extracted by computing $\mathbf{Hy}^T$.

The design of embedding distortion is an important part of the minimizing distortion framework, and could directly affect the performance of the embedding algorithm. Given a PD, the embedding distortion caused by modification of PD is described in the following subsection.

3.2 Distortion Function

Existing highly practical and successful scheme to image steganography is under the framework of minimal distortion embedding. The framework consist of a well-designed distortion function and a method for encoding the message to minimize the total distortion. With the development of STCs, the codec can embed near the rate-distortion bound for additive distortion. So the remaining task left to the steganographers is the design of the distortion. Generally, adaptive image steganography tends to embed data into complex textural regions. Similarly, it is intuitive that modifications in complex areas are likely to cause less suspicions in AMR steganography. For a specific pitch delay of subframe, the richer its difference is, the more suitable it can be used to embed message.

A. Pitch Delay's Short Term Stability. Due to the quasi-periodic property of voiced speech segments, pitch period of voiced speech segments should be stable for a short time. In AMR codec, pitch delay is the prediction of pitch period, so the pitch delay sequence of voiced speech segments should be stable

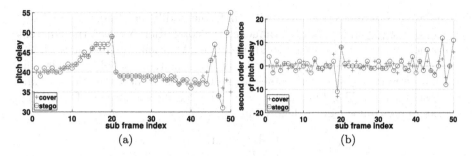

Fig. 5. Comparison in pitch delay statistics changes between cover and stego audio. (a) are the changes between the pitch delay of cover and stego audio, (b) are the changes in the second order difference pitch delay between cover and stego audio.

to some degree. The local continuity between adjacent PD has been proven in [17]. The authors first defined a steganalytic feature which is the difference of pitch delay (DPD) and constructed a Markov transition probability matrix of the second-order difference of pitch delay (MSDPD) to describe the difference between cover and stego audio. As can be seen from the Fig. 5, it is clearly that the less statistics change caused by PD modification, the less embedding impact can be achieved. Inspired by Ren *et al.*'s work, we apply the second-order DPD to measure the embedding impact on PD. To be specific, assume that there are n subframes, denoted as vector $\mathbf{p} = (p_1, p_2, ..., p_i, ..., p_n), i = 1, ..., n$. The second-order DPD can be calculated as follows:

$$DPD_i^2 = |p_{i+2} - 2p_{i+1} + p_i| \qquad (4)$$

the larger distortion will be obtained for PDs with less differences, which means that the PDs with similar value are not suitable for embedding. As a result, if the embedding modifications are made in PDs with less differences, the security against statistical steganalysis is expected to be enhanced.

B. Characteristics of Adjacent Subframe. As described in Sect. 2, in the close loop search of the AMR, the second and fourth subframes are performed based on the previous subframe $T_{CLi}, i = 1, 3$. The specific process can refer to Fig. 6. It indicated that there is a very strong correlation exists between

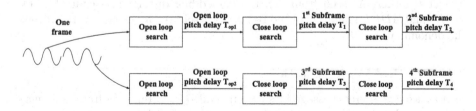

Fig. 6. Diagram of adaptive codebook search

the adjacent subframes compared with subframe in different frame. Specifically, the embedding operations would influence the correlation between the adjacent subframe, such as the first and second subframe . Additionally, existing work [22] have confirmed this phenomenon. It is intuitive that, we should consider the relation between adjacent subframes as another important factor in designing out cost function. The difference between the specified adjacent PD (ADPD) subframes in a frame can be denoted in (5).

$$ADPD_{i,j} = \begin{cases} |AP_{i,1} - AP_{i,2}|, & j = 1,2 \\ |AP_{i,3} - AP_{i,4}|, & j = 3,4 \end{cases} \tag{5}$$

where $AP_{i,j} = (p_{i,1}, p_{i,2}, p_{i,3}, p_{i,4})$ is the index of adjacent pitch delay in one frame sorted by time. To be specific, AP is limited to the first and second subframe and the third and forth subframe. As analysis above, the modification of PD with larger difference in adjacent subframes could cause larger embedding impact, and thus leaving a trail for steganalyzer. In order to reduce the embedding impact, the message embedded in those PD values which are associated with large differences of adjacent PD is better.

3.3   Definition of Additive Distortion Function

Based on the framework of minimizing embedding distortions stegaography, the embedding impact can be measured by a non-negative additive distortions implemented as independent modifications. Thanks to STCs, the overall minimum distortion can be realized by this advanced steganographic codes. In our proposed method, the distortion function of AMR PD embedding domain can be calculated by (6).

$$D(\mathbf{x}, \mathbf{y}) = \sum_{i=1}^{n} \sum_{j=1}^{4} \rho_{i,j}(\mathbf{x}_{i,j}, \mathbf{y}_{i,j}) * |\mathbf{x}_{i,j} - \mathbf{y}_{i,j}| \tag{6}$$

where the variable $0 \leq \rho_{i,j} \leq \infty$ is the designed cost function to fully measure the changing PD $\mathbf{x}_{i,j}$ to $\mathbf{y}_{i,j}$, i denotes the ith frame, j denotes the jth subframe in a frame. Next, the embedding costs $\rho_{i,j}$ is computed as (7).

$$\rho_{i,j}(PD_{i,j}, PD'_{i,j}) = \alpha(DPD_{i,j}^2 + \varepsilon)^{-1} + \beta(ADPD_{i,j} + \varepsilon)^{-1}, (\alpha + \beta = 1) \tag{7}$$

where α ia and β are adjustment parameters in order to control embedding impact together. As seen from (7), the embedding distortion is controlled by DPD^2 and $ADPD$ simultaneously. Besides, ε is selected as a constant to prevent the denominator is 0.

3.4   Practical Implementation

In practice, the secret message bits are embedded in a frame-by-frame manner. For each subframe, the embedding and extraction with one single frame are described as follows.

A. Procedure of Data Embedding. The full description of embedding procedure combined with one single frame is illustrated in Fig. 7.

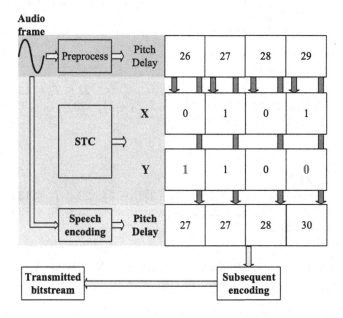

Fig. 7. Instance diagram of embedding with one single frame.

(1) Preprocess. For each subframe, store the corresponding PD, and calculate the corresponding cost scalar according to (7). After that, the PD vector $\mathbf{p} = (p_1, ..., p_n)$, and the associated cost vector $\boldsymbol{\rho} = (\rho_1, ..., \rho_n)$ are obtained. Based on $\mathbf{p}$, construct the cover vector as $\mathbf{x} = (x_1, ..., x_n)$.

(2) STCs coding. According to (2), STCs is subsequently used to embed an αN-bit message $\mathbf{m}$ by modifying $\mathbf{x}$ into $\mathbf{y}$ as $\mathrm{Emb}(\mathbf{x}, \mathbf{m}) = \mathbf{y}$.

(3) Speech Encoding. Encoding the original frame again. For each T, the possible modification T is controlled by y_i. Specifically, if $y_i = x_i$, the corresponding T remain unchanged, otherwise a suboptimal $\tilde{T}$ is searched. Taking the first and second subframe at 12.2 kbit/s mode as an example. The suboptimal $\tilde{T}_0$ and $\tilde{T}_1$ are shown in (8), (9), (10) and (11) respectively.

$$\tilde{T}_0 = \begin{cases} \{18, 20, 22, 24\}, & T_{olo} < 21 \\ \{T_{olo} - 2, T_{olo}, T_{olo} + 2\}, & 21 \leq T_{olo} \leq 140, T_{olo}\%2 = 0 \\ \{T_{olo} - 3, T_{olo} - 1, T_{olo} + 1, T_{olo} + 3\}, & 21 \leq T_{olo} \leq 140, T_{olo}\%2 = 1 \\ \{138, 140, 142\}, & T_{olo} > 140 \end{cases}$$

$$(8)$$

$$\tilde{T}_0 = \begin{cases} \{19, 21, 23\}, & T_{olo} < 21 \\ \{T_{olo} - 3, T_{olo} - 1, T_{olo} + 1, T_{olo} + 3\}, & 21 \le T_{olo} \le 140, T_{olo}\%2 = 0 \\ \{T_{olo} - 2, T_{olo}, T_{olo} + 2\}, & 21 \le T_{olo} \le 140, T_{olo}\%2 = 1 \\ \{137, 139, 141, 143\}, & T_{olo} > 140 \end{cases}$$

$$(9)$$

$$\tilde{T}_1 = \begin{cases} \{18, 20, 22, 24, 26\}, & T_0 < 23 \\ \{T_0 - 4, T_0 - 2, T_0, T_0 + 2, T_0 + 4\}, & 23 \le T_0 \le 139, T_0\%2 = 0 \\ \{T_0 - 5, T_0 - 3, T_0 - 1, T_0 + 1, T_0 + 3, T_0 + 5\}, & 23 \le T_0 \le 139, T_0\%2 = 1 \\ \{134, 136, 138, 140, 142\}, & T_0 > 139 \end{cases}$$

$$(10)$$

$$\tilde{T}_1 = \begin{cases} \{19, 21, 23, 25, 27\}, & T_0 < 23 \\ \{T_0 - 5, T_0 - 3, T_0 - 1, T_0 + 1, T_0 + 3, T_0 + 5\}, & 23 \le T_0 \le 139, T_0\%2 = 0 \\ \{T_0 - 4, T_0 - 2, T_0, T_0 + 2, T_0 + 4\}, & 23 \le T_0 \le 139, T_0\%2 = 1 \\ \{135, 137, 139, 141, 143\}, & T_0 > 139 \end{cases}$$

$$(11)$$

Finally, the compressed frame is obtained with N PDs carrying αN secret message bits.

B. Procedure of Data Extracting. The extraction of message is relatively simple. The recipient decoder the received frame to obtain all the n PD values, and reconstructs the binary channel $\mathbf{y}$. At last, the secret message can be extracts as $\mathbf{m} = \mathbf{yH}^T$.

4   Experiments

To evaluate the performance of the proposed steganographic algorithm, we employed different speech sample files with PCM format as cover media for steganography to conduct experiments. Several experiments with different audio databases are performed in this section. In the experiments, we use the we use RBR (Relative embedding rate) to denote the embedding ratio, which represents the ratio of length of message m to the length of cover audio n. For example, to test our scheme with a RBR of 0.2. If the number of subframes is 100, the length of message is 20, the RBR $\alpha = m/n = 20/100 = 0.2$.

4.1   Experimental Setup

The test audio databases is comprised of 2000 WAV audios from two public speech databases. 1000 of these WAV audios are derived from CMU speech databases [20], the rest of them are obtained from Tsinghua open speech database [3]. Each WAV audio is mono, 8 kHz, 16 bit quantization, and saved in

PCM format with a length of 10 s. These WAV audios contain digital speeches from different people and different languages, including English and Chinese. All of these WAV audios are used to produce cover and stego AMR audio databases respectively. The following three audio base will be explored in the next section.

1. CSB. 2000 WAV audios are encoded by 3GPP public floating-point AMR codec [5] with encoding rate modes 10.2 kbit/s and 12.2 kbit/s. The total number of cover AMR samples is $2000 * 2 = 4000$.
2. HSB. The steganography of Huang's [10] is implemented under same rate modes of CSB. Secret messages are embedded with various RBR of 10%, 20%, 40%, 50%, 60%, 80% and 100% for each rate mode from CSB. The total number of stego AMR samples in HSB is $2000 * 2 * 7 = 28000$.
3. ASB. The steganography of our proposed adaptive embedding method is implemented under same rate modes of CSB. All WAV audios from CSB are embedded with an RBR of 10%, 20%, 40%, 50%, 60%, 80% and 100% for each rate mode. So the total amount of stego samples in this database is $2000 * 2 * 7 = 28000$.

4.2 Audio Quality

Perceptual evaluation speech quality (PESQ) [18] is commonly used as a measure of quality degradation of speech signals by comparing an original signal with a degraded signal, and the value of PESQ can be regarded as a prediction of the perceived quality. We applied PESQ to test the signals decoded after the stego codec. In the experiment, the output PESQ of 100 cover audios and corresponding 100 stego audios generated by the two steganographic algorithms are measured. The distribution of PESQ score between stego audios the PDAS and Huang's schemes under 12.2 kbit/s and 10.2 kbit/s are shown in Figs. 8 and 9 respectively. From the comparisons in the Fig. 8, we can find that fluctuation of PDAS's PESQ is less than Huang's PESQ, and the median of PDAS is greater than Huang's in most case. The results indicates our proposed method maintain a better hearing quality. The minimal embedding impact and search of sub-optimal PD ensures that once a PD is modified, the caused error will be handled automatically. As a major advantage, the proposed PDAS methods do not affect PESQ much.

4.3 Statistical Security

The steganalytic work consists of attacking against our proposed embedding scheme PDAS and Huang's steganographic schemes. For security evaluation, the recently proposed MSDPD feature [17] is leveraged, which performs a high effectiveness and strong security in detecting PD-based schemes. The LibSVM toolbox [1] is employed for classification. Default parameters of SVM with Gaussian kernel are set in all experiments.

The experiment results under 12.2 kbit/s and 10.2 kbit/s are shown in Table 1. We use the test error rate (TER) to measure the detection performance,

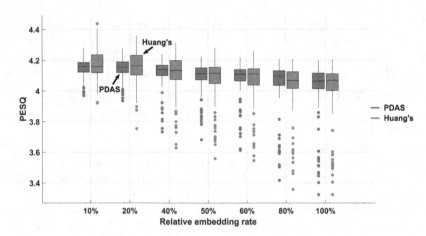

Fig. 8. The distribution of PESQ for different steganography schemes for 12.2 kbit/s mode.

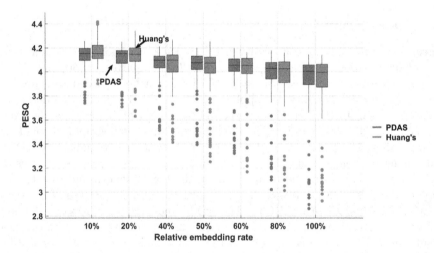

Fig. 9. The distribution of PESQ for different steganography schemes for 10.2 kbit/s mode.

which is defined as the proportion of the tested AMR audios incorrectly classified for each of the categories. The calculation of TER is shown in (12).

$$TER = \frac{P_{FA} + P_{MD}}{2} \tag{12}$$

where P_{FA} and P_{MD} are the false alarm probability and the miss detection probability respectively. TER shows the error rate of the steganalysis scheme which is used to detect the tested steganography schemes. So if the TER is

Table 1. Average TER for our proposed PDAS scheme and Huang's scheme [10] under the steganalysis method [17].

RBR	Scheme under 12.2 kbit/s		Scheme under 10.2 kbit/s	
	PDAS	Huang	PDAS	Huang
10%	**0.4183** (± 0.0114)	0.3609 (± 0.0087)	**0.4340** (± 0.0097)	0.3535 (± 0.0116)
20%	**0.3384** (± 0.0126)	0.2140 (± 0.0072)	**0.3648** (± 0.0114)	0.1979 (± 0.0098)
40%	**0.1147** (± 0.0081)	0.0550 (± 0.0049)	**0.1309** (± 0.0077)	0.0540 (± 0.0041)
50%	**0.0670** (± 0.0049)	0.0279 (± 0.0032)	**0.0706** (± 0.0048)	0.0298 (± 0.0036)
60%	**0.0317** (± 0.0046)	0.0191 (± 0.0032)	**0.0326** (± 0.0040)	0.0179 (± 0.0050)
80%	**0.0071** (± 0.0019)	0.0069 (± 0.0032)	**0.0074** (± 0.0019)	0.0068 (± 0.0023)
100%	**0.0033** (± 0.0014)	0.0031 (± 0.0015)	**0.0048** (± 0.0019)	0.0043 (± 0.0031)

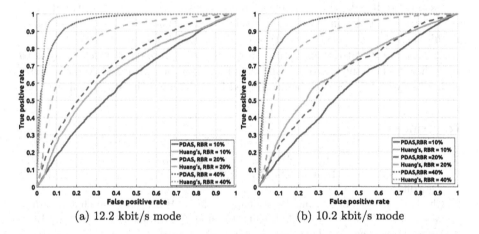

(a) 12.2 kbit/s mode   (b) 10.2 kbit/s mode

Fig. 10. ROC curves against MSDPD steganalytical method.

larger, it means the steganography method is more safer to escape from the detecting of the steganalysis scheme.

Then 500 pairs of the AMR audios (stego and clean) are randomly selected for the training stage, and another disjoint 500 pairs are also randomly selected for testing. Every detection experiment is always conducted over 10 splits on the training set and testing set. The last result is shown in Table 1, for each steganalysis scheme, the TER of the PDAS scheme is bigger than the existing schemes [10] under the same RBR. Besides, the receiver operating characteristic (ROC) curves using steganalyzers are depicted in Fig. 10. In comparisons with Huang's schemes, the detection rates and the ROC curves indicate that our proposed method reduces the probability of detection significantly, which implies a higher level of steganographic security.

4.4 Hiding Capacity

From the principle of the proposed scheme, the secret information is embedded in each sub-frame one bit by one bit. For example, in 12.2 kbit/s mode, there is one frame for 20 ms. In each frame, there are 4 sub-frame for 5 ms. It means that for 20 ms AMR audio, there are $\frac{1}{20*10^{-3}} * 4 = 200$ bit/s bit can be embedded. So the hiding capacity of the proposed PDAS scheme is equal to Huang's scheme [10] and greater than Yan's scheme [22] (100 bit/s).

5 Conclusion

In this paper, a novel PD-based adaptive steganographic scheme is proposed. To against the current effective steganalytic method, the results of detection is significantly reduced, which benefits from effective STCs and suboptimal pitch delay searched. Experimental results show that satisfactory levels of steganographic security and speech quality are achieved with adequate payloads.

As part of our future work, the more embedding impact of pitch delay is to be further studied and the distortion definition is to be optimized. What's more, the multi-layered STCs is to be attempted for enhancing the statistical security.

References

1. Chang, C.C., Lin, C.J.: LIBSVM: a library for support vector machines. ACM Trans. Intell. Syst. Technol. **2**, 27:1–27:27 (2011). http://www.csie.ntu.edu.tw/cjlin/libsvm
2. Chi, Y.U., Huang, L.S., Yang, W., Chen, Z.L., Miao, H.B.: A 3G speech data hiding method based on pitch period. J. Chin. Comput. Syst. **33**(7), 1445–1449 (2012)
3. Wang, D., Zhang, X.: Thchs-30: A Free Chinese Speech Corpus (2015). http://arxiv.org/abs/1512.01882
4. Filler, T., Judas, J., Fridrich, J.: Minimizing additive distortion in steganography using syndrome-trellis codes. IEEE Trans. Inf. Forensics Secur. **6**(3), 920–935 (2011)
5. MSCSP Functions: Adaptive multi-rate (AMR) speech codec. Voice Activity Detector (VAD) (2012)
6. Group, I.T.S., et al.: Coding of speech at 8 kbits/s using conjugate-structure algebraic-code-excited linear-prediction (CS-ACELP). In: International Telecommunication Union Telecommunication Standardization Sector, Draft Recommendation, Version 6 (1995)
7. Guo, L., Ni, J., Shi, Y.Q.: An efficient JPEG steganographic scheme using uniform embedding. In: IEEE International Workshop on Information Forensics and Security, pp. 169–174 (2012)
8. Hess, W., OShaughnessy, D.: Pitch determination of speech signals: Algorithms and devices by Wolfgang Hess (1984)
9. Holub, V., Fridrich, J., Denemark, T.: Universal distortion function for steganography in an arbitrary domain. EURASIP J. Inf. Secur. **1**(1), 1 (2014)
10. Huang, Y., Liu, C., Tang, S., Bai, S.: Steganography integration into a low-bit rate speech codec. IEEE Trans. Inf. Forensics Secur. **7**(6), 1865–1875 (2012)

11. DRSC ITU-T for multimedia communications transmitting at 5.3 and 6.3 kbit/s. ITU-T Recommendation G 723 (2006)

12. Iwakiri, M., Matsui, K.: Embedding a text into conjugate structure algebraic code excited linear prediction audio codes. Trans. Inf. Process. Soc. Jpn **39**, 2623–2630 (1998)

13. Liang, X.H.Y., Xia, M.: Steganalysis of speech compressed based on voicing features. J. Comput. Res. Develop. **46**(s1), 173–176 (2009)

14. Liu, C.H., Bai, S., Huang, Y.F., Yang, Y., Song-Bin, L.I.: An information hiding algorithm based on pitch prediction. Comput. Eng. **39**(2), 137–140 (2013)

15. Nishimura, A.: Data hiding in pitch delay data of the adaptive multi-rate narrowband speech codec. In: International Conference on Intelligent Information Hiding & Multimedia Signal Processing, pp. 483–486 (2009)

16. Nishimura, A.: Steganographic band width extension for the AMR codec of low-bit-rate modes. In: INTERSPEECH 2009, Conference of the International Speech Communication Association, Brighton, United Kingdom, September, pp. 2611–2614 (2009)

17. Ren, Y., Yang, J., Wang, J., Wang, L.: AMR steganalysis based on second-order difference of pitch delay. IEEE Trans. Inf. Forensics Secur. **12**(6), 1345–1357 (2017)

18. Rix, A.W., Beerends, J.G., Hollier, M.P., Hekstra, A.P.: Perceptual evaluation of speech quality (PESQ)-a new method for speech quality assessment of telephone networks and codecs. In: IEEE International Conference on Acoustics, Speech, and Signal Processing, Proceedings (ICASSP 2001), vol. 2, pp. 749–752. IEEE (2001)

19. Song-Bin, L.I., Jia, Y.Z., Jiang-Yun, F.U., Dai, Q.X.: Detection of pitch modulation information hiding based on codebook correlation network. Chin. J. Comput. **37**(10), 2107–2116 (2014)

20. Sullivan, T.: The CMU audio databases (1996)

21. Wu, Z.J., Yang, W., Yang, Y.X.: ABS-based speech information hiding approach. Electron. Lett. **39**(22), 1617–1619 (2003)

22. Yan, S., Tang, G., Sun, Y.: Steganography for low bit-rate speech based on pitch period prediction. Appl. Res. Comput. **32**(6), 1774–1777 (2015)

An Empirical Study of Steganography and Steganalysis of Color Images in the JPEG Domain

Théo Taburet[1], Louis Filstroff[3], Patrick Bas[1(✉)], and Wadih Sawaya[2]

[1] Univ. Lille, CNRS, Centrale Lille, UMR 9189 CRIStAL, 59000 Lille, France
Patrick.Bas@ec-lille.fr
[2] IMT Lille-Douais, Univ. Lille, CNRS, Centrale Lille, UMR 9189 CRIStAL, 59000 Lille, France
[3] IRIT, Université de Toulouse, CNRS, Toulouse, France

Abstract. This paper tackles the problem of JPEG steganography and steganalysis for color images, a problem that has rarely been studied so far and which deserves more attention. After focusing on the 4:4:4 sampling strategy, we propose to modify for each channel the embedding rate of J-UNIWARD and UERD steganographic schemes in order to arbitrary spread the payload between the luminance and the chrominance components while keeping a constant message size for the different strategies. We also compare our spreading payload strategy w.r.t. two strategies: (i) the concatenation of the cost map (CONC) or (ii) equal embedding rates (EER) among channels. We then select good candidates within the feature sets designed either for JPEG or color steganography. Our conclusions are threefold: (i) the GFR or DCTR features sets, concatenated on the three channels offer better performance than ColorSRMQ1 for JPEG Quality Factor (QF) of 75 and 95 but ColorSRMQ1 is more sensitive for QF = 100, (ii) the CONC or EER strategies are suboptimal, and (iii) depending of the quality factors and the embedding schemes, the empirical security is maximized when between 33% (QF = 100, UERD) and 95% (QF = 75, J-UNIWARD) of the payload is allocated to the luminance channel.

Keywords: Steganography · Steganalysis · JPEG · Color · Features

1 Introduction

Since image steganography may be used to hide potentially sensitive messages inside mainstream image formats, it is surprising to notice that the majority of academic contributions in steganography and steganalysis deals with exotic image formats such as lossless raw coding (PGM, PPM) or grayscale JPEG images. Moreover, if a steganographic implementation addresses the most popular image format of the Web, i.e. color JPEG images, it is usually done without distinguishing the color components.

© Springer Nature Switzerland AG 2019
C. D. Yoo et al. (Eds.): IWDW 2018, LNCS 11378, pp. 290–303, 2019.
https://doi.org/10.1007/978-3-030-11389-6_22

More accurately, whenever embedding is realized on color numerical images in the pixel domain (usually for steganalysis purposes), it is most of the time implemented independently on each component [1,4,5] but more advanced schemes use a synchronization strategy to have more coherent embedding changes across the different channels [13]. Popular implementations of color JPEG steganography such as F5 [15] or J-UNIWARD [8] alter DCT coefficients without taking into account their related color channels or the related component statistics.

Regarding the steganalysis of color images, Ker et al. underlined in [10] that most of the research carried out over the past ten years focused on grayscale images, and that methods taking into account correlation between channels were left to be desired. Regarding spatial steganography and RGB components, Goljan et al. developed the Spatial and Color Rich Models (SCRMQ1) [5], which can be seen as a spatial extension of the Spatial Rich Model (SRM) [3] that uses Color Co-occurrence Matrices. These features, as well as other specific feature sets, such as the Gaussian filter bank features [1] (which is an extension of the SCRMQ1), or the CFA-aware features [4], have been particularly designed for color pixel-based steganography. Recently a steganalysis scheme using deep convolutional networks [16] has been proposed, it uses 3 disjoint layers (one for each color components) that are pooled together in the next layers. However the complexity learning phase makes this approach prohibitive to benchmark a large variety of different embedding strategies.

To the best of our knowledge there is no color-specific steganalysis method for JPEG images. For grayscale JPEG images however, among the most advanced feature sets are the DCTR (DCT residuals) [7] and the GFR (Gabor Filter residuals) [14]. The DCTR extraction method computes residuals from convolutions with 8×8 DCT basis vectors and the features are generated by computing histograms on each residual. The same methodology is adopted for GFR by using oriented Gabor kernels instead.

The overall lack of solutions for color JPEG steganography and steganalysis can also be explained by the diversity of color JPEG images that are not all coded in a unique way. For example, since the chroma sub-sampling option is also variable between images (see Sect. 2), the dimensions of the color components of a JPEG image are dependent on the acquisition device or the developing software.

In this paper we propose to extend the popular J-UNIWARD [8] and UERD [6] algorithms to color JPEG, and to evaluate their detectability by designing appropriate feature sets. The next section explains how to obtain different versions of the embedding scheme by spreading the payload among the color components. Section 3 presents feature sets used in this framework, they are derived from popular feature sets in the literature (SCRMQ1, DCTR and GFR). Section 4 provides the different results and associated conclusions related to the paper, both on the best embedding strategy and the most sensitive feature sets for steganalysis.

2   Practical Optimization of the Embedding Schemes

Without loss of generality, we have decided to study here the 4:4:4 JPEG sampling format. This choice is motivated by the fact that, as presented in Table 1, certain sources such as the photo sharing website Flickr mainly use this sampling strategy. However, note that the proposed methodology (choice of the spreading factor in Sect. 2, choice of the most sensitive feature sets in Sect. 3), can also be adopted for other sampling formats.

Table 1. Statistics of chroma sampling strategies for 10,000 "Explored" images downloaded at full resolution from Flickr.com

Chroma sub-sampling	4:4:4	4:2:2	4:2:0
Proportion	65%	8%	27%

Furthermore, because of their excellent performances, we decided to adapt J-UNIWARD and UERD algorithms, respectively proposed by Holub et al. and Guo et al. J-UNIWARD is a ternary adaptive embedding scheme which computes costs for each DCT coefficients based on the impact of a ± 1 modification on the wavelet decomposition of the spatial representation of the image. UERD uses a different approach to compute the cost, which is based on the DCT coefficients variation within a block and its neighboring blocks.

2.1   Parametrization of the Payload Distribution for YC_bC_r Components

Because a JPEG color image is composed of 3 color components, it is not straightforward to spread the payload among Y, C_b and C_r. Note that in order to provide a fair comparison, the same message size has to be embedded for each spreading strategy. This problem can be seen as a problem of batch steganography [9], and hence we can use several strategies to allocate the total payload within the three color components. We list below 3 natural ways to deal with this issue:

- **Cost Map Concatenation (CONC):** A first strategy is to compute a common cost map by firstly concatenating the YC_bC_r components, secondly computing a joint distortion map, and finally computing the embedding probability for the embedding rate α.
- **Equal Embedding Rate (EER):** One straightforward way to perform the embedding is to set the same payload rate for the three color channels, but this strategy omits the fact that the chroma components contain on average less information than the luminance component and that it is quantized in a different way. Table 2 shows average number of non-zero-AC (nzAC) coefficients for BOSSBase in the JPEG 4:4:4 domain. Firstly, we can observe that

the number of luminance nzAC coefficients represents between around 36% (QF = 100) and 80% (QF = 75) of total number of nzAC coefficients. Secondly, since chroma components are less informative, for an equal embedding rate the embedding should be more detectable for the chroma channels. This rational which will be practically assessed in Sect. 4, motivates the following more flexible strategy.

- **Arbitrary Repartition of the Payload Between the 3 Channels (ARB):** This strategy, which is detailed in the rest of this section, consists in using a new embedding parameter to arbitrary spread the payload across the YC_bC_r channels.

Table 2. Statistics (average number of nzAC coefficients) of BOSSBase for quality factor of 75, 95 and 100, 4:4:4 chroma sampling. BOSSBase in color JPEG was generated by first exporting to PPM format using the standard BOSSBase conversion routine

Component	Mean (QF = 75)	Ratio	Mean (QF = 95)	Ratio	Mean (QF = 100)	Ratio
Y	41340	79%	96893	62%	183715	36%
C_b	6087	11%	29284	19%	157970	31%
C_r	5001	10%	29105	19%	167419	33%

We propose to distribute the payload among luminance and chrominance components in the following way. Given N_Y, N_{C_b} and N_{C_r} the number of non-zero AC coefficients (nzAC) for respectively Y, C_b and C_r, and α the total embedding rate per nzAC for the three channels, we set:

- P: the message size, i.e. the payload, in bits, which has to stay constant for all strategies,
- α: the total embedding rate, in bit per nzAC coefficient, as it is classically defined in steganography
- a couple of parameters (β, γ) such that $\gamma(1 - \beta)$ defines the embedding rate associated to the luminance channel (in bit per nzAC luma coefficient) and $\gamma\beta$ the embedding rate associated to the two chrominance channels (in bit per nzAC chroma coefficient). Note that $\beta = 0$ implies that all the payload is embedded in the luminance channel ($\gamma = \alpha$), and $\beta = 1$ means that the whole payload is carried by the chroma channels. γ can be seen as a necessary degree of freedom used to choose $\beta \in [0, 1]$ and to be able to compare embeddings at equal message sizes.

The embedded message size (in bits) is then given by:

$$P = \gamma\left[(1 - \beta) N_Y + \beta\left(N_{C_b} + N_{C_r}\right)\right]. \tag{1}$$

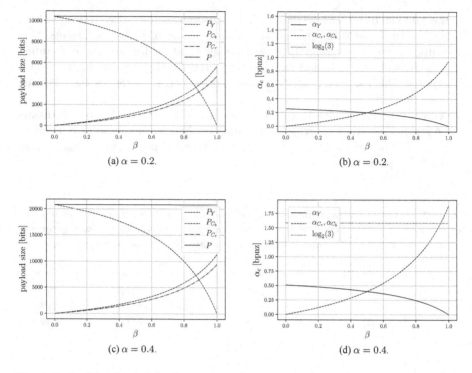

Fig. 1. Left: allocations of the message sizes among the different channels. Right: values of the different embedding rates w.r.t. the parameter β. For this example, the number of nzAC coefficient is close to the one obtained for QF = 75: $N_Y = 41000$, $N_{C_b} = 6000$, $N_{C_r} = 5000$.

The embedding rate per nzAC α is then:

$$\alpha = \frac{P}{N_Y + N_{C_b} + N_{C_r}} = \frac{\gamma\left[(1-\beta)\,N_Y + \beta\left(N_{C_b} + N_{C_r}\right)\right]}{N_Y + N_{C_b} + N_{C_r}}. \tag{2}$$

We consequently have four parameters $(\alpha, \beta, P, \gamma)$ and one degree of freedom to choose the embedding rate or the payload. We can set the message size P and choose β, and α and γ will be calculated using (2) and (1) respectively. In a more conventional way, we can set the embedding rate α and choose β, and P and γ will be computed using (2) and (1) respectively. If we worked on grayscale images, we would set $\beta = 0$ which means $P = \alpha N_Y$.

Note also that the equal embedding rate strategy is equivalent to have $\beta = 0.5$ since in this case all embedding rates are equal to α.

Moreover, the proportion of the payload R_L carried by the luminance channel is given by:

$$R_L = \frac{(1-\beta)\,N_Y}{(1-\beta)\,N_Y + \beta\left(N_{C_b} + N_{C_r}\right)}. \tag{3}$$

Figure 1 illustrates evolutions of message sizes and embedding rates for the three components w.r.t. the parameter β for two embedding rates of 0.2 and 0.4 bit per nzAC and for arbitrary (N_Y, N_{C_b}, N_{C_r}). We can notice that the embedding rate can be larger than the maximum embedding rate for J-UNIWARD and UERD ($\log_2(3)$ bits), but this happens only for low quality factors, high embedding rates and β close to 1. In Sect. 4 we shall see that these configurations provide very low practical security and will consequently never be used in practice.

3   Feature Sets for Steganalysis of Color JPEGs

We decide to first benchmark the steganographic scheme by adapting methods dedicated either for color spatial or JPEG grayscale steganographic schemes.

Our first choice is the Color Rich Model, which is composed of the *SRMQ1* features, augmented by a collection of 3D co-occurrences of residuals between color channels to obtain a set of 18,157 features referred in [5] as SCRMQ1. Since the images we analyze are in the JPEG domain, we propose an alternative version of the SCRMQ1 where residuals are computed in the YC_bC_r color space. That means that the RGB components are first converted into YC_bC_r and then all residual filtering and co-occurrence computation are performed in the exact same way as for SCRMQ1.

Table 3 shows for UERD and J-UNIWARD the difference between computing the SCRMQ1 in the RGB domain or in the YC_bC_r domain, one can see on this example (that generalizes to other embedding rates) the necessity of computing features in the appropriate subspace. This can be explained by the fact the spatial discrepancies captured by the *SRMQ1* features are more significant when applied in the same color space than the embedding. Since no synchronization strategy is applied between the color components, the co-occurrences between the color channels are more effective as well.

Table 3. Impact of computing the SCRMQ1 feature set in the appropriate domain for Color-JPEG steganography. $\alpha = 0.4$, $\beta = 0.7$, QF = 95

Color space	RGB	YC_bC_r
P_E (UERD)	14.38%	8.13%
P_E (J-UNIWARD)	32.39%	8.02%

Because both DCTR and GFR feature sets provide excellent performance on grayscale images, we also decide to use these features on color images by simply concatenating the features computed for each channel. Here, by definition the features are computed directly in the YC_bC_r color space (only the inverse DCT transform is computed before filtering with DCT kernels for C-DCTR or Gabor kernels for C-GFR), and we end up with $3 \times 8000 = 24,000$ features for

Color-DCTR features (abbreviated C-DCTR) and $3 \times 17000 = 51,000$ for Color-GFR (abbreviated C-GFR). Note that even if C-DCTR and C-GFR do not compute co-occurrence matrices between color channels as SCRMQ1, discrepancies between embedding strategies between different channels can be captured by the concatenation operation. For example one can expect that by setting the embedding parameter $\beta = 0$, C-DCTR and C-GFR feature sets will capture a discrepancy between the statistical properties of the luminance channel w.r.t the chroma channels.

4 Results

4.1 Experimental Protocol

In order to evaluate the proposed scheme we generate a version of BOSSBase [2] from the available RAW images and we changed the script by directly generating a JPEG image from the cropped and scaled 512×512 PPM image. For all these experiments we choose:

- three JPEG quality factors, 75, 95 and 100,
- two embedding rates, $\alpha = 0.2$ and $\alpha = 0.4$ bit per nzAC coefficient.
- two steganographic schemes J-UNIWARD and UERD (see Sect. 2)

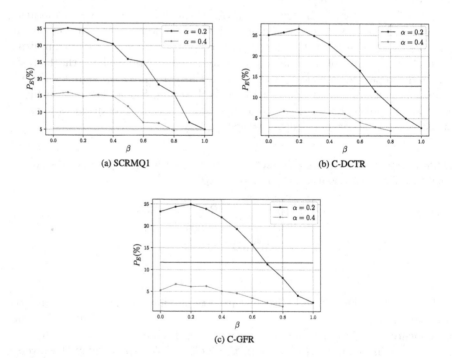

Fig. 2. J-UNIWARD: Comparison w.r.t. β for different feature sets, JPEG QF $= 75$. Horizontal lines are results for the CONC strategy.

- the parameter β fluctuating in the range $[0,1]$ to assess the impact of payload allocation, recalling that $\beta = 0.5$ is tantamount to the Equal Embedding Rate strategy. For $\alpha = 0.4$, we do not benchmark the scheme for $\beta = 0.9$ or $\beta = 1.0$ since it can be that in this case the embedding rate in the chroma components is larger than $\log_2(3)$ bits.
- for comparison purposes the CONC strategy is also benchmarked.

All detectors are trained as binary classifiers implemented using the FLD ensemble [12], with default settings. The ensemble by default minimizes the total classification error probability under equal priors:

$$P_E = \min_{P_{FA}} \frac{1}{2}(P_{FA} + P_{MD}),$$

where P_{FA} and P_{MD} denote respectively the false-alarm and missed-detection probabilities. P_E is averaged over ten different training and testing sets, in which the 10,000 cover images and the associated 10,000 stego images are randomly divided into two equal halves for pair-training and testing. We report this value as $\overline{P}_E$ for values of γ satisfying (1) and (2).

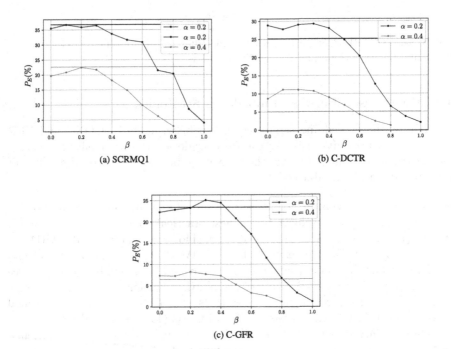

Fig. 3. UERD: Comparison w.r.t. β for different feature sets, JPEG QF = 75. Horizontal lines are results for the CONC strategy.

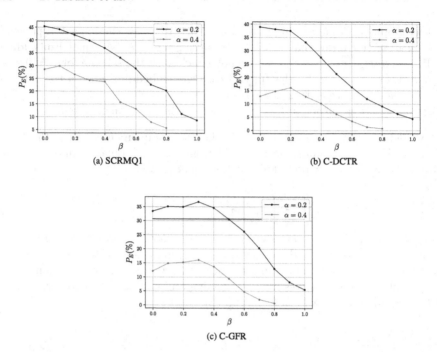

Fig. 4. J-UNIWARD: Comparison w.r.t. β for different feature sets, JPEG QF = 95. Horizontal lines are results for the CONC strategy.

4.2 Comparison Between Embedding Strategies

We look at the embedding strategies chosen between ARB, CONC and EER (i.e. $\beta = 0.5$) that gives the highest P_E considering the most efficient feature sets, i.e. the minimum of P_E over the 3 feature sets. From these results, different comparisons can be established:

- As a general conclusion, for all feature sets the arbitrarily spreading of the payload can allow to achieve the highest practical security.
- For QF = 75 (see Figs. 2 and 3), it is reached for $\beta \simeq 0.2$ for J-UNIWARD and $\beta \simeq 0.3$ for UERD. For example for J-UNIWARD, using equations (3) and (2), it means that on average 94% of the payload is carried by the luminance channel which itself carries 79% of the nzAC coefficients.
- For QF = 95 (see Figs. 4 and 5), gives the same conclusions w.r.t. the optimal values of β. In this case however, 85% of the payload is carried by the luminance channel for J-UNIWARD, which conveys 62% of the nzAC coefficients.
- For QF = 100 (see Figs. 6 and 7), the maximal empirical security is reached for $\beta \simeq 0.3$ for J-UNIWARD and $\beta \simeq 0.4$ for UERD. In this case 50% of the payload is carried by the luminance channel on average for J-UNIWARD and 33% for UERD.

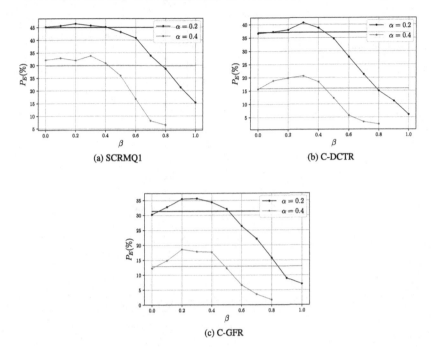

Fig. 5. UERD: Comparison w.r.t. β for different feature sets, JPEG QF $= 95$. Horizontal lines are results for the CONC strategy.

Moreover, two important remarks can be drawn from these extensive sets of results:

- We can see that the naive strategies of setting $\beta = 0$ (all the payload is embedded in the luminance channel) or $\beta = 0.5$ (the embedding rates are equal) are suboptimal. For example for J-UNIWARD at $\alpha = 0.2$ and QF $= 75$ using the best feature set (C-GFR), the gap between $\beta = 0.0$ and $\beta = 0.2$ (the optimal strategy) $\Delta P_E \simeq 2\%$, between $\beta = 0.2$ and $\beta = 0.5$ is $\Delta P_E \simeq 6\%$. These two conclusions are not surprising: pushing all the payload in the luminance channel is equivalent to not taking into account possible dependencies between luminance and chroma components. Furthermore this leads to a concentration of changes on the same component, hence a higher detectability. On the other hand, the EER strategy would be optimal only if the capacity of the scheme would be directly proportional to the number of nzAC, and we know that it is not true in practice (see for example the Ker laws [11]).
- The CONC strategy (concatenation of the c,osts then embedding), represented by the vertical lines on the different plots, is also clearly sub-optimal for the different embedding rates, embedding schemes or quality factors. For example for J-UNIWARD at $\alpha = 0.2$ and QF $= 75$, the gap between $\beta = 0.2$ and CONC is $\Delta P_E \simeq 13\%$. This can be explained by (i) the fact that empirical costs computed by J-UNIWARD and UERD have be designed w.r.t.

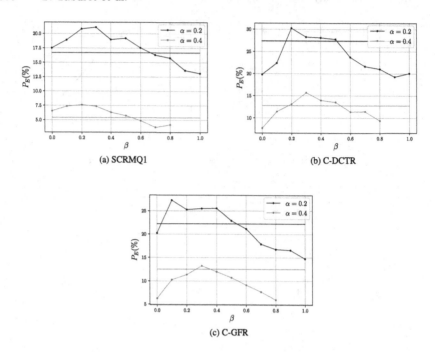

Fig. 6. J-UNIWARD: Comparison w.r.t. β for different feature sets, JPEG QF = 100. Horizontal lines are results for the CONC strategy.

grayscale image steganography and they do not take into account potential dependencies between color channels and (ii) the fact that luma and chroma components do not use the same quantization matrices except for QF = 100. The mixing between costs computed using completely different quantization steps can explain the non-adaptivity of the CONC strategy. When $QF \neq 100$ we can see that the CONC strategy is however closer to the optimal solution for UERD than for J-UNIWARD.

As a more general comparison, we can see that as for grayscale JPEG steganography the practical security of UERD is slightly more important than the practical security of J-UNIWARD, especially for low embedding rates. For example at QF = 95 using C-GFR, the gap is $\Delta P_E \simeq 3\%$ for $\alpha = 0.2$, at QF = 100, the gap is $\Delta P_E \simeq 4\%$ for $\alpha = 0.2$.

4.3   Comparison Between Feature Sets

We now draw few conclusions on the steganalysis side, depending on the JPEG QF.

For QF = 75 and QF = 95: the C-GFR feature sets outperforms the C-DCTR feature sets by a small margin for UERD ($\Delta P_E \simeq 3\%$ at QF = 75, $\Delta P_E \simeq 5\%$ at QF = 95 for optimal β), and the SCRMQ1 features set by a large margin.

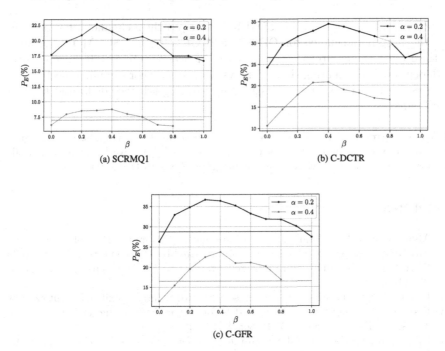

Fig. 7. UERD: Comparison w.r.t. β for different feature sets, JPEG QF $= 100$. Horizontal lines are results for the CONC strategy.

C-DCTR shows superior performance w.r.t. the two other feature sets except for J-UNIWARD at QF $= 95$ and $\beta \geq 0.3$ where C-DCTR is more performant. However for the embedding values of β offering the best empirical security, C-GFR are rather efficient.

For QF $= 100$: SCRMQ1 features are more sensitive than the two other feature sets. This can be explained by the fact that lot of information from the uncompressed image is kept at QF $= 100$ since all quantization steps are equal to 1. Consequently, SCRMQ1 computed in the YC_bC_r appears to be one ideal candidate for accurate steganalysis.

5   Conclusion and Perspectives

This paper has proposed an empirical analysis of JPEG steganography and steganalysis on color images. Our conclusions are three-fold: (i) using constant embedding rate across channel or concatenating the cost maps are not optimal embedding strategies since they do not take into account statistical dependencies between the color channels, (ii) especially for JPEG QF of 75 and 95, most of the payload should be concentrated in the luminance channel to maximize empirical security, (iii) over the three reputed feature sets used in color or JPEG steganalysis, the concatenation of GFR features on the 3 channels offer on average the best performance for QF = 75 and QF = 95, but SCRMQ1 computed in the YC_bC_r domain offers superior performances for QF = 100. Future works will focus on implementing similar analyses for other color sampling mechanisms such as 4:2:2 or 4:2:0, and to design deep learning schemes dedicated to color JPEG images.

Acknowledgments. The authors would like to thank Rémi Duprès, who designed the pipeline used to perform this set of extensive tests. This work was also partially supported by the French ANR DEFALS program (ANR-16-DEFA-0003).

References

1. Abdulrahman, H., Chaumont, M., Montesinos, P., Magnier, B.: Color image steganalysis based on steerable gaussian filters bank. In: Proceedings of the 4th ACM Workshop on Information Hiding and Multimedia Security, pp. 109–114. ACM (2016)
2. Bas, P., Pevny, T., Filler, T.: Bossbase (May 2011). http://exile.felk.cvut.cz/boss
3. Fridrich, J., Kodovsky, J.: Rich models for steganalysis of digital images. IEEE Trans. Inf. Forensics Secur. **7**(3), 868–882 (2012)
4. Goljan, M., Fridrich, J.: CFA-aware features for steganalysis of color images. In: IS&T/SPIE Electronic Imaging. pp. 94090V–94090V. International Society for Optics and Photonics (2015)
5. Goljan, M., Fridrich, J., Cogranne, R., et al.: Rich model for steganalysis of color images. In: National Conference on Parallel Computing Technologies (PAR-COMPTECH), pp. 185–190. IEEE (2015)
6. Guo, L., Ni, J., Su, W., Tang, C., Shi, Y.Q.: Using statistical image model for jpeg steganography: uniform embedding revisited. IEEE Trans. Inf. Forensics Secur. **10**(12), 2669–2680 (2015)
7. Holub, V., Fridrich, J.: Low-complexity features for jpeg steganalysis using undecimated DCT. IEEE Trans. Inf. Forensics Secur. **10**(2), 219–228 (2015)
8. Holub, V., Fridrich, J., Denemark, T.: Universal distortion function for steganography in an arbitrary domain. EURASIP J. Inf. Secur. **2014**(1), 1–13 (2014)
9. Ker, A.D., et al.: Batch steganography and pooled steganalysis. In: Camenisch, J.L., Collberg, C.S., Johnson, N.F., Sallee, P. (eds.) IH 2006. LNCS, vol. 4437, pp. 265–281. Springer, Heidelberg (2007). https://doi.org/10.1007/978-3-540-74124-4_18
10. Ker, A.D., et al.: Moving steganography and steganalysis from the laboratory into the real world. In: Proceedings of the first ACM workshop on Information hiding and multimedia security, pp. 45–58. ACM (2013)
11. Ker, A.D., Pevný, T., Kodovský, J., Fridrich, J.: The square root law of steganographic capacity. In: Proceedings of the 10th ACM workshop on Multimedia and security, pp. 107–116. ACM (2008)
12. Kodovsky, J., Fridrich, J., Holub, V.: Ensemble classifiers for steganalysis of digital media. IEEE Trans. Inf. Forensics Secur. **7**(2), 432–444 (2012)
13. Li, B., Wang, M., Li, X., Tan, S., Huang, J.: A strategy of clustering modification directions in spatial image steganography. IEEE Trans. Inf. Forensics Secur. **10**(9), 1905–1917 (2015)

14. Song, X., Liu, F., Yang, C., Luo, X., Zhang, Y.: Steganalysis of adaptive jpeg steganography using 2D gabor filters. In: Proceedings of the 3rd ACM workshop on information hiding and multimedia security, pp. 15–23. ACM (2015)
15. Westfeld, A.: F5—a steganographic algorithm. In: Moskowitz, I.S. (ed.) IH 2001. LNCS, vol. 2137, pp. 289–302. Springer, Heidelberg (2001). https://doi.org/10.1007/3-540-45496-9_21
16. Zeng, J., Tan, S., Liu, G., Li, B., Huang, J.: Wisernet: Wider separate-then-reunion network for steganalysis of color images. arXiv preprint arXiv:1803.04805 (2018)

Identification and Security

VPCID—A VoIP Phone Call Identification Database

Yuankun Huang[1], Shunquan Tan[2], Bin Li[1(✉)], and Jiwu Huang[1]

[1] Guangdong Key Laboratory of Intelligent Information Processing and Shenzhen Key Laboratory of Media Security, College of Information Engineering, Shenzhen University, Shenzhen 518060, China
libin@szu.edu.cn

[2] National Engineering Laboratory for Big Data System Computing Technology, College of Computer Science and Software Engineering, Shenzhen University, Shenzhen 518060, China

Abstract. Audio forensic plays an important role in the field of information security to address disputes related to the authenticity and originality of audio. However, some audio forensics methods presented in existing references were evaluated under either non-forensic oriented databases or private databases which were not publicly available. It creates difficulty for researchers to make comparison between different methods. In this paper we established VPCID, a VoIP phone call identification database for audio forensic purpose. As there is an increasing trend of phone scams or voice phishing via VoIP, through which the caller's identity can be hidden or forged easily, it is demanded to address the issues of identifying VoIP phone calls. The VPCID database is comprising of 1152 VoIP call recordings and 1152 mobile phone call recordings, each of which has more than two minutes. Recordings were collected from 48 different speakers using different smart phones and by considering varies recording conditions such as VoIP software, locations etc. We used MFCC (Mel-Frequency Cepstral Coefficients) and ACV (Amplitude Co-occurrence Vector) based features respectively equipped with SVM (Support Vector Machine) classifier to perform classification on the database. We also evaluated our own database on a CNN (convolutional neural network), but the performance is not too much satisfactory. Therefore the VoIP phone call identification problem is challenging and it calls for more effective solutions to address the problem. We hope our proposed database will convey more than this paper and inspire the future studies, which is openly available in below link, http://media-sec.szu.edu.cn/VPCID.html, and we welcome the use of this database.

Keywords: Audio forensics · VoIP · Call recording · Identification

This work was supported in part by the NSFC (U1636202, 61572329, 61772349), Shenzhen R&D Program (JCYJ20160328144421330). This work was also supported by Alibaba Group through Alibaba Innovative Research (AIR) Program.

C. D. Yoo et al. (Eds.): IWDW 2018, LNCS 11378, pp. 307–321, 2019.
https://doi.org/10.1007/978-3-030-11389-6_23

1   Introduction

With the popularity of mobile phone and the development of Internet technology, many new fraud methods based on audio have emerged [1]. One of numerous challenges is VoIP (Voice over Internet Protocol) phone call fraud [2]. Unlike traditional landline or mobile telephone call, VoIP phone call is transmitted over the Internet connection via VoIP servers, which allows users to communicate without using a telephone number or a SIM (Subscriber Identity Module) card. In these types of systems, criminals can easily forge their caller numbers without verification, and so that their true identities (IDs) are disguised. Fraud victims are usually confused by the caller IDs faked as being from polices, banks, or companies with well-known telephone numbers [3]. Therefore, identifying whether a phone call is via VoIP or not can help to verify the identity of a caller and prevent possible frauds.

As a branch of digital multimedia forensics technologies, audio forensics focuses on analysing the authenticity, originality, and reliability of audio. Audio forensics methods may help to address the issue of VoIP phone call identification. However, a possible difficulty that may hinder the development of effective audio forensics methods is that there is no suitable dataset for evaluation. In fact, although there are plenty of audio databases, only a few of them are specifically designed for forensic purpose.

Many audio forensics methods presented in existing references were evaluated on non-forensic oriented databases. For example, TIMIT [4] database, which was originally designed for automatic speech recognition systems, has been used in audio codec identification [5] and double compressed AMR detection [6]. WSJ-CAM0 speech corpus of British English [7] was originally designed for speech recognition and it was exploited for detecting recaptured audio [8]. NOIZEUS [9] consists of speeches added with noise under different SNR conditions, which was originally built for speech enhancement and was used for electronic disguised voice identification [10].

In recent years, some datasets have also been constructed to address specific audio forensics issues. For instance, LIVE RECORDS [11] and MOBIPHONE [12] were built for identifying different smart phones. SAS Corpus [13] was built for detecting spoofed speech. ASVspoof 2017 Corpus [14] was designed for audio replay detection. In addition, many audio forensics experts built their own databases and evaluated their proposed methods on them. For example, Luo et al. [15] built a dataset for smart phone identification and verification. Hicsonmez et al. [16] constructed a dataset consisting of 1,000 audio samples from 500 songs for audio codec identification.

Unfortunately, as far as we know, for the problem of VoIP phone call identification, there is no publicly available database for evaluation. Moreover, since audio transmitting between caller and callee undergoes a series of complex transformations such as transcoding, degradation and so on, it is difficult to simulate the transmitted audio on existing datasets. Therefore, building a specific database for VoIP phone call identification is of great interest for forensics research society. To this aim, we have built a database called VPCID (VoIP

Phone Call Identification Database). The database contains two different type of call recordings, half of which are mobile phone call recordings and the other half are VoIP phone call recordings. The call recordings are collected from 48 volunteers using different smart phones when they make phone calls. In order to simulate the real-world situations as much as possible, we set different locations for volunteers in controlled environments and we also considered using a variety of VoIP software programs. Each call lasted more than two minutes and finally we obtain a database with total 76-h call time and 2,304 audio files. A detailed description of the database is presented in this paper. We have also tried two feature based audio forensics methods and a CNN based method to differentiate VoIP phone call from mobile phone call. The results indicate that existing methods do not handle the problem well. Therefore, it calls for more advanced methods be developed in the near future.

The rest of this paper is organized as follows. We provide a brief introduction of audio transmission in telephony network in Sect. 2. In Sect. 3, we describe the details of our database. In Sect. 4, we present experimental results for evaluating existing audio forensics methods on our database. The conclusion is given in Sect. 5.

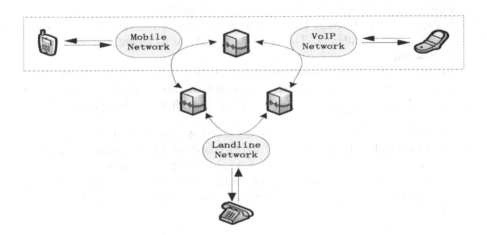

Fig. 1. A description of telephony systems.

2 Audio Transmission in Telephony Networks

In this section, we briefly introduce some basics of the audio transmission process in telephony networks.

As shown in Fig. 1, there are three types of telephony networks, including landline networks, mobile networks, and VoIP networks. Audio signal is first encoded into bit-streams and different network have different codecs. For example G.711 is widely used in landline networks, while GSM HR, GSM FR, and

AMR are used in mobile networks. The codecs used in VoIP networks include G.711, G.726, G.729, iLBC, Speex, and so on. A gateway is a networking device used for data transmission between different networks. The encoded audio data is transcoded at gateways when it is transmitted through different networks. Apart from going through complex encoding and decoding processes, audio undergoes various forms of degradation when it is transmitted in telephony networks. Although some methods such as [17–21] have been proposed to identify the codecs and transcoded audios [16], it seems that it is less effective to identify VoIP call based on codecs because there are many forms of degradation in telephony networks as disturbance factors for codec identification.

A possible solution is to identify the source of the received audio directly. But the received audio from telephony network is also affected by many factors, some of which are listed as follows:

- Device. The hardware devices used in telephony networks play an important role. For the caller and callee, the brands and the models of their phones should be taken into account for audio quality.
- VoIP software. There are a variety of VoIP software programs can be used for communication. Different software programs may utilize different codec which leads to different coding efficiency and quality.
- Location. With different locations of caller and callee, the communication channels can be different. Therefore the quality of a call varies from location to location.
- Network traffic. The network traffic varies from time to time. To avoiding network collapse, congestion control techniques are used. If the number of user suddenly increases at a sudden, the call quality may be affected.

As we can see, there are a lot of factors that may affect the audio signal received by a callee. To build a database for VoIP call identification, we need to take these factors into account as many as possible. Since almost everyone uses a smart phone for communication, we limit our study on the communication between mobile network and VoIP network, which is shown in the dash box of Fig. 1.

3   The VPCID Database

In this section, we give a detailed description of VPCID—the VoIP Phone Call Identification Database. We first introduce the data collecting process and the distributions of recording data. Then we give the annotations of the data.

3.1   Data Collection

The VPCID database is designed to provide various kinds of mobile phone call recording data and VoIP phone call recording data for forensics researchers so that they can develop and evaluate their methods for identifying the source of a phone call. For simulating the real-world situations as much as possible, we take into account the following factors and set various configurations when collecting our data:

1. The influence of smart phone devices.
2. The influence of speakers.
3. The influence of background noise.
4. The influence of network traffic.
5. The influence of VoIP software.
6. The influence of recording formats.

Table 1. The brands and the models of 48 smart phones.

Index	Brand	Model	Index	Brand	Model
#1	iPhone	6s plus ML6G2CH/A	#25	iPhone	5s A1530
#2	Huawei	Honor 8 FRD-AL00	#26	MI	MI6
#3	iPhone	6s MKT12LL/A	#27	iPhone	6 MG492ZP/A
#4	MI	Redmi Note3	#28	MX	6 M685C
#5	iPhone	6 plus MGAK2ZP/A	#29	iPhone	7 MN8L2ZP/A
#6	MI	Redmi Note2	#30	MI	MI 5S
#7	iPhone	7 MNGQ2CH/A	#31	Huawei	P9 EVA-AL10
#8	MI	MI 6	#32	Huawei	Honor 8 FRD-AL10
#9	iPhone	6 plus MGA82CH/A	#33	iPhone	6s plus MKU72ZP/A
#10	MI	MI Note LTE	#34	Nubia	Z9mini
#11	iPhone	6s ML7H2CH/A	#35	MI	Redmi Note4
#12	OnePlus	1 A0001	#36	Huawei	Honor 8 FRD-AL10
#13	iPhone	6 MG4H2ZP/A	#37	iPhone	6 MG4J2ZP/A
#14	MI	MI 4S	#38	Samsung	GT-I9070
#15	iPhone	6 MG4J2ZP/A	#39	Oppo	R9tm
#16	Huawei	Honor 6 H60-L11	#40	MX	3 M356
#17	iPhone	6 MG4J2CH/A	#41	MI	MIX2
#18	Nubia	Z11 mini NX549J	#42	Lenovo	Zuk z2 pro
#19	iPhone	6s MKQP2J/A	#43	iPhone	6s NKU92ZP/A
#20	Huawei	Honor 9 STF-AL00	#44	Huawei	Honor 8 PRA-AL00
#21	Samsung	GALAXY S4 I9500	#45	iPhone	6 plus MGAK2ZP/A
#22	MI	MI 4	#46	Oppo	R9sk
#23	iPhone	SE MLXQ2CH/A	#47	iPhone	6s ML7M2CH/A
#24	MI	Redmi Note 4X	#48	Huawei	Honor 6 H60-L03

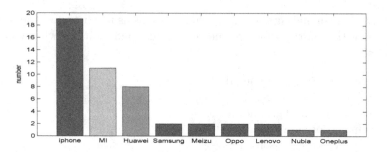

Fig. 2. Distribution of different brands.

The database is collected with the help of 48 volunteers from Shenzhen Univeristy, including 6 females and 42 males. They are identified as speakers and indexed by a number from S1 to S48. Among them, S4, S33, S39, S44, S45, and S47 are females. The volunteers provide their smart phones for data collection, and as a result, there are 48 different smart phones. The devices are indexed by a number from #1 to #48. In Table 1, we show the brands and the specific models of the smart phones used by the volunteers. Figure 2 shows the distribution of smart phone brands.

In order to consider different background noise, we set 4 locations for callers and 2 locations for callees, leading to a combination of 8 different source-and-destination configurations for data collection. The scenes of each location are shown as Fig. 3. To take account the network traffic, the phone calls are conducted in three different time periods of the day, i.e., morning (8:00–12:00), afternoon (13:00–17:00), and night (19:00–23:00).

In our data collection process, a volunteer players the role of a caller, who is required to make a mobile phone call and then a VoIP phone call for each time period. Each phone call should last at least 2 min. Only the caller speaks, while the callee records the speech with the smart phone being dialed. In order to eliminate the influence of speakers, two volunteers share the same data collection configuration. The detailed data collection processes are designed as follow.

Step 1. The caller X in Location A uses a smart phone x to make a phone call to callee Y in Location E via mobile network. The callee records the speech of X with the called smart phone y. This step simulates the process of the communication between two mobile networks.

Step 2. The caller X in Location A uses the smart phone x to make a VoIP phone call to callee Y in Location E by using a VoIP software program. The callee records the speech of X with the called smart phone y. This step simulates the process of the communication from a VoIP network to a Mobile network.

Step 3. The caller X changes his or her calling position to Location B, Location C, and Location D, respectively. And then X repeats Step 1 and Step 2.

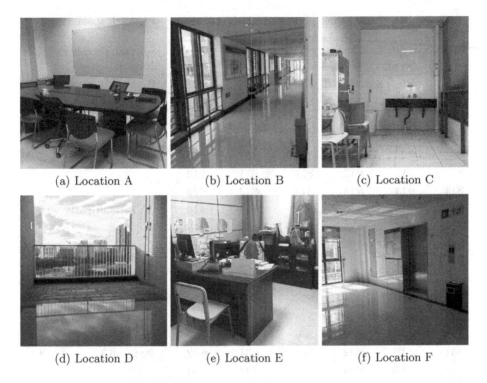

(a) Location A   (b) Location B   (c) Location C

(d) Location D   (e) Location E   (f) Location F

Fig. 3. The scene of different locations

Step 4. The callee Y changes his or her recorded position to Location F, and then repeats from Step 1 to Step 3.

Step 5. The caller X and the callee Y repeat the above steps in the other two time periods.

We use 8 different kinds of VoIP software for the caller. Table 2 shows the smart phones and the VoIP software used by each volunteer. The recordings are recorded under a variety of parameters and are saved in AMR, MP3, or AAC format, which depends on the native recording software of the called smart phone. Detailed parameters of the recordings and corresponding speakers are shown in Table 3.

Data collection starts from April 2017 and ends in June 2018. After all 48 volunteers complete the above process, we obtain a database with more than 76.8 h call recordings, taken a storage space of approximately 600 MB. The database consists of 2304 (48 volunteers × 2 calls × 4 caller positions × 2 callee positions × 3 time periods = 2304) call recordings, including 1152 mobile phone call recordings and 1152 VoIP phone call recordings. Specifically, we have 144 mobile phone call recordings and 144 VoIP phone call recordings for each source-and-destination configuration. Among the recorded data, 54.2% of the recordings are saved in AMR format, 41.7% are MP3, and the rest are AAC.

Table 2. List of smartphones and VoIP software used by each speaker.

Speaker	Caller's device	Callee's device	Speaker	Caller's device	Callee's device	Software on caller's device
S1	#1	#2	S2	#1	#2	Wetalk v28.0.0
S3	#3	#4	S4	#3	#4	
S5	#5	#6	S6	#5	#6	
S7	#7	#8	S8	#7	#8	
S9	#9	#10	S10	#9	#10	Start v1.5.0
S11	#11	#12	S12	#11	#12	
S13	#13	#14	S14	#13	#14	
S15	#15	#16	S16	#15	#16	WeiweiMultiparty v2.0
S17	#17	#18	S18	#17	#18	
S19	#19	#20	S20	#19	#20	
S21	#21	#22	S22	#22	#21	
S23	#23	#24	S24	#23	#24	Vhua v4.7.5
S25	#25	#26	S26	#25	#26	
S27	#27	#28	S28	#27	#28	
S29	#29	#30	S30	#29	#30	
S31	#31	#32	S32	#31	#32	Skype v6.3.5
S33	#33	#34	S34	#33	#34	
S35	#35	#36	S36	#36	#35	
S37	#37	#38	S37	#37	#38	Uwewe v4.5
S39	#39	#40	S40	#39	#40	
S41	#41	#42	S42	#41	#42	Ailiao v6.8.6
S43	#43	#44	S44	#43	#44	
S45	#45	#46	S46	#45	#46	Alicall v6.9.9
S47	#47	#48	S48	#47	#48	

3.2 Data Annotation

Since the VPCID database is built under different recording conditions, we annotate every recording file in the database with the corresponding recording condition so that researchers can conveniently retrieve a specific file. The syntax of the filename is designed as:

[type][software][speaker][caller location][callee location][timeperiod].[format]

where each field is explained as follows.

- type: mobile|voip. It represents the type of phone call.
- software: wetalk|start|weiweimultiparty|vhua|skype|uwewe|ailiao|alicall. It represents the used VoIP software if the call is a VoIP phone call. It is absent if the call is mobile phone call.

Table 3. Parameters of different recordings.

Sampling rate	Bit depth	Channel	Bit rate	Format	Speaker
16 kHz	16 bits	Mono	13.2 kbps	AMR	S1, S2, S19 S20, S31, S32, S33 S34, S36, S43, S44
8 kHz	16 bits	Mono	8 kbps	MP3	S3, S4, S5, S6, S9 S10, S22, S23, S24
48 kHz	16 bits	Mono	32 kbps	MP3	S7, S8, S13, S14 S25, S26, S29, S30
16 kHz	16 bits	Stereo	25 kbps	AAC	S11, S12
8 kHz	16 bits	Mono	12.8 kbps	AMR	S15, S16, S17 S18, S21, S37, S38 S39, S40, S41, S42 S45, S46, S47, S48
44.1 kHz	16 bits	Mono	64 kbps	MP3	S27, S28
16 kHz	16 bits	Stereo	24 kbps	MP3	S35

- *speaker*: 1|2|3| ⋯ |47|48. It represents the index of speakers.
- *caller location*: a|b|c|d. It represents the location of a speaker when the speaker is making a call.
- *callee location*: e|f. It represents the location of callee when the speaker is making a call.
- *time period*: 1|2|3. It represents the first call or the second call or the third call in a specific location since we record three times at different times for each location.
- *format*: amr|aac|mp3. It represents the format used for storage which depends on the used smart phone.

For example, *voip_skype_3_c_e_2.mp3* represents a recording for speaker S3 in location C making a VoIP phone call via Skype in the second time period to the callee, while the callee being in location E and saving the speech in a MP3 file. In this way, one can easily divide the VPCID database into training sets, validation sets, and test sets, by retrieving corresponding files according to the filenames. It is convenient for researchers to evaluate the robustness of their proposed methods under different recording conditions.

4   Experiments on the Database

In this part, we investigate whether some existing forensics or audio classification methods [22–24] can be used to identify the VoIP phone calls on the proposed database.

4.1   Evaluation Methods

Two kinds forensic features with SVM classifier and a convolutional neural network (CNN) have been used for evaluation. Their details are as follows.

MFCC Features. In [25], MFCC (Mel-Frequency Cepstral Coefficients) features are used to evaluate microphone and environment classification. MFCC was designed based on human auditory system, and it is widely used not only for speech recognition and speaker recognition systems but also for many audio forensics applications. The procedure of extracting MFCC features is shown in Fig. 4, which includes the following steps:

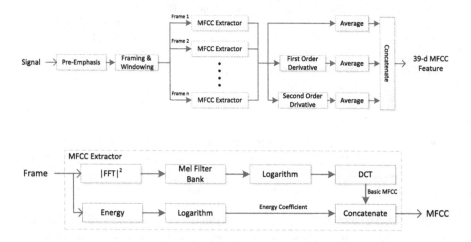

Fig. 4. Procedure of extracting MFCC features

Step 1. Increase the magnitude of the high frequency part of signal by a pre-emphasis filter and segment the signal into frames with a window function. We use Hamming window in our implementation.

Step 2. Take the fast Fourier transform (FFT) of each frame and calculate the power spectrum of FFT.

Step 3. Calculate Mel-scale spectrum by applying Mel filter banks to the FFT power spectrum. We use triangular filter banks in our implementation.

Step 4. Compute the logarithm of Mel-scale spectrum. Perform discrete cosine transform (DCT) on the log Mel-scale spectrum to obtain basic MFCC coefficients.

Step 5. Compute the energy of the input frame signal and then take logarithm of the output. The resulting coefficient is called energy coefficient.

Step 6. Concatenate the basic MFCC coefficients with the energy coefficient. The resulting coefficients for each frame are called MFCC coefficients. There are 13 MFCC coefficients for each frame.

Step 7. Take the average value of MFCC coefficients over all frames and obtain a 13-D feature vector.

Step 8. Compute the first order frame-to-frame differential signal [26] of MFCC coefficients, and take the average value over all frames. A 13-D feature vector can be obtained.

Step 9. Compute the second order frame-to-frame differential signal of MFCC coefficients and take the average value over all frames. Another 13-D feature vector can be obtained.

Step 10. Concatenate the features extracted from Step 6 to 8 to obtain 39-D MFCC features.

In our implementation, we set the frame length to be 30 ms and the frame shift to be 15 ms.

ACV Features. ACV (Amplitude Cooccurrence Vector) is proposed in [23] for detecting audio postprocessing operations. The details of ACV feature extraction procedures are as follows.

Step 1. Normalize the given audio signal and filter the normalized signal using a high-pass filter.

Step 2. Choose a threshold T to quantize the high-passed signal $X(x_1, x_2, ..., x_n)$ by

$$y_i = \begin{cases} -1 \; , \; x_i \leq -T \\ 0 \; , \; -T \leq x_i < T \\ 1 \; , \; x_i \geq T \end{cases} \tag{1}$$

where y_i represents the i-th sample of quantized signal $Y(y_1, y_2, ..., y_n)$.

Step 3. Compute the w-D co-occurrence features for $Y(y_1, y_2, ..., y_n)$. Since $y_i \in \{-1, 0, 1\}$, there are a total number of 3^w patterns.

In our implementation, we set the threshold $T = 0.02$ and the window size $w = 5$ to obtain 243 ($3^5 = 243$) dimensional ACV features.

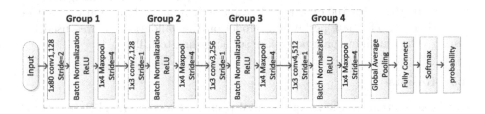

Fig. 5. Architecture of ESR-CNN.

Environmental Sound Recognition CNN (ESR-CNN). In [24], a series of convolutional model have been proposed for environmental sound recognition. We choose the "M5 model" to detect VoIP phone call. As shown in Fig. 5, the

M5 model accepting raw waveform as input is composed of four convolutional modules. Each convolutional module consists of a convolutional layer, a batch normalization layer, a ReLU activation function, and a max pooling layer. The kernel size and stride in each convolutional layer and max pooling layer can be found in Fig. 5. At the end of the last group, a global average pooling layer is adopted while a fully connected layer and a softmax function are used for classification. In our implementation, the number of output channel was set to 128 in the first and the second convolutional layer, 256 in the third convolutional layer, and 512 in the last convolutional layers.

4.2   Experimental Setup

We investigated the performance of MCFF features, ACV features, and ESR-CNN respectively on VPCID in detecting VoIP phone calls. We decoded each audio file from our database to waveform (with 16 bits per sample and 8,000 Hz sampling rate). Then we divided each waveform into segments. The duration of each segment was two seconds. In this way, we obtained a total number of 71,249 mobile phone call segments and 71,411 VoIP phone call segments. We randomly selected 71,000 mobile phone call segments and corresponding 71,000 VoIP phone call segments for our experiments. Among them, 60% mobile phone call segments and the corresponding VoIP phone call segments were randomly selected for training, while the rest segments were for testing.

In our experiments, we used LIBSVM [27] as the classifier for MFCC feature and ACV feature. Specifically, we chose C-SVM equipped with RBF kernel. In order to obtain optimal hyper-parameters, we set different pairs of C and γ, where $(C, \gamma) \in \{(2^i, 2^j) | i \in (-5, -3, -1, ..., 15), j \in (5, 3, 1, ..., -15)\}$. The best performing model in three-fold cross-validation on the training set was used for testing.

For ESR-CNN, we used the same 60% data for training and then selected others 20% mobile phone call segments and VoIP phone call segments for validation. The best performing model was used for testing on the rest segments. The batch size was set to 100 in our implementation. We used training data to train ESR-CNN with 100 epochs and evaluate them every 100 iterations on the validation set. The best performing model on the validation set was used for testing. The remaining parameters are set according to [24].

4.3   Results

In this subsection we show experimental results by measuring TPR (true positives rate), TNR (true negatives rate), and ACC (detection accuracy), which are respectively defined as:

$$TPR = \frac{TP}{TP + FN} \tag{2}$$

$$TNR = \frac{TN}{TN + FP} \tag{3}$$

$$ACC = \frac{TP + TN}{TP + FN + TN + FP} \tag{4}$$

where TP, TN, FP, FN represent the number of true positive segments, true negative segments, false positive segments, and false negative segments, respectively. In this paper, the VoIP phone call recording is defined as positive class. The experimental results are shown in Table 4. From the table, it can be observed that the MFCC scheme and the ACV scheme respectively achieved the accuracy of 69.35% and 67.27%. Since audio go through a series of complex encoding and decoding process, various forms of degradation and others transformations in telephony networks, the MFCC and ACV can not capture the difference between mobile phone calls and VoIP phone calls. From Table 4 we can find that the ESR-CNN achieved the accuracy of 85.51%. However, this result is still unsatisfactory. It is obvious that the audio forensics issues of VoIP phone call identification is challenging.

Table 4. Results for different methods.

Method	TPR	TNR	ACC
MFCC+SVM	71.82%	66.89%	69.35%
ACV+SVM	77.02%	57.52%	67.27%
ESR-CNN	85.86%	85.10%	85.51%

5 Conclusions

In this paper, we introduce a new database named VPCID which was built for audio forensics researchers to address the issues of VoIP phone call identification. The database contains 2,304 recordings, half of which are mobile phone call recordings and the others are VoIP phone call recordings, each of which last two minutes. The database was built under a variety of recording conditions which include different speakers, different devices, different software, and different calling and recording locations. We have also evaluated two state-of-the-art audio forensic features and a CNN based method on VPCID. The experimental results show that the VoIP phone call identification problem on VPCID dataset is challenging.

Since the recorded audio data in VPCID were collected by 48 individual speakers and then recorded by 26 smart phones, the database may also be used for others audio forensic purpose. For instance, they can be used for the issues of device source identification and speaker verification. The VPCID database is publicly online available at http://media-sec.szu.edu.cn/VPCID.html. We welcome the use of this database and hope it can help the research community to advance the techniques on VoIP phone call identification and other related audio forensics issues. We acknowledge that the audio in VPCID is mainly recorded under the low background noise with Chinese language. The next version of the database may be extended by considering more outdoor scenes and using more languages.

References

1. Shahani, A.: Why phone fraud starts with a silent call (2015). https://www.npr. org/sections/alltechconsidered/2015/08/24/434313813/why-phone-fraud-starts-with-a-silent-call
2. vd Groenendaal, H.: Why phone fraud starts with a silent call (2014). https:// mybroadband.co.za/news/telecoms/112935-voip-fraud-explained.html
3. McGlasson, L.: Vishing scam: four more states struck (2010). http://www. bankinfosecurity.com/articles.php?art_id=2138
4. Garofolo, J.S., Lamel, L.F., Fisher, W.M., Fiscus, J.G., Pallett, D.S.: Darpa timit acoustic-phonetic continous speech corpus CD-ROM. nist speech disc 1-1.1. NASA STI/Recon technical report n 93 (1993)
5. Jenner, F., Kwasinski, A.: Highly accurate non-intrusive speech forensics for codec identifications from observed decoded signals. In: 2012 IEEE International Conference on Acoustics, Speech and Signal Processing (ICASSP), pp. 1737–1740. IEEE (2012)
6. Luo, D., Yang, R., Li, B., Huang, J.: Detection of double compressed AMR audio using stacked autoencoder. IEEE Trans. Inf. Forensics Secur. **12**(2), 432–444 (2017)
7. Robinson, T., Fransen, J., Pye, D., Foote, J., Renals, S.: WSJCAMO: a British English speech corpus for large vocabulary continuous speech recognition. In: 1995 International Conference on Acoustics, Speech, and Signal Processing, ICASSP 1995, vol. 1, pp. 81–84. IEEE (1995)
8. Lin, X., Liu, J., Kang, X.: Audio recapture detection with convolutional neural networks. IEEE Trans. Multimedia **18**(8), 1480–1487 (2016)
9. Hu, Y., Loizou, P.C.: Subjective comparison and evaluation of speech enhancement algorithms. Speech Commun. **49**(7–8), 588–601 (2007)
10. Cao, W., Wang, H., Zhao, H., Qian, Q., Abdullahi, S.M.: Identification of electronic disguised voices in the noisy environment. In: Shi, Y.Q., Kim, H.J., Perez-Gonzalez, F., Liu, F. (eds.) IWDW 2016. LNCS, vol. 10082, pp. 75–87. Springer, Cham (2017). https://doi.org/10.1007/978-3-319-53465-7_6
11. Hanilci, C., Ertas, F., Ertas, T., Eskidere, Ö.: Recognition of brand and models of cell-phones from recorded speech signals. IEEE Trans. Inf. Forensics Secur. **7**(2), 625–634 (2012)
12. Kotropoulos, C., Samaras, S.: Mobile phone identification using recorded speech signals. In: 2014 19th International Conference on Digital Signal Processing (DSP), pp. 586–591. IEEE (2014)
13. Wu, Z., et al.: SAS: a speaker verification spoofing database containing diverse attacks. In: 2015 IEEE International Conference on Acoustics, Speech and Signal Processing (ICASSP), pp. 4440–4444. IEEE (2015)
14. Kinnunen, T., et al.: The ASVspoof 2017 challenge: assessing the limits of replay spoofing attack detection (2017)
15. Luo, D., Korus, P., Huang, J.: Band energy difference for source attribution in audio forensics. IEEE Trans. Inf. Forensics Secur. **13**(9), 2179–2189 (2018)
16. Hicsonmez, S., Sencar, H.T., Avcibas, I.: Audio codec identification from coded and transcoded audios. Digital Signal Process. **23**(5), 1720–1730 (2013)
17. Scholz, K., Leutelt, L., Heute, U.: Speech-codec detection by spectral harmonic-plus-noise decomposition. In: Conference Record of the Thirty-Eighth Asilomar Conference on Signals, Systems and Computers. vol. 2, pp. 2295–2299. IEEE (2004)
18. Svečko, R., Kotnik, B., Chowdhury, A., Mezgec, Z.: GSM speech coder indirect identification algorithm. Informatica **21**(4), 575–596 (2010)

19. Zhou, J.: Automatic speech codec identification with applications to tampering detection of speech recordings. Ph.D. thesis (2011)
20. Sharma, D., Naylor, P.A., Gaubitch, N.D., Brookes, M.: Non intrusive codec identification algorithm. In: 2012 IEEE International Conference on Acoustics, Speech and Signal Processing (ICASSP), pp. 4477–4480. IEEE (2012)
21. Drăghicescu, D., Pop, G., Burileanu, D., Burileanu, C.: GMM-based audio codec detection with application in forensics. In: 2015 38th International Conference on Telecommunications and Signal Processing (TSP), pp. 1–5. IEEE (2015)
22. Davis, S.B., Mermelstein, P.: Comparison of parametric representations for monosyllabic word recognition in continuously spoken sentences. In: Readings in speech recognition, pp. 65–74. Elsevier (1990)
23. Luo, D., Sun, M., Huang, J.: Audio postprocessing detection based on amplitude cooccurrence vector feature. IEEE Signal Process. Lett. **23**(5), 688–692 (2016)
24. Dai, W., Dai, C., Qu, S., Li, J., Das, S.: Very deep convolutional neural networks for raw waveforms. In: 2017 IEEE International Conference on Acoustics, Speech and Signal Processing (ICASSP), pp. 421–425. IEEE (2017)
25. Kraetzer, C., Oermann, A., Dittmann, J., Lang, A.: Digital audio forensics: a first practical evaluation on microphone and environment classification. In: Proceedings of the 9th Workshop on Multimedia & Security, pp. 63–74. ACM (2007)
26. Furui, S.: Speaker-independent isolated word recognition based on emphasized spectral dynamics. In: IEEE International Conference on Acoustics, Speech, and Signal Processing. ICASSP 1986, vol. 11, pp. 1991–1994. IEEE (1986)
27. Chang, C.C., Lin, C.J.: Libsvm: a library for support vector machines. ACM Trans. Intell. Syst. Technol. (TIST) **2**(3), 27 (2011)

Secure Multilayer Perceptron Based on Homomorphic Encryption

Reda Bellafqira[1,2]([⊠]), Gouenou Coatrieux[1,2], Emmanuelle Genin[2], and Michel Cozic[3]

[1] IMT Atlantique, 655 Avenue du Technopole, 29200 Plouzane, France
{reda.bellafqira,gouenou.coatrieux}@imt-atlantique.com
[2] Unit INSERM 1101 Latim, 29238 Brest Cedex, France
emmanuelle.genin@inserm.fr
[3] MED.e.COM, 29470 Plougastel Daoulas, France
mcozic@wanadoo.fr

Abstract. In this work, we propose an outsourced Secure Multilayer Perceptron (SMLP) scheme where privacy and confidentiality of the data and the model are ensured during its training and the classification phases. More clearly, this SMLP: (i) can be trained by a cloud server based on data previously outsourced by a user in an homomorphically encrypted form; its parameters are homomorphically encrypted giving thus no clues about them to the cloud; and (ii) can also be used for classifying new encrypted data sent by the user while returning him the encrypted classification result. The originality of this scheme is threefold: To the best of our knowledge, it is the first multilayer perceptron (MLP) secured homomorphically in its training phase with no problem of convergence. It does not require extra-communications with the user. And, is based on the Rectified Linear Unit (ReLU) activation function that we secure with no approximation contrarily to actual SMLP solutions. To do so, we take advantage of two semi-honest non-colluding servers. Experimental results carried out on a binary database encrypted with the Paillier cryptosystem demonstrate the overall performance of our scheme and its convergence.

Keywords: Secure neural network · Multilayer perceptron · Homomorphic encryption · Cloud computing

1 Introduction

Nowadays, cloud technology allows outsourcing the processing and the storage of huge volume of data, these ones being personal data or data issued from

This work has received a French government support granted to the CominLabs excellence laboratory and managed by the National Research Agency in the "Investing for the Future" program under reference ANR0LABX0701, and to the ANR project INSHARE, ANR15CE1002402.

© Springer Nature Switzerland AG 2019
C. D. Yoo et al. (Eds.): IWDW 2018, LNCS 11378, pp. 322–336, 2019.
https://doi.org/10.1007/978-3-030-11389-6_24

many sources for big data analysis purposes. In healthcare for example, different initiatives aim at sharing medical images and Personal Health Records (PHR) between either health professionals or hospitals with the help of cloud [9]. They take advantage of the medical knowledge, volume of data represents so as to develop new decision making tools based on machine learning techniques. Among such techniques, there is the multilayer perceptron (MLP) method which belongs to Neural Network (NN) family and which is a core element of deep learning methods; methods that are broadly studied and used nowadays. A MLP consists of multiple layers of interconnected perceptrons (see Fig. 2). A perceptron is a classifier that maps its inputs with a vector of weights followed by an activation function. The output of a perceptron is the input of the next perceptron layer. As all machine learning algorithms, MLP works in two distinct ways: the training phase and the classification of new data. In a supervised mode, the training phase aims at inferring the network parameters from a labeled database by optimizing some objective function. Once trained, a MLP scheme is used so as to classify new data.

Despite the attractive benefits provided by MLP, one of the actual limits of its outsourcing in a cloud environment stands on the security of the data used for the training phase or for classification purposes as well as of the MLP parameters. At the same time, the parameter of a process, like those of a trained MLP, may have some important added value for a company. There is thus an interest to develop secured MLP (SMLP) methods that can be trained remotely using outsourced data while respecting data privacy and confidentiality.

Different approaches have been proposed to secure neural network methods. Some of them are based on additive secret sharing that allows several parties to jointly compute the value of a target function $f(.)$ without compromising the privacy of its input data. For instance, [17] presents a privacy preserving NN learning protocol where each participant performs most of the learning computations in the clear domain except the NN weight update which is performed with secret additive sharing (e.g. secure sum and secure matrix addition). One limit of this solution is that, at each iteration, all updated weights are revealed to all participants which may leak information about the training data. To reduce such information leakage, [18] proposes to share through a server only a small fraction of the parameters; parameters on which the NN weights update can be performed using a synchronous stochastic gradient descent (ASGD) instead of a stochastic gradient descent. This method consequently establishes a compromise between accuracy and privacy. Higher the number of shared parameters, better is the classification accuracy but lower is privacy. Recently, in [1], the authors demonstrate that in [18], even a small portion of shared gradients of weights (gradients that are used to update the weight values) can leak useful information about training data. To overcome this problem, they suggest a solution based on homomorphic encryption to secure ASGD. The interest of homomorphic encryption is that it allows performing operations (e.g. $+$, $\times$) onto encrypted data with the guarantee that the decrypted result equals the one carried out with unencrypted data [2–4,6]. In [1], all users: (i) share the same homomorphic cryptosystem public and secret keys (ii) train locally a NN over their data (iii) computes their weight gradients and send them in homomorphic encrypted form to the server. When the server receives the encrypted gradients, it updates the weights in the encrypted domain and (iv) sends them back to the users. Since each user has the secret key, they decrypt the weights and train again their NN based on the new weights. In this scheme, homomorphic encryption is just used for the NN update, one computation of the NN learning process. Beyond, due to the fact this solution is based on AGSD [1,17], it suffers of the delayed gradient problem, i.e. a converge issue of the training phase problem [22].

An alternative to these approaches is to train neural networks in the clear domain and by next use them with encrypted data. Most solutions make use of homomorphic encryption. In this work, we are focusing on conducting all the computations of the training phase in the homomorphic encrypted domain. To the best of our knowledge, such an issue has only been theoretically studied in [21] where is shown that NN can be trained using fully homomorphic encryption data and by approximating activation functions with polynomials as homomorphic encryption only allows linear operations.

However, due to the fact fully homomorphic cryptosystems add noise to the data after each multiplication or addition operation. Both the computational complexity and the length of cipher-texts increase with the number of desired operations to guarantee the correct polynomial evaluation. In order to maintain a fixed cipher-text length, a practical implementation requires a de-noising process so as to be feasible or restrict the computation just on low degree polynomials. Moreover, the efficiency of the homomorphic computations depends on the multiplicative depth. To avoid a multiplicative depth too big which increases the computation complexity, after a certain number of iteration, the encrypted updated weights are sent to the parties to be decrypted and re-encrypted. Nevertheless, this solution leads to a higher communication complexity of the scheme.

Beyond this theoretical work, all other proposals [5,8] focus on securing the NN classification phase. For instance, [5] proposes three privacy homomorphic encryption based classifiers: the linear model and two low degree models. In [8] a fully homomorphic convolutional neural networks classifier (CNN) is proposed.

In this paper, we propose a secure multilayer perceptron (SMLP) method, the training and classification procedures of which do not suffer of convergence issues. To do so, we take advantage of the rectified linear unit (ReLU). Beyond its accuracy and its contribution to MLP efficiency [11], ReLU can be secured with homomorphic encryption and two non-colluding semi-honest servers avoiding thus the need to use of an approximation procedure of the perceptron's output as proposed by the above methods. Another originality of our SMLP, is that its output is also encrypted. That is not the case of actual solutions that provide unencrypted output. Furthermore, our SMLP is entirely outsourced in the sense it does not require extra-communications overhead in-between the servers and the user to conduct the training and classification phases. The user just has to send his data homomorphically encrypted to the cloud server that will train the

SMLP or classify data, without the cloud being able to infer information about the SMLP model parameters, the data or the classification result.

The rest of this paper is organized as follows. Section 2 regroups preliminaries related to Multilayer Perceptron and the Paillier cryptosystem on which relies the implementation of our SMLP. We also provide the basic properties and the operations one can implement over Paillier encrypted data when using two non-colluding semi-honest servers. In Sect. 3, we detail our secure multilayer perceptron. Section 4 provides some experimental results conducted to model the "AND" logic function on a binary database, and the security analysis of our proposal. Section 5 concludes this paper.

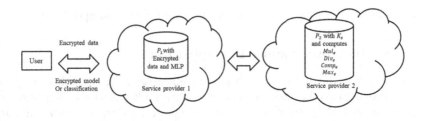

Fig. 1. Secure neural network architecture in a cloud environment

2 Preliminaries on the Paillier Cryptosystem and Multilayer Perceptron

2.1 The Paillier Cryptosystem

Being asymmetric, the Paillier cryptosystem [16] makes use of a pair of private and public keys. Let p and q be two large primes. Let also $K_p = pq$, $\mathbb{Z}_{K_p} = \{0, 1, ..., K_p - 1\}$, $\mathbb{Z}^*_{K_p}$ denotes the set of integers that have multiplicative inverses modulo K_p in $\mathbb{Z}_{K_p}$. We select also $g \in \mathbb{Z}^*_{K_p^2}$ such that

$$gcd(L(g^\lambda \mod K_p^2), K_p) = 1 \tag{1}$$

where: $gcd(.)$ is the greatest common divisor function; $\lambda = lcm(p-1, q-1)$ is the private key (K_s), with $lcm(.)$ the least common multiple function; the pair (K_p, g) defines the public key; and, $L(s) = \frac{s-1}{K_p}$. Let $m \in \mathbb{Z}_{K_p}$ the message to be encrypted. Its cipher-text is derived as

$$c = E[m, r] = g^m r^{K_p} \mod K_p^2 \tag{2}$$

where $E[.]$ is the encryption function, $r \in \mathbb{Z}^*_{K_p}$ is a random integer. Since r is not fixed, the Paillier cryptosystem satisfies the so-called "semantic security". More clearly, depending on the value of r, the encryption of the same plain-text message yields to different cipher-texts even though the public encryption key is the same. The plain-text m is recovered using the decryption function $D[.]$ defined as follow

$$m = D[c, \lambda] = \frac{L(c^\lambda mod K_p^2)}{L(g^\lambda mod K_p^2)} \quad mod \ K_p \tag{3}$$

The Paillier cryptosystem has an additive homomorphic property. Considering two plain-texts m_1 and m_2, then

$$E[m_1, r_1].E[m_2, r_2] = E[m_1 + m_2, r_1.r_2] \tag{4}$$

$$E[m_1, r_1]^{m_2} = E[m_1.m_2, r_1^{m_2}] \tag{5}$$

For the sake of simplicity, in the sequel we denote $E[m, r]$ simply by $E[m]$.

2.2 Operations over Paillier Encrypted Data

As stated above, the Paillier cryptosystem allows implementing linear operations. It can however be used so as to compute multiplications, divisions and comparisons with the help of two non-colluding semi-honest servers P_1 and P_2.

– Multiplication operator in Paillier encrypted domain $Mul_e^{P_1, P_2}(.;.)$
  Let us consider two messages a and b and their respective Paillier encrypted versions $E[a]$ and $E[b]$ obtained with the user public key K_p. In order to compute $E[a \times b]$ without revealing any information about a and b, one can take advantage of blinding and of two servers P_1 and P_2. Assuming that P_1 possesses $(E[a], E[b])$, the objective is that P_2 returns $E[a \times b]$ to P_1 while ensuring that no clues about a and b are revealed to P_1 and P_2. Under the hypothesis P_2 knows the user secret key K_s and that it does not collude with P_1, this objective can be reach according to the following procedure we will refer as $Mul_e^{P_1, P_2}(a; b)$:
  1. *Data randomization* - P_1 firstly randomizes $E[a]$ and $E[b]$ such that

$$a' = E[a] \times E[r_a] = E[a + r_a] \tag{6}$$
$$b' = E[b] \times E[r_b] = E[b + r_b] \tag{7}$$

  where r_a and r_b are two random numbers only known from P_1 and uniformly chosen in $\mathbb{Z}_{K_p}$. Then P_1 sends a' and b' to P_2.
  2. *Multiplication computation phase* - On its side, using the user private key K_s, P_2 decrypts a' and b' and multiplies the result

$$M = (a + r_a)(b + r_b) \tag{8}$$

  P_2 next encrypts M into $E[M]$ using the user public key K_p and sends it to P_1.
  3. *Multiplication denoising* - In order to get $E[a \times b]$, P_1 just has to remove the extra-random factors as follow

$$E[a \times b] = E[M] \times E[b]^{-r_a} \times E[a]^{-r_b} \times E[-r_a \times r_b] \qquad (9)$$

– Division operator in Paillier encrypted domain: $Div_e^{P_1,P_2}(.;.)$
  Different ways, based on two servers, have been proposed so as to compute
  the division. The one used in this paper works as follows [19]. Let us consider
  P_1 has an encrypted message $E[a]$ and that it wants to divide a by d. At this
  time d can be encrypted or not, that is to say known or unknown from P_1.
  Again, we don't want P_1 and P_2 to learn details about a. The computation of
  $E[a/d]$ from $E[a]$ and d is also based on blinding. As above, it is assumed that
  P_2 possesses the decryption key K_s. Our division operation $Div_e^{P_1,P_2}(a;d)$ is
  thus a procedure defined as

  1. *Data blinding* - P_1 randomly chooses a number $r \in \mathbb{Z}_{K_p}$ and computes
  $E[z] = E[a + r] = E[a]E[r]$. P_1 then sends $E[z]$ to P_2.
  2. *Division computation* - P_2 decrypts $E[z]$ with the user private key K_s
  and computes $c = z/d$. P_2 encrypts the division result $E[c]$ and sends it
  to P_1.
  3. *Division denoising* - P_1 computes $E[a/d]$ such as:

$$E[a/d] = E[c] \times E[-r/d]. \qquad (10)$$

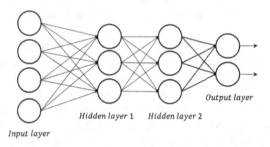

Fig. 2. Example of MultiLayer perceptron (MLP)

2.3 Multilayer Perceptron (MLP)

The common architecture of a MLP is given in Fig. 2. It is constituted of perceptrons organized in different layers: the input and the output layers and, in-
between them, a given number of hidden layers (two in the given example of
Fig. 2). The first layer takes as input the user data set $X = \{x_n\}_{n=1...N}$ where
each vector $x_n = \{x_n(1), x_n(2), ..., x_n(q)\}$ represents the nth training vector with
q the number of perceptron inputs. The output layer provides the class of the
input data t'_n (i.e. $MLP(x_n) = t'_n$ where $MLP(.)$ refers to the function that
computes the output of the network).

A perceptron is a classifier that maps its input to an output value, for example the output of the ith perceptron of the lth layer is given as Z:

$$Z = A_i^l(N_i^l) = A_i^l(\sum_j W_{j,i}^{l-1}.A_j^{l-1})$$ (11)

where $W_{j,i}^{l-1}$ denotes the weight between the jth perceptron in layer $l-1$ and the ith perceptron in layer l. $A_i^l()$ is the activation function of the ith perceptron of the lth layer. Notice that many activation functions have been proposed (e.g. Sigmoid, Tanh, ReLU). In this work, we opted for the rectified linear unit (ReLU) activation function, one of the most used function due to its accuracy and its efficiency [11]. Another reason is that it can be secured by means of homomorphic operators. We will come back in details on this point in Sect. 3. ReLU is defined such as

$$A(y) = \begin{cases} y & \text{if} \quad y \geq 0 \\ 0 \text{ otherwise} \end{cases}$$ (12)

To make such a MLP scheme operational, it should be trained so as to find the perceptron weight values. This training can be supervised or unsupervised. In the former case, the classes of data the MLP should distinguished are *a priori* known. Thus to train a MLP scheme, the user provides labeled data $T = \{t_n\}_{n=1...N}$ where N is the size of the training set and t_n indicates the label of the nth training input data x_n. In the second case, the perceptron identifies by itself the different classes of data. The solution we proposed in this work is trained on labeled data.

The supervised training of NN relies on two phases that are iteratively applied: the feed-forward and the back-propagation phases. Before starting the first feed-forward phase, all perceprons' weights are initialized with random values, for instance. Then training data are provided as input to the MLP. By next, the error between the original label and the ones computed by the MLP is calculated using an objective function (called also cost function) (e.g. cross entropy, Mean Square Error, Minkowski distance). This error is then used in the back-propagation phase, so as to update all perceptrons' weights applying gradient descent. Once weights updated, a new feed-forward starts using the same labeled data.

Many solutions have been proposed so as to decide when to stop the training phase [7]. Among these conditions, one can fix a number of iterations ("aka epochs"): the MLP will stop once a number of epochs have elapsed. An alternative stands in thresholding the training set Mean Squared Error (MSE) (i.e. MSE between the training set labels and the MLP outputs). The smaller MSE, the network better performs. Thus the training stops when MSE is smaller than a given threshold value. Instead, it has been proposed to use the Training Set Accuracy; that is the number of correctly classified data over the total number of data in the training set for an epoch. In this work, we opted for a fix number of iterations.

Once a MLP model or scheme trained, i.e. once the perceptrons' weights known, it can be used so as to classify new data. This classification process simply consists in applying the feed-forward phase with new data as input, considering that the MLP output will give the data class.

3   Secure Multilayer Perceptron

3.1   General Framework and System Architecture

The general framework we consider in this work is given in Fig. 1, where a user outsourced into the cloud Paillier encrypted data; data on which the user wants the cloud service provider to train our secure multilayer perceptron (SMLP). Once trained, this SMLP will be used by the user so as to classify new data. The user will also send it encrypted to the cloud. In our view, the data, the classification data result as well as all the parameters of the SMLP should be unknown from the cloud. As it can be seen in Fig. 1 and as we will see in the sequel, the computations of both the SMLP training and classification phases are distributed over two servers, P_1 and P_2, of two distinct cloud service providers. We consider them as honest but curious [14]. More clearly, they will try to infer information about the data, the classification results as well as about the SMLP parameters. In our scenario, P_1 interacts with the user, stores and handles his data. P_2 cooperates with P_1 so as to conduct some operations (division, multiplication, etc. ...) involved into the training or classification phases of ours MLP.

3.2   Proposed Secure Multilayer Perceptron

Securing a multilayer perceptron consists in implementing the feed-forward and back-propagation phases over encrypted data. The MLP that we propose to secure, both in its learning and classification phase, is based on: (i) perceptrons, the activation function of which ReLU, (ii) the mean squared error (MSE) as cost function. The secure version of this MLP, we describe it in the following, works with the Paillier cryptosystem and takes advantage of the above two servers based system architecture so as to exploit the secure multiplication and division operators depicted in Sect. 2. As we will see, different issues have to be overcome in order to ensure the convergence of such a Secure MLP. In particular, we propose a new "Max" function operator so as to secure ReLU.

Secure MLP Feed-Forward Phase. The feed-forward phase consists in calculating the MLP output for a given input. Based on the fact a MLP is constituted of different layers of perceptrons, securing the feed-forward phase relies on securing each perceptron independently. As seen in Sect. 2, the ith perceptron in the lth layer performs a weighted sum of the input vector $\{A_j^{l-1}(N_j^{l-1})\}_{j=1...S}$ where S is the number of perceptron in the $l-1$ layer (see Eq. (11)), the result of which is provided to an activation function (see Eq. (12)). Considering that all pieces of information provided by the user are Paillier encrypted, i.e. $\{E[A_j^{l-1}(N_j^{l-1})]\}_{i=1...S}$, the weighted sum in the encrypted domain becomes:

$$E[N_i^l] = \prod_{i=0}^{n} Mul_e^{P_1,P_2}(E[W_{j,i}^{l-1}], E[A_j^{l-1}(N_j^{l-1})]) \tag{13}$$

where P_1 and P_2 are the two independent servers (see Fig. 1), $E[N_i^l]$ is the secure weighted sum and $\{E[W_{j,i}^{l-1}]\}_{j=1...n}$ the encrypted perceptron weights which are also confidential.

In this computation as well as in all others, one important constraint to consider stands on the fact that the Paillier cryptosystem only works with plain-text and cipher-text constituted of positive integers in $\mathbb{Z}_{K_p}$. More clearly, all data and parameters of the SMLP should be represented by integers. To overcome this issue, taking as example the input data, these ones are turned into integer values by scaling and quantizing them as follow

$$X = [Qx] \tag{14}$$

where $[.]$ is the rounding function and Q is an expansion or scaling factor. Beyond, even if the SMLP parameters and inputs are integers, their processing may lead to negative values. In order to represent such values in $\mathbb{Z}_{K_p}$, integer values greater than $(K_p+1)/2$ will correspond to negative values and the others to positive values.

By next, the secure perceptron's output is computed by applying a secure version of the ReLU activation function to the encrypted weighted sum $E[N_i^l]$. One key issue to overcome in securing ReLU (see Eq. (12)) stands in the calculation of the function $Max(a,b)$ in-between two integer values a and b in the Paillier encrypted domain. Different solutions have been proposed so as to securely compare encrypted data [4,10,13,20]. Most of them are based on blinding and two non-colluding parties. However, with all these approaches, the comparison result is provided in a clear form. More clearly, if P_1 asks P_2 to compare $E[a]$ and $E[b]$, P_1 will know if $E[a]$ is or not greater than $E[b]$. In our framework, this leads to an information leak. Indeed, P_1 is not authorized to get some information about the SMLP parameters. To solve this problem, the authors of [15] propose a protocol so as to compare two input values in a secure distributed fashion between two or more participants using the Paillier cryptosystem and secret sharing schemes. However, this scheme has several issues: (i) they consider the public key of the Paillier cyrptosystem as a secret key, a concept in contradiction with the one of public key, (ii) they assume that the computation of the multiplicative inverse of a ciphertext is possible without the knowledge of the public key, which mathematically speaking is not possible. Indeed the inverse is defined in the multiplicative group $\mathbb{Z}_{K_p}^*$ where K_p is the public key of Paillier cryptosystem; (iii) they compute the multiplication in the Paillier cryptosystem domain without explaining "how" the Paillier cryptosystem is homomorphically additive. In this work, we propose a novel comparison operator $Comp_e^{P_1,P_2}$ which overcomes these issues. Its output is encrypted and it will be used so as to compute $Max_e^{P_1,P_2}$ operator in our secure version of ReLu. $Comp_e^{P_1,P_2}$ works accordingly two steps:

– *Data randomization.* The objective of this step is to apply blinding to data P_1 will send to P_2. To do so, and as given in [15], P_1 selects two random values r and r' from $\mathbb{Z}_{K_p}$ such that r is significantly greater than r' ($r >> r'$) and that it verifies the constraint

$$log_2(K_p) > log_2(r) + l + 2 \tag{15}$$

where l is the number of bits used to encode the input. Then, P_1 computes

$$E[r(a - b) - r'] = (E[a]E[b]^{-1})^r \times E[r']^{-1} \tag{16}$$

and sends the result to P_2.
- *Secure comparison.* P_2 decrypts the data and compare them to 0 and sends an encrypted bit i such as:

$$Comp_e^{P_1,P_2}(E[a], E[b]) = E[i] = \begin{cases} E[1] & if \quad r(a - b) - r' > 0 \\ E[0] & if \quad else \end{cases} \tag{17}$$

Then P_2 sends $E[i]$ to P_1.
Based on $Comp_e^{P_1,P_2}(E[a], E[b])$, P_1 can compute the $Max_e^{P_1,P_2}$ operator $Max_e^{P_1,P_2}(E[a], E[b])$:

$$Max_e^{P_1,P_2}(E[a], E[b]) = E[max(a, b)]$$
$$= Mul_e^{P_1,P_2}(E[a]E[b]^{-1}, E[i]) \times E[b]$$

$$= E[i(a - b) + b] = \begin{cases} E[a] & if \quad i = 1 \\ E[b] & if \quad i = 0 \end{cases} \tag{18}$$

With $Comp_e^{P_1,P_2}(E[a], E[b])$, P_1 accesses to the encrypted version of the maximum value between two integers without knowing which value is greater than the other one. Such a security level is achieved based on fact the Paillier cryptosystem uses random values which multiply after each multiplication (i.e. $E[a, r_1]E[b, r_2] = E[a + b, r_1 r_2]$ - see Sect. 2). Finally, based on the $Max_e^{P_1,P_2}$ operator, the output of our secure ReLU based perceptron is given by:

$$E[max(0, y)] = Max_e^{P_1,P_2}(E[0], E[y]) \tag{19}$$

Based on this results, a secure MLP is based on secure perceptron layers.

Secure Back-Propagation Phase. As stated in Sect. 3, the objective of the back-propagation phase is to update the MLP weights of each perceptron. In the supervised mode, for a given input, one computes the error between the MLP output and the input data label according to an objective or cost function. In this work, the Mean Square Error (MSE) is used. Then, the MLP weights are updated so as to minimize this function.

Let us consider a MLP network composed of M_L layers (see Fig. 2) and an *a priori* known vector input data x_n along with its label t_n. If t'_n corresponds to the MLP output (see Fig. 2), then the error e_n in the clear domain is such that

$$e_n = MSE(t'_n, t_n) = ||t'_n - t_n||_2^2. \tag{20}$$

This cost function can be expressed in the Paillier encrypted domain by

$$E[e_n] = Mul_e^{P_1,P_2}(E[t'_n - t_n], E[t'_n - t_n]) \tag{21}$$

Let us recall, that in our framework, P_1 holds $E[t'_n]$ and $E[t_n]$. It computes $E[t'_n - t_n]$ thanks to the homomorphic Paillier properties, and interacts with P_2 so as to compute $E[e_n] = Mul_e^{P_1,P_2}(E[t'_n - t_n], E[t'_n - t_n])$.

Once the error computed e_n, the next step stands in back propagating it so as to update the MLP weights of each perceptron. This update is based on the descent gradient. The updated value of a MLP weight $w_{i,j}^l$ is given by

$$w_{i,j}^l = w_{i,j}^l - \frac{1}{\lambda^{-1}} \frac{\partial e_n}{\partial w_{i,j}^l} \tag{22}$$

where: $w_{i,j}^l$ represents the weight between the ith perceptron in layer l and the jth perceptron in layer $l + 1$; λ is the learning rate factor.

The descent gradient can be computed with the help of the chain rule algorithm so as to calculate all partial derivatives, even those of intermediary layers. According to this algorithm, the gradient is given as

$$\frac{\partial e_n}{\partial w_{i,j}^l} = N_i^l . \delta_j^{l+1} \tag{23}$$

δ_j^{l+1} is the fraction of the network error that is caused by the jth perceptron in the layer $l + 1$. The computation of the error depends on the location of the perceptron in the network and is such as

$$\delta_i^l = \begin{cases} A_i'(t'_n(i))(t_n(i) - t'_n(i)) & if \quad l = M_L \\ A_i'(N_i^l) \sum_j w_{i,j}^l \delta_j^{l+1} & if \quad l = M_L \end{cases} \tag{24}$$

where $A_i(.)$ is the activation function of the ith perceptron and t_n denotes the label of the data placed at the input of the MLP. Notice that, derivate of the ReLU function is $A_i'(y) = 1_{(y>0)}$, where $1_{(.)}$ represents the unit step function the value of which is zero for negative input or one, otherwise. The same update operation in the encrypted domain becomes

$$E[w_{i,j}^l] = E[w_{i,j}^l] Div_e^{P_1,P_2}(E[\frac{\partial e_n}{\partial w_{i,j}^l}], \lambda) \tag{25}$$

The back-propagation phase in the encrypted domain can be easily derived

$$E[\frac{\partial e_n}{\partial w_{i,j}^l}] = Mul_e^{P_1,P_2}(E[N_i^l], E[\delta_j^{l+1}]) \tag{26}$$

where

$$E[\delta_i^l] = \begin{cases} Mul_e^{P_1,P_2}(E[A_i'(t'_n(i))]E[(t_n(i) - t'_n(i))]) & if \quad l = M_L \\ Mul_e^{P_1,P_2}(E[A_i'(N_i^l)], \prod_j Mul_e^{P_1,P_2}(E[w_{i,j}^l], E[\delta_j^{l+1}])) & if \quad l = M_L \end{cases} \tag{27}$$

It is important to underline that the encrypted version of the unit step function $E[1_{(y>0)}]$ is equivalent to $E[1_{(y>0)}] = Comp_e^{P_1,P_2}(E[0], E[y])$.

By iteratively applying the secure feed-forward and back-propagation phases, it is possible to train our SMLP without compromising the security of the input data, of the SMLP parameters and of its output. It is the same when classifying new data.

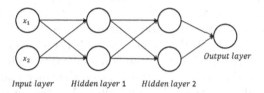

Fig. 3. SMLP architecture used to learning the AND function

4 Experimental Results and Security Analysis

The proposed SMLP solution has been implemented so as to learn the $And - Logic$ function in a supervised training mode. This function takes as input two real numbers x_1 and x_2 in the interval $[0, 1]$ and its output is a binary value such that:

$$y = [x_1]AND[x_2] \tag{28}$$

where $[.]$ denotes the rounding function.

4.1 Dataset and MLP Architecture

The training data set is constituted of 10000 lines of three columns each, where each line represents a training input sample. The first two columns contain two real values between 0.0 and 1.0, while the last column contains their AND value.

Figure 3 provides the architecture of the implemented SMLP. It is composed of an input layer and of two hidden layers, both containing two perceptrons, followed by an output layer of one perceptron. As stated above, the network is based on our secure ReLU activation function (see Sect. 3). In all following tests, the expansion factor Q was fixed to 10^6 so as to ensure the SMLP works with integer values with a training phase limited to 100 epochs and 8000 samples of the training data set are used for the learning phase and the 2000 other for the testing phase. The expected result is that, upon the entry of two values contained between 0.0 and 1.0, the activation of the output layer after feed-forward contains the value of the AND between the two inputs, that is, either 0 or 1.

4.2 Secure MLP Performance

The performance of our secure MLP, which is expressed in terms of classification accuracy and also convergence, depends on the learning rate. Precision is the number of correct predictions made divided by the total number of predictions made. We recall that the learning rate factor λ plays a critical role in the convergence of the network. Indeed, it influences the modification step in the weights update in the back-propagation phase (see Sect. 3). We tested several λ values in the range $[10^{-12}; 10^{-4}]$. We give in Table 1, the precision of our SMLP in average after 10 tries, and if yes or no it has converged after the training. It can be seen that SMLP converges for values of λ smaller than $\lambda = 10^{-8}$. We thus recommend taking initial weights distributed in the range $[10^{-5}, 10^5]$ and a learning rate factor $\lambda = 10^{-10}$.

Table 1. Convergence and precision of our SMLP for different learning rate factor values

λ	10^{-12}	10^{-10}	10^{-8}	10^{-6}	10^{-4}
Convergence (Y/N)/Accuracy	Yes/72%	Yes/83%	Yes/93.1%	No	No

We also have trained the equivalent MLP in the clear domain under the same conditions with a learning rate factor of 0.005 and 100 epochs. The obtained MLP precision is about 98.3% with of course no convergence issues. It can be seen based on Table 1, that SMLP always provides lower performance. This can be explained by the use of an expansion factor so as to convert real values into integer values. Anyway, these results show that it is possible to train a MLP in a secure outsourced way.

4.3 Security Analysis Under the Semi-honest Model

The following analysis considers the semi-honest cloud adversary model as presented in Sect. 3. Due to the fact all data (i.e. input data and SMLP parameters) are encrypted with the Paillier cryptosystem the security of which has been demonstrated in [16], the security of the feed-forward and back-propagation phases stand on the security of the operators $Mul_e^{P_1,P_2}(.)$, $Div_e^{P_1,P_2}(.)$ and $Comp_e^{P_1,P_2}(.)$.

- Security of $Mul_e^{P_1,P_2}(.)$ - As shown in Sect. 2, $Mul_e^{P_1,P_2}(E[a], E[b])$ relies on a data blinding operation. P_1 applies on $E[a]$ and $E[b]$ to compute $E[a \times b]$. To do so, P_1 generates two random values r_a and r_b from $\mathbb{Z}_{K_p}$ and computes $E[a + r_a]$ and $E[b + r_b]$. P_2 decrypts by next these values. Since r_a and r_b are randomly chosen in $\mathbb{Z}_{K_p}$ and only known from P_1, they give no clues to P_2 regarding a and b.
- Security of $Div_e^{P_1,P_2}(.)$ - We let the reader refer to [19], where Thijs Veugen proved the security of the operator $Div_e^{P_1,P_2}(.)$.

- Security of $Comp_e^{P_1,P_2}(.)$ and consequently of $Max_e^{P_1,P_2}(.,.)$ – As explained in Sect. 3, $Max_e^{P_1,P_2}(E[a], E[b]) = E[max(a,b)]$ depends on the $Comp_e^{P_1,P_2}(;)$ operator. Let us consider P_1 possesses the couple $(E[a], E[b])$ and that he wants to compute $Max_e^{P_1,P_2}(E[a], E[b])$. To do so, it computes $E[r(a-b) - r']$ where r and r' are chosen uniformly from $\mathbb{Z}_{K_p}$ under the constraint that $r >> r'$. P_2 accesses to $r(a-b) - r'$ from which it cannot deduce any information about a and b nor about $a - b$ since it does not know r and r'. P_2 compares this value to zero. This comparison gives not more information to P_2. By next, in order to avoid that P_1 knows the comparison result, P_2 encrypts using the user public key the bit 0 or 1 (see Sect. 3) and it sends it to P_1. P_1 can derive the results of the function $Max_e^{P_1,P_2}(E[a], E[b])$, because all these computations are conducted over encrypted data, P_1 has no idea about a, b and $Max(a, b)$.

The rest of the computations (e.g. MSE, error derivatives) are based on either encrypted or randomized data. As consequence, if P_1 and P_2 do not collude, no information related to the user data or to the SMLP model is disclosed. Since all operations involved in the computation of the feed-forward and back-propagation phases are in cascade, then according to the sequential Composition theorem [12], SMLP is completely secure under the semi-honest model.

5   Conclusion

In this paper, we have proposed a new Secure Multilayer Perceptron (SMLP) which can be deployed in the cloud. Its main originality, compared to actual homomorphic encryption based SMLP schemes, is that it can be trained with homomorphically encrypted data with no extra communications between the user and the servers. With this scheme, all data; input data and SMLP output and parameters, are encrypted. Our SMLP is based on: an original secure version of the $Max(.,.)$ function we propose, the result of which is encrypted and a ReLU activation function secured with no linear approximation. Such a SMLP has been implemented so as to learn or model the AND function in-between real values. Experimental results demonstrate that SMLP converges in its training phase under some parameter initialization constraints. Beyond the complexity of our SMLP, which is based on homomorphic encryption, these preliminary results are very encouraging.

References

1. Aono, Y., Hayashi, T., Wang, L., Moriai, S., et al.: Privacy-preserving deep learning via additively homomorphic encryption. IEEE Trans. Inf. Forensics Secur. **13**(5), 1333–1345 (2018)
2. Bellafqira, R., Coatrieux, G., Bouslimi, D., Quellec, G.: Content-based image retrieval in homomorphic encryption domain. In: 2015 37th Annual International Conference of the IEEE Engineering in Medicine and Biology Society (EMBC), pp. 2944–2947. IEEE (2015)
3. Bellafqira, R., Coatrieux, G., Bouslimi, D., Quellec, G.: An end to end secure CBIR over encrypted medical database. In: 2016 IEEE 38th Annual International Conference of the Engineering in Medicine and Biology Society (EMBC), pp. 2537–2540. IEEE (2016)

4. Bellafqira, R., Coatrieux, G., Bouslimi, D., Quellec, G., Cozic, M.: Proxy re-encryption based on homomorphic encryption. In: Proceedings of the 33rd Annual Computer Security Applications Conference, pp. 154–161. ACM (2017)
5. Bost, R., Popa, R.A., Tu, S., Goldwasser, S.: Machine learning classification over encrypted data. In: NDSS (2015)
6. Bouslimi, D., Bellafqira, R., Coatrieux, G.: Data hiding in homomorphically encrypted medical images for verifying their reliability in both encrypted and spatial domains. In: 2016 IEEE 38th Annual International Conference of the Engineering in Medicine and Biology Society (EMBC), pp. 2496–2499. IEEE (2016)
7. Castellano, G., Fanelli, A.M.: Variable selection using neural-network models. Neurocomputing 31(1), 1–13 (2000)
8. Chabanne, H., de Wargny, A., Milgram, J., Morel, C., Prouff, E.: Privacy-preserving classification on deep neural network. IACR Cryptol. ePrint Archive 2017, 35 (2017)
9. Decencière, E., et al.: TeleOphta: machine learning and image processing methods for teleophthalmology. IRBM 34(2), 196–203 (2013)
10. Ding, W., Yan, Z., Deng, R.H.: Encrypted data processing with homomorphic re-encryption. Inf. Sci. 409, 35–55 (2017)
11. Glorot, X., Bordes, A., Bengio, Y.: Deep sparse rectifier neural networks. In: Proceedings of the Fourteenth International Conference on Artificial Intelligence and Statistics, pp. 315–323 (2011)
12. Goldreich, O.: Foundations of Cryptography. Basic Applications, vol. 2. Cambridge University Press, New York (2009)
13. Hsu, C.Y., Lu, C.S., Pei, S.C.: Image feature extraction in encrypted domain with privacy-preserving sift. IEEE Trans. Image Process. 21(11), 4593–4607 (2012)
14. Huang, Y., Evans, D., Katz, J., Malka, L.: Faster secure two-party computation using garbled circuits. In: USENIX Security Symposium, vol. 201 (2011)
15. Kerschbaum, F., Biswas, D., de Hoogh, S.: Performance comparison of secure comparison protocols. In: 20th International Workshop on Database and Expert Systems Application, pp. 133–136. IEEE (2009)
16. Paillier, P.: Public-key cryptosystems based on composite degree residuosity classes. In: Stern, J. (ed.) EUROCRYPT 1999. LNCS, vol. 1592, pp. 223–238. Springer, Heidelberg (1999). https://doi.org/10.1007/3-540-48910-X_16
17. Schlitter, N.: A protocol for privacy preserving neural network learning on horizontal partitioned data. In: PSD (2008)
18. Shokri, R., Shmatikov, V.: Privacy-preserving deep learning. In: Proceedings of the 22nd ACM SIGSAC conference on computer and communications security, pp. 1310–1321. ACM (2015)
19. Veugen, T.: Encrypted integer division. In: 2010 IEEE International Workshop on Information Forensics and Security (WIFS), pp. 1–6. IEEE (2010)
20. Wu, F., Zhong, H., Shi, R., Huang, H.: Secure two-party computation of the quadratic function's extreme minimal value. In: 2012 9th International Conference on Fuzzy Systems and Knowledge Discovery (FSKD), pp. 2975–2978. IEEE (2012)
21. Xie, P., Bilenko, M., Finley, T., Gilad-Bachrach, R., Lauter, K., Naehrig, M.: Crypto-nets: Neural networks over encrypted data. arXiv preprint arXiv:1412.6181 (2014)
22. Zheng, S., et al.: Asynchronous stochastic gradient descent with delay compensation. arXiv preprint arXiv:1609.08326 (2016)

Surveillance Video Authentication Using Universal Image Quality Index of Temporal Average

Sondos Fadl[1,2]([⊠]), Qi Han[1]([⊠]), and Qiong Li[1]

[1] School of Computer Science and Technology, Harbin Institute of Technology,
Harbin, China
qi.han@hit.edu.cn
[2] Faculty of Computers and Information, Menoufia University,
Menofia, Egypt
sondos.magdy@ci.menofia.edu.eg

Abstract. Inter-frame forgery is a common type of surveillance video forgery where a tampered process occurs in a temporal domain such as frame deletion, insertion, and shuffling. However, there are a number of methods that have been proposed for detecting this type of tampering, most of the methods have been found to be deficient in terms of either accuracy or running time. In this paper, a new approach is proposed as an efficient method for detecting frame deletion, insertion, and shuffling attacks. Firstly, the video is extracted into frames and the temporal average for each non-overlapping subsequence of frames is computed for examination instead of exhaustive checking which can be reduced the running time. Then, the universal image quality index is used for detecting the inter-frame forgery and determining its location. The experimental results show the efficiency of the proposed method for detecting inter-frame forgery with high accuracy and low running time.

Keywords: Passive forensics · Inter-frame forgery detection ·
Temporal average · Universal image quality index

1 Introduction

Video surveillance systems are widely used for controlling crimes. The availability of video editing tools has made the work of editing to be very easy. On the other hand, some people misuse these tools to change events by inserting, deleting, or shuffling a sequence of video frames to destroy the evidence. This forces the necessity of verifying the authenticity and integrity of a surveillance video especially if it is used as an evidence in the court. However, more efforts have been spent on detecting image forgeries compared with video forgeries; the challenges of video forensics compared with image forensics are a large number of data to be examined based on the spatial and temporal domain which need to high computational time.

© Springer Nature Switzerland AG 2019
C. D. Yoo et al. (Eds.): IWDW 2018, LNCS 11378, pp. 337–350, 2019.
https://doi.org/10.1007/978-3-030-11389-6_25

In [11,12], video forgeries have been classified into two types of attacks: (1) Intra-frame forgeries, these attacks are done in either spatial or spatio-temporal domain, such as region splicing (where foreign regions from one video are composited into the original video to modify its content) and copy-move (where portions of a frame are copied and pasted into other locations in the same frame or where particular regions from a sequence of frames are copied and pasted into another sequence in the same video); and (2) Inter-frame forgeries, these attacks are done in temporal domain, such as duplication (where a clip is copied and pasted into another location in the same video), insertion (where a foreign clip is inserted into the original video), deletion (where some of the frames are deleted), and shuffling (where the order of some frames is changed to change the order of events). Inter-frame forgery is commonly used in surveillance videos because of its convenience and imperceptibility.

Forged video can be examined by active techniques such as digital watermarking or media fingerprints [1,2,6,10] and passive detection techniques [8,16,18]. Digital watermark and fingerprint are not available making passive detection techniques (use statistical information) dominant.

Wang et al. extracted the discontinuity points using the optical flow variation sequence to detect anomalies and identify the inter-frame based forgery [17]. Their method requires a high computational time because of the optical flow estimations. Zheng et al. used block-wise brightness variance descriptor for detecting frame deletion and insertion, but it has a low precision rate in the localization of forgery [23]. Liu et al. used zernike opponent chromaticity moments (ZOCM) and a coarseness feature analysis. Then, abnormal points were extracted based on the difference in ZOCM among adjacent frames [5]. Their method used Tamura Coarse feature analysis to reduce false positives which increases the method's precision, but also increases the execution time. Zhao et al. used Hue-Saturation-Value (HSV) color histogram comparison to detect tampered frames in a shot. Then, Speeded Up Robust Features (SURF) feature extraction and Fast Library for Approximate Nearest Neighbors matching (FLANN) were used for double-checking [22]. Their method has a high accuracy, but requires high computational time; besides it fails to detect a deleted shot which has a small number of frames.

Ulutas et al. used the Bag-of-Words (BoW) model to detect the forged videos [15]. Their method can only detect duplication forgery type and fails in other types. Fadl et al. [4] used discrete cosine transform coefficients (DCT) as features for the residual frames to detect the tampered clips. Their method detects the duplicated clips only and fails in other forgeries. In [14], the authors used binary features of frames and determined the similarity among them; their method detects duplication forgery only.

Most of the current inter-frame forensics techniques are based on the exhaustive examination of the spatial and temporal properties among video frames. Hence, checking all frames in spatial and temporal domains is computationally expensive. In this paper, we detect inter-frame (deletion, insertion, and shuffling) forgery with high accuracy and low running time. The proposed method detects inconsistencies using image quality measurements for the average images of non-overlapping subsequence frames instead of entire frames.

The rest of this paper is organized as follows: In Sect. 2, some related works are briefly reviewed. The proposed method is detailed in Sect. 3. We present the experimental results in Sect. 4 and conclude this paper in Sect. 5.

2   Related Works

2.1   Temporal Average

In the field of digital video forensics, most of the previous methods have not achieved high accuracy and low running time simultaneously. So, if we have a sequence of images, and we want to collect these images in one image for reducing the number of comparisons and reducing the processing time. One way to determine the collected image is an average of images which called temporal average (TP). It can be described for N number of images as

$$TP = \frac{1}{N} \sum_{i=1}^{N} F_i, \tag{1}$$

where each point in the TP image is the average of points in the same positions in each of the image F. The result of TP image shows the background with a pale version of a moving object, as shown in Fig. 1. The pale version of the object occurs when the image brightness is affected by its movements, but the object is still there. If we use more images, then the presence of the object will become much pallid. TP has been used in many application of computer vision such as moving object detection and background estimation [7]. In this paper, TP is used to detect inter-frame forgeries for the first time in the literature.

2.2   Image Quality Measure

Image quality measure is an important field in image processing that is used for many applications such as compression, de-noising and so on. It can be classified into two types: full-reference, and no-reference [20, 21]. In the first type, the comparison between the reference image (original image) and the distorted image (tested image) is required, meaning that the reference image must be known. In the second type, the reference image is not available and not required.

In this paper, we focus on the full-reference image quality assessment, considering that the reference and tested images are two adjacent TP images in the video. There are two classes of quality assessment techniques: mathematically techniques and human visual system based techniques. Mathematically methods are attractive because they are easy to calculate, have low computational time and independent of viewing conditions [20]. We use the universal image quality index (UQI) which has been proposed by Bovik et al. [19] to detect inter-frame forgeries.

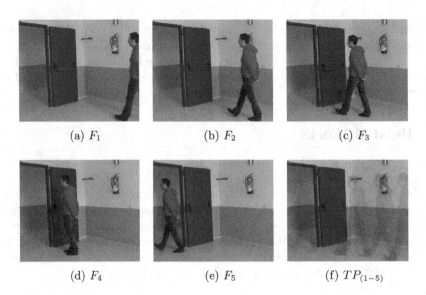

(a) F_1 (b) F_2 (c) F_3

(d) F_4 (e) F_5 (f) $TP_{(1-5)}$

Fig. 1. An example of the temporal average for the sequence of images.

UQI. Assume x and y are the original and test images with the same size $(m \times n)$, the quality index Q can be described as:

$$Q = \frac{4\sigma_{xy}\mu_x\mu_y}{(\sigma_x^2 + \sigma_y^2)(\mu_x^2 + \mu_y^2)}, \tag{2}$$

where μ, σ^2 represent the average of pixels and the variance of each x and y; σ_{xy} is the covariance of x and y. They can be described as follows:

$$\mu_x = \frac{1}{m \times n}\sum_{i=1}^{m}\sum_{j=1}^{n}x_{ij}, \qquad \mu_y = \frac{1}{m \times n}\sum_{i=1}^{m}\sum_{j=1}^{n}y_{ij},$$

$$\sigma_x^2 = \frac{1}{(m \times n) - 1}\sum_{i=1}^{m}\sum_{j=1}^{n}(x_{ij} - \mu_x)^2,$$

$$\sigma_y^2 = \frac{1}{(m \times n) - 1}\sum_{i=1}^{m}\sum_{j=1}^{n}(y_{ij} - \mu_y)^2,$$

and

$$\sigma_{xy} = \frac{1}{(m \times n) - 1}\sum_{i=1}^{m}\sum_{j=1}^{n}(x_{ij} - \mu_x)(y_{ij} - \mu_y).$$

Q is applied to local regions using the sliding window method with size $(b \times b)$. If w is the total number of windows in an image, then the overall Q is given by

$$Q = \frac{1}{w}\sum_{i=1}^{w}Q_i. \tag{3}$$

The output range of Q is $[-1, 1]$, where the best value is 1 which indicates a high similarity between x and y; if the similarity decreases, the value of Q becomes lower.

3 Proposed Method

The proposed method uses image quality measure (UQI) of temporal averages for non-overlapping subsequence frames to detect the inter-frame illegal attacks (i.e. frame deletion, insertion, and shuffling) instead of checking all entire frames for saving the running time. We assume that the digital video has been taken from a surveillance stationary camera with a static background. Firstly, the video is extracted into frames, then TP is computed for each non-overlapping subsequence of frames. UQI of each two adjacent TP images is applied to extract abnormal events as illegal candidates because of video continuity and regularity; if the video is subjected to deletion, insertion or shuffling, the similarity will become lower and Q values at the border of the tampered clip will become lower than others. Finally, the locations of inter-frame attack are determined by the least Q value of corresponding frames of TP candidates and their neighbors. The steps of our proposed will be illustrated in the next subsections.

3.1 TP Candidate Selection

The input video is extracted into frames as $F = \{F_i | i = 1, 2, \ldots, N_f\}$. Then, F is divided into non-overlapping subsequences with size N (e.g. if the size of each subsequence is N, the first subsequence starts from 1 to N, the second starts from $N + 1$ to 2N, the third starts from $2N + 1$ to 3N, and so on.), and TP is calculated for each subsequence by Eq.(1) as $TP = \{TP_i | i = 1, 2, \ldots, (N_f/N)\}$.

According to Eqs.(2) and (3), Q of each two adjacent TPs is computed (where $x = TP_i$ and $y = TP_{i+1}$) as $Q = \{Q_i | i = 1, 2, \ldots, (N_f/N) - 1\}$. If $|mean(Q) - min(Q)|$ is less than a threshold T_{shf}, frame shuffling is detected; if it is less than a threshold T_{del}, frame deletion is detected; if it is less than a threshold T_{ins}, frame insertion is detected. For each Q_i, if its value is less than a threshold τ ($\tau = min(Q)/c$), the corresponding TP_i is selected as a forged candidate (where c is a small constant between 0.95 and 1 to make sure that the selection points have the minimum values of Q). According to persistence phenomenon of human vision [23] and the number of frames that have a small variation with short time intervals such 0.4 s, we assume $N = 10$ in our schema to achieve simultaneously high accuracy with low execution time. It is noticed the value of N should be ($N > 1$ and $N \leq N_f/3$) to make sure that the proposed method works well because the number of comparisons must be greater than 2 to detect the abnormal measure, and the number of frames of TP should be greater than 1 to achieve our proposed for reducing time. Figure 2 illustrates the diagram of calculating Q values for TP candidates selection.

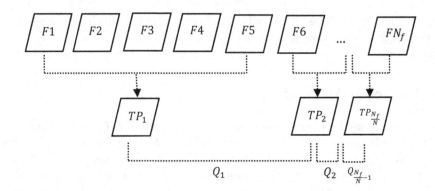

Fig. 2. An illustration for TP candidates selection.

3.2 Determination of Attack Location

After TP candidates selection, a further analysis is necessary to determine the attack locations. The corresponding frames of the selected TP_i, and its neighbors are grouped in S_F as:

$$S_F = \begin{cases} F(TP_i, TP_{i+1}), & \text{if } i = 1 \\ F(TP_{i-1}, TP_i, TP_{i+1}), & \text{if } i > 1 \text{ and } i \le (N_f/N) - 1 \end{cases} \quad (4)$$

Then, Q values are computed among each two adjacent frames in S_F using Eqs.(2) and (3). Attack location is selected as the minimum value of Q.

The abnormal points are detected at the border of the fake clip (i.e. start and end) for shuffling and insertion forgeries; and the start of the deleted clip. Figure 3 shows an example of deletion attack detection; Fig. 3a shows TP candidate selection at 20th; Fig. 3b shows the location of attack at 200th frame. Figure 4 shows an example of insertion attack detection; Fig. 4a shows TP candidates selection at 12th and 17th; Fig. 4b,c show the locations of insertion attack which observed at the beginning and the ending of the inserted clip at the frames 122nd and 172nd. Frame shuffling forgery is the most difficult to detect because its frames are original but they have been put in different times; this process causes distortion of the video regularity; in this paper, we consider shuffling attack to be a flipping. Figure 5 shows an example of shuffling attack detection; Fig. 5a shows TP candidates selection, where the order of frames from 102nd to 145th are changed and TPs are selected at 10th and 14th; Fig. 5b,c show the locations of the beginning and the ending of the shuffled clip at the frames 102nd and 145th. Finally, the block diagram of the proposed method is summarized in Fig. 6.

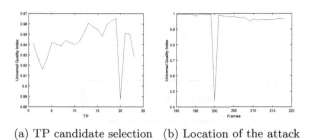

(a) TP candidate selection   (b) Location of the attack

Fig. 3. An example of deletion attack detection.

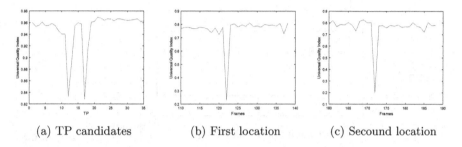

(a) TP candidates   (b) First location   (c) Secound location

Fig. 4. An example of insertion attack detection.

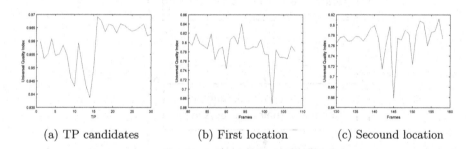

(a) TP candidates   (b) First location   (c) Secound location

Fig. 5. An example of shuffling attack detection.

4   Experimental Results

4.1   Video Dataset

We selected some videos from SULFA [9], LASIESTA [3], and IVYLAB [13] for creating our forgery dataset because of unavailability of a single dataset to detect inter-frame forgeries. It contains 15 tampered videos under deletion, insertion and shuffling forgeries. For example, Fig. 7 shows the original and tampered video from SULFA, where the order of frames from 124th to

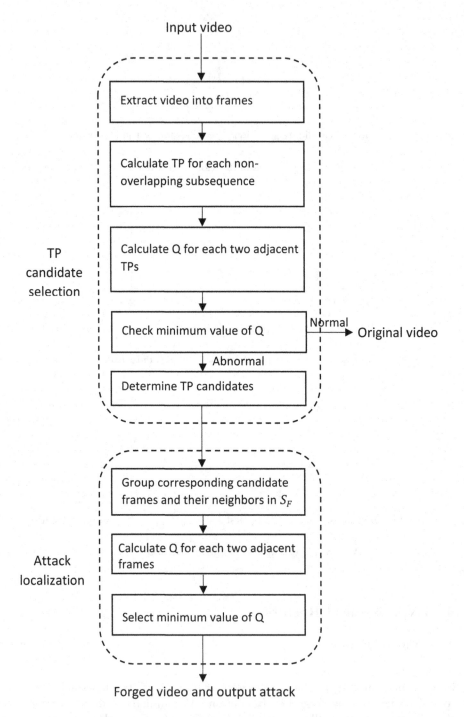

Fig. 6. The block digram of the proposed method.

145th has been changed to change the ball moving direction. Figure 8 shows the original and tampered video from IVYLAB, where the frames from 417th to 536th have been deleted to eliminate the fact that the person climbed to the top floor. Figure 9 shows the original and tampered video from LASI-ESTA, where the foreign frames from 261st to 455th have been inserted into the original video in order to prove that the girl came back again and entered the room. Our test dataset can be available at https://drive.google.com/open?id=1_JAhq0223kMADdZcjWABtenzstvYZqb7; the details of forged videos of our dataset are listed in Table 1.

4.2 Results Analysis

The detection results of the proposed method for all videos in our dataset with execution times are listed in Table 2. The proposed method is able to achieve the detection of inter-frame forgeries with a low running time; the average runtime of each frame is less than 0.03 s. It is noticed that the detection results of our method cannot be affected by weather conditions such as rain (V8), or light conditions (V9); furthermore, it can detect the deleted clip which has a small number of frames such as V3 (five frames have been deleted); these results demonstrate the robustness of our proposed method.

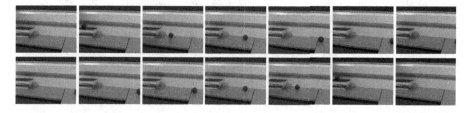

Fig. 7. An example of video from SULFA dataset; original frames in the first row; tampered frames in the second row.

Fig. 8. An example of video from IVYLAB dataset; original frames in the first row; tampered frames in the second row.

Fig. 9. An example of video from LASIESTA dataset; original frames in the first row; tampered frames in the second row.

Table 1. The details of tested videos

Video	Original length	Tampered length	Resolution	fps	Forgery type	Forgery location
V1	319	319	320 × 240	30	shuffling	124–145
V2	321	241	320 × 240	29.97	deletion	107–186
V3	361	355	320 × 240	29.97	deletion	105–110
V4	332	332	320 × 240	29.97	shuffling	75–273
V5	203	203	320 × 240	30	shuffling	85–135
V6	315	510	320 × 240	29.97	insertion	183–377
V7	313	349	320 × 240	29.97	insertion	130–165
V8	1400	1400	352 × 288	30	shuffling	921–989
V9	300	350	352 × 288	30	insertion	21–70
V10	275	470	352 × 288	30	insertion	261–455
V11	350	232	352 × 288	30	deletion	156–273
V12	525	555	352 × 288	30	insertion	406–435
V13	729	648	704 × 576	25	deletion	20–100
V14	708	588	704 × 576	30	deletion	417–536
V15	662	662	704 × 576	30	shuffling	511–600

4.3   Evaluation Metrics

To evaluate the performance of the proposed method, we used precision, recall and $F_1 score$. The precision and recall rates refer to the correctly detected videos among all the detected videos, and all tampered videos, respectively. They are given by the formulas

$$precision = \frac{TP}{TP + FP}, \tag{5}$$

$$Recall = \frac{TP}{TP + FN}, \tag{6}$$

and

$$F_1 = 2 * \frac{precision * Recall}{precision + Recall}. \tag{7}$$

where TP and FP denote the number of correctly and falsely detected video forgeries, respectively. FN denotes the number of undetected video forgeries.

4.4 Detection Performance

In this section, we report the detection performance of the proposed method; the thresholds for detecting the type of forgery were configured empirically as follows: $T_{shf} = 0.04$, $T_{del} = 0.09$, and $T_{ins} = 0.35$. We compare our method with similar previous methods in [5,17,22,23] under frame deletion forgery type in Table 3; under frame insertion forgery type in Table 4; under frame shuffling forgery type in Table 5. From the above tables, the proposed method achieves the highest rates under all types of forgery compared with the previous methods. Although there are some failures in detecting the frame deletion from a static scene because of a high similarity between its frames; this situation is contrary to reality because there is no need to delete a clip from a static scene.

Table 2. The detection results of the tested videos

Video	TP candidates	Forgery localization	Execution time	
			Total time(s)	Time(s/frame)
V1	12, 15	123, 145	7.86	0.02
V2	10	106	5.01	0.02
V3	11	104	7.23	0.02
V4	7, 27	74, 273	9.40	0.02
V5	8, 12	85, 135	4.51	0.02
V6	18, 38	182, 377	10.79	0.02
V7	13, 16	129, 165	7.01	0.02
V8	92, 98	920, 953	31.6	0.02
V9	2, 7	20, 70	8.29	0.02
V10	26, 45	260, 455	10.39	0.02
V11	14	155	5.36	0.02
V12	40, 43	405, 435	13.23	0.02
V13	2	19	22.89	0.03
V14	41	416	21.81	0.03
V15	51, 60	510, 600	23.49	0.03

Table 3. The detection performance for our proposed compared with others under deletion attack.

Method	Precision	Recall	F_1 score
Wang [17]	0.89	0.85	0.86
Zheng [23]	0.83	0.89	0.85
Liu [5]	0.97	0.93	0.95
Zhao [22]	0.96	0.98	0.97
Ours	0.98	0.99	0.98

Table 4. The detection performance for our proposed compared with others under insertion attack.

Method	Precision	Recall	F_1 score
Wang [17]	0.93	0.90	0.91
Zheng [23]	0.82	0.92	0.86
Liu [5]	0.96	0.97	0.96
Zhao [22]	0.97	0.98	0.97
Ours	0.99	0.99	0.99

4.5   Running Time

The average running time of our method and the methods in [5,17,22,23] are listed in Table 6. Our proposed has the lowest time compared with others because the temporal averages of non-overlapping subsequence frames are checked instead of checking all entire frames which can reduce the running time. For example, if each frame needs to t time for checking and a video has N_f frames, the video needs $t * N_f$ time for checking in the previous methods; but in our proposed the video needs $(t * (N_f/N)) + L_t$ time for checking and determining the tampered locations, where $L_t = 2N * t$ or $3N * t$ according to the position of the selected TP as mentioned in Sect. 3.2.

Table 5. The detection performance for our proposed compared with others under shuffling attack.

Method	Precision	Recall	F_1 score
Wang [17]	0.73	0.75	0.74
Zheng [23]	0.82	0.81	0.81
Liu [5]	0.89	0.78	0.83
Zhao [22]	0.92	0.93	0.92
Ours	0.96	0.97	0.96

Table 6. Average execution time of the different methods.

Method	Time (s)	
	Total Time	Time/frame
Wang [17]	90830.4	189.23
Zheng [23]	441.6	0.92
Liu [5]	427.2	0.89
Zhao [22]	220.8	0.46
Ours	12.5	0.026

5   Conclusion

In this paper, we have proposed an efficient method for frame deletion, insertion, and shuffling forgeries detection. UQI of TP is used for detecting illegal attacks in a surveillance video. TP of each non-overlapping subsequence frames is computed after the video is extracted into frames. Q values are calculated among each two adjacent TPs for selecting illegal candidates and among their corresponding frames for determining the attack locations.

The experimental results show that the proposed method outperforms the state of art methods with the lowest running time. In the future, we intend to increase our dataset by adding some modifications to the tampered clips such as noise, etc.

Acknowledgments. This work was supported by the National Natural Science Foundation of China [grant numbers 61471141, 61361166006, 61301099]; Key Technology Program of Shenzhen, China, [grant number JSGG20160427185010977]; Basic Research Project of Shenzhen, China [grant number JCYJ20150513151706561].

References

1. Baudry, S.: Frame-accurate temporal registration for non-blind video watermarking. In: Proceedings of the on Multimedia and Security, MM&Sec 2012, pp. 19–26. ACM, New York (2012). https://doi.org/10.1145/2361407.2361411

2. Baudry, S., Chupeau, B., Lefèbvre, F.: A framework for video forensics based on local and temporal fingerprints. In: Proceedings of the 16th IEEE International Conference on Image Processing, ICIP'09, pp. 2853–2856. IEEE Press, Piscataway (2009)

3. Cuevas, C., Yanez, E.M., Garcia, N.: Labeled dataset for integral evaluation of moving object detection algorithms: lasiesta. Comput. Vis. Image Underst. **152**(Supplement C), 103–117 (2016). https://doi.org/10.1016/j.cviu.2016.08.005. http://www.gti.ssr.upm.es/data/lasiesta_database.html

4. Fadl, S.M., Han, Q., Li, Q.: Authentication of surveillance videos: detecting frame duplication based on residual frame. J. Forensic Sci. **63**(4), 1099–1109 (2018). https://doi.org/10.1111/1556-4029.13658

5. Liu, Y., Huang, T.: Exposing video inter-frame forgery by zernike opponentchromaticity moments and coarseness analysis. Multimedia Syst. **23**(2), 223–238 (2017). https://doi.org/10.1007/s00530-015-0478-1

6. Mao, J., Xiao, G., Sheng, W., Hu, Y., Qu, Z.: A method for video authenticity based on the fingerprint of scene frame. Neurocomputing **173**(Part 3), 2022–2032 (2016). https://doi.org/10.1016/j.neucom.2015.09.001

7. Nixon, M.S., Aguado, A.S.: Chapter 9-moving object detection and description. In: Nixon, M.S., Aguado, A.S. (eds.) Feature Extraction & Image Processing for Computer Vision, 3rd edn., pp. 435–487. Academic Press, Oxford (2012). https://doi.org/10.1016/B978-0-12-396549-3.00009-4

8. Pathak, A., Patil, D.: Review of techniques for detecting video forgeries. Int. J. Comput. Sci. Mobile Comput. **3**(2), 422–438 (2014)

9. Qadir, G., Yahaya, S., Ho, A.T.S.: Surrey university library for forensic analysis (SULFA) of video content. In: IET Conference on Image Processing (IPR), pp. 1–6 (2012). https://doi.org/10.1049/cp.2012.0422,. http://sulfa.cs.surrey.ac.uk/index.php

10. Shi, Y., Qi, M., Yi, Y., Zhang, M., Kong, J.: Object based dual watermarking for video authentication. Optik - Int. J. Light Electron Opt. **124**(19), 3827–3834 (2013). https://doi.org/10.1016/j.ijleo.2012.11.078

11. Singh, R.D., Aggarwal, N.: Video content authentication techniques: a comprehensive survey. Multimedia Syst. **24**(2), 211–240 (2018). https://doi.org/10.1007/s00530-017-0538-9

12. Sitara, K., Mehtre, B.: Digital video tampering detection: an overview ofpassive techniques. Digital Investig. **18**(Supplement C), 8–22 (2016). https://doi.org/10.1016/j.diin.2016.06.003

13. Sohn, H., Neve, W.D., Ro, Y.M.: Privacy protection in video surveillancesystems: analysis of subband-adaptive scrambling in JPEG XR. IEEE Trans. Circuits Syst. Video Technol. **21**(2), 170–177 (2011). https://doi.org/10.1109/TCSVT.2011.2106250. http://ivylab.kaist.ac.kr/demo/vs/dataset.htm

14. Ulutas, G., Ustubioglu, B., Ulutas, M., Nabiyev, V.: Frameduplication/mirroring detection method with binary features. IET Image Process. **11**(5), 333–342 (2017). https://doi.org/10.1049/iet-ipr.2016.0321

15. Ulutas, G., Ustubioglu, B., Ulutas, M., Nabiyev, V.V.: Frame duplication detection based on bow model. Multimedia Syst. **24**(5), 549–567 (2018). https://doi.org/10.1007/s00530-017-0581-6

16. Wahab, A.W.A., Bagiwa, M.A., Idris, M.Y.I., Khan, S., Razak, Z., Ariffin, M.R.K.: Passive video forgery detection techniques: a survey. In: 10th International Conference on Information Assurance and Security, pp. 29–34. IEEE (2014). https://doi.org/10.1109/ISIAS.2014.7064616

17. Wang, W., Jiang, X., Wang, S., Wan, M., Sun, T.: Identifying video forgery process using optical flow. In: Shi, Y.Q., Kim, H.-J., Pérez-González, F. (eds.) IWDW 2013. LNCS, vol. 8389, pp. 244–257. Springer, Heidelberg (2014). https://doi.org/10.1007/978-3-662-43886-2_18

18. Wang, W., Farid, H.: Exposing digital forgeries in video by detecting duplication. In: Proceedings of the 9th workshop on Multimedia and Security, pp. 35–42. ACM, Dallas, Texas (2007)

19. Wang, Z., Bovik, A.C.: A universal image quality index. IEEE Signal Process. Lett. **9**(3), 81–84 (2002). https://doi.org/10.1109/97.995823

20. Wang, Z., Bovik, A.C., Sheikh, H.R., Simoncelli, E.P.: Image quality assessment: from error visibility to structural similarity. IEEE Trans. Image Process. **13**(4), 600–612 (2004). https://doi.org/10.1109/TIP.2003.819861

21. Zahir, S.A., Kashanchi, F.: A new image quality measure. In: 2013 26th IEEE Canadian Conference on Electrical and Computer Engineering (CCECE), pp. 1–5 (2013). https://doi.org/10.1109/CCECE.2013.6567730

22. Zhao, D.N., Wang, R.K., Lu, Z.M.: Inter-frame passive-blind forgery detection for video shot based on similarity analysis. Multimedia Tools and Applications (2018). https://doi.org/10.1007/s11042-018-5791-1

23. Zheng, L., Sun, T., Shi, Y.-Q.: Inter-frame video forgery detection based on blockwise brightness variance descriptor. In: Shi, Y.-Q., Kim, H.J., Pérez-González, F., Yang, C.-N. (eds.) IWDW 2014. LNCS, vol. 9023, pp. 18–30. Springer, Cham (2015). https://doi.org/10.1007/978-3-319-19321-2_2

Special Session: Deep Generative Models for Forgery and Its Det

Reconstruction of Fingerprints from Minutiae Using Conditional Adversarial Networks

Hakil Kim[(✉)], Xuenan Cui, Man-Gyu Kim, and Thi Hai Binh Nguyen

School of Information and Communication Engineering, Inha University,
100 Inha-ro, Michuhol-gu, Incheon 22212, South Korea
hikim@inha.edu

Abstract. Fingerprint recognition systems have been known to be exposed to several security threats. Those are fake fingerprints, attacking at communication channels and software modules, and stealing fingerprint templates from database storages. For a long time, stolen templates are not seriously investigated because it was believed that fingerprint templates did not reveal the original fingerprints used to extract the templates. However, recent studies have proved that a fingerprint can be reconstructed from its minutiae, although the reconstructed fingerprints may have many spurious minutiae and unnatural patterns. This paper proposes an algorithm based on conditional generative adversarial networks (conditional GANs) to reconstruct fingerprints from sets of minutiae. The fingerprints generated by the proposed networks are very similar to the real fingerprints and can be used to fool fingerprint recognition systems. The acceptance rates of the generated fingerprints range from 42% to 98%, depending on the features and security levels used in the matching algorithms.

Keywords: Fingerprint reconstruction ·
Conditional adversarial network · Synthetic fingerprint

1 Introduction

Verifying the identity of one person can be done in different ways which can be categorized into three classes. The first category is based on what a person knows; this class includes but not limited to password, and PIN. The second category is based on what a person has, such as a smart card, token, and certificate. The last class is based on whom a person is, called biometrics. Biometrics is identifying individuals using their biological characteristics, such as fingerprint, face, iris, vein, and behavioral characteristics, such as speech. Biometrics offers certain advantages such as negative recognition and non-repudiation that cannot be provided by tokens and passwords.

Among the biological characteristics, the fingerprint is one of the most popular traits due to its permanence and uniqueness. More than 50 years have passed since the first automatic fingerprint recognition system introduced by Trauring

© Springer Nature Switzerland AG 2019
C. D. Yoo et al. (Eds.): IWDW 2018, LNCS 11378, pp. 353–362, 2019.
https://doi.org/10.1007/978-3-030-11389-6_26

[11]; fingerprint recognition systems have been widely incorporated into forensic, civilian, and many commercial applications [8]. The deployment of portable
devices capable of capturing fingerprint images, such as mobile phones, leads to
a growing demand for fingerprint-based authentication applications.

Despite the advantages, fingerprint recognition systems encounter several
problems. One of them is presentation attack which is spoofing the systems with
fake fingerprints. Other threats are attempting to change the system decision by
attacking communication channels or software modules and stealing fingerprint
templates from database storages. Stolen templates can be used to replace the
true templates when a person attacks commutation channels or software modules. However, this paper presents another threat which comes from synthetic
fingerprints created from fingerprint templates. For a long time, people believed
that a template, particularly minutiae, did not disclose the original fingerprint
used to extract the template. That is, given a template, it is impossible to generate a fingerprint that is the same as the original fingerprint from which the
template comes. However, the experiments in this paper prove that this statement is no longer correct.

Research on reconstructing fingerprint images from minutiae started in 2001
with the study of Hill [5]. After this very first attempt, there are several studies on
this problem [1,3,4,7,10]. Existing algorithms consist of two main steps, which
are fingerprint orientation map reconstruction and ridge pattern reconstruction.
Orientation maps, which describe the basic structure of fingerprints, can be
reconstructed using the Zero-pole model [3,5]. However, these methods require
that singular points, i.e., core and delta, exist in fingerprints. Other approaches
estimate orientation maps by sets of three or eight neighborhood minutiae [4,7,
10]. Each set of minutiae provides the orientation field of a fingerprint block. Cao
et al. [1] learned a dictionary of orientation patches from high-quality fingerprints
and used the dictionary to reconstruct fingerprint orientations. Figure 1 shows
the orientation reconstructed by different algorithms.

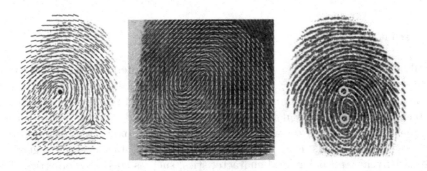

Fig. 1. Reconstructed orientation using different algorithms: (a) Zero-pole model [3],
(b) minutiae in eight sectors [4], (c) orientation patch dictionary [1]

After obtaining orientation maps, linear interpolation starting from a minutia point can be applied to generate ridge lines [10]. Ridge pattern also can be reconstructed by an algorithm called iterative pattern growing, which iteratively applies Gabor filters to an image formed by minutiae [3]. Since it is possible to represent a fingerprint image as a 2D amplitude and frequency modulated (AM-FM) signal, Feng et al. [4] and Li et al. [7] used the AM-FM model to reconstruct fingerprint ridges. In the work of Cao et al. [1], ridge patterns are restored from a continuous phase patch dictionary which is learned from a set of enhanced rolled fingerprints. Several examples of reconstructed fingerprints are shown in Fig. 2.

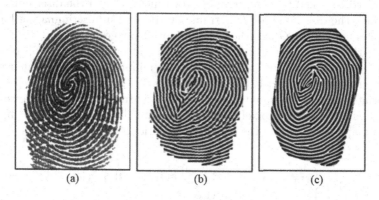

(a)   (b)   (c)

Fig. 2. Examples of reconstructed fingerprints: (a) Real fingerprint image from which minutia set was extracted, (b) fingerprint reconstructed by AM-FM model [4], (c) fingerprint reconstructed by continuous phase patch dictionary [1].

The existing works can reconstruct fingerprint images from sets of minutiae; however, the fingerprint areas in the output images are smaller than the original fingerprint areas because there is often no minutia point near the fingerprint boundary. Besides, there are spurious minutiae introduced in the outputs. The reconstructed images do not look real either. This paper proposes an algorithm to reconstruct fingerprints from minutiae by applying conditional GANs which were designed for the problem of image-to-image translation [6]. The fingerprint reconstruction can be considered as an image-to-image translation, in which a fingerprint image is generated from an image that contains minutia information. In this study, we successfully build a single network to produce fingerprint images from minutia sets. The experiments show that the generated fingerprints resemble the real fingerprints well.

The rest of the paper is organized as follows. Section 2 describes the architecture of the proposed network and the process of generating fingerprints from minutia sets. Section 3 explains how the network was trained and provides the evaluation on generated fingerprints. Conclusions and future works are stated in Sect. 4.

2 Proposed Network for Fingerprint Reconstruction

Network Architecture. Before presenting the proposed fingerprint reconstruction network, we define our problem as follows. Let x be a fingerprint image; $S_x = \{(i, j, \theta_{ij})\}$ be the set of minutiae extracted from x, where (i, j) and θ_{ij} are the location and direction of the ith minutia. Our problem is building a deep neural network capable of generating a fingerprint image from S_x. The generated fingerprint should be as similar to the original one x as possible.

The proposed network for reconstructing fingerprints from minutiae is based on the original work from [6]. The network consists of a generator G and a discriminator D and is trained in an adversarial manner. That is, the generator G is trained to generate fingerprint images which can fool the discriminator D; meanwhile, the discriminator D is trained to do well in discriminating between the images created by G and the real fingerprint images.

Since this study adopts the network proposed by Isola et al. [6], inputs of the generator G should be images instead of minutia sets. Thus, minutia sets are converted into images before feeding into G. Given a minutia set S_x of a fingerprint image x, the minutia map m_x created from S_x is an image that has the same size as x. The pixel values of m_x are defined in Eq. 1. Samples of minutia maps are shown in the experiment section.

$$m_x(i_b, j_b) = \begin{cases} \lfloor \frac{\theta_{ij}}{2} \rfloor + 1 & \text{if } (i, j) \in S_x \text{ and } |i_b - i| \leq 5, |j_b - j| \leq 5 \\ 0 & \text{otherwise} \end{cases} \tag{1}$$

The generator G has 16 modules, and the discriminator D has five modules. Each module is formed by 4×4 convolutional filters, a batch normalization, and an activation function. Tables 1 and 2 detail the structure of the generator and discriminator. The generator G accepts a 256×256 minutia map as its input and produces a grayscale fingerprint image, called the reconstructed fingerprint. There are special connections, named skip connections, between modules in the generator G. These connections happen between the module $G - k$ and $G - (16 - k)$, where k is from 1 to 7. If there is a skip connection between $G - k$ and $G - (16 - k)$, the output of $G - k$ is concatenated with the output of $G - (16 - k)$, and the merged output will be the input of $G - (16 - k + 1)$.

The inputs of the discriminator D are pairs of images. Each pair consists of a minutia map and a real or generated fingerprint image. If the fingerprint image is the real one used to extract the minutiae, this pair is a "real" pair. However, if the fingerprint image comes from G, this pair is a "fake" pair. The output of D is the probability of being "fake" or "real" of a pair.

Fingerprint Reconstruction. The discriminator D plays a role in the training stage only. In the reconstruction stage, the generator G is used as an independent generator. Let S_x be a set of minutiae which is extracted from a fingerprint image. The process of reconstructing the fingerprint from S_x includes two steps.

Table 1. Structure of the generator G

Module	Input size	Output size	Conv. filter size/stride	# of filters	Activation function
G-1	$256 \times 256 \times 1$	$128 \times 128 \times 64$	$4 \times 4/2$	64	Leaky ReLU
G-2	$128 \times 128 \times 64$	$64 \times 64 \times 128$	$4 \times 4/2$	128	Leaky ReLU
G-3	$64 \times 64 \times 128$	$32 \times 32 \times 256$	$4 \times 4/2$	256	Leaky ReLU
G-4	$32 \times 32 \times 256$	$16 \times 16 \times 512$	$4 \times 4/2$	512	Leaky ReLU
G-5	$16 \times 16 \times 512$	$8 \times 8 \times 512$	$4 \times 4/2$	512	Leaky ReLU
G-6	$8 \times 8 \times 512$	$4 \times 4 \times 512$	$4 \times 4/2$	512	Leaky ReLU
G-7	$4 \times 4 \times 512$	$2 \times 2 \times 512$	$4 \times 4/2$	512	Leaky ReLU
G-8	$2 \times 2 \times 512$	$1 \times 1 \times 512$	$4 \times 4/2$	512	Leaky ReLU
G-9	$1 \times 1 \times 512$	$2 \times 2 \times 512$	$4 \times 4/2$	512	ReLU
G-10	$2 \times 2 \times 1024$	$4 \times 4 \times 512$	$4 \times 4/2$	512	ReLU
G-11	$4 \times 4 \times 1024$	$8 \times 8 \times 512$	$4 \times 4/2$	512	ReLU
G-12	$8 \times 8 \times 1024$	$16 \times 16 \times 512$	$4 \times 4/2$	512	ReLU
G-13	$16 \times 16 \times 1024$	$32 \times 32 \times 256$	$4 \times 4/2$	256	ReLU
G-14	$32 \times 32 \times 512$	$64 \times 64 \times 128$	$4 \times 4/2$	128	ReLU
G-15	$64 \times 64 \times 256$	$128 \times 128 \times 64$	$4 \times 4/2$	64	ReLU
G-16	$128 \times 128 \times 128$	$256 \times 256 \times 1$	$4 \times 4/2$	1	Tanh

Table 2. Structure of the discriminator D

Module	Input size	Output size	Conv. filter size/stride	# of filters	Activation function
D-1	$256 \times 256 \times 2$	$128 \times 128 \times 64$	$4 \times 4/2$	64	Leaky ReLU
D-2	$128 \times 128 \times 64$	$64 \times 64 \times 128$	$4 \times 4/2$	128	Leaky ReLU
D-3	$64 \times 64 \times 128$	$32 \times 32 \times 256$	$4 \times 4/2$	256	Leaky ReLU
D-4	$32 \times 32 \times 256$	$31 \times 31 \times 512$	$4 \times 4/1$	512	Leaky ReLU
D-5	$31 \times 31 \times 512$	$30 \times 30 \times 1$	$4 \times 4/2$	1	Sigmoid

The first step builds a map from S_x by following the minutia map creation process described above (Eq. 1). In the second step, the generator G is used to produce a fingerprint image from the minutia map. Figure 3 displays the fingerprint reconstruction flowchart.

3   Experiments

3.1   Training of the Proposed Network

The training process uses 3,600 image pairs; each includes a fingerprint image and the corresponding minutia map. All fingerprints in the training set are from a private database, namely CVLab database. The images were captured by an

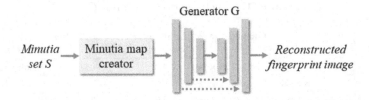

Fig. 3. The flowchart of reconstructing a fingerprint from minutiae.

Fig. 4. Examples of image pairs used in training. Each pair consists of a fingerprint image and the corresponding minutia map.

optical sensor and are 280 pixels in width and 320 pixels in height; the resolution is 500 dpi. The minutia map is created from a fingerprint image as described in Sect. 2. Minutiae are extracted from fingerprints using the VeriFinger SDK extractor [9]. Samples of training pairs are shown in Fig. 4.

Because the training image size is 280×320 but the proposed network inputs have the size of 256×256, the training images and their minutia maps are resized to 320×320 by padding them with ones and zeros, respectively. After padding, they are downscaled to the size of the network inputs. The deep learning framework used in both training and testing is TensorFlow 1.7. The computing platform is a desktop with Windows 10, Intel Core i5 3.30 GHz, 12 GB RAM, and NVIDIA GTX 1080.

3.2   Evaluation of the Reconstructed Fingerprints

1900 fingerprint images were selected randomly from the CVLab database to evaluate the performance of the reconstructed fingerprints. These test fingerprints come from 380 fingers, i.e., each finger has five impressions. 1900 corresponding minutia sets are extracted from test fingerprints using the VeriFinger extraction algorithm [9]. These minutia sets are used to generate fingerprint images as described in Sect. 2. Several examples of real fingerprints, their corresponding minutia maps, and the generated fingerprints produced by the proposed generator G are in Fig. 5.

The purpose of this study is to prove that the fingerprint image obtained from a set of minutiae can resemble the original fingerprint from which the minutiae are extracted. Therefore, the matching results between fingerprints generated by the proposed network and real fingerprints are used to evaluate the goodness of the reconstructed fingerprints. Let x and y be the different impressions of

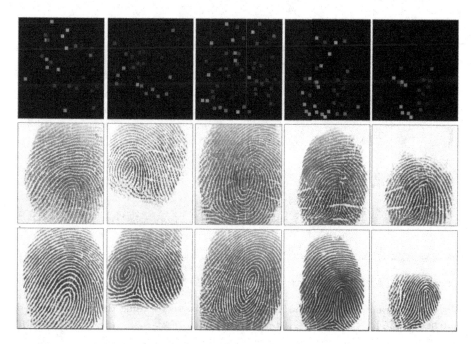

Fig. 5. Samples of reconstructed fingerprints. First rows: minutia maps; second row: fingerprints generated from the minutia maps by the proposed network; third row: real fingerprints from which the minutiae were extracted.

the same finger; m_x be the minutia map corresponding to x; $G(m_x)$ be the image generated from m_x by the generator G. There are two types of matching performed in the experiments. The first is matching the generated fingerprint against the same impression from which the minutiae are extracted, i.e., match $G(m_x)$ against x. The second type involves matching the generated fingerprint against a different impression of the finger from which the minutiae are extracted, i.e., match $G(m_x)$ against y. The matching scores can be used to measure how good the generated images are. The higher is the matching score, the better is the reconstructed fingerprint. The experiments use two matching algorithms, one is a minutiae-based matcher [2], and the other is a fusion feature-based matcher [9].

The histograms of matching scores using the minutiae-based matcher and fusion features-based matcher are in Figs. 6 and 7, respectively. The matching score between $G(m_x)$ and x is called type 1 genuine matching score and shown in red in the histograms. The matching score between $G(m_x)$ and y is called type 2 genuine matching score and shown in blue. Furthermore, the imposter matching scores are computed to show the similarities between pairs of fingerprints of different fingers. The observation reveals that the distributions of imposter matching scores between pairs of a reconstructed fingerprint and a real fingerprint are similar to those of real fingerprint pairs (displayed as green and black in Figs. 6 and 7).

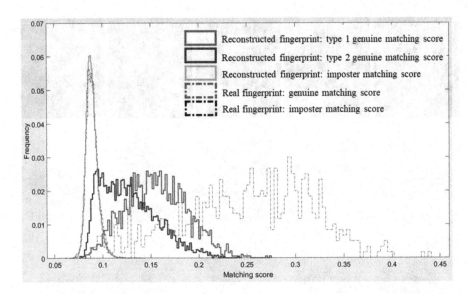

Fig. 6. Histogram of genuine and imposter matching scores using the minutiae-based matcher.

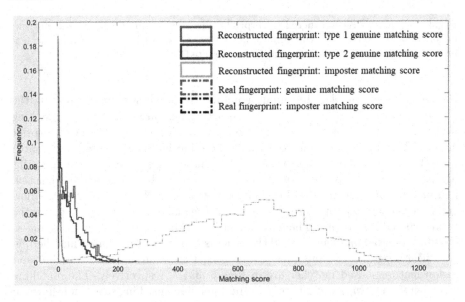

Fig. 7. Histogram of genuine and imposter matching scores using the fusion features-based matcher.

The acceptance rates computed at several security levels based on matching scores are also used to measure the reconstructed fingerprints (Eq. 2). The threshold value (thr$_{@FAR}$) are linked to the false acceptance rates (FAR) of the matching algorithm. The higher is the threshold, the lower is FAR and higher FRR (false rejection rate). That is, a high threshold indicates a strict security system. The acceptance rate shows the capability of fooling a fingerprint recognition system of the fingerprints produced by the proposed network.

$$AR_{@FAR} = \frac{\text{Number of pairs that have matching scores above thr}_{@FAR}}{\text{Total number of pairs}} \quad (2)$$

Table 3 contains the acceptance rates of the minutiae-based and fusion features-based matcher at three security levels. Since only the information of minutiae is used to reconstruct fingerprint images, it is expected that the acceptance rates when using minutiae-based matching algorithms are higher than the fusion features-based. The type 2 genuine matching scores usually are smaller than the type 1 genuine scores because there are translations, rotations, and distortions in different impressions of the same finger. The acceptance rates on the test database have supported our theory.

Table 3. Acceptance rates when using different matching algorithms. Type 1 means matching the reconstructed fingerprint against the same impression from which the minutiae are extracted. Type 2 means matching the reconstructed fingerprint against a different impression of the finger from which the minutiae are extracted.

	FAR (security level)	Acceptance rate	
		Type 1	Type 2
Minutiae-based matcher	0.1%	98.4%	83.9%
	0.01%	94.5%	69.1%
	0.001%	91.3%	62.4%
Fusion features-based matcher	0.1%	86.1%	71.4%
	0.01%	75.6%	56.7%
	0.001%	61.5%	41.9%

4   Conclusions and Future Works

This paper proposed a deep learning-based approach to generate fingerprint images from sets of minutiae. The fingerprints generated by the proposed network are similar to the real fingerprints from which minutia sets were extracted. These similarities were proved by two matching algorithms, one is based on minutiae only, and the other is based on multiple features. The acceptance rates of generated fingerprints show that generated fingerprints are significant threats to fingerprint recognition systems. Hence, it leads to the requirement of protecting fingerprint templates. In this study, only minutia locations and directions were used to generate fingerprints; we will include minutia types in the future works. Also, applying deep neural networks to create massive databases of synthetic fingerprints for evaluating the performance of fingerprint recognition systems will be considered.

References

1. Cao, K., Jain, A.K.: Learning fingerprint reconstruction: from minutiae to image. IEEE Trans. Inf. Forensics Secur. **10**(1), 104–117 (2015)
2. Cappelli, R., Ferrara, M., Maltoni, D.: Minutia cylinder-code a new representation and matching technique for fingerprint recognition. IEEE Trans. Patt. Anal. Mach. Intell. **32**(12), 2128–2141 (2010)
3. Cappelli, R., Lumini, A., Maio, D., Maltoni, D.: Fingerprint image reconstruction from standard templates. IEEE Trans. Patt. Anal. Mach. Intell. **29**(9), 1489–1503 (2007)
4. Feng, J., Jain, A.K.: FM model based fingerprint reconstruction from minutiae template. In: Tistarelli, M., Nixon, M.S. (eds.) ICB 2009. LNCS, vol. 5558, pp. 544–553. Springer, Heidelberg (2009). https://doi.org/10.1007/978-3-642-01793-3_56
5. Hill, C.J.: Risk of masquerade arising from the storage of biometrics, Master degree thesis, Department of Computer Science, Australian National University, Australia, November 2001
6. Isola, P., Zhu, J., Zhou, T., Efros, A.A.: Image-to-image translation with conditional adversarial networks. In: 2017 IEEE Conference on Computer Vision and Pattern Recognition (CVPR), pp. 5967–5976, July 2017
7. Li, S., Kot, A.C.: An improved scheme for full fingerprint reconstruction. IEEE Trans. Inf. Forensics Secur. **7**(6), 1906–1912 (2012)
8. Maltoni, D., Maio, D., Jain, A., Prabhakar, S.: Handbook of Fingerprint Recognition. Springer, London (2003)
9. Neurotechnology: Verifinger SDK. https://www.neurotechnology.com/verifinger.html. Accessed 09 May 2018
10. Ross, A., Shah, J., Jain, A.K.: From template to image: reconstructing fingerprints from minutiae points. IEEE Trans. Patt. Anal. Mach. Intell. **29**(4), 544–560 (2007)
11. Trauring, M.: Automatic comparison of finger-ridge patterns. Nature **197**, 938–940 (1963)

Unsupervised Domain Adaptation for Object Detection Using Distribution Matching in Various Feature Level

Hyoungwoo Park[1]([⊠]), Minjeong Ju[1], Sangkeun Moon[2], and Chang D. Yoo[1]

[1] Korea Advanced Institute of Science and Technology, Daejeon, South Korea
hyoungwoo.park@kaist.ac.kr
[2] Korea Electric Power Corporation (KEPCO), Daejeon, South Korea

Abstract. As the research on deep learning has become more active, the need for a lot of data has emerged. However, there are limitations in acquiring real data such as digital forensics, so domain adaptation technology is required to overcome this problem. This paper considers distribution matching in various feature level for unsupervised domain adaptation for object detection with a single stage detector. The object detection task assumes that training and test data are drawn from the same distribution; however, in a real environment, there is a domain gap between training and test data which leads to degrading performance significantly. Therefore, we aim to learn a model to generalize well in target domain of object detection by using *maximum mean discrepancy* (MMD) in various feature levels. We adjust MMD based on *single shot multibox detector* (SSD) model which is a single stage detector that learns to localize objects with various size using a multi-layer design of bounding box regression and infers object class simultaneously. The MMD loss on high-level features between source and target domain effectively reduces the domain discrepancy to learn a domain-invariant feature in SSD model. We evaluate the approaches using Syn2real object detection dataset. Experimental results show that reducing the domain shift in high-level features improves the cross-domain robustness of object detection, and domain adaptation works better with simple MMD method than complex method as GAN.

Keywords: Object detection · Unsupervised domain adaptation · Maximum mean discrepancy

1 Introduction

Object detection is one of the fundamental problems in computer vision. Object detection is a task to localize all object instances in an image and also classify their categories. Due to the development of convolutional networks (CNNs), many CNN-based supervised object detection algorithms have been

© Springer Nature Switzerland AG 2019
C. D. Yoo et al. (Eds.): IWDW 2018, LNCS 11378, pp. 363–372, 2019.
https://doi.org/10.1007/978-3-030-11389-6_27

proposed and they have achieved considerable performances. While they drastically improve the performances, the deep learning based algorithms rely on a huge amount of labeled data. Annotating a large amount of real data is an expensive and time-consuming procedure. Especially in the field of digital forensics, it is also difficult to acquire real data itself. Crawling synthetic data can be an alternative to real data; however, there is a difference in distributions between synthetic and real data. Such a distribution mismatch referred to as domain shift leads to performance degradation. Domain adaptation attempts to alleviate this domain discrepancy and reduces the burden of collecting and annotating the real data.

In this paper, we address an unsupervised domain adaptation problem for object detection. The instance level annotation that is composed of a category label and a location of a bounding box is given in the source domain while the target domain does not have any annotations. We build an end-to-end deep learning model based on single shot multibox detector (SSD) [5] with distribution matching in various feature level. The domain shift could occur on feature level in single stage detector, which motivates us to minimize the domain gap on various feature level. The multi-level feature maps in single stage detector contain different instance level information (e.g. size of an object and appearance of an object). Therefore, we match a variety of feature levels using maximum mean discrepancy (MMD) [7] to learn robust features that are domain-transferable. This leads to reduce domain gap and the detector become generalized for the target domain. We conduct experiments on Syn2real [6] which is the visual domain adaptation dataset for object detection. The experimental results show that the matching distribution in high-level features improves cross-domain adaptation performance.

The rest of the paper is organized as follows. The previous algorithms for unsupervised domain adaptation for object detection are introduced in Sect. 2. Our method is described in Sect. 3. In Sect. 4, we discuss our experimental results on the benchmark dataset. Section 5 concludes the paper.

2 Related Works

2.1 Object Detection

Most object detection algorithms have been driven by deep learning models recently [1–5]. The object detection algorithms would be categorized into (1) two-stage detectors and (2) one-stage detectors. The two-stage detectors [1–3] are region-based CNNs and these algorithms extract region proposals from the image and a network is trained to classify each region of interest (RoI) independently. R-CNN [1] is a baseline model of region-based CNN detectors and it is extended to share the convolution feature map among all RoIs in Fast R-CNN [2]. Faster R-CNN [3] proposes region proposal networks (RPN) for learning to produce object proposals with end-to-end detection and it achieves considerable results in object detection algorithm. In single stage detectors, the algorithms conform detection without explicit region proposal step. YOLO [4] consists of a single convolutional network that simultaneously predicts multiple bounding boxes and class probabilities for those boxes. SSD [5] is one of the most representative one-stage detectors and it is also composed of the single CNN architecture that localizes the objects in an image as well as classifies the categories of the objects. SSD has less number of weights and faster speed than those of Faster R-CNN and it has competitive performance.

2.2 Unsupervised Domain Adaptation

Unsupervised domain adaptation has been widely studied for classification in computer vision. Recent methods are based on deep learning architectures and aim to improve the domain adaptability with various methods. Previous algorithms have focused on learning transferable feature by minimizing the discrepancy between the source and target feature distributions. Tzeng *et al.* [9] have used the MMD loss as regularization term for minimizing the discrepancy of two distributions of features between the source and target domain. On the other hand, Sun *et al.* [10] propose a *correlation alignment* (CORAL) loss to match the mean and covariance of two distribution in feature space between the source and target domain. Ganin *et al.* [11] use adversarial training to learn a domain-invariant representations. The *domain adversarial neural network* (DANN) is composed of a shared network for extracting transferable representation with two classifiers. One classifier is trained to predict the class of the data from the source domain and the other is trained to predict where the input data is from. The domain classification loss makes the shared feature extractor in adversarial training by using *gradient reversal layer* (GRL). In this paper, we focus on the object detection problem in unsupervised domain adaptation, which is more challenging as both categories of the object and the location of the bounding box are jointly predicted.

2.3 Unsupervised Domain Adaptation for Object Detection

There has been an approach to domain adaptation for object detection. Chen *et al.* [8] have proposed minimizing discrepancy using GRL in image level and instance level to learn domain-invariant features. Also, they propose consistency regularization in both levels to learn the cross-domain robustness for bounding box regressor.

3   Method

3.1   Preliminaries

Generative Adversarial Networks (GAN). Generative adversarial networks (GAN) [13] is composed of generator G and discriminator D that are trained by an adversarial process for the minimax game. A generator G receives noise $\mathbf{z}$ and produces samples $G(\mathbf{z})$. A discriminator D outputs the probability that an input is drawn from real data **x**. The goal of a generator is to generate samples that have the same distribution from real data, and the goal of the discriminator is to distinguish whether the input is drawn from real data or fake samples from the generator. Both networks are trained by solving.

$$\min_{G} \max_{D} \mathbb{E}_{\mathbf{x} \sim p_{\text{data}}}[\log D(\mathbf{x})] + \mathbb{E}_{\mathbf{z} \sim p(\mathbf{z})}[\log(1 - D(G(\mathbf{z})))]. \tag{1}$$

3.2 Single Shot Detector (SSD)

For domain adaptation of object detection task, SSD was used as a baseline model. SSD is composed of a combination of VGG-16 [12] and several additional convolutional feature layers. In SSD, 6 features with a variety of sizes in the network are extracted to detect objects of different sizes, where the more deeper the features in the network, the bigger the size of the objects can be detected. As keeping the area based on a square bounding box, several bounding boxes (default boxes) are considered according to aspect ratios. When the number of categories is c and the number of default boxes used is k, output per one pixel in features has $4k$ location information with coordinates of each bounding box and ck class information. Using this, output dimension of each feature map with size $m * n$ is $(c + 4)kmn$. As used feature map sizes are $38 * 38$, $19 * 19$, $10 * 10$, $5 * 5$, $3 * 3$, and $1 * 1$, the total number of observed bounding boxes in SSD is $8732 * (c + 4)$. Applying score and nms threshold, bounding boxes are refined to detect more precisely (Fig. 1).

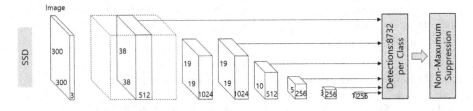

Fig. 1. Single Shot Detector (SSD)

SSD loss $\mathcal{L}$ is calculated as weighted sum of confidence loss $\mathcal{L}_{conf}$ and localization loss $\mathcal{L}_{loc}$ as follows. Confidence loss is the softmax for the score of multiple classes and localization loss is the Smooth L1 loss. N means the number of default boxes which is matched and α is set to 1.

$$\mathcal{L} = \frac{1}{N}(\mathcal{L}_{conf} + \alpha \mathcal{L}_{loc})$$

Using this formula with multiple feature maps, detection loss considering both location and class category of each bounding box is obtained.

3.3 Loss Function

Our task is to detect objects in the target domain data with trained model in source domain data. Let's assume that $\mathbf{x}_s$ and $\mathbf{y}_s$ are source image inputs and its annotation that contains location of boxes $\mathbf{b}_s$ and labels $\mathbf{l}_s$. For the target domain, $\mathbf{x}_t$ is input images and $\mathbf{y}_t$ is annotation with box location $\mathbf{b}_t$ and $\mathbf{l}_t$. For unsupervised domain adaptation problem, $\mathbf{y}_t$ is not given.

When doing our task, main problem is that there exists some gap in feature levels between source domain and target domain. Therefore, it is crucial to reduce the gap between domains (Fig. 2).

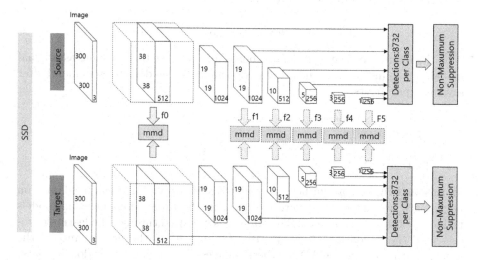

Fig. 2. Method using MMD in SSD

Maximum Mean Discrepancy (MMD) Loss. To diminish the domain gap of features, we apply maximum mean discrepancy (MMD) into features of SSD. Let features that extracted to predict location of the bounding boxes in SSD be $\{f^{(i)}\}_{i=0}^{5}$ in order of shallow level in network. Based on original MMD equation $MMD(f_s, y) = E\{K(x, x)\} + E\{K(y, y)\} - 2E\{K(x, y)\}$ with kernel K, MMD loss can be defined as follows:

$$\mathcal{L}_{mmd}^{(i)}(f_{source}^{(i)}, f_{target}^{(i)}) = \mathbb{E}\{K(f_{source}^{(i)}, f_{source}^{(i)})\} + \mathbb{E}\{K(f_{target}^{(i)}, f_{target}^{(i)})\}$$
$$- 2\mathbb{E}\{K(f_{source}^{(i)}, f_{target}^{(i)})\}, \text{for } i = 0, 1, ..., 5. \quad (2)$$

In this network, Gaussian kernel is used.

$$\text{Gaussian Kernel } K(\mathbf{x}_i, \mathbf{x}_j) = e^{\frac{-\|\mathbf{x}_i - \mathbf{x}_j\|^2}{2\sigma^2}}$$

This MMD loss matches the distribution of features in different domains. Therefore, if MMD loss is applied into higher feature level, higher level features of source domain and target domain are matched to be similar. This allows the detector to better detect objects in the target domain.

Detection Loss. As with other domain adaptation tasks, the detection performance of the source domain basically has a significant impact on the detection performance of the target domain. Therefore, the detection loss $L_{detection}$ for the source domain is obtained so that the detector works well for source domain data through learning. When source data is inserted into SSD as an input, the detection loss is calculated as a combination of L_{conf} and L_{loc}.

Total Loss. Combining SSD detection loss related to location and class of bounding boxes from source data and MMD loss to match features between different domains, total loss can be defined.

$$\mathcal{L}_{total} = \mathcal{L}_{detection} + \lambda \mathcal{L}_{mmd}^{(i)}, \text{ for } i = 0, 1, ..., 5.$$

N is the number of matched default boxes and α is set to 1 as same as original model. λ is found to 0.01 when best performance of the detector was found after several experiments.

4   Experiments

4.1   Dataset

In this experiment, a synthetic-to-real (Syn2Real) visual domain adaptation benchmark was adopted to detect objects in the target domain using models trained by the source domain. The training set is used through the learning process, and the validation set is operated for measuring the performance of the model. In that dataset, CAD-Synthetic images are used as source domain data. It is generated by 1,907 rendering 3D models of the 12 object classes; aeroplane, bicycle, bus, car, horse, knife, motorcycle, person, plant, skateboard, train and

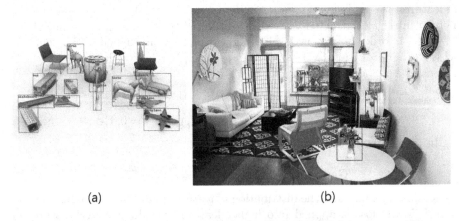

(a)   (b)

Fig. 3. A Syn2Real visual domain adaptation benchmark 2018 detection track dataset (a) CAD-Synthetic images (b) filtered MS COCO images

truck. With a variety of conditions such as angles, lighting, scaling, rotating, translating, and texturing, numerous synthetic source domain images can be obtained easier. The size of all images is fixed at 540 by 540. It does not take into account the ratio of object sizes in the real world. For example, the train can be smaller than the horse like in the image Fig. 3(a).

Target domain dataset was a refined version of Microsoft COCO dataset which is real images as shown in Fig. 3(b). As original MS COCO dataset is composed of 80 category and 12 categories of the Syn2Real benchmark dataset are the subset of the COCO dataset category, COCO dataset images were cropped only for the 12 category objects of Syn2Real visual domain adaptation benchmark dataset. Each image has a different width and height.

4.2   Results

Quantitative Results. In the experiments, SSD300 was used with ImageNet pretrained model. The IoU threshold for NMS is set to 0.45 as same as original SSD [5]. Score threshold for guaranteeing the confidence of bounding box outputs is employed as 0.2. For fine-tuning, SGD is used with initial learning rate 1e–3, 0.9 momentum, 1e–4 weight decay and batch size 24. For SSD, score threshold and nms threshold are set to 0.2 and 0.45. Pascal VOC's mAP metric is used to evaluate detection performance. Table 1 shows the results; AP for each class and mAP for baselines and our methods according to feature level used. To analyze our method more precisely, we additionally proceeded the experiments using DANN [11] in order to match the features in SSD levels using discriminator.

Performance of source only model is evaluated without MMD loss term (only detection loss). MMD loss term for domain adaptation is applied into each SSD feature level; 0, 4, and 5. As shown in Table 1, mAP value increases, as MMD loss is applied to deeper level of features. This implies that the domain adaptation method using MMD for deeper layer shows better performance while matching distributions of different features effectively.

For DANN, as similar to the results of the MMD experiment, the domain adaptation performance was higher when the distributions of deeper level features were matched. However, due to the unstable properties of GAN, the mAP

Table 1. Object detection performance in mAP for domain adaptation method

	mAP (%)
Source only	8.030
grl w/ f_0	8.379
grl w/ f_4	8.626
grl w/ f_5	8.663
MMD w/ f_0	8.423
MMD w/ f_4	8.670
MMD w/ f_5	8.823

Table 2. Object detection image result in mAP for domain adaptation method

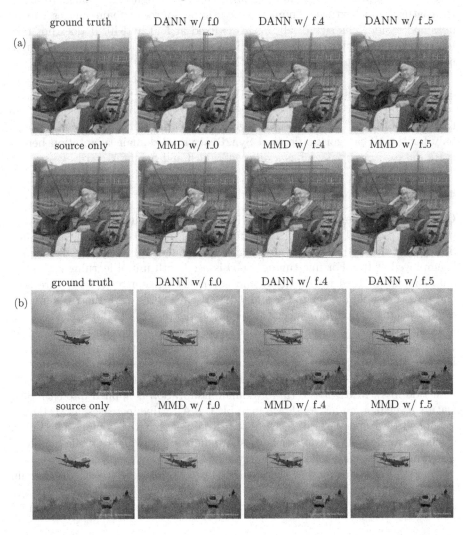

performance of DANN was not as good as that of MMD. Therefore, it can be said that a more simple approach than the unstable method such as GAN is effective in the domain adaptation problem.

Qualitative Results. Table 2 shows the image results by our methods. The images used in Table 2 are the part of the MS COCO 2017 validation dataset as target domain used to measure our method. For the source only model, it does not detect real objects well. It shows improved performance after training SSD with our methods. As can be seen from the mAP values, the results observed in the data image with predicted bounding boxes were also better when applied to MMD than DANN and to a deep layer with f5 rather than f0.

5   Conclusion and Future Work

We consider distribution matching in various feature levels for unsupervised domain adaptation for object detection. We adjust MMD based on an SSD model which is a single stage detector that learns to localize objects with various size using the multi-layer design of bounding box regression and infers object class simultaneously. The distribution matching in high-level features between the source and target domain alleviates the domain discrepancy in SSD model. We evaluate the approaches using Syn2real object detection dataset. Experimental results show that reducing the domain shift in high-level features improves the cross-domain robustness of object detection using the simple method as MMD. We will perform the experiments on other object detection datasets.

Acknowledgement. This research was supported by the Korea Electric Power Research Institute (KEPRI) of the Korea Electric Power Corporation (KEPCO).

References

1. Girshick, R., et al.: Rich feature hierarchies for accurate object detection and semantic segmentation. In: Proceedings of the IEEE Conference on Computer Vision and Pattern Recognition (2014)
2. Girshick, R.: Fast R-CNN. In: Proceedings of the IEEE International Conference on Computer Vision (2015)
3. Ren, S., et al.: Faster R-CNN: towards real-time object detection with region proposal networks. In: Advances in Neural Information Processing Systems (2015)
4. Redmon, J., et al.: You only look once: unified, real-time object detection. In: Proceedings of the IEEE Conference on Computer Vision and Pattern Recognition (2016)
5. Liu, W., et al.: SSD: single shot multibox detector. In: Leibe, B., Matas, J., Sebe, N., Welling, M. (eds.) ECCV 2016, Part I. LNCS, vol. 9905, pp. 21–37. Springer, Cham (2016). https://doi.org/10.1007/978-3-319-46448-0_2
6. Peng, X., et al.: Syn2Real: A New Benchmark for Synthetic-to-Real Visual Domain Adaptation. arXiv preprint arXiv:1806.09755 (2018)
7. Quiñonero-Candela, J., et al.: Covariate shift and local learning by distribution matching (2008)
8. Chen, Y., et al.: Domain adaptive faster R-CNN for object detection in the wild. In: Proceedings of the IEEE Conference on Computer Vision and Pattern Recognition (2018)
9. Tzeng, E., et al.: Simultaneous deep transfer across domains and tasks. In: Proceedings of the IEEE International Conference on Computer Vision (2015)
10. Sun, B., Saenko, K.: Deep CORAL: correlation alignment for deep domain adaptation. In: Hua, G., Jégou, H. (eds.) ECCV 2016, Part III. LNCS, vol. 9915, pp. 443–450. Springer, Cham (2016). https://doi.org/10.1007/978-3-319-49409-8_35

11. Ganin, Y., et al.: Domain-adversarial training of neural networks. J. Mach. Learn. Res. **17**(1), 2096–2030 (2016)
12. Simonyan, K., Zisserman, A.: Very deep convolutional networks for large-scale image recognition. arXiv preprint arXiv:1409.1556 (2014)
13. Goodfellow, I., et al.: Generative adversarial nets. In: Advances in Neural Information Processing Systems (2014)

Towards Robust Neural Networks with Lipschitz Continuity

Muhammad Usama and Dong Eui Chang$^{(\boxtimes)}$

School of Electrical Engineering,
Korea Advanced Institute of Science and Technology,
Daejeon, Republic of Korea
dechang@kaist.ac.kr

Abstract. Deep neural networks have shown remarkable performance across a wide range of vision-based tasks, particularly due to the availability of large-scale datasets for training and better architectures. However, data seen in the real world are often affected by distortions that not accounted for by the training datasets. In this paper, we address the challenge of robustness and stability of neural networks and propose a general training method that can be used to make the existing neural network architectures more robust and stable to input visual perturbations while using only available datasets for training. Proposed training method is convenient to use as it does not require data augmentation or changes in the network architecture. We provide theoretical proof as well as empirical evidence for the efficiency of the proposed training method by performing experiments with existing neural network architectures and demonstrate that same architecture when trained with the proposed training method perform better than when trained with conventional training approach in the presence of noisy datasets.

Keywords: Deep neural networks · Robust neural networks ·
Lipschitz continuity

1 Introduction

Recent advances in deep learning have immensely increased the representational capabilities of the neural networks and made them powerful enough to be applied to different vision-based tasks including image classification [1–4], object detection [5,6], image captioning [7] as well as to deep reinforcement learning [8,9]. Some important factors that explain the rapid development of deep learning include emergence of dedicated mathematical frameworks for deep neural networks [10], availability of large scale annotated datasets [11,12], improvements in the network architectures [3,13] and open source deep learning libraries [14,15].

Availability of large amounts of high-quality and distortionless image data is often assumed and the visual quality of training images is often overlooked while designing deep learning based applications. It has been shown that models trained with *clean* data suffer with depreciation in their performance when

© Springer Nature Switzerland AG 2019
C. D. Yoo et al. (Eds.): IWDW 2018, LNCS 11378, pp. 373–389, 2019.
https://doi.org/10.1007/978-3-030-11389-6_28

Table 1. Effect of input image quality on the deep learning model prediction. We trained resnet-20 architecture with standard and proposed training procedure and tested them on a CIFAR-10 dataset image. Model trained with standard method fails to correctly classify the image as the severity of distortion increases while that trained with proposed method correctly classifies all images with high confidence.

Gaussian Noise std		$\sigma = 0.0$	$\sigma = 0.2$	$\sigma = 0.4$	$\sigma = 0.6$
Input to the model					
standard training	Model Prediction	ship	ship	bird	bird
	confidence for 'ship'	0.9999	0.5608	0.1266	0.0252
proposed training	Model Prediction	ship	ship	ship	ship
	confidence for 'ship'	0.9999	0.9986	0.8710	0.7215

tested on samples that are distorted with blur or noise distortions [16,17]. In most real-world applications, the images undergo various forms of distortions owing to formatting, compression and post-processing that are routinely applied to visual datasets and often are unobservable to a human eye. Therefore, the availability of clean data is no longer guaranteed. One way to alleviate this problem can be to train the networks with noisy data expected to be seen in the real-world. However, the commonly used large scale datasets [11,12] for training the deep learning models do not provide training data with these artifacts and distortions. Therefore, it is imperative to develop training techniques that can give more robust deep learning models while using only available large scale popular datasets that do not cater for these distortions.

The problem discussed in this work is about improving the robustness and stability of deep neural networks. This is a fundamental problem in computer vision and has recently received increased interest by the community [18–20]. Our focus is on improving the training process rather than the DNN architecture. We introduce a general training technique that can be applied to any standard state-of-the-art deep learning model and lets them learn a mapping that is more robust and insensitive to input visual perturbations and distortions. We note that a deep neural network can be considered as a mathematical model and the least we can expect from a stable mathematical model is that a small perturbation or distortion in its input will not produce a large change in its behavior. In order to realize this, we utilize some fundamental concepts including Lipschitz functions and Lipschitz continuity. According to the perturbation theory, if the input is perturbed by a small amount, the output of the system stays *close* to its nominal output when there is no perturbation in the input provided that the system dynamics are continuous and locally Lipschitz. In order to motivate the dynamics of the deep neural network to remain locally Lipschitz, we include an additional term in the loss function called $L_{Lipschitz}$. We provide theoretical justification for the proposed training method in Sect. 4, proving that for admissible distortions in the neighborhood of input image, the Locally Lipschitz neural network is guaranteed to be stable, thus improving the performance in presence of noisy data. We verify the theoretical results by performing extensive experiments on MNIST, CIFAR-10 and STL-10 datasets.

We summarize the paper findings in Table 1 where resnet-20 network architecture, trained without the proposed method, when presented with distorted input images fails to classify them as the severity of the distortion increases. Even for correctly classified distorted images, the prediction confidence is very low. On the other hand, the same architecture trained with the proposed method when presented with same distorted images correctly classifies them with reasonable prediction confidence.

2   Related Work

While training the deep neural networks, availability of high quality and artifact-free image data is often assumed. However, this may not always be true due to distortions the images encounter during accusation, transmission and storage phases. Moreover, with the increasing demand of DNN based mobile applications, the assumption for high quality of the availability of high quality input data needs to be relaxed. [16,17] showed that the deep neural networks trained on clean datasets are all susceptible to poor performance when tested to blur and noise distortions while being resilient to compression artifacts such as JPEG and contrast. They propose to train the networks on low quality data to alleviate this problem, which may cause networks to perform poorly to high quality data. The VGG [18] architecture was shown to perform better than AlexNet [4] or GoogleNet [1] to the considered types of distortions. [1] showed that standard architectures trained on high-quality data suffered significant degradation in performance when tested with distorted data due to blurring or camera motion. They showed that fine-tuning the trained models with a mix of blurry and sharp training examples helps to regain the lost performance to a degree at the cost of minor computational overhead. [21] proposed two approaches to alleviate poor performance due to blurred and noisy images: re-training and fine-tuning with noisy images, showing that fine-tuning is more practical than re-training. [22] also shows that fine-tuned networks on distorted data outperform the original networks when tested on noisy data, but these fine-tuned networks show poor performance on quality distortions that they have not been trained for. [22] propose the concept of mixture of experts ensemble, where various experts are trained on different types of distortions and the final output of the model is the weighted sum of these expert models' outputs. A separate gating network is used to determine these weights. [19] presents BANG which is the training algorithm that assigns more weight to the correctly classifies samples. Since the correctly classified training samples do not contribute much to the loss as compared to the incorrectly classified training samples, therefore, training is more focused on learning those samples that are badly classified. [19] proved that increasing the contribution of correctly classified training samples in the batch helps flatten the decision space around these training samples, thus training more robust DNNs. In addition to above mentioned issues, [23] showed the inability of many machine learning models to deal with slightly, but intentionally, perturbed examples which are called adversarial examples. These adversarial examples are indistinguishable to human observers from their original counterparts. Authors in [23] were first to introduce a method of finding adversarial perturbations while [24] introduced a computationally cheaper adversarial example generation algorithm called Fast Gradient Sign Method (FGSM). Our work differs drastically from [20] as instead of flattening the neural network dynamics function f altogether, we are more focused on setting a soft upper bound on the gradient of f that does not adversely affects the representational power of the neural network. Our work also differs from data augmentation as we propose a way to improve the training process without using any extra training samples, while data augmentation uses standard training techniques and instead increases the number of training samples.

3   Background

In this section, we present the basic concepts of Lipschitz functions and Lipschitz continuity.

Let S be an open set in some $\mathbb{R}^n$. A function $f : \mathbb{R}^n \to \mathbb{R}^m$ is called Lipschitz continuous on S if there exists a nonnegative constant $L_f \in \mathbb{R}_{\geq 0}$, called a Lipschitz constant of function f on S, such that the following condition holds:

$$\|f(x) - f(y)\| \leq L_f \|x - y\| \tag{1}$$

for all $x, y \in \mathbb{S}$. We call the function f to be locally Lipschitz continuous if for each $z \in \mathbb{R}^n$, there exists a constant r such that f in Lipschitz continuous on the open ball $B_r(z)$ of center z and radius r, where $B_r(z)$ is mathematically written as $B_r(z) = \{y \in \mathbb{R}^n : \|y - z\| < r\}$. The function f is said to be globally Lipschitz continuous if it is Lipschitz continuous on its entire domain $\mathbb{R}^n$. We note that if the function $f(x)$ is Lipschitz continuous with a Lipschitz constant L_f, then it is also Lipschitz continuous with any L such that $L \geq Lf$.

Lipschitz continuity is a measure designed to measure the change of the function values versus the change in the independent variable. Let $f : \mathbb{R}^n \to \mathbb{R}^m$ be a Lipschitz continuous function with a Lipschitz constant L_f, so it satisfies (1), i.e.

$$\frac{\|f(x) - f(y)\|}{\|x - y\|} \leq L_f \tag{2}$$

for all $x \neq y \in \mathbb{R}^n$. In other words, the average rate of change in the value of f for any pair of points x and y in $\mathbb{R}^n$ does not exceed the Lipschitz constant L_f. Here we note that the Lipschitz constant L_f depends upon the function f. It may vary from being large for one function to being small for another. If L_f is small, then $f(x)$ may only vary a little as the input is changed. But if L_f is large, the function output $f(x)$ may vary a lot with only a small change in its input x. In particular, when the Lipschitz function f is real-valued, i.e. $m = 1$, then by taking the limit of (2) as $y \to x$ we obtain $\|f'(x)\| \leq L_f$, where $f'(x)$ is the derivative function of $f(x)$. In other words, the magnitude of (instantaneous) rate of change in f does not exceed the Lipschitz constant L_f when the Lipschitz continuous function f is differentiable.

Lipschitz continuity, therefore, quantifies the idea of sensitivity of the function $f(x)$ with respect to its argument using the Lipschitz constant L_f. We note here that the Lipschitz constant L_f represents only the upper bound on how much the function $f(x)$ can change with the change in its input, the actual change might also be smaller than that indicated by L_f.

4   Approach

Neural networks can be considered as a sequence of layers that attempt to learn the arbitrary mapping $f \colon X \to Y$. The network is parameterized with many parameters that are optimized given the training data $x \in X$ and $y \in Y$. Therefore, imposing the condition of Lipschitz continuity on the neural network dynamics implies that a small perturbation in the input will not result in large change at the output of the network, thus increasing the robustness and the stability of the network. Theoretical justification for our approach is provided in the following theorem.

Theorem 1. *Let $\Lambda = \{y_1, y_2, \ldots, y_l\}$ be the set of l labels used and let $\rho = 1/2 \min\limits_{1 \leq i < j \leq l} \|y_i - y_j\|$ be half of the minimum distance between any two labels. Let $f(x)$ be the neural network dynamics. Let L_n be the chosen Lipschitz constant hyperparameter. If $f(x)$ is Lipschitz, then for all distortions d in input space such that $\|d\| < \rho/L_n$, x and $\tilde{x}$ are guaranteed to be mapped to the same label where $\tilde{x}$ is the distorted input of the form $x + d$.*

Proof. From the Lipschitz assumption, we have $\|f(x + d) - f(x)\| \leq L_n/\|d\|$. Since we have $\|d\| < \rho/L_n$, we get $\|f(x+d) - f(x)\| < \rho$. Since $f(x)$ is *discrete-valued* in Λ, taking into consideration the definition of ρ, we conclude that both x and $\tilde{x}$ get mapped to the same label in set Λ.

The Lipschitz property of $f(x)$ guarantees that for any distortion d such that $\|d\| < \rho/L_n$, the output of the distorted input lies within a sphere of radius ρ about the output of the nominal input where ρ gives the half of the maximum distance between any two labels. Thus, it is guaranteed that distorted input gets mapped to the same label as the nominal input. For the case when the network is trained without the proposed method, we do not impose any *upper bound* on the slope of $f(x)$. Therefore, we have Lipschitz constant $L_n = \infty$ which in Theorem 1 gives $\|d\| = 0$, which trivially implies that there is no distortion d for which the network is guaranteed to be robust.

5   Method

Let $\mathbb{R}^{H \times W \times C} \to R^l$, where l denotes the number of labels, represents the mapping performed by the deep neural network. Let $x \in \mathbb{R}^{H \times W \times C}$ be the input that the network takes, for example an image in the case of a convolutional neural network. In order to encourage the network to be locally Lipschitz continuous, we perturb the network input during the training process with zero mean Gaussian Noise to get a perturbed copy of the input, $\bar{x}$, i.e.

$$\bar{x} = x + N(0, \sigma) \tag{3}$$

where we note that in (3), $N(0, \sigma)$ has same dimensions as the input image x i.e. $N(0, \sigma) \in \mathbb{R}^{H \times W \times C}$ and each component of $N(0, \sigma)$ is a single valued zero mean Gaussian random variable $\mathcal{N}(0, \sigma)$ with standard deviation σ. Here, σ is treated as a hyperparameter in the experiments.

In general, the derivative $f'(x)$ of a function $f(x)$ at a point a point x is defined by

$$f'(x) = \lim_{y \to x} \frac{f(y) - f(x)}{y - x},$$

it can be approximated by

$$f'(x) \approx \frac{f(y) - f(x)}{y - x},$$

where y is a point *near* x. Hence, if we take $y = \bar{x} = x + N(0, \sigma)$ from (3), we then have

$$\|f'(x)\| \approx \frac{\|f(\bar{x}) - f(x)\|}{\|\bar{x} - x\|} =: k(x). \tag{4}$$

In order to encourage the neural network to become locally Lipschitz continuous, we add an additional term, called $L_{Lipschitz}$, in the usual loss function, termed here as L_{usual}, to get an aggregated loss function L, i.e.

$$L = L_{usual} + L_{Lipschitz},$$

where L_{usual} is the loss term corresponding to the task to be performed by the network, for example cross-entropy loss, while $L_{Lipschitz}$ is defined as:

$$L_{Lipschitz} = \beta * \max(0, k(x) - L_n) \tag{5}$$

where β is the weighting factor for the added loss term $L_{Lipschitz}$, L_n serves the purpose of the Lipschitz constant for the neural network dynamics, and $k(x)$ is given in (4). We treat both β and L_n as hyperparameters.

The effect of the hyperparameters will be studied in Sect. 7.

Table 2. Classification accuracies for experiments with MNIST. Results are shown for various levels of distortions in test dataset as described by the value of σ_{test}. Here $\sigma_{test} = 0.0$ corresponds to undistorted test data. We used $\beta = 10$ for MNIST experiments.

Network training details	σ_{test}		
	0.0	0.5	1.0
Standard method	0.97	0.92	0.65
$\sigma_{train} = 0.5$, $L_n = 0.01$	0.98	0.95	0.70
$\sigma_{train} = 0.75$, $L_n = 0.005$	0.98	0.96	0.78
$\sigma_{train} = 0.75$, $L_n = 0.01$	0.98	0.96	0.77

6 Experiments

In order to evaluate our approach, we tested our proposed training procedure with MNIST [25], CIFAR-10 [26] and STL-10 [27] datasets. Details about these experiments and their results are explained in following subsections. When we train the network without using the proposed training method, we refer to the training method as *standard training method*.

Justification for Using Gaussian Noise: In experiments, we use Gaussian noise to corrupt test data. To see why Gaussian model can approximate realistic distortions, we see that any distortion of an image x can always be expressed as $\bar{x} = T_\sigma(x)$, where $T_\sigma(\cdot)$ is a map *close to the identity map*, i.e. $T_0(x) = x$, parameterized by a parameter σ. Hence, for all small values of σ, $\bar{x} = T_\sigma(x) = T_0(x) + O(|\sigma|) = x + O(|\sigma|)$ in Taylor expansion of $T_\sigma(x)$ in σ around $\sigma = 0$, where $O(|\sigma|)$ represents the terms of order 1 or higher in σ and can be interpreted as a perturbation term that vanishes when $\sigma = 0$. Hence, it is reasonable to use Gaussian noises $N(0, \sigma)$ to simulate various realistic distortions to the image x.

Due to space constraints, some tables and figures are given in the supplementary material and will be referenced in the subsequent sections as required.

6.1 MNIST

Experiment Details. We used a convolutional neural network consisting of one convolutional layer, one fully-connected layer and an output layer for experiments with MNIST dataset. 5 epochs of 550 iteration were performed and learning rate was set to 10^{-4}. For training the network with standard training method, we set $\beta = 0$ in (5). Network was trained with and without the proposed training mechanism. $(\sigma_{train}, \beta, L_n) \in \{0.5, 0.75\} \times \{10\} \times \{0.005, 0.01\}$ were used as hyperparameters.

We tested trained networks with test data distorted with zero mean Gaussian noise with standard deviation values of $\sigma_{test} = 0.0, 0.5$ and 1.0. Networks trained with various percentages of training data were also tested.

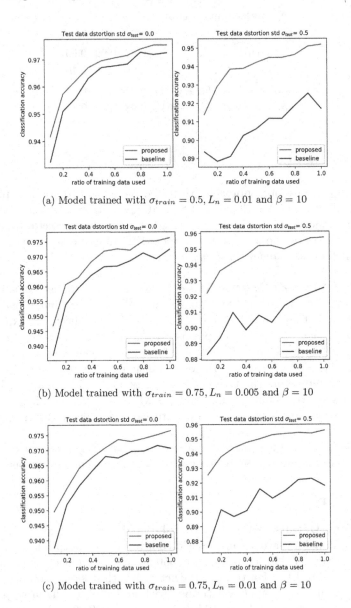

(a) Model trained with $\sigma_{train} = 0.5, L_n = 0.01$ and $\beta = 10$

(b) Model trained with $\sigma_{train} = 0.75, L_n = 0.005$ and $\beta = 10$

(c) Model trained with $\sigma_{train} = 0.75, L_n = 0.01$ and $\beta = 10$

Fig. 1. Plots of classification accuracy versus ratio of training data used in training process.

Table 3. Top-1 accuracies for models trained with $\sigma_{train} = 0.25$ on CIFAR-10 dataset

For ResNet-20 architecture

Training	L_n	Test data distortion σ_{test}								
		$\sigma_{test} = 0.0$			$\sigma_{test} = 0.3$			$\sigma_{test} = 0.5$		
		$\beta = 1$	$\beta = 5$	$\beta = 10$	$\beta = 1$	$\beta = 5$	$\beta = 10$	$\beta = 1$	$\beta = 5$	$\beta = 10$
Standard	-	**92.77**	**92.77**	**92.77**	38.28	38.28	38.28	18.01	18.01	18.01
Proposed	0.01	88.02	82.49	88.18	50.56	45.80	**58.56**	23.49	21.68	**29.70**
	0.1	88.86	88.21	89.00	**63.01**	**59.05**	57.92	**34.73**	**31.17**	25.84

For Preresnet-20 architecture

Training	L_n	Test data distortion σ_{test}								
		$\sigma_{test} = 0.0$			$\sigma_{test} = 0.3$			$\sigma_{test} = 0.5$		
		$\beta = 1$	$\beta = 5$	$\beta = 10$	$\beta = 1$	$\beta = 5$	$\beta = 10$	$\beta = 1$	$\beta = 5$	$\beta = 10$
Standard	-	**92.59**	**92.59**	**92.59**	30.80	30.80	30.80	15.91	15.91	15.91
Proposed	0.01	86.91	87.86	88.34	**63.52**	58.86	59.47	32.84	26.99	26.33
	0.1	86.55	88.11	87.80	58.51	**61.25**	**64.98**	**35.14**	**32.76**	**39.41**

We also investigated the effects of using only a proportion of training data for training purpose. We trained the networks with various percentages of training data and tested them on entire test data. We randomly sample a percentage of training data at the start of training. We hypothesize that a robust neural network trained with only a portion of training data should be able to generalize well across the entire test dataset.

Results. Table 2 presents classification accuracies for models trained with different combinations of hyperparameters. We see that networks trained with Lipschitz continuity loss perform better than the network obtained with standard training procedure. With undistorted test data, the gain in performance is small but as the severity of distortion increases, the networks trained with proposed method show significant performance improvement over network trained with standard training process. As the value of L_n is increased keeping other hyperparameters the same, the performance slightly deteriorates in accordance with the conclusion of Theorem 1, where the region of admissible distortions d decreases as L_n is increased i.e. $\|d\| \leq \rho/L_n$.

In order to test the robustness of proposed training procedure, we trained the networks with various portions of training data. These models were then tested with entire test dataset, undistorted as well as distorted ($\sigma_{test} = 0.5$). Figure 1 shows that networks trained with Lipschitz loss always perform better than those trained with standard training process, thus proving their robustness.

6.2   CIFAR-10

Experiment Details. We used ResNet-20 [3] and PreResNet-20 [17] as our network architectures for classification task with CIFAR-10 dataset. Both networks have 16-16-32-64 channels and 0.26 million parameters each. Each model

Table 4. Top-1 accuracies for models trained with $\sigma_{train} = 0.05$ on CIFAR-10 dataset

For ResNet-20 architecture

Training	L_n	Test data distortion σ_{test}								
		$\sigma_{test} = 0.0$			$\sigma_{test} = 0.3$			$\sigma_{test} = 0.5$		
		$\beta = 1$	$\beta = 5$	$\beta = 10$	$\beta = 1$	$\beta = 5$	$\beta = 10$	$\beta = 1$	$\beta = 5$	$\beta = 10$
Standard	-	**92.77**	**92.77**	**92.77**	**38.28**	38.28	38.28	**18.01**	18.01	18.01
Proposed	0.01	92.39	92.44	92.68	32.5	36.56	34.09	15.68	19.65	16.33
	0.1	92.57	92.32	**93.02**	34.15	**38.48**	**42.06**	13.67	**20.63**	**21.56**

For Preresnet-20 architecture

Training	L_n	Test data distortion σ_{test}								
		$\sigma_{test} = 0.0$			$\sigma_{test} = 0.3$			$\sigma_{test} = 0.5$		
		$\beta = 1$	$\beta = 5$	$\beta = 10$	$\beta = 1$	$\beta = 5$	$\beta = 10$	$\beta = 1$	$\beta = 5$	$\beta = 10$
Standard	-	**92.59**	92.59	**92.59**	30.80	30.80	30.80	15.91	15.91	15.91
Proposed	0.01	92.50	92.40	92.56	**41.31**	**35.18**	**34.66**	**22.25**	**18.39**	**16.46**
	0.1	92.36	**92.66**	92.34	34.92	28.37	33.67	17.54	16.12	14.83

Table 5. Top-1 accuracies for models trained with $\sigma_{train} = 0.5$ on CIFAR-10 dataset

For ResNet-20 architecture

Training	L_n	Test data distortion σ_{test}								
		$\sigma_{test} = 0.0$			$\sigma_{test} = 0.3$			$\sigma_{test} = 0.5$		
		$\beta = 1$	$\beta = 5$	$\beta = 10$	$\beta = 1$	$\beta = 5$	$\beta = 10$	$\beta = 1$	$\beta = 5$	$\beta = 10$
Standard	-	**92.77**	**92.77**	**92.77**	38.28	38.28	38.28	18.01	18.01	18.01
Proposed	0.01	82.97	82.72	82.55	**70.31**	**67.60**	66.89	**46.47**	**43.91**	41.15
	0.1	81.36	83.20	84.62	58.55	60.09	**72.40**	36.25	40.75	**45.53**

For Preresnet-20 architecture

Training	L_n	Test data distortion σ_{test}								
		$\sigma_{test} = 0.0$			$\sigma_{test} = 0.3$			$\sigma_{test} = 0.5$		
		$\beta = 1$	$\beta = 5$	$\beta = 10$	$\beta = 1$	$\beta = 5$	$\beta = 10$	$\beta = 1$	$\beta = 5$	$\beta = 10$
Standard	-	**92.59**	**92.59**	**92.59**	30.80	30.80	30.80	15.91	15.91	15.91
Proposed	0.01	82.43	80.88	80.00	**70.83**	**64.34**	**72.08**	**45.54**	**33.10**	47.19
	0.1	80.08	85.17	82.42	53.92	58.37	65.94	31.77	26.48	**47.28**

was trained for 300 epochs with batch size of 128 and learning rate of 0.1. Learning rate was decreased by a factor of 10 first at epoch 150 and then at epoch 225. $(\sigma_{train}, \beta, L_n) \in \{0.05, 0.25, 0.5\} \times \{1, 5, 10\} \times \{0.001, 0.1\}$ were used as hyperparameters. For training the network with standard training method, we set $\beta = 0$ in (5).

We tested the trained networks with corrupted test data generated by distorting the test data set with zero mean Gaussian Noise having standard deviation values ranging from $\sigma_{test} = 0.0$ to $\sigma_{test} = 0.5$ with step size of 0.01.

Table 6. Top-1 accuracies for models trained with $\sigma_{train} = 0.25$ on STL-10 dataset

Test data distortion σ_{test}										
Training	L_n	$\sigma_{test} = 0.0$			$\sigma_{test} = 0.3$			$\sigma_{test} = 0.5$		
		$\beta = 1$	$\beta = 5$	$\beta = 10$	$\beta = 1$	$\beta = 5$	$\beta = 10$	$\beta = 1$	$\beta = 5$	$\beta = 10$
Standard	-	**80.44**	**80.44**	**80.44**	50.67	50.67	50.67	34.94	34.94	34.94
Proposed	0.01	75.65	77.41	78.19	66.11	59.00	62.91	**48.77**	40.94	**44.52**
	0.1	78.88	79.71	77.21	**68.34**	**65.47**	**64.60**	47.42	**46.26**	42.24

Results. Table 3 shows the top-1 classification accuracies for networks trained with $\sigma_{train} = 0.25$ and σ_{test} values of $0.0, 0.3$ and 0.5. Similarly, Tables 4 and 5 show results in similar fashion for $\sigma_{train} = 0.05$ and $\sigma_{train} = 0.5$ respectively. Figures 2, 3 and 4 show plots for test accuracies versus $\sigma_{test} = 0.0 - 0.5$ for networks trained with $\sigma_{train} = 0.05, 0.25, 0.5$ respectively for better visualization.

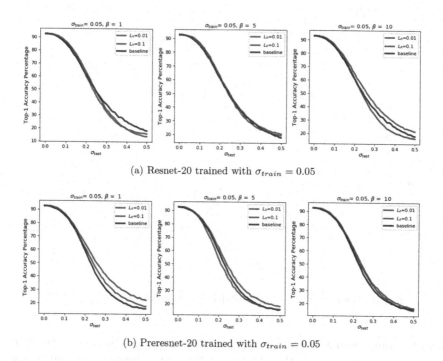

(a) Resnet-20 trained with $\sigma_{train} = 0.05$

(b) Preresnet-20 trained with $\sigma_{train} = 0.05$

Fig. 2. Plots of the top-1 CIFAR-10 test accuracies for models trained with $\sigma_{train} = 0.05$ and with standard training. (a) shows results for resnet-20 and (b) shows results for preresnet-20.

We see that the models trained with $\sigma_{train} = 0.05$ perform comparable to the original baseline with the undistorted test data. As the distortion severity is increased, they perform better than the baseline confirming that they are more

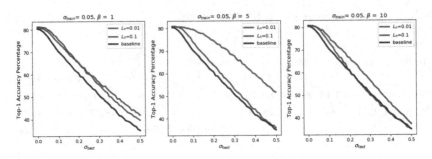

Fig. 3. Plots of the top-1 STL-10 test accuracies for $\sigma_{train} = 0.05$

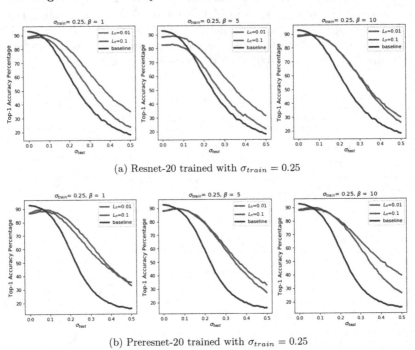

(a) Resnet-20 trained with $\sigma_{train} = 0.25$

(b) Preresnet-20 trained with $\sigma_{train} = 0.25$

Fig. 4. Plots of the top-1 CIFAR-10 test accuracies for $\sigma_{train} = 0.25$

robust to input visual distortions. As the value of σ_{train} is increased, we get the models that tend to lose performance with the undistorted dataset but perform much better as the distortion severity in increased. Therefore, models trained with increased values of σ_{train} are much more robust and insensitive to input distortions with some loss in performance with undistorted input data. We also note that as the value of β is increased, the performance difference of models trained with different L_n values tends to diminish as they start to performance equally well. This is due to high value of β that makes the effect of different L_n values in the training loss ineffective.

Table 7. Top-1 accuracies for models trained with $\sigma_{train} = 0.05$ on STL-10 dataset

Test data distortion σ_{test}										
Training	L_n	$\sigma_{test} = 0.0$			$\sigma_{test} = 0.3$			$\sigma_{test} = 0.5$		
		$\beta = 1$	$\beta = 5$	$\beta = 10$	$\beta = 1$	$\beta = 5$	$\beta = 10$	$\beta = 1$	$\beta = 5$	$\beta = 10$
Standard	-	80.44	80.44	80.44	50.67	50.67	50.67	34.94	34.94	34.94
Proposed	0.01	80.44	80.88	**80.79**	**56.54**	**67.81**	**56.56**	**41.74**	**51.58**	**37.25**
	0.1	**81.34**	**80.90**	80.64	55.46	52.88	49.86	39.51	39.51	34.84

Table 8. Top-1 accuracies for models trained with $\sigma_{train} = 0.5$ on STL-10 dataset

Test data distortion σ_{test}										
Training	L_n	$\sigma_{test} = 0.0$			$\sigma_{test} = 0.3$			$\sigma_{test} = 0.5$		
		$\beta = 1$	$\beta = 5$	$\beta = 10$	$\beta = 1$	$\beta = 5$	$\beta = 10$	$\beta = 1$	$\beta = 5$	$\beta = 10$
Standard	-	**80.44**	**80.44**	**80.44**	50.67	50.67	50.67	34.94	34.94	34.94
Proposed	0.01	73.16	72.08	70.90	60.19	66.97	65.89	**48.83**	53.21	51.33
	0.1	71.75	75.35	71.83	**62.79**	**69.10**	**67.88**	46.40	**55.95**	**52.21**

6.3 STL-10

Experiment Details. We used PreResNet-32 [1] as our baseline architecture for classification task with STL-10 dataset. The network has 16–16–32–64 channels and 0.46 million parameters. Training conditions and hyperparameters' values are same as for CIFAR-10 experiments. Test data was also generated similar to CIFAR-10 experiments.

Results. Table 6 shows the top-1 classification accuracies for networks trained with $\sigma_{train} = 0.25$ and σ_{test} values of 0.0, 0.3 and 0.5. Similarly, Tables 7 and 8 show results in similar fashion for networks trained with $\sigma_{train} = 0.05$ and $\sigma_{train} = 0.5$ respectively. Figures 5, 6 and 7 in the supplementary material show plots for test accuracies versus $\sigma_{test} = 0.0-0.5$ for networks trained with $\sigma_{train} = 0.05, 0.25, 0.5$ respectively for better visualization.

We see that the models trained with $\sigma_{train} = 0.05$ perform comparable to the original baseline with the undistorted test data. As the distortion severity is increased, they perform better than the baseline confirming that they are more robust to input visual distortions. As the value of σ_{train} is increased, we get the models that tend to lose performance with the undistorted dataset but perform much better as the distortion severity in increased. Therefore, models trained with increased values of σ_{train} are much more robust and insensitive to input distortions with some loss in performance with undistorted input data. We also note that as the value of β is increased, the performance difference of models trained with different L_n values tends to diminish as they start to performance equally well. This is due to high value of β that makes the effect of different L_n values in the training loss ineffective.

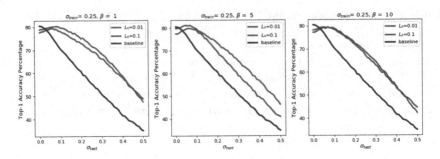

Fig. 5. Plots of top-1 STL-10 test accuracies for $\sigma_{train} = 0.25$

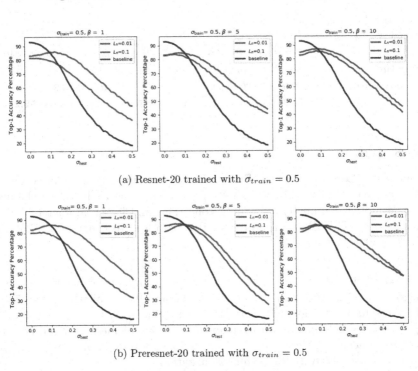

(a) Resnet-20 trained with $\sigma_{train} = 0.5$

(b) Preresnet-20 trained with $\sigma_{train} = 0.5$

Fig. 6. Plots of the top-1 CIFAR-10 test accuracies for $\sigma_{train} = 0.5$

7   Sensitivity Analysis of Hyperparameters

The impact of hyperparameters is best studied using the sensitivity analysis. The hyperparameters introduced in this study are $(\sigma_{train}, \beta, L_n) \in \{0.05, 0.25, 0.5\} \times \{1, 5, 10\} \times \{0.01, 0.1\}$. For sensitivity analysis, let's take nominal values of hyperparameters be $(\sigma_{train}, \beta, L_n) = (0.25, 5, 0.01)$. Let acc denote the percentage accuracy of the model trained with Lipschitz term in loss function. We change the hyperparameters σ_{train}, β and L_n as follows: $\Delta\sigma_{train} = 0.25, \Delta\beta = 5$ and

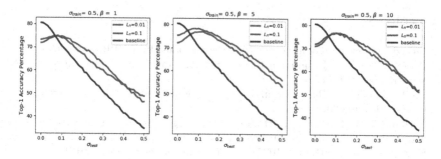

Fig. 7. Plots of the top-1 STL-10 test accuracies for $\sigma_{train} = 0.5$

$\Delta L_n = 0.09$. Experiments are performed with new hyperparameters values on CIFAR-10 dataset. The sensitivities of model performance with respect to σ_{train}, β and L_n are given as:

$$\Delta acc/\Delta\sigma_{train} = 87.20, \quad \Delta acc/\Delta\beta = 2.55$$

and

$$\Delta acc/\Delta L_n = -28.89$$

respectively.

We see that the network performance is most sensitive to change in σ_{train}. Performance is least sensitive to change in β. Performance is fairly sensitive to change in L_n where the negative value of $\Delta acc/\Delta L_n$ indicates that the performance deteriorates as L_n increases, which is consistent with the conclusion of Theorem 1 in Sect. 4 where the radius of admissible distortions d is inversely proportional to the magnitude of L_n i.e. $\|d\| \leq \rho/L_n$.

8   Conclusion

In this paper, we presented a method for training neural networks using Lipschitz continuity that can be used to make them more robust to input visual perturbations. We provide theoretical justification and experimental demonstration about the effectiveness of our method using existing neural network architectures in the presence of input perturbations. Our approach is, therefore, easy-to-use and effective as it improves the network robustness and stability without using data augmentation or additional training data.

Acknowledgement. This research has been in part supported by the ICT R&D program of MSIP/IITP [2016-0-00563, Research on Adaptive Machine Learning Technology Development for Intelligent Autonomous Digital Companion].

References

1. Szegedy, C., et al.: Going deeper with convolutions. In: CVPR, June 2015
2. Wang, F., et al.: Residual attention network for image classification. CoRR, abs/1704.06904 (2017)
3. He, K., Zhang, X., Ren, S., Sun, J.: Deep residual learning for image recognition. In: CVPR, June 2016
4. Krizhevsky, A., Sutskever, I., Hinton, G.E.: Imagenet classification with deep convolutional neural networks. In: Pereira, F., Burges, C.J.C., Bottou, L., Weinberger, K.Q. (eds.) NIPS 2012, pp. 1097–1105. Curran Associates Inc. (2012)
5. Redmon, J., Divvala, S., Girshick, R., Farhadi, A.: You only look once: unified, real-time object detection. In: CVPR, June 2016
6. Ren, S., He, K., Girshick, R., Sun, J.: Faster R-CNN: towards real-time object detection with region proposal networks. In: Cortes, C., Lawrence, N.D., Lee, D.D., Sugiyama, M., Garnett, R. (eds.) NIPS 2015, pp. 91–99. Curran Associates Inc. (2015)
7. Vinyals, O., Toshev, A., Bengio, S., Erhan, D.: Show and tell: a neural image caption generator. CoRR, abs/1411.4555 (2014)
8. Mnih, V., et al.: Human-level control through deep reinforcement learning. Nature **518**(7540), 529–533 (2015)
9. Silver, D., et al.: Mastering the game of go without human knowledge. Nature **550**, 354 (2017)
10. Caterini, A.L., Chang, D.E.: Deep Neural Networks in a Mathematical Framework. SCS. Springer, Cham (2018). https://doi.org/10.1007/978-3-319-75304-1
11. Deng, J., Dong, W., Socher, R., Li, L., Li, K., Fei-Fei, L.: Imagenet: a large-scale hierarchical image database. In: CVPR, pp. 248–255, June 2009
12. Lin, T.-Y., Maire, M., Belongie, S., Hays, J., Perona, P., Ramanan, D., Dollár, P., Zitnick, C.L.: Microsoft COCO: common objects in context. In: Fleet, D., Pajdla, T., Schiele, B., Tuytelaars, T. (eds.) ECCV 2014. LNCS, vol. 8693, pp. 740–755. Springer, Cham (2014). https://doi.org/10.1007/978-3-319-10602-1_48
13. He, K., Zhang, X., Ren, S., Sun, J.: Identity mappings in deep residual networks. CoRR, abs/1603.05027 (2016)
14. Paszke, A., et al.: Automatic differentiation in pytorch, Alban Desmaison (2017)
15. Abadi, M., et al.: TensorFlow: Large-scale machine learning on heterogeneous systems (2015). Software tensorflow.org
16. Dodge, S.F., Karam, L.J.: Understanding how image quality affects deep neural networks. CoRR, abs/1604.04004 (2016)
17. Vasiljevic, I., Chakrabarti, A., Shakhnarovich, G.: Examining the impact of blur on recognition by convolutional networks. CoRR, abs/1611.05760 (2016)
18. Simonyan, K., Zisserman, A.: Very deep convolutional networks for large-scale image recognition. CoRR, abs/1409.1556 (2014)
19. Rozsa, A., Günther, M., Boult, T.E.: Towards robust deep neural networks with BANG. CoRR, abs/1612.00138 (2016)
20. Zheng, S., Song, Y., Leung, T., Goodfellow, I.J.: Improving the robustness of deep neural networks via stability training. CoRR, abs/1604.04326 (2016)
21. Zhou, Y., Song, S., Cheung, N.-M.: On classification of distorted images with deep convolutional neural networks. CoRR, abs/1701.01924 (2017)
22. Dodge, S.F., Karam, L.J.: Quality resilient deep neural networks. CoRR, abs/1703.08119 (2017)

23. Szegedy, C., et al.: Intriguing properties of neural networks. CoRR, abs/1312.6199 (2013)
24. Goodfellow, I., Shlens, J., Szegedy, C.: Explaining and harnessing adversarial examples. In: International Conference on Learning Representations (2015)
25. LeCun, Y., Cortes, C.: MNIST handwritten digit database (2010)
26. Krizhevsky, A.: Learning multiple layers of features from tiny images. Technical report (2009)
27. Coates, A., Ng, A., Lee. H.: An analysis of single-layer networks in unsupervised feature learning. In: Gordon, G., Dunson, D., Dudk, M. (eds.) Proceedings of the Fourteenth International Conference on Artificial Intelligence and Statistics, vol. 15 of Proceedings of Machine Learning Research, pp. 215–223, Fort Lauderdale, FL, USA, 11–13 Apr 2011. PMLR (2011)

Author Index

Printed in the United States
By Bookmasters